THE IDEA OF AUTHORSHIP IN COPYRIGHT

For my family
Rina, Moshe and Orly

The Idea of Authorship in Copyright

LIOR ZEMER
Interdisciplinary Centre, Radzyner School of Law, Herzliya, Israel
Boston University, School of Law, USA

ASHGATE

Published by
Ashgate Publishing Limited
Gower House
Croft Road
Aldershot
Hampshire GU11 3HR
England

Ashgate Publishing Company
Suite 420
101 Cherry Street
Burlington, VT 05401-4405
USA

Ashgate website: http://www.ashgate.com

British Library Cataloguing in Publication Data
Zemer, Lior
The idea of authorship in copyright. - (Applied legal philosophy)
1. Copyright 2. Authorship 3. Intellectual property
I. Title
346'.0482

Library of Congress Cataloging-in-Publication Data
Zemer, Lior.
The idea of authorship in copyright / by Lior Zemer.
p. cm. -- (Applied legal philosophy)
Includes bibliographical references and index.
ISBN-13: 978-0-7546-2376-2
1. Authorship. 2. Copyright. 3. Authorship--Philosophy.
4. Copyright--Philosophy. I. Title.

K1440.Z46 2007
346.04'82--dc22

2006032545

ISBN 978-0-7546-2376-2

Printed and bound in Great Britain by MPG Books Ltd, Bodmin, Cornwall.

Contents

Preface

In a world of intellectual achievers whose creations are safeguarded by robust regimes of rights of exclusion, the public is collectively isolated from and deprived of recognition of its social and cultural contribution to the process of creating intellectual properties. In this book I argue that copyrighted entities represent the authorial collectivity. I advocate the authorial role of the public in the process of copyright creation. This role has been largely ignored and taken for granted. I take the temerity to introduce and develop a socio-legal argument suggesting a property right for the public in *every* copyrighted enterprise.

This book is about copyright theory. It presents a model of public authorship. The upshot consists of a mix of morally viable copyright-specific justice reasons. The discussion is founded upon the argument that a copyright work is a joint enterprise of the public and the author. Every copyright work depends on and is reflective of the decisive authorial contribution the public makes to the formation of authorial and artistic materials. The author's exposure to and consumption of cultural and social elements is what makes the copyright creation successful. These elements are nurtured and stimulated by the public and constitute an integral part of the public's collective identity. Copyright works should therefore, not be regarded as exclusive private property. Since copyright works profit from significant public contribution, both public and authors should own them under a joint title.

As a way to approach the above issues, Chapter 1 introduces my general argument, maps the theories dominating our copyright culture and positions my argument amongst them. Chapter 2 discusses the conceptual aura surrounding copyright discourse, and considers what benefits we can extract from answering the question whether copyright is an essentially contested concept. In Chapter 3 I define the scope of copyright entitlement. I consider to what extent the entitlement paradigm within copyright law mimics the patterns of the common law allocation of entitlement within the institution of traditional property. I argue that copyright confers a bundle of rights on rightholders, and emphasise that this bundle imposes correlative duties on the public.

In order to account for the public authorial role, we have to eliminate well-established misconceptions dominating our copyright realm. Chapter 4 inquires into the role of the public in copyright creation. It examines the social nature of copyright and argues that authorial and artistic works require contribution from two sources: public and authors. I argue that every copyrighted work is limited *ab initio* due to its dependence on the public authorial contribution. Chapter 5 takes the arguments of the preceding chapter a step forward and presents a social constructionist theory and bases on it limits to copyright. In Chapter 6 I attempt to rein in the tendency to assume that Locke's property theory provides a coherent justification for copyright.

I challenge the many modern copyright-Lockeans who claim that Locke did not account for copyright.

Chapter 7 takes joint authorship as its organising principle. Here I provide a comparative analysis of the requirements for joint authorship and show how the public/author relationship satisfies them all. I then present several alternatives to the present ownership pattern in copyright, reflecting the actual collaborations and the proprietary aspirations of the two parties that deserve property right in copyrighted works – public and authors. Chapter 8 concludes the present study. In this chapter I provide a summary of the main arguments I present and the significance of the public authorship model to contemporary copyright law and policy. I also outline further broader conclusions highlighting the misconceptions we cherish in our vision of copyright.

It should be stated that in this book I do not intend to undermine traditional property. In essence, I reject the allocation of exclusive property rights in copyrighted materials. I also do not intend to announce the 'death of the author' or the end of copyright. I agree that copyright protection is a necessary economic desideratum and should be encouraged by the incentives and rewards that the system provides. I agree on the assumption that cultural and social properties ought to be brought within the domain of some kind of property institution. This, however, does not mean allocation of rights operating on the axis of ultimate private exclusivity.

Although much of the discussion transcends the law of any particular jurisdiction, the statutory and doctrinal examples are drawn principally from particularities of English copyright law. Where applicable, examples from other jurisdictions are given.

Lior Zemer
Interdisciplinary Centre, Radzyner School of Law, Israel
Boston University, School of Law, USA
January 2007

Acknowledgements

This book is about the concept of authorship and the acute contemporary need to redefine its scope and boundaries. It is a product of a journey. In this journey, which began almost a decade ago, I did not travel without company. There were many passengers, institutions, events, and conversations taking part in the process of building and defending arguments and their eventual expression in this book. I have been fortunate to invite new passengers in almost every corner of the journey and I accumulated debts of gratitude to many people. I owe most, of course, to the supervisor of my doctorate, Leslie Green, for his encouragement, invaluable suggestions and constructive criticism, and for making my research an exciting academic experience. Leslie, I have learned much from you and from our many discussions, and I am confident that it will take many more years for me to fully realise their true impact on my current and future research.

I began exploring the seeds of the arguments presented in this book at Oxford while writing a research project under the supervision of David Vaver. A major part in the very idea of this research began during that period when David introduced me to the contours of academic research, and astutely criticised versions of earlier parts of my research. David, the many lessons I learned from you and skills I obtained during my research keep guiding me whenever I embark on new research. It was during that time that I have met a colleague who became a close friend. Wendy Gordon introduced me to copyright philosophy and the lore of John Locke's legal and social agendas. I am grateful to you for accompanying my research since then, for being such a source of inspiration and support, and a true friend.

Many colleagues and friends have been generous with their time, support, and critical intervention. Mary Jane Mossman, Abraham Drassinower, Carys Craig, Rosemary Coombe, Leslie Jacobs, Joshua Getzler, and the late James Harris deserve special mention for having read and criticised previous versions of the arguments I present here. I hope this work justifies their efforts. I am also indebted to Craig Scott, Liora Salter, Michael Spence, Margaret Llewelyn, David Townend, Elise Histed, Jeremy Philips, Ilanah Simon, Glynis Truter, Robin White, Cosmo Graham, Daniel Goldsein, Herwig Hoffman, Benjamin Geva, Haya Leibowitz, Merav Kropero, Inbal Fogel, Eitan and Nitza Ben-Moshe, Chava and Joseph Pardo, David Freedman, Nitza Shapiro-Libaee, Amnon Rubinstein, Amir Licht, Guy Seidman, Eyal Kimel, Ofer Raban, Lea Dooley, Holly Paisey, Jo Goacher, Ronit Golik, Jacob Abir, Sylvie Da Lomba, Tana Spanic, Alen Zysblat, Irena Zolotova, Adina Fleisher, Marc Cogen, Fiona Smith, Edward Vernon, John Vernon, Elisha Shor, Suzie Navot, Michael Meurer, David Bone, Tamar Frankel, June Dilevsky, Fred and Joyce Zemmans, and Judge John D Cooke and Judge S von Bahr of the European Court of Justice. I would like to thank my students in Leicester, Birmingham, Boston and Toronto for allowing me their views when presenting my arguments in class. I learnt much from you. Rabbi Pink of Leicester, Rabbi Posner of Boston and their families deserve a special mention for their support and warm welcoming to their communities. I would also like to thank the editorial team at Ashgate, John Irwin, Alison Kirk, and Gemma Lowle, for their help and efforts in publishing this book, and to Tom Campbell for allowing me the privilege to publish this book in the series 'Applied Legal Philosophy'.

I am keenly aware, too, of the many institutional debts I have incurred in writing this book. I am grateful to Osgoode Hall Law School for the resources and financial support which it has provided. I would also like to thank Oxford Intellectual Property Research Centre at St. Peter's College, Boston University School of Law, University of Leicester Faculty of Law, the Hebrew University Faculty of Law, Radzyner School of Law of the Interdisciplinary Centre in Herzliya, the British Society of Legal Scholars, and the British Academy, for their intellectual companionship and financial support. Sections of this book were presented at Boston University School of Law, Queen Mary Intellectual Property Research Institute, University of London, and the Radzyner School of Law, Interdisciplinary Centre in Herzliya. In every instance I profited from the discussions that followed.

There are three special people who each deserve a very special mention here. Sharon Pardo, Christine Vernon and Merav Tauber. Without your support and encouragement this research would not have reached this stage.

I owe much to the support I received from Joseph Shaked, my grandfather David Zemer, and to a person that will not see this project complete, my grandmother, Sofia Beni whose vision will always stay with me. Finally, this book is dedicated to three people whose inspiration and support keep guiding me, my parents Rina and Moshe, and my sister Orly. Thank you for being there for me. All the time.

Parts of the introduction to this book were published in 'On the Value of Copyright Theory' (2006) 1 *Intellectual Property Quarterly* 55; Chapter 2 is an expanded version of 'The Conceptual Game in Copyright' (2006) 28(3) *Hastings Communications and Entertainment Law Journal* 409; an earlier version of Chapters 5 and 6 appeared in 'The Copyright Moment' (2006) 43 *San Diego Law Review* 247, and in 'Towards a Conception of Authorial Knowledge in Copyright' (2006) 3(2) *Buffalo Intellectual Property Law Journal* 83; Part of Chapter 6 appeared in 'The Making of a New Copyright Lockean' (2006) 29(3) *Harvard Journal of Law & Public Policy* 891; and parts of Chapter 7 were published in 'We-Intention and the Limits of Copyright' (2006) 24(1) *Cardozo Arts & Entertainment Law Journal* 99, in 'Contribution and Collaboration in Joint Authorship: Too Many Misconceptions' (2006) 1(4) *Journal of Intellectual Property Law & Practice* 283, and in 'Rethinking Copyright Alternatives' (2006) 14(1) *International Journal of Law and Information Technology* 137.

Lior Zemer
January 2007

Table of Cases

Chapter 1

Introduction

Against Sole Authorship

Every copyrighted entity represents the creative collectivity. It is a joint enterprise of both the individual author and the public. Contemporary conceptions of copyright reject the collective nature of authorial and artistic creations and invoke copyright to signify entitlement of a certain kind, to mark an individual territory and disregard its social nature. The framework within which the regulation of copyright is examined is embedded with misconceptions and contradictions. At the heart of this definitional complexity is copyright laws' perennial struggle to define the boundaries of when the right to own begins, and when the social realm takes priority. The avenues to resolving this struggle are affected by various implications arising from this complexity. Reaching an effectual balance depends on the success of any definition of copyright in taking into account and rewarding the contribution of key participants in the process of authorial creation.

The law's inability to strike a proper balance between private and public interests in copyright is controlled by the fact that classical notions of property are embedded in policies on cultural and social appropriation. Copyright focuses on authors as a privileged category. It confers a fenced private dominion on rightholders and posits the singular author at the very centre of the copyright creation process. It rejects the very nature of copyright creation as a collectively imagined and produced activity. Hence, the reason for the slogan coined by Boyle: 'Authors tend to win.'[1]

As a legal and social institution, copyright is governed by diametrically opposing conceptions of rights. It is a technical name that does not reveal the concept's intrinsic difficulties. It declares ownership over authorial and artistic resources and confers exclusive entitlement and control to a definitive category of creators, engaged in genuine activity vested in original works. It is a system that sanctifies and preserves the right to ownership. It is a system that allows traditional conceptions of property and ownership to control its social commitments.[2]

Copyright denies the contribution of the public to the copyright creation process and imposes and maintains an imbalance between private and public interests. The

---

1 J Boyle, *Shamans, Software and Spleens: Law and the Construction of the Information Society* (Cambridge Mass.: Harvard University Press, 1996) 116.

2 The key questions to ask are: 'Should we have a system of property rights in the products of intellectual labour? If so, what sorts of things should it cover? And what bundles of rights and other incidents of ownership should be included?' LC Becker, 'Deserving to Own Intellectual Property' (1993) 68 *Chicago-Kent Law Review* 609, 609-610.

role the public plays in the copyright creation process has been explored from various standpoints, but no concept has been sufficiently developed to be incorporated into a paradigm of copyright ownership. We are bound to rethink the way in which our copyright system allocates exclusive private rights in cultural and social items. As Coombe argues: 'If, as human selves in human communities, we are constituted by and constitute ourselves with shared cultural symbols, then it is important that legal theorists consider the nature of the cultural symbols "we" "share" in consumer societies and the recognition the law affords them.'[3] In this book I argue that copyright creation is a collective enterprise. I approach copyright from a social perspective and claim a right for the public in every copyrighted entity, not merely for the sake of philosophical or academic debate, but for matters of proprietary entitlement and control.

Every copyrighted entity is a social construction. It depends on the consumption of cultural and social properties that make an author capable of interpreting and absorbing the significance of these properties, then translating his creative ability into the language of copyright creation.[4] The set of rights copyright confers on authors does not reflect the inevitable causal relationship between authors and public. Moreover, as Scafidi asserts, '[t]his exclusive celebration of one individual not only obscures the role of the community and society at large in the development of intellectual property, but it also shifts attention away from the need for a robust public domain…'[5] Preservation of the collective, and conservation of a rich and diverse array of cultural and social properties rarely conjure a romantic view similar to that of the lone author.

Many plausible arguments justify exclusive property rights over tangibles such as land and chattels. Intellectual property in general, and authorial and artistic works in particular, differ from tangible assets. The distinctions between intellectual and traditional property are three.[6] First, since a copyrighted work is a form of expression, there is a clear and decisive public role – more than in any other form of property – in shaping methods of expression such as languages, and musical and artistic styles.

Second, copyrighted works such as literature, music and films, are the defining components of our culture and social reality. Treating them as assets that can be subject to exclusive ownership essentially means that our culture and social reality can be owned with the perquisites of buying, selling, transferring and excluding. Not only do the expressions of our culture and social environment define our society as a whole, they are also part of what defines our individual personalities and aspirations.

---

3 RJ Coombe, 'Objects of Property and Subjects of Politics: Intellectual Property Laws and Democratic Dialogue' (1991) 69 *Texas Law Review* 1853, 1864.

4 See for example P Jaszi, 'Towards a Theory of Copyright: The Metamorphoses of "Authorship"' (1991) *Duke Law Journal* 455.

5 S Scafidi, 'Intellectual Property and Cultural Goods' (2001) 81 *Boston University Law Review* 793, 804.

6 I shall use the term 'property' interchangeably with 'traditional', 'tangible' or 'corporeal' property and the term 'intellectual property' interchangeably with 'intangible', 'incorporeal' or 'abstract' property.

Subjecting these elements to exclusive private property has a direct detrimental impact on the development of our society and its individual members.[7]

Third, the law has recognised that copyright and property, while fulfilling similar ambitions, are different doctrinal areas. The law has designed a different set of rules specifically applicable to copyrights to accommodate their social implications. In that special set of rules, the duration of the right is perhaps of the greatest difference. While perpetuity is not an alien concept in traditional property, in copyright it is.[8] As Hughes observes: 'Perhaps the greatest difference between the bundles of intellectual property rights and the bundles of rights over other types of property is that intellectual property always has a self-defined expiration, a built-in sunset.'[9] Despite the limited duration of the right, it is frequently argued that it creates the danger of conferring on authors a quasi-perpetual right. In fact, as Lessig remarks, this danger is already with us: copyrights have come to be thought of 'not as rights that get defined or balanced against other state interests, but as rights that are, like natural property rights, permanent and absolute.'[10]

---

7 As Vaidhyanathan writes: '…there must be a formula that would acknowledge that all creativity relies on previous work, builds "on the shoulders of giants", yet would encourage – maximize – creative expression in multiple media and forms. But because twentieth-century copyright law has been a battle of strong interested parties seeking to control a market, not a concerted effort to maximize creativity and content for the benefit of the public, we have lost sight of such a formula along the way.' S Vaidhyanathan, *Copyrights and Copywrongs: The Rise of Intellectual Property and How it Threatens Creativity* (New York and London: New York University Press, 2001) 116.

8 An author enjoys copyright in his works for 70 years 'from the end of the calendar year in which the author dies.' Copyright, Designs and Patents Act 1988 (1988, c.48) s 12(2) (hereinafter – 'CDPA 1988').

9 J Hughes, 'The Philosophy of Intellectual Property' (1988) 77 *Georgetown Law Journal* 287, 296. However, there exists one exception to this rule. The CDPA 1988 provides a unique exception to the standard usage of copyright term, designed especially for Sir James Matthew Barrie's play *Peter Pan*. The exception provides the trustees of The Hospital for Sick Children, Great Ormond Street, London, a perpetual 'right to a royalty in respect of the public performance, commercial exploitation, broadcasting or inclusion in cable programme service of the play "Peter Pan" by Sir James Matthew Barrie, or of any adaptation of that work, notwithstanding that copyright in the work expired on 31 December 1987.' CDPA s 301. The right will terminate if the Hospital ceases to have a separate identity or no longer has as its purpose the care of sick children.

Seville remarks in that respect that '[t]he policy questions are vexing…since authorship draw from the literary commons, it is arguably inappropriate to attribute "ownership" of a character to a single author, at least if it is to extend beyond the boundaries of the character's expression in the author's copyright works' and 'quite apart of the dangers of unwittingly restricting other's use of character types, room must be left for humour, parody, comment, and reference.' C Seville, 'Peter Pan's Rights: "To Die Will Be an Awfully Big Adventure"' (2003) 51(1) *Journal of the Copyright Society of the USA* 1, 7.

10 L Lessig, 'Copyright's First Amendment' (2001) 48 *UCLA Law Review* 1057, 1068.

Although it is not entirely wrong to argue that '[o]ur lives are in every respect dominated by an intuitive sense of property and belonging',[11] when intellectual properties are at stake, ownership and control should not be defined under exclusive terms. I shall argue that copyrighted entities are manifestations of the collective creativity; they are socially and culturally constructed. So we may ask, if works of art and authorship are collectively produced, ought they to be collectively owned? Admittedly, as Underkuffler remarks: property is a legal conclusion but '[t]he idea that property rights…are presumptively free from collective claims has been decisively abandoned, if ever it was true.'[12] I largely base my arguments on the claim that every copyrighted entity is socially constructed and historically contingent.[13] This claim raises serious doubts regarding declarations such as 'I own the copyright' or 'this is my copyright.'

A starting point for the understanding of copyright from a constructionist perspective is the role of collaboration in copyright creation and its place as a key characteristic of the creative society. In fact, collaborative authorship is not an invention of modern times. Masten tells us that collaboration 'was a prevalent mode of textual production in the sixteenth and seventeenth centuries, only eventually displaced by the mode of singular authorship with which we are more familiar.'[14] Vickers asserts that collaborative authorship was a 'standard practice in Elizabethan, Jacobean, and Caroline drama.'[15] Jaszi tells us that in recent times works of art and

---

11 K Gray, 'Equitable Property' (1994) 47(2) *Current Legal Problems* 157, 158.

12 LS Underkuffler, *The Idea of Property: Its Making and Power* (Oxford: Oxford University Press, 2003) 2. See also by the same author, 'On Property: An Essay' (1990) 100 *Yale Law Journal* 127.

This can be supported by Gordon's remark that 'what strikes the backward-looking observer as curious is simply this: that in the midst of such a lush flowering of absolute dominion talk in theoretical and political discourse, English legal doctrines should contain so very few plausible instances of absolute dominion rights. Moreover, it is curious that English and colonial social practices contained so many property relations that actually seemed to traduce the ideal of absolute individual rights. The real building-blocks of basic eighteenth-century social and economic institutions were not absolute dominion rights but, instead property rights fragmented and split among many holders; property rights held and managed collectively…; property relations of dependence and subordination; property subject to arbitrary and discretionary direction or destruction…; property surrounded by restriction on use and alienation; property qualified and regulated for communal or state purposes…' RW Gordon, 'Paradoxical Property', in J Brewer and S Staves (eds.), *Early Modern Conceptions of Property* (London: Routledge, 1996) 96.

13 As Hacking, writing on social constructionism, tells us: 'none of the examples is my own. I deliberately take historical case studies made by other people', and that '[c]ollectively my audiences were participating in the making of this book.' I Hacking, *The Social Construction of What?* (Cambridge Mass.: Harvard University Press, 1999) ix, 172.

14 J Masten, *Textual Intercourse: Collaboration, Authorship, and Sexualities in Renaissance Drama* (Cambridge: Cambridge University Press, 1997) 4.

15 B Vickers, *Shakespeare, Co-Author: A Historical Study of Five Collaborative Plays* (Oxford: Oxford University Press, 2002) 137.

authorship are increasingly becoming 'collective, corporate, and collaborative.'[16] In the relationship between collaborators, whether artists, musicians, choreographers or architects both artists win: their relationship and collaboration make them better individual artists. Copyright laws acknowledge this and reward them with an exclusive right.

Yet, in every creative collaborative incident there is one contributor who does not win: the public. The collaboration between two artists – for example, Picasso and Matisse whose collaborative efforts were the subject of a recent three-city exhibition, conveying to the audience the long obsession the two artists had for each other's works, focusing on instances where one artist surges and the other responds, consciously or not, to the other[17] – cannot be isolated from the wider cultural and social matrix in which they are created. Collaboration that reaches artistic fruition is *always* dependent on collectively produced and owned social and cultural properties. I reject romantic notions of creativity and authorship which stress the subjective experience of the author in order to perpetuate patterns of social denial and further diminishing the rights of the general public.[18] As Palmer most poignantly remarks: if rights are to be recognised in works of art and authorship anywhere 'they should be in the audience, and not in the artist, for it is on the audience that the art work depends for its continued existence, and not the artist.'[19]

On this account, authors cannot claim, and in fact are not entitled to, any *exclusive* ownership rights of the products of their creative labour. After all, both the public and its members laboured on each creation. While the individual author invests qualities from his original make-up, his subjective interpretation of the external reality, his talent, and financial resources, the public invests the social and cultural capital, necessary to transform an individual into an 'author' and make him realise and translate his talent into the language of authorial creation.[20]

---

16 P Jaszi, 'On the Author Effect: Contemporary Copyright and Collective Creativity' in M Woodmansee and P Jaszi (eds.), *The Construction of Authorship* (Durham and London: Duke University Press, 1994) 29, 38.

17 Reported in *The New York Times*, 'Arts & Leisure', S Boxer Sunday, 'Artists Dueling, Curators Dealing: A Show is Born', February 9, 2003, Section 2, 1 and 32.

18 Lord Macaulay does not deny the good in a copyright system. However, the right is equivalent to a monopoly right and a monopoly is an evil: 'For the sake of the good we must submit to the evil; but the evil ought not to last a day longer than is necessary for the purpose of securing the good.' Lord Macaulay, A Speech Delivered in the House of Commons on 5th February 1841 in Lady Trevelyan (ed.), *The Works of Lors Macaulay* (London: Longmans, Green and Co, 1866) 195, 199.

19 TG Palmer, 'Are Patents and Copyrights Morally Justified? The Philosophy of Property Rights and Ideal Objects' (1990) 13 *Harvard Journal of Law & Public Policy* 817, 848.

20 Thus regarded, no copyrighted work stands alone. The idea that authors create original works is but a fiction. The creation of every copyright work, as Litman observes, is more akin to 'translation and recombination.' J Litman, 'The Public Domain' (1990) 39 *Emory Law Journal* 965, 966.

I shall argue that every copyrighted work is limited *ab initio* due to the dependency on the contribution of the public. The copyright bargain must reflect the fact that each copyright work is dependent on the public's social and cultural input, and each work owes much to its predecessors while each informs its successors. The question, then, 'who authors copyrighted materials?' is not idle. Viewing the public role in this way raises the question that motivates my research – why should the public not be granted authorial rights similar to those granted to individual creators? It is my main argument that *every copyright work is a joint enterprise*. For every copyright work there are at least two contributors: the individual author and the public.

In a recent work Gordon reminds us the 'gift all artists receive, namely, a tradition and world they have not made.'[21] How to translate this gift into the language of power and control in copyright is a task I undertake in the present book. Copyright laws sanctify the lore behind the principle 'as you sow, so shall you reap.'[22] I argue that the principle applies to both the public and authors. Donne's words in his second *Satire*, judging poetry plagiarism, show how Renaissance writers regarded the theft of intellectual property. Donne's remarks support the argument why both public and authors deserve a right in the products of their labour:

But he is worst, who (beggardly) doth chaw
Others' wits' fruits, and his ravenous maw
Rankly digested, doth those things out spew,
As his own things; and they are his own, 'tis true,

In other words, every intellectual property is derivative. As Leval wittily puts the matter: 'Not since Athena sprung from the head of Zeus has an artist emerged fully formed. There is no such thing as a wholly original thought. Every idea takes a substantial part from what has gone before. Intellectual man, like biological man, displays the genes of his forebears. Titian's Venus and Goya's Maja are both present in Manet's Olympia. Cezanne's geometric reductions are found in Picasso's cubism. T.S. Elliot tells us that while lesser writers borrow, great writers steal.' PN Leval, 'Fair Use or Foul? The Nineteenth Donald C Brace Memorial Lecture' (1989) 36 *Journal of the Copyright Society of the USA* 167, 169.

21 WJ Gordon, 'Render Copyright unto Caesar: On Taking Incentives Seriously' (2004) 71(1) *The University of Chicago Law Review* 75, 77.

22 In the historic case of *Millar v Taylor* the Court advocates an author-oriented approach. Mansfield J held: 'Because it is just, that an author should reap the pecuniary profits of his own ingenuity and labour. It is just, that another should not use his name, without his consent. It is fit, that he should not only choose the time, but the manner of publication; how many; what volume; what print. It is fit, he should choose to whose care he will trust the accuracy and correctness of the impression; to whose honesty he will confine.' *Millar v Taylor* (1769) 98 Eng Rep 201, 252. Willes J adds that 'it is certainly not agreeable to natural justice, that a stranger should reap the beneficial pecuniary produce of another man's work.' Ibid 218.

The court's decision in *Millar* was reversed by the House of Lords in *Donaldson v Beckett*, where it was held that there is no place for natural law in copyright jurisprudence. *Donaldson v Beckett* (1774) 1 Eng Rep 837 (both cases involved James Thomson's poem '*The Seasons*'). See M Rose, *Authors and Owners: the Invention of Copyright* (Cambridge Mass.: Harvard University Press, 1993) 78-85.

For if one eat my meat, through it be known
The meat was mine, th'excrement is his own.[23]

The concerns I expressed above are known to scholars familiar with the rhetoric encircling the scope of the 'right' in copyright. I believe all feel some sense of uncertainty as to the direction copyright law is taking us. Some even proclaim 'the death of copyright',[24] warn us about 'the escalating copyright wars',[25] argue that the institution of intellectual property is 'in crisis',[26] simply remark that 'old-fashioned' copyright does no longer exist,[27] or just tell us that the future of copyright depends on our intention and how we choose to redefine it.[28] These predictions reflect different schools of thought, but scholars still adhere to the idea that traditional concepts of property and ownership best accommodate contemporary copyright issues. I argue that we must be aware of the fact that property, when used in the 'copyright talk' is not a mere metaphor. As Rose observes, the property metaphors we use

> [A]re not just ornamental; they structure the way we think about matters and they have consequences…they are deeply embedded in the way we think about ourselves as well as the way we think about copyright. We cannot simply escape from these metaphors because we cannot escape from history and from ourselves. A persuasive solution to the problems our metaphors pose will be one that does not simply reject the old tropes but finds new ways to understand them.[29]

I shall not 'reject the old tropes' in their entirety, but refute misconceptions dominating copyright theory. I will attempt to structure a new theoretical paradigm and, although I am aware of the fact that copyright balances veer from the apocalyptic to the utopian, I shall argue that, since the institution of private property is both natural and human-created, it is something that a culture can change when the day comes that we finally see how increasingly destructive our existing ownership norms have become.[30]

---

23 J Donne, Satire 2, 25-30, in AJ Smith (ed.), *John Donne: The Complete English Poems* (Harmondsworth, 1971) 158, cited in Vickers (n 15 above) 524.

24 GS Lunney Jr., 'The Death of Copyright: Digital Technology, Private Copying, and the Digital Millennium Copyright Act' (2001) 87 *Virginia Law Review* 813.

25 PK Yu, 'The Escalating Copyright Wars' (2004) 32 *Hofstra Law Review* 907.

26 D Vaver, 'Patently Absurd' [2000] *Oxford Today* 21-22. Inaugural Lecture, University of Oxford.

27 D Nimmer, 'The End of Copyright' (1995) 48 *Vanderbilt Law Review* 1385, 1420.

28 M Geist, The Ninth Annual Honorable Helen Wilson Nies Memorial Lecture in Intellectual Property, 'All Rights Reserved? Cultural Monopoly and the Troubles with Copyright' (2006) 10 *Marquette Intellectual Property Law Review* 411.

29 M Rose, 'Copyright and Its Metaphors' (2002) 50 *UCLA Law Review* 1, 3, 15.

30 As Warren and Brandeis remark: 'An individual shall have full protection in person and in property…but it has been found necessary from time to time to define anew the exact nature and extent of such protection.' S Warren and L Brandeis, 'Privacy – The Right to' (1890) 4 *Harvard Law Review* 193.

Before I embark on my analysis of copyright I shall review and analyse prominent approaches to copyright. I shall divide the various theories dominating copyright thought into several groups and map the strengths and weaknesses of each of them. This will enable me to unveil the dangers inherent in insufficient clarity when we talk copyright theory, highlight conflicting interests, mark common standards to all theories, and then benchmark my arguments in relation to these theories and establish my contribution to the study of copyright theory and policy.

The Landscape of Copyright Theory

The Many Faces of Copyright Theory

Arguments favouring conferring property rights on intellectual creations are manifold. They contain great value for development of intellectual property systems and shaping their limits. Like all doctrinal thought-experiments, I am unable, within the framework of the present book, to fully explore all theories and sub-theories that may affect my arguments. I shall not refute the wisdom behind adopting traditional concepts of property to assess ideational entities, but advocate a limited conception of property for copyrighted works. I shall argue that limitations on copyright ownership and control stem not only from considerations of social justice, but also from the very nature of authors and copyrighted material as social constructs.

There are many approaches to intellectual property theory.[31] Together they prove that 'copyright is very much of a mixed blessing.'[32] For Menell, intellectual property theory should be divided into utilitarian and non-utilitarian theories.[33] In the latter he includes natural right/labour theory; unjust enrichment; personhood theory; libertarian theories; distributive justice; democratic theories; radical/socialist theories; and ecological theories.[34] It is arguable whether intellectual property theory lends itself to categorization, and it seems that any attempt to categorise is bound to be misleading or incomplete. Theories are often related to each other, and there will always be at least one approach that stands independently of any existing theory.

---

31 On the philosophy of intellectual property, in particular copyright, see generally L Zemer, 'The Value of Copyright Theory' (2006) 1 *Intellectual Property Quarterly* 55; JM Garon, 'Normative Copyright: A Conceptual Framework for Copyright Philosophy and Ethics' (2003) 88 *Cornell Law Review* 1278; W Fisher, 'Theories of Intellectual Property' in S Munzer (ed.), *New Essays in the Legal and Political Theory of Property* (Cambridge: Cambridge University Press, 2001) 168; G Pessach, 'A Theoretical Basis for Copyright' (2001) 31(2) *Mishpatim* 359 (in Hebrew); PS Menell, 'Intellectual Property: General Theories' in B Bouckaert and G de Geest (eds.), *Encyclopedia of Law & Economics: Volume II* (Edward Elgar: Cheltenham, UK, 2000) 129; P Drahos, *A Philosophy of Intellectual Property* (Dartmouth: Ashgate 1996); Palmer (n 19 above); Hughes (n 9 above).

32 SG Breyer, 'The Uneasy Case for Copyright' (1970) 87 *Harvard Law Review* 281, 351.

33 Menell (n 31 above) 129.

34 Ibid 156-163.

Six major approaches dominate the literature on intellectual property theory: the instrumental/utilitarian approach; the labour theory of property; the personhood theory; social-institutional-planning; traditional proprietarianism; and authorial constructionism. This division is open to debate and is by no means conclusive. These approaches 'grow out of and draw support from lines of arguments that have long figured in the raw materials of intellectual property law – constitutional provisions, case reports, preambles to legislation…judicial opinions, statutes, and appellate briefs.'[35]

I shall suggest a seventh theoretical approach advocating limits to copyright based on *social constructionism*. The argument that authors and copyrighted works are social constructs lies at the heart of my approach. As social constructs, authors' claims for property in their creations are limited *ab initio* by their reliance on the contribution of the public to the realisation of authorial abilities and actual copyrighted materials. This approach differs from any of the six approaches. It combines three of them: the labour theory of property, traditional proprietarianism, and authorial constructionism. As opposed to copyright theorists who discuss the latter approach as a threshold for a greater individual authorial autonomy, I present a social constructionist argument for limiting this autonomy by allocating authorial rights to the public, reflecting its pivotal role in the formation of works protected under copyright laws. I will elaborate my reasoning at length in a short while. Before doing so, however, I wish to summarise the foundations of the six theoretical approaches in order to highlight their special contribution to our copyright dialogue.

Utilitarianism Utilitarian theorists endorse the creation of intellectual property rights in order to induce innovation and intellectual productivity.[36] They limit

35 Fisher (n 31 above) 173-175. Still, the power of these theories is not limitless: 'Ambiguities, internal inconsistencies, and the lack of crucial empirical information severely limit their prescriptive power.' Ibid 177.

36 Justifying copyright on the premises of the utilitarian theory can be traced back to the first modern copyright law, the Statute of Anne, 1709. The title of the legislation reads: 'An Act for the Encouragement of Learning, by vesting the Copies of printed Books in the Authors, or Purchasers, of such Copies, during the Times therein mentioned', holding the law to be 'For the Encouragement of Learning Men to Compose and Write Useful Books.'

The United State's Constitution explicitly bases the logic of copyright and patent regimes on utilitarian foundations. In the words of the US Constitution: Congress is empowered '[T]o promote the Progress of Science and useful Arts, by securing for limited Times to Authors and Inventors the exclusive Right to their respective Writings and Discoveries.' US Constitution Art 1 s 8 cl 8. Indeed, the US Congressional Committee entrusted on the 1909 Copyright Act remarked: 'The enactment of copyright legislation by Congress under the terms of the Constitution is not based upon any natural right that the author has in his writings…but upon the ground that the welfare of the public will be served and progress of science and useful arts will be promoted…by securing to authors for limited periods the exclusive rights to their writings.' HR Rep No 222, 60th Cong, 2nd Sess 7 1909. See for example, *Mazer v Stein* (1954) 347 US 201, 209. In the famous *Feist* case the US Supreme Court held: 'the primary objective of copyright is not to reward the labors of authors, but to promote the Progress of Science and

conferment of rights in order to strike a balance between the economic interests of rightholders claiming exclusive rights, and the greater interest of the public. As Palmer explains: 'The utility gains from increased incentives for innovation must be weighted against the utility losses incurred from monopolization of innovations and their diminished diffusion.'[37] In a Benthamite style,[38] utilitarian theorists argue that limited monopolies spur innovation, and in order to foster innovation the system must recognise exclusive rights in intellectual creations – rights which are limited in duration and scope and are balanced against rightholders' economic aspirations and power.

Utilitarian arguments are consequentialist and hold the view that the good is whatever yields the greatest net utility. They differ from non-utilitarian arguments in that the latter emphasises creators' moral rights to control their work. They see the right bestowed on the creators of intellectual property as a reward for their efforts. Despite the social costs of monopoly power, as well as jurisdictional differences, I have little doubt that economic reward and control characterises *every* intellectual property regime. Legal protection for inventions encourages new investments and provides incentives for further development. Disclosure requirements in patent law advance dissemination of knowledge and trigger new research initiatives and scientific discoveries. Propagation of literary and artistic works is dependent, in many instances, on economic reward. Copyright protection promotes creativity, social exchange and interaction.[39] Trademark protection encourages the development of

---

useful Arts…To this end copyright assures authors the right to their original expression.' *Feist Publications, Inc v Rural Telephone Service Co* 499 US 340 349-350 (1991).

On the interpretation of the US clause see for example KB Lutz, 'Patents and Science: A Clarification of the Patent Clause of the U.S. Constitution' (1949) 18 *George Washington Law Review* 50; EC Walterscheid, 'To Promote the Progress of Science and Useful Arts: The Background and Origin of the Intellectual Property Clause of the United States Constitution' (1994) 2 *Journal of Intellectual Property* 1; and LA Durham, '"Useful Arts" in the Information Age' (1999) *Brigham Young University Law Review* 1419.

37 Palmer (n 19 above) 849-850.

38 In the words of Bentham: 'That which one has invented, all the world can imitate. Without the assistance of the laws, the inventor would almost always be driven out of the market by his rival, who finding himself, without any expense, in possession of a discovery which has cost the inventor much time and expense, would be able to deprive him of all his deserved advantages, by selling at a lower price.' J Bentham, A *Manual of Political Economy* (New York: GP Putnam, 1839) 71 cited in Menell (n 31 above).

39 Breyer rejects the noneconomic arguments of copyright and concludes: '[N]one of the noneconomic goals served by copyright law seems an adequate justification for a copyright system. The system provides a fairly useful way to protect an author's dignitary rights, and it can provide extra compensation to some writers. Yet alternative legal arrangements can readily be devised to protect the personal nonpecuniary interests of the author. Moreover, the merits of the claim to extra compensation have not been clearly established, nor has copyright proved particularly effective in providing compensation for the "great work" of unusual social value. If we are to justify copyright protection, we must turn to its economic objectives.' Breyer (n 32 above) 291. See also BW Tyerman, 'The Economic Rationale for Copyright

branding and distinctive products. Without trademark protection, companies might avoid producing quality goods, limiting commercial intercourse. Legal protection of trade secrets secures property rights in informational entities, thereby creating economic incentives to develop and produce additional know-how.

In their seminal essay on the economics of copyright, Landes and Posner contend that the nature of public goods renders them vulnerable for replication and use by free riders, thereby creating the risk of not recovering the production costs.[40] This will adversely affect production of socially valuable intellectual entities. The allocation of exclusive rights of authorship is necessary in order to avoid such economically inefficient outcomes.[41] According to Landes and Posner, '[c]opyright protection – the right of the copyright's owner to prevent others from making copies – trades off the costs of limiting access to a work against the benefits of providing incentives to create the work in the first place.'[42] They recognise the need to strike a balance between public and private interests, as the central problem in copyright: 'Striking the correct balance between access and incentives is the central problem in copyright law. For copyright law to promote economic efficiency, its principal legal doctrines must, at least approximately, maximize the benefits from creating additional works minus both the losses from limiting access and the costs of administering copyright protection.'[43]

Protection for Published Books: A Reply to Professor Breyer' (1971) 18 *UCLA Law Review* 1100; and SG Breyer, 'Copyright: A Rejoinder' (1972) 20 *UCLA Law Review* 75.

40 W Landes and R Posner, 'An Economic Analysis of Copyright Law' (1989) 18 *Journal of Legal Studies* 325. On economic theories of copyright, see also WJ Gordon and RG Bone, 'Copyright' in B Bouckaert and G de Geest (eds.), *Encyclopedia of Law & Economics: Volume II* (Edward Elgar: Cheltenham, UK, 2000) 189; GS Lunney Jr., 'Reexamining Copyright's Incentives-Access Paradigm' (1996) 49 *Vanderbilt Law Review* 483; SE Sterk, 'Rhetoric and Reality in Copyright Law' (1996) 94 *Michigan Law Review* 1197, 1204; JW Harris, *Property and Justice* (Oxford: Oxford University Press, 1996) 296-299; GK Hadfield, 'The Economics of Copyright: An Historical Perspective' (1992) 38 *Copyright Law Symposium* (ASCAP) 1; RM Hurt and N Schuchman, 'The Economic Rationale of Copyright' (1966) 56 *American Economic Review* 421; A Plant, 'The Economic Aspects of Copyright in Books' (1934) 1 *Economica* 167. See also Fisher (n 31 above) 169, 173-184; Menell (n 31 above) 130-156; Pessach (n 31 above) 361-383; and Drahos (n 31 above) 119-144.

41 Landes and Posner apply similar line of reasoning to trademarks. See W Landes and R Posner, 'Trademark Law: An Economic Perspective' (1987) 30 *Journal of Law & Economics* 265.

42 Landes and Posner (n 40 above) 326.

43 Ibid. The line of reasoning they employ can be traced back to, J Bentham (n 38 above); AC Pigou, *The Economics of Welfare* (London: Macmillan, 1921); and JB Clark, *Essential of Economic Theory* (New York: Macmillan, 1927). For example, Pigou writes: 'The patent laws aim, in effect, at bringing marginal trade net product and marginal social net product more closely together. By offering the prospect of reward for certain types of invention they do not, indeed, appreciably stimulate inventive activity, which is, for the most part, spontaneous, but they do direct it into channels of general usefulness.' Ibid 161.

The incentive structure in utilitarian arguments focuses on promoting the general public good, not on placing the individual creator as an independent object entitled to a right. That is, '[i]ntellectual property rights are rewards, or more accurately opportunities to gain a reward in the market-place.'[44] Such a view raises questions about the efficiency of utilitarianism in fostering the social goals they posit at the heart of their claims. Boyle asks: 'will we only tolerate limitations on intellectual property rights when those limitations are necessary to minimize transaction costs or accomplish well-defined public goals?'[45] Scholarly analysis supporting a utilitarian approach 'tries to preserve incentives for creators, even establishing a typology of "fair uses" – assigning or denying property rights in part according to whether those uses would tend to reduce the reward available to the author.'[46]

True, as Samuelson recently observed, '[t]he principal justification for intellectual property law in the Anglo-American tradition is economic. Without a grant of exclusive rights, innovators would have too little incentive to invest in socially beneficial innovations…'[47] However, as Boyle observes, such a view largely ignores the opposite perspective, as 'we see that one important purpose of "fair use" law is to make sure that future creators have available to them an adequate supply of raw materials. From this perspective, too many "incentives" could convert the public domain into a fallow landscape of private plots.'[48] The problem in utilitarian

---

Boyle explains and criticizes: 'Landes and Posner describe copyright as constructed by the tension between the need to grant legally protected interests to authors in order to motivate them and the need to limit the rights of authors so as to allow future creators legal access to the raw materials they need. This seems reasonable enough, but it also leaves them dangerously close to the mushy "balancing" analysis from which economics was supposed to provide surcease.' J Boyle, 'A Theory of Law and Information: Copyright, Spleens, Blackmail, and Insider Trading' (1992) 80 *California Law Review* 1413, 1447.

Judging the delicate balance in intellectual property on economic terms does not only cover newly created intellectual properties that meet the challenges of originality and inventiveness, but also improvements introduced by authors and inventors. See MA Lemley, 'The Economics of Improvement in Intellectual Property Law' (1997) 75 *Texas Law Review* 989.

44 Drahos (n 31 above) 122. Utilitarian considerations may be market-based or contain broader social goals. Market-instrumental approaches are frequently used as justification in the field of intellectual property. For example, Harris, while rejecting natural right-based justifications for intellectual property, argues that 'if it can be demonstrated, for example, that a pharmaceutical corporation will invest research and development costs in the manufacture of a new drug only if it is granted a patent, or that an author or composer will create an artistic work only if he is accorded copyright, and if in either case considerations parallel…to conditions for augmenting social wealth through incentives apply, then justice requires that the patent or the copyright be awarded.' Harris (n 40 above) 297.

45 Boyle (n 1 above) 38.

46 Ibid.

47 P Samuelson, 'Should Economics Play a Role in Copyright Law and Policy' (2003-2004) 1 *University of Ottawa Law & Technology Journal* 1.

48 Boyle (n 1 above). In the words of Hugenholtz, the public domain is being encroached by the 'private domain' in a way that bona fide purchasers are 'drowning in a sea of intellectual

justifications for copyright, as Boyle rightly remarks, is that they emphasise the property component of the prerequisites of information production and not the role of the public domain. Indeed, Landes and Posner stated that the role of the public domain is a neglected consideration.[49] Boyle then remarks that:

> One explanation of this emphasis, even in the best and most sophisticated copyright literature, might be the power of the vision of authorship...The romantic vision of authorship emphasizes creativity and originality and deemphasizes the importance of sources, genre, and conventions of language and plot. Thus when economists and legal scholars come to do their analysis, most of them see the issue as the extent of property necessary to motivate and reward the creative spirit, rather than the extent of the public domain necessary to give the magpie genius raw material she needs.[50]

Labour-based justifications Non-utilitarian theories of intellectual property have proliferated in recent years. The remaining five categories of copyright theory, and the seventh approach I purport to present, are non-utilitarian. The labour theory of property is perhaps the most famous amongst these categories. This book is a variation of this approach. Although it may seem unusual to base contemporary copyright arguments on a text written over three centuries ago, John Locke's theory of property has inspired courts, legions of scholars and policy makers.[51] The many faces of Lockean thought, from communitarianism to capitalism,[52] are often reflected in intellectual property scholarship.[53]

The Lockean labour theory can be regarded as the union of two basic theses. The first is that everyone has a natural property right in his own 'person' and in the labour

---

property.' PB Hugenholtz, 'Copyright and Freedom of Expression in Europe' in R Dreyfuss, LD Zimmerman and H First (eds.), *Expanding the Boundaries of Intellectual Property: Innovation Policy for the Knowledge Society* (Oxford: Oxford University Press, 2001) 343, 344.

49 Landes and Posner (n 39 above).

50 Boyle (n 1 above) 244 n 2.

51 In a very recent attempt to define the scope of copyright protection, the Canadian Federal Court explicitly refers to Locke's labour theory of property. *CCH Canadian Ltd v Law Society of Upper Canada* [2004] 1 SCR 339.

52 *Cf* J Tully, *An Approach to Political Philosophy: Locke in Contexts* (Cambridge: Cambridge University Press, 1993); with CB Macpherson, *The Political Theory of Possessive Individualism: Hobbes to Locke* (Oxford: Oxford University Press 1972).

53 See most recently, L Zemer, 'The Making of a New Copyright Lockean' (2006) 29(3) *Harvard Journal of Law & Public Policy* 891; J Tehranian, 'ET TU, Fair Use? The Triumph of Natural-Law Copyright (2005) 38 *U C Davis Law Review* 465; J Lipton, 'Information Property: Rights and Responsibilities' (2004) 56 *Florida Law Review* 135, 177-181; BG Damstedt, 'Limiting Locke: A Natural Law Justification for the Fair Use Doctrine' (2003) 112 *Yale Law Journal* 1179; A Drassinower, 'A Right-Based View of the Idea/Expression Dichotomy in Copyright Law' (2003) 16 *Canadian Journal of Law and Jurisprudence* 3; RA Spinello, 'The Future of Intellectual Property' (2003) 5 *Ethics and Information Technology* 1; CJ Craig, 'Locke, Labour and Limiting the Author's Right: A Warning Against a Lockean Approach to Copyright Law' 28 *Queens Law Journal* (2002) 1; and Gordon (n 21 above).

of his body – the famous metaphor of labour mixture.[54] The second is that property rights are limited by specific social norms.[55] Locke tells his readers that in the state of nature men share a common right in all things.[56] Thus, justifying the individual's right to property is notoriously difficult: once one takes a particular item from the common, one violates the right of other commoners, to whom this particular item also belongs. Locke resolves this seeming contradiction by introducing the idea of expenditure of labour. Labour justifies the penetration of a physical object into the labourer's realm, and the result is ownership – the deer the Indian killed is his in the sense that it is a part of himself, and a plan for a tulip garden in the centre of Brussels is the planner's own, as it now constitutes part of himself.[57] In essence, Locke refutes the theory of universal compact as a necessary condition for legitimate appropriation.[58]

A labourer's right, however, is not unconditional. It is subject to the 'no-harm principle',[59] which ensures that one's natural property right is protected as long as it is regulated by certain social norms and does not conflict with the common good. Locke introduces a set of duties and conditions to be satisfied and complied with before one can exercise the right to appropriate from the common in order to make one's own property.[60] Locke argues that a labourer may appropriate only the amount that he can come to use – 'Nothing was made by God for Man to spoil or destroy.'[61] This is known as the 'no-spoliation Proviso.' And, man has a right to appropriate from the common as long as 'enough and as good' is left in common for others.[62] This is known as the 'enough and as good Proviso.' With these Locke secures the principle that, except in extreme circumstances, all persons have a duty not to harm others. The significance of the Provisos is negligible in the realm of ideas since

54 J Locke, *Two Treatises of Government*, edited with an Introduction and Notes by P Laslett (Cambridge: Cambridge University Press, 2nd ed., 1988) 265-428. All subsequent references to the *Second Treatise*, and in particular to Chapter V, 'Of Property', are simply by book, chapter and section (e.g., 2nd T: i 7).

55 2nd T: v 27.

56 2nd T: v 13, 25.

57 Denicola asserts that 'the act of aggregating isolated pieces of information' should be grounds for copyright protection, in part because of considerations of 'natural right to the fruits of one's labour' and unjust enrichment. R Denicola, 'Copyright in Collections of Facts: A Theory for the Protection of Nonfiction Literary Works' (1981) 81 *Columbia Law Review* 516, 519-520, 528, 530. See also WJ Gordon, 'On Owning Information: Intellectual Property and the Restitutionary Impulse' (1992) 78 *Virginia Law Review* 149, 166-167, 266-273.

58 'But I shall endeavor to shew, how Men might come to have a *property* in several parts of that which God gave to Mankind in common, and that without any express Compact of all the Commoners.' 2nd T: v 25.

59 WJ Gordon, 'A Property Right in Self-Expression: Equality and Individualism in the Natural Law of Intellectual Property' (1993) 12 *Yale Law Journal* 1533, 1544-1545.

60 See also Harris' criticism. Harris (n 40 above) 182-212, 296-299.

61 2nd T: v 31.

62 2nd T: v 27.

by their nature ideas are infinitely consumable. My concern is with the *expressive*, copyrightable, form of the ideas.

Property rooted in labour is the challenge intellectual property scholars find in Locke's theory of property. They are mainly attracted by Locke's attempt to reconcile the tension between private acquisition and public interest: the right of the labourer, the good of the public, and the conservation of the public domain. Scholars use Locke's labour theory to argue that intellectual property rights are never absolute and focus on the nonrivalrous nature of ideational entities and their ability to survive the Lockean test.[63]

Hughes and Gordon were the first to argue that the Lockean property argument is particularly attractive when we discuss copyright ownership.[64] They created an interpretive tradition on which modern copyright-Lockeans keep devising theories about copyright. However, in a recent essay, Damstedt claims that '[r]evising Locke for a theory of intellectual property has become vital.'[65] Despite their great contribution to copyright theory, the arguments of Hughes, Gordon and Damstedt are fundamentally flawed for their failure to take account of Locke's explicit reference to copyright in his theory of property and in other essays. With only two clear exceptions, subsequent scholarship on Locke and intellectual property confines its exploration of the Lockean position on copyright to the twenty-six sections of Chapter V.[66] I shall reject widely accepted interpretations of Locke's property used in discussions on copyright. While it might be far-fetched to claim that he predicted contemporary trends in copyright, a reading of Locke's minor essay 'Liberty of the Press' may lead one to crown Locke the 'Boyle of copyright.'[67]

---

63 This is what accounts for the non-rivalrous nature of the consumption of ideational entities: works of art and authorship are nonrivalrous goods which are products 'more like inexhaustible 'public goods' that are ordinarily un-owned', and thereby eliminate the scarcity problem. WJ Gordon, 'Intellectual Property' in P Cane and M Tushnet (eds.), *The Oxford Handbook of Legal Studies* (Oxford: Oxford University Press, 2003) 617, 621. See also PM Romer, 'Endogenous Technological Change' (1990) 98(5) *Journal of Political Economy*, S71, S73-S74.

In other words, it is argued that as non-rivalrous goods, works of art and authorship 'can be used by an infinite number of people in an infinite number of ways without harming the use value of any other person, including the initial producer.' Damstedt (n 53 above) 1182.

64 Hughes (n 9 above); Gordon (n 59 above).

65 Damstedt (n 53 above) 1180.

66 The first exception is an article written by Wilf in which he considers both Chapter V and Locke's *Essay Concerning Human Understanding* for the justification of a community wide right in trademarks. S Wilf, 'Who Authors Trademarks?' (1999) 17 *Cardozo Arts & Entertainment Law Journal* 1. The second exception is an article by Shiffrin in which she discusses a part of Chapter V, Locke's minor essay entitled 'Liberty of the Press.' SV Shiffrin, 'Lockean Arguments for Private Intellectual Property' in Munzer (n 31 above) 138-167.

67 J Locke, 'Liberty of the Press' (published 1694-1695) in M Goldie (ed.), *John Locke: Political Essays* (Cambridge: Cambridge University Press, 1997) 329.

The personhood approach Another traditional theory is premised on the assumption that the allocation of entitlements and control over resources in the external environment, in the guise of property, is necessary for the development of personality. The personhood school of thought derives from Kantian and Hegelian philosophies. For Hegel, private property is acquired by joining one's individual will to a given external object.[68] The person who mixes his labour with land, deserves a reward for attaching his existence to the object.[69] Personality for Hegel, Palmer explains, 'does not simply require external objects for its development. Its development is its objectification through externalization of its will.'[70]

Radin reformulates Hegel's normative connection between property and personality and argues that property is protected because it is already part of the individual's personality.[71] She distinguishes between personal (inalienable) property and fungible (market value) property. A personal object of property is where 'its loss causes pain that cannot be relieved by the object's replacement',[72] while fungible property 'is perfectly replaceable with other goods of equal market value.'[73] Radin asserts that '[t]he more closely connected with personhood, the stronger the entitlement.'[74] From this standpoint, intellectual property rights are justifiable as manifestations of one's personality in one's intellectual expressions, and as barriers to expropriation of inalienable features of one's personality, invested in his authorial creations. From this philosophical underpinning, German and French copyright laws evolved, and their impact on Anglo-American laws was eventually grounded in a separate system of moral rights.

Hughes provides us with a useful treatment of the Hegelian personality argument and its applicability to intellectual property. He argues that the 'Hegelian personality theory applies more easily because intellectual products, even the most technical,

68 GWF Hegel, *Philosophy of Right* (1821) (Oxford: Oxford University Press, TM Knox trans., 1967) 44, 50, 51-58. For further analysis see, PG Stillman, *Property, Freedom, and Individuality in Hegel's and Marx's Political Thoughts*, in JR Pennock and JW Chapman (ed.), *Property*, Nomos, XXII, (New York: New York University Press, 1980) 130-167.

69 See J Waldron, *The Right to Private Property* (Oxford: Clarendon Press, 1988) 343-389.

70 Palmer (n 19 above) 838.

71 MJ Radin, 'Property and Personhood' (1982) 34 *Stanford Law Review* 957, 965 (hereinafter – 'Radin 1982'). Radin's purpose is to attack the dominance of utilitarian theories of property claiming that not al! entitlements can be subject to market exchange. This view was fully developed by her in 'Market Inalienability' (1987) 100 *Harvard Law Review* 1849; and *Reinterpreting Property* (Chicago: Chicago University Press, 1993).

72 Radin 1982, ibid 959.

73 Ibid 960.

74 Ibid 986.

seem to result from the individual's mental processes.'[75] Intellectual properties, Hughes argues, are a 'receptacle for personality.'[76]

Scholars debating intellectual property and personhood employ different approaches. For example, Fisher asks: 'When an author has revealed her work to the world, does it nevertheless continue to fall within the zone of her "personhood" – so that she may legitimately claim a right to restrict its further communication?'[77] Netanel replies to this question in the affirmative and claims that 'authors in fact have a strong interest in continuing sovereignty over their expression.'[78] In contrast, Weinreb writes that 'once the individual has communicated her expression publicly, it takes on a "life of its own" and that thereafter, unless it remains tied to the author in some special way, its further communication does not involve her autonomous self. Were the author given such control in the name of autonomy, it would, I think, come down to an economic interest, the author herself commodifying what was declared uncommodifiable.'[79]

Social and institutional planning Cultural diversity is a key feature in copyright discourse. The fourth theoretical division, social-institutional-planning, is largely devoted to discussing ways to maintain a strong civic culture that benefits from a reasonably balanced social and institutional intellectual property regime. Those who are engaged in social and institutional planning, draw upon various legal and political theories. This category is close to Fisher's sub-category of copyright theory entitled: 'Social Planning Theory.'[80] He includes in this category theories that formulate 'a vision of a just and attractive culture'[81] in which controversial elements comprise the vision: consumer welfare, a cornucopia of information and ideas, a rich artistic tradition, distributive justice, diverse cultural meaning, semiotic democracy

75 Hughes (n 9 above) 365.

76 Ibid 340. Subsequent academic writings employed the personhood theory for, amongst other, questions of alienability; restrictions upon copyright interests; legitimacy of the personhood theory to copyright; rights in works produced in the course of employment; and for testing parameters for personhood interests such as creativity and originality. See for example, K Port, 'The Unnatural Expansion of Trademark Rights: Is a Federal Dilution Statute Necessary?' (1994) 18 *Seton Hall Legislative Journal* 433, 475-478; S Cherensky, 'A Penny for Their Thoughts: Employee-Inventors, Preinvention Assignment Agreement, Property and Personhood' (1993) 81 *California Law Review* 597; TF Cotter, 'Pragmatism, Economics, and the Droit Moral' (1997) 76 *North Carolina Law Review* 8; Drahos (n 31 above) 73-94; Palmer (n 19 above) 835-849; Pessach (n 31 above) 403-410; Fisher (n 31 above) 171-172, 184-189; Menell (n 31 above) 158-159.

77 Fisher, ibid 190.

78 See NW Netanel, 'Copyright Alienability Restrictions and the Enhancement of Author Autonomy: A Normative Evaluation' (1993) 24 *Rutgers Law Journal* 347, 400.

79 L Weinreb, 'Copyright for Functional Expression' (1998) 111 *Harvard Law Review* 1149, 1222 n.310.

80 W Fisher, 'Property and Contract on the Internet' (1998) 73 *Chicago-Kent Law Review* 1203 (hereinafter – 'Fisher 1998'); Fisher (n 31 above) 172-173, 192-194.

81 Fisher 1998, ibid 1215.

and respect.[82] He then explains that the 'Social Planning Theory' 'is similar to utilitarianism in its teleological orientation, but dissimilar in its willingness to deploy visions of a desirable society richer than the conceptions of "social welfare" deployed by utilitarians.'[83]

Copyright promotes expression, but copyrightable expressions limit subsequent democratic and expressive discourse. Social and institutional planning theorists advocate a less rigid set of intellectual property laws, elite patronage and cultural hierarchy, in order to facilitate expansive social interaction and cultural exchange. Amongst the many scholars who debate the importance of democratic dialogue and the existence of an open expressive environment, two key works stand out. Coombe presents a post-modernist approach to intellectual property and stresses the implications of a restricted public domain,[84] and Netanel brings invaluable insights from democratic theory to our views of intellectual property protection.[85] Both Coombe and Netanel advocate a greater democratic dialogue, a freer communicative sphere, the need to eliminate restrictions on creative expression, a stronger public domain and a radical change of the perception of copyright proprietary entitlements in order to enable more widespread participation in the production of knowledge and ideas.[86]

Traditional proprietarianism Although scholars differ one from another in their theoretical approach to the idea of copyright, they seem to agree that copyright is a form of property.[87] They tend to adopt conceptions of ownership and title of traditional property to questions of copyright ownership, without taking account of the social nature of copyright. Although 'traditional proprietarianism' may not seem as an independent theoretical approach to copyright, it connects between the different

---

82 Fisher 1998, ibid 1212-1218. He recognises that these elements have been 'the subjects of furious debate among political philosophers' and intellectual property theories will certainly not solve controversies surrounding these elements. Fisher (n 31 above) 193.

83 Fisher, ibid 172.

84 Coombe (n 3 above); and by the same author, *The Cultural Life of Intellectual Properties: Authorship, Appropriation and the Law* (Durham and London: Duke University Press, 1998).

85 NW Netanel, 'Copyright and Democratic Civil Society' (1996) 106 *Yale Law Journal* 283; and by the same author 'Assessing Copyright's Democratic Principles in the Global Arena' (1998) 51 *Vanderbilt Law Review* 217.

86 See also in this vein N Elkin-Koren, 'Copyright Law and Social Dialogue on the Information Superhighways: The Case Against Copyright Liability of Bulletin Board Operators' (1995) 13 *Cardozo Arts & Entertainment Law Journal* 345; Y Benkler, 'Free as the Air to Common Use: First Amendment Constraints on Enclosure of the Public Domain' (1999) *New York University Law Review* 354; NW Netanel, 'Locating Copyright Within the First Amendment Skein' (2001) 54 *Stanford Law Review* 1.

87 In a recent work Lemley challenges this attitude. He claims that intellectual property has come of age and we do not have to look for justifications in other theories such as property. We should follow traditional utilitarian explanations of intellectual property. See MA Lemley, 'Property, Intellectual Property, and Free Riding' (2005) 83 *Texas Law Review* 1031.

approaches. Every copyright theory sanctifies conceptions of property entitlement, familiar to discussions on traditional property.

The purpose of identifying 'traditional proprietarianism' as an approach to copyright theory is to emphasise that every theory relates in one way or another to the bundle of rights associated with the right to traditional tangible property, and with traditional principles of trespass and encroachment into one's private dominion.[88] At present, as I will argue, even scholars who advocate a radical socialist approach to copyright remain steadfast to conceptions of ownership of traditional property.

Authorial constructionism The sixth theoretical approach one may find in the current corpus of debates on copyright theory is authorial constructionism. Scholars that are affiliated with this approach criticise the romantic notion of 'the author' and define the property constituent of the copyright system from a social perspective. For scholars engaged in research on authorial constructionism, the author is deconstructed into a vessel through which many influences and experiences are poured.

Jaszi and Woodmansee investigate the origin and meaning of authorship. They argue that '[m]ost writing today – in business, government, industry, the law, the sciences and social sciences – is collaborative, yet it is still being taught as if it were solitary, originary activity.'[89] The baseline of Woodmansee's and Jaszi's argument is that authorial creations are collaborative in nature. They view the authorial creative activity as a multi-player activity. While Woodmansee examines the evolution of the concept of 'authorship' and its many definitions as a collaborative activity,[90] Jaszi argues that the romantic vision of the author undermines the nature of copyright creation as a collaborative activity.[91] Their collaborative approach to copyright is, however, somewhat individualistic because they treat authors or groups of authors in their individual capacity, rather than as members of a larger social group and do not question the right of this group for matters of copyright ownership. Their ideal of the constructed author is more based on the interaction with fellow authors, than with society at large. Their view thus questions the wisdom of authorship and its origin, but does not sufficiently challenge the monopoly position of authors in the copyright creation process.

---

88 Palmer labels this approach the 'piggy-back' theory. Palmer (n 19 above) 820, 851-855.

89 M Woodmansee and P Jaszi, 'Introduction' in Woodmansee and Jaszi (n 16 above) 1, 9. Kaplan also writes: 'most of today's 'intellectual work including the distinctively imaginative is now being done by teams, a practice apt to continue and grow.' B Kaplan, *An Unhurried View of Copyright* (New York: Columbia University Press, 1967) 117.

90 M Woodmansee, 'On the Author Effect: Recovering Collectivity' in Woodmansee and Jaszi, ibid 15; and by the same author 'The Genius and the Copyright: Economic and Legal Conditions of the Emergence of the "Author"', (1984) 17 *Eighteenth-Century Studies* 425. See also, P Kewes, '"A Play, Winch I Presume to Call Original": Appropriation, Creative Genius, and Eighteenth-Century Playwriting' (2001) 34(1) *Studies in the Literary Imagination* 17.

91 Jaszi (n 16 above). See also by the same author (n 4 above).

Drawing upon these views of authorship, Boyle criticises the idea of romantic authorship and its effect on the scope of copyright in modern times.[92] He reminds us that authorial entities do not stand alone. They are built on contributions from various sources; and thus are 'socially constructed and historically contingent.'[93] Many scholars support, albeit sometimes not explicitly, the idea behind authorial constructionism, that copyrighted entities do not stand alone, and that realisation of these works necessitates contribution from the collective. For example, Chaffee remarks that 'the world goes ahead because each of us builds on the work of our predecessors',[94] Litman argues that there is no ultimate originality,[95] Coombe criticises the propertisation of shared symbols and cultural elements,[96] Craig argues that intellectual works are necessarily the products of collective labour and so ought to be owned collectively,[97] and Gordon reminds us that artists receive 'a tradition and world they have not made.'[98] These examples demonstrate the inapplicability of the romantic notion of authorship and the need to evaluate authorship in a social context. As Durham puts it: 'Authorship, according to this "un-romantic" point of view, is less a manifestation of the author's personal vision, created *ex nihilo*, than it is a synthesis of prior texts and cultural influences.'[99]

Although many copyright scholars purport to recognise the ideology behind the construction of authorship, they still retain dominant stereotypes of authorship and authors. For example, Samuelson writes: 'Boyle does not oppose authors' rights except to the extent that romantic notions about authorship lead to inefficient or unjust legal outcomes, as sometimes occur when we fail to appreciate fully the sources from which authors draw or the contributions of audiences.'[100] Indeed, Boyle asserts that allocation of property rights to authors has 'a clear element of existential truth – our experience of authors, inventors, and artists who do transform their fields and our world, together with the belief…that the ability to remark the conditions of

---

92 Boyle (n 1 above). *Cf* MA Lemley, 'Romantic Authorship and the Rhetoric of Property' (1997) 75 *Texas Law Review* 873.

93 Ibid 114.

94 Z Chafee Jr., 'Reflections on the Law of Copyright: I' (1945) 45 *Columbia Law Review* 503, 511.

95 Litman (n 20 above). Litman views the creative act as an act dependent on the works of others, and concludes that 'this is the essence of authorship.' Ibid 966. Similarly Yen remarks: 'Any frank appraisal of authorship must conclude that each author's work contains both the author's original creations and material drawn from other authors.' A Yen., 'The Interdisciplinary Future of Copyright Theory' in Woodmansee and Jaszi (n 16 above) 159, 166.

96 Coombe (n 3 above).

97 Craig (n 53 above) 36.

98 Gordon (n 21 above) 77.

99 A Durham, 'The Random Muse: Authorship and Indeterminacy' (2002) 44 *William and Mary Law Review* 569, 616.

100 P Samuelson, 'The Quest for Enabling Metaphors for Law and Lawyering in the Information Age' (1996) 94 *Michigan Law Review* 2029, 2055-2056.

individual life and collective existence is to be cherished and rewarded.'[101] However, Boyle does not fully translate his rejection of the romantic notion of authorship into a paradigm of ownership that takes into account the right of the public.[102]

Social constructionism In this book I present a model for public authorship, emphasising the sociality of copyright. I fully recognise the fundamental necessity of allocating property rights for authors in order to maintain stable social and cultural realities and do not reject rewards to authors in the form of property rights. As Ginsburg recently asserted: 'whether one sees copyright as a personality right conferring on the author the ownership of the fruits of her labor, or as an economic incentive scheme to promote the production of works of authorship, or as a public works program designed to fill the public domain (or, most accurately, as a combination of the three), giving credit where it is due is fully compatible with both the author-regarding and the public-regarding aspects of these goals.'[103]

The public authorship model I introduce and defend in this book combines of arguments postulated, amongst other, by Woodmansee, Jaszi, Boyle, and Coombe. As a right-base approach, it defines the scope of authors' rights and the rights of the public in copyrighted materials and argues for a public property right in every copyrighted entity. The views expressed by scholars who examine authorial constructionism, in particular Woodmansee and Jaszi, contribute immensely to the understanding of the sociality of the creative act and inspired my vision of what copyright *should* be. At the same time, however, while Woodmansee and Jaszi examine the 'construction of authorship' I emphasise the '*social* construction of authorship.' As opposed to Woodmansee and Jaszi who define the creative act as collaborative in nature but emphasise the collaboration between authors in their individual capacity, I examine the vital and unavoidable collaboration between authors and the public in the collective sense, and highlight their mutual role in the formation of copyrighted entities. This role renders every copyrighted entity a social construct and require us to take account of the public's role when we structure the entitlement edifice in copyright. I attempt to show that social constructionism is a unique definitional tool on which to base limitations to copyright ownership. My analysis is designed to lay the foundations for a coherent copyright balance and reward all actors involved in the making of authorial and artistic properties.

In Search of Philosophical Clarity

The claim that existing intellectual property theories do not provide sufficient philosophical clarity cannot be dismissed. First, each of the theories shares common

101 Boyle (n 1 above) 60.

102 I further explore this aspect in 'The Copyright Moment' (2006) 43(3) *San Diego Law Review* 247.

103 JC Ginsburg, 'The Right to Claim Authorship in US Copyright and Trademarks Law' (2004) 41 *Houston Law Review* 263, 307.

elements, which blur the boundaries between them.[104] Second, scholars do not agree on any given theory, but rather combine the various theoretical patterns to develop new themes. Third, intellectual property theories are not designed to address foundational arguments about private property or wider philosophical issues. Scholars and practitioners draw elements from various theories and take the parts that seem applicable for a given situation. A good example is the way copyright scholars apply Locke's labour theory to copyright. They tend, as I will argue, to consider only parts of Locke's property philosophy and on that basis wrongly argue that he ignored intellectual property or did not think of the public good.

Perhaps an acceptable theory should be pluralistic in its foundations. I agree that there is no unitary justification for intellectual property. For this reason, one finds traces of utilitarianism, together with principles from a personhood theory in the Lockean approach.[105] The various justifications may create a multi-tiered system for intellectual property theory.[106] Even if we favour a pluralistic approach, we must not let misconceptions of ownership and control to override social needs we, the collective, ought to secure. Fisher expresses various misgivings with regards to the capacity of theories to contribute to the practical evolution of intellectual property laws, but then asserts:

> That conclusion, however, does not imply that the theories have no practical use. In two respects, I suggest, they retain considerable value. First, while they have failed to make good on their promises to provide comprehensive prescriptions concerning the ideal shape of intellectual-property law, they can help identify nonobvious attractive resolutions of particular problems. Second, they can foster valuable conversations among the various participants in the lawmaking process…through continued conversations among scholars, legislators, judges, litigants, lobbyists, and the public at large, there may lie some hope of addressing the inadequacies of the existing theories...Only by continuing to discuss…can we hope to make progress.[107]

Menell expresses a more favourable approach towards the contribution of theories to the development of the intellectual property system. He identifies the necessity to extend the reach of current theories in intellectual property and recognises the important role theories play in providing fresh insights 'for the evolution of new privately and socially constructed institutions to develop effective governance structures.'[108] Like any other theory, discrepancies between the various copyright theories exist. The important message emanating from new inquiries into copyright theory is their impact on reformulating social and political principles, highlighting

104 Fisher 1998 (n 80 above) 1215.

105 Hughes (n 9 above) 329.

106 See for example, DB Resnik, 'A Pluralistic Account of Intellectual Property' (2003) 46 *Journal of Business Ethics* 319.

107 Fisher (n 31 above) 194-199.

108 Menell (n 31 above) 163.

societal needs that courts alone cannot predict, and clarifying controversial conceptual gaps in the way we understand copyright and its limits.

A Road Map

This book argues for a public property right in copyrighted entities. It emphasises the sociality of copyright creation and the role and contribution of the public to the creation of every copyright work. I apply this approach to propose needed conceptual and institutional reforms in copyright law. After the introductory chapter and the examination of the six main approaches dominating the landscape of current copyright theory, Chapter 2 begins an exploration of the conceptual complexity in copyright and discusses the nature of copyright as an essentially contested concept and argues that if we really strive to confront the challenge of rethinking the wisdom of our copyright regime, we have to clarify what lies at the heart of copyright's inner conceptual structure.

Chapter 3 considers the broad question of what comprises copyright. Copyright, I argue, is a bundle of rights and duties that cannot be isolated one from the other. This chapter explores the inherent difficulties we encounter when we associate copyright with traditional property. Although I defend the allocation of property in artistic and authorial entities, I oppose the allocation of similar protective powers afforded to traditional property to copyright. I argue that in order to balance rightholders' demands and the public interest we must rethink the strength and content of copyright's bundle of rights.[109]

The broad theoretical issues I discuss in this book are relevant to every branch of our intellectual property system, but they are most urgent in copyright. Copyrighted works are the most dependent on the public's contribution *and* at the same are protected by a system that consistently denies this contribution. Although arguments can be made against exclusive ownership of trademarks, their social value and impact are minor in comparison to copyright. With patent protection, the paradox between public contribution and public benefit is less acute. The patent system requires that

109 True, '[m]any contemporary *intellectual*-property theorists also participate in… arguments about the appropriate shape of property law in general' Menell (n 31 above) 176. In this book I make no claim to an exhaustive taxonomy of property rights theories, nor do I intend to undermine traditional property. My analysis is confined to copyright law. I chose to discuss definable questions with the hope of generating future debate that would cover other branches of intellectual property. Tawney puts this matter aptly: 'Property is the most ambiguous of categories…It covers a multitude of rights which have nothing in common except that they are exercised by persons and enforced by States…They may be conditioned like the grant of patent rights, or absolute like the ownership of ground rents, terminable like copyright, or permanent like a freehold…The course of wisdom is neither to attack private property in general, nor to defend it in general; for things are not similar in quality, merely because they are identical in name.' RH Tawney, 'Property and Creative Work', in CB Macpherson, *Property: Mainstream and Critical Positions* (Oxford: Basil Blackwell, 1978) 133, 136.

an invention add some distinct value to the public. In contrast, copyright appears to defy any requirement of value. This does not imply that patents should be exclusively owned or that protection of copyright works should be contingent on value. It does suggest, however, that it is vital to start the journey towards expanding the public domain with the branch of intellectual property that most saliently repudiates the contribution made by the public.

Chapters 4 and 5 explore the special relationship between the individual author and the collective, and criticise the lack of awareness we show towards the social nature of copyright. Chapter 4 takes the romantic notion of authorship as its organising principle. It argues that no copyrighted material can be created *ex nihilo*, and criticises the law and scholars who treat copyright creation as a solitary activity. I argue that the public satisfies the requirement for authorship and that a copyrighted item can never be 'originally created' in the sense that its organising components have no prior owner. The casual relations between already existing works, templates, social and cultural processes, and newly created works by authors, artists and the like, render the label 'original' fictitious.

Chapter 5 applies social construction theory to the findings of Chapter 4. Probably no copyright scholar wholly rejects the argument that copyright works are socially constructed and historically contingent. It is an implicit argumentative component in copyright discourse. However, the crucial question to ask is what *is* socially constructed in copyright? It is obvious that the institution of copyright is a social construction, an evolution of historical events, but it is less obvious that authors and their works are social constructions as well. Although statements frequently made by copyright scholars attest to the fact that they are aware of social construction, no theory of copyright has been sufficiently developed which reflects the full implications of this.

Social constructionism, as it applies to copyright, must not only relate to the interaction between authors as individuals within a large social group but also the interaction between them and the group in its collective capacity. Chapter 5 examines the role of collaboration between authors and the public and challenges misconceptions concerning prevalent definitions of the public domain. It explains 'the copyright moment' and argues that copyrighted entities are born in the instant in which the input from two sources, public and authors, is combined into a unitary whole. One of the major conclusions from Chapters 4 and 5 is that every copyrighted entity is limited *ab initio* due to its dependence on the public's authorial contribution.

Chapter 6 challenges the tendency to claim that Locke's property theory does not provide a coherent justification for our copyright system. On the contrary; Locke's explicit writings show a normatively relevant awareness of the socially constructed character of copyright. Chapter 6 begins with an overview of common scholarly trends in the application of Lockean property to copyright and challenges the many modern copyright-Lockeans who argue that Locke never thought of copyright or that his discussion on tangible property either suffices for an understanding of copyright or illegitimate for copyright because of its individualistic nature.

This chapter examines whether Locke can be re-imagined. It asks whether Locke's general philosophy of property and concepts of ownership and control can address social and cultural concerns this book raises with regards to the ownership of copyrighted entities. First, it explores Locke's letter entitled 'Liberty of the Press', which reveals his vision of copyright. Second, it rejects certain classic interpretations of his theory of property as applied to copyright. Third, it argues that Locke's theory of knowledge has a constructivist element that has implications for his wider ideas of property and ownership, and that this actually supports the argument that the making of copyright is a collective enterprise and that the public deserves a property entitlement in every work resulting from this enterprise.

One of the main conclusions from these chapters will be that the nature of a copyright work as a social construction means that both public and authors labour on its creation. Thus, I argue, copyrighted works should be *jointly owned* between public and authors. Chapter 7 examines the conditions the law imposes on authors for recognition of joint authorship in order to ascertain whether the public/authors collaborative paradigm satisfies these conditions. It argues that we should recognise the public authorial contribution to the making of copyrighted materials, and avoid perpetuating patterns of authorial denial embedded in our existing conception of copyright. It shows, by comparative analysis, how the role played by the public in copyright creation qualifies it as a joint author, even in jurisdictions in which tests of joint authorship are most stringent. This chapter concludes with a brief review of several alternatives to copyright, which may accommodate the concerns I express in this book and account for the public joint right. I provide my preferred formula, which grounds the public authorial role as an undisputable and entrenched guarantee. In concluding, Chapter 8 explains the significance of this study for copyright theory and policy. It then outlines broader conclusions, highlighting the misconceptions we nurture in copyright.

Chapter 2

Conceptualising Copyright

A Conceptual Challenge

Dealing with a complex discipline like copyright requires attention to the conceptual aura surrounding it. Copyright scholars develop new concepts, reject existing ones and introduce into the copyright playing field conflicting views and attitudes. We like, as Waldron asserts 'to keep our armory of concepts in good shape'[1] in order to defend our personal understanding and claim that those of others lack clarity. In this chapter I examine the nature of copyright as a 'concept' and discuss the benefits that can be derived from understanding copyright as a vague conceptual framework, or, alternatively as an arsenal of competing interpretations and permutations, rendering its meaning 'essentially contested.' In this book I offer a new definitional paradigm for copyright. As Garon observes, '[u]nless there is a valid conceptual basis for copyright laws, there can be no fundamental immorality in refusing to be bound by them…'[2]

'Concept' versus 'Conception'

Philosophers sometimes distinguish between 'concepts' and 'conceptions' as analytical tools.[3] The distinction concerns levels of abstraction. The concept of X is more general, more abstract and does not tell us what X requires in particular circumstances. The concept displays an inherent complexity. Hart, for example, argues that there is 'certain complexity in the structure of the idea of justice.'[4] Justice is an abstract idea which to many would mean maintaining or restoring a certain

---

1 J Waldron, 'Is the Rule of Law an Essentially Contested Concept (in Florida)?' (2002) 21 *Law and Philosophy* 137, 138 (hereinafter – 'Waldron 2002').

2 JM Garon, 'Normative Copyright: A Conceptual Framework for Copyright Philosophy and Ethics' (2003) 88 *Cornell Law Review* 1278, 1283.

3 Dworkin takes fairness as an example of a concept and explains: 'The difference is a difference not just in the detail of the instructions given but the kind of instructions given. When I appeal to the concept of fairness I appeal to what fairness means, and I give my views on that issue no special standing. When I lay down a conception of fairness, I lay down what I mean by fairness, and my view is therefore the heart of the matter. When I appeal to fairness I pose a moral issue; when I lay down my conception of fairness I try to answer it.' R Dworkin, Taking Rights Seriously (London: Duckworth, 1977) 135.

4 HLA Hart, *The Concept of Law* (Oxford: Oxford University Press, 2nd ed. 1994) 160.

balance or proportion. A central element in the way we perceive justice is 'Treat like cases alike; though we need to add to the latter and treat different cases differently.'[5] But this remains an empty form unless we understand that 'any set of human beings will resemble each other in some respects and differ from each other in others.'[6] We have to identify elements of resemblance and elements of difference. This is a crucial point since without identifying these elements 'we cannot proceed to criticize laws or other social arrangements as unjust.'[7] Treating justice as a general abstract concept, according to Hart, means that the concept consists of two parts: '[A] uniform or constant feature, summarized in the precept 'Treat like cases alike' and a shifting or varying criterion used in determining when, for any given purpose, cases are alike or different. In this respect justice is like the notions of what is genuine, or tall, or warm, which contains an implicit reference to a standard which varies with the classification of the thing to which they are applied.'[8]

It can be argued that a concept reflects a general abstract idea, an uncontroversial idea or principle, or the agreement people share that the concept X exists. The conceptions of X reflect different views of the concept.[9] They take X to denote a parent concept from which competing conceptions may emerge. A good example Dworkin uses is the way courts apply the Constitution, and 'if courts try to be faithful to the Constitution, they will for that very reason be forced to decide between competing conceptions of political morality.'[10]

We normally tend to agree on the 'concept', yet disagree on the detailed 'conception' because we see things differently. 'Justice' is a concept, but its applicability to copyright admits of many different conceptions. Rawls employs the concept/conception paradigm and tells us that its greatest benefit is in helping us to map competing applications of a given concept. The 'distinction between concept and the various conceptions of justice settles no important questions. It simply helps to identify the role of the principles of social justice.'[11] Rawls believes that people radically differ in respect of their conception of the good life and remarks:

> Men disagree about which principles should define the basic terms of their association. Yet we may still say, despite this disagreement, that they each have a conception of justice...a characteristic set of principles for assigning basic rights and duties and for

---

5 Ibid 159.

6 Ibid.

7 Ibid.

8 Ibid 160.

9 In *Diversity: The Invention of a Concept* Wood argues that we are not free people who chart the direction we chose to go. Wood's attempt is an example of common confusion between 'concept' and 'conception: his book is *not* to construct a 'concept' but to invent a 'conception' of the existing concept 'diversity', and claim that society's diversity is defined by us being members of a social group – creatures of the historical evolution of these groups. P Wood, *Diversity: The Invention of a Concept* (San Francisco: Encounter Books, 2003).

10 Dworkin (n 3 above) 136 (emphasis added).

11 J Rawls, *A Theory of Justice* (Oxford: Oxford University Press, 1971 (ed 1999)) 5.

> determining what they take to be the proper distribution of the benefits and burdens of social cooperation. Thus it seems natural to think of the concept of justice as distinct from the various conceptions of justice and as being specified by the role which these different sets of principles, these different conceptions, have in common.[12]

Property is a good example of a concept around which competing conceptions of entitlements and their limits contend.[13] We share an agreement on the existence of property as a concept but it does not tell us how property is understood in particular situations. That is, we tend to agree on the general concept, but disagree on its various conceptions. Conceptions of property play a decisive role in copyright debates. Ideals of property affect ideals of copyright. Just as property can be justified as a derivation from labour, desert, liberty, utility, efficiency, personality and human nature,[14] so copyright is justifiable on grounds of utility, labour, personality, social and institutional planning, authorial constructionism and social constructionism. The competing conceptions of the appropriate scope of copyright acknowledge the existence of a concept.

In recent works on property, Harris and Underkuffler offer different accounts, to some extent competing, of the concept of property. Neither denies that the concept of property exists and has a recognisable general meaning, but each devises conceptions representing different approaches regarding the definition and regulation of property. For Harris the institution of property is composed of 'the twin notions of trespassory rules and the ownership spectrum.'[15] He explains:

> By 'trespassory rules' is meant any social rules, whether or not embodied in law, which purport to impose obligations on all members of society, other than an individual or group who is taken to have some form of open-ended relationship to a thing, not to make use of that thing without the consent of the individual or group. The most hallowed such trespassory rule embodies the commandment 'thou shalt not steal'...By 'the ownership spectrum' is meant the open-ended relationships presupposed and protected by trespassory rules. All attempts in the history of theorizing about property to provide an univocal explication of the concept of ownership, applicable within all societies and to all resources, have failed. Yet, property talk, lay and legal, deploys ineliminable ownership conceptions.[16]

---

12 Ibid.

13 Although no universally accepted theory of property has been constructed, most philosophical speculations affirm the existence of property. I offer an examination of this proposition in Chapter 3 and its effect on the evolution of the concept of copyright.

14 Carter's examination of property is a good example of how property is a concept justifiable through competing conceptions. A Carter, *The Philosophical Foundations of Property Rights* (London: Harvester Wheatsheaf, 1989).

15 JW Harris, *Property and Justice* (Oxford: Oxford University Press, 1996) 5.

16 Ibid.

Harris argues that both conceptions explain the concept of property. Underkuffler challenges Harris's conceptions.[17] She defines the concept of property as 'a general legal matter'[18] governed by two conceptions: (i) the 'common conception' which defines the rights of the individual, separated from the communal sphere and securing the individual's private autonomy against collective interests;[19] and (ii) the 'operative conception' in which property performs a weaker function. This conception represents individuals' rights fluid in time and mutable as circumstances dictate, in order to account for the general public welfare.[20] Underkuffler also argues that both conceptions are necessary in order to reach a coherent understanding of the concept of property, and to find a balance within that concept.

Underkuffler presents two conceptions of property and considers Harris' twin conceptions to have only one general meaning which parallels the 'common conception' she advocates. She writes: 'by defining ownership as an "open-ended set of *prima facie* use-privileges [and] control powers", Harris represents a *particular* conception of property (the "common" conception of property) as, in fact, the *only* one.'[21] It seems that Underkuffler's criticism of Harris and formulation of two conceptions of property, reaffirms the inherent employment of the concept/conception paradigm in her argument:

> The different conceptions of property that we have identified provide radically different protection for individual interests under legal guarantee such as the Taking Clause. If the common conception of property is used, individual interests are afforded strict protection. If the operative conception is used, individual interests are – as a practical matter – afforded none.
>
> Our choice of a conception of property is not, in short, a simply 'descriptive' or 'neutral' one. We determine – through our choice of a conception of property – what is assumed and what is not, what is 'radical' and what is not, what is presumptively legitimate and what is not, what is 'owed' (as a normative matter) to the individual and what is not.[22]

The agreement people share on the existence of property as a general concept is precisely the agreement they share on copyright. The concept of copyright exists and has a common framework in which it operates. But the manner in which it is developed or regulated is subject to many conflicting views. In other words, there is no dispute that the institution of copyright exists, but it 'means many things to many people. To some it signifies a component of the rights of man, deriving from natural

---

17 LS Underkuffler, *The Idea of Property: Its Making and Power* (Oxford: Oxford University Press, 2003) 37-63, 132-134.

18 Ibid 54.

19 Ibid 38-46.

20 Ibid 46-51.

21 Ibid 60. For further illustration on the application of the concept/conception to 'ownership', see J Waldron, *The Right to Private Property* (Oxford: Oxford University Press, 1988) 47-53.

22 Ibid 61-63.

law and sustaining the work of the human mind by protecting authors in respect of all uses of their works. To others it represents a commercially inspired monopoly for the better regulation of the exploitation of the author's work in the market place.'[23] That is, any attempt to introduce a conclusive conception of copyright is notoriously elusive. As a system that depends on collectively produced and owned social and cultural properties, and has to balance between the individual's proprietary interests and society's need for recognition of its contribution to each and every copyrighted work, it is ubiquitous and complex, socially and economically important, and thus deemed controversial.

Just as there is an almost indefinite number of conceptions of the good life there are many conceptions of the concept 'just copyright' amongst authors, consumers, academics and legislators.[24] The simple reason, in Madison's words, lies in the fact that 'copyright doctrine suggests stories of artists, artisans, tradespeople, and industries with different and overlapping interests, all expressed through the prism of a single body of law.'[25] If copyright is composed of various conceptions, copyright, as a 'concept', is open for great challenges. I shall not press the concept/conception paradigm any further, but rather pose another question which is a variation on this theme: is copyright an essentially contested concept?

Gallie's Ideal of Essential Contestability

Gallie coined the term 'essentially contested concept' according to which, there are certain concepts, such as art and democracy, 'the proper use of which inevitably involves endless disputes about their proper uses on the part of their users.'[26]

---

23 JAL Sterling, *World Copyright Law* (London: Sweet and Maxwell, 1998) xi.

24 It is important to clarify that copyright can be used as a conception where property is the concept, and property can be used as a conception where justice, equality or democracy are the concepts. In this study I concentrate on copyright as a concept and analyse the rival conceptions that it generates.

25 MJ Madison, 'Comment: Where Does Creativity Come From? And Other Stories of Copyright' (2003) 53 *Case Western Reserve Law Review* 747, 748.

26 WB Gallie, 'Essentially Contested Concepts' (1955-1956) 56 *Proceedings of the Aristotelian Society* 167, 169. Hampshire used a similar idiom referring to 'essentially questionable and corrigible concepts', according to which, there are 'some concepts that are permanently and essentially subject to question and dispute and are recognised to be at all times questionable', for example morality and politics. S Hampshire, *Thought and Action* (New York: Viking Press, 1959) 230-231. For Gray, the contestability nature of concepts to which Gallie and Hampshire refer is 'consisted in its being somewhat inherently liable to rival interpretations.' J Gray, 'Political Power, Social Theory, and Essential Contestability' in D Miller and L Siedentop (eds.), *The Nature of Political Theory* (Oxford: Clarendon Press, 1983) 75, 94. The concept 'essential contestability' was also examined by many others. For further illustration see, A MacIntyre's, 'The Essential Contestability of Some Social Concepts' (1973) 84 *Ethics* 1; E Garver, 'Essentially Contested Concepts: the Ethics and Tactics of Argument' (1990) 23 *Philosophy & Rhetoric* 251; and RG Wright, 'Is Natural Law Theory of Any Use

Property, for example, as Dagan asserts: 'is too controversial and has too many manifestations and configurations...Property is an essentially contested concept that is open to competing interpretations and permutations.'[27] Gallie regarded a concept as 'essentially contested' when it fulfils four main conditions: (i) it must be a value-concept: 'it must be appraisive in the sense that it signifies or accredits some kind of valued achievement';[28] (ii) the achievement has to be internally complex;[29] (iii) 'any explanation of its worth must therefore include reference to the respective contributions of its various parts or features;[30] and (iv) any such achievement has to be '"open" in character',[31] i.e., to allow considerable modifications that cannot be defined in advance.[32] Gallie then adds condition (v) to the first four, which ensures that every person recognises that his use of the concept is contested by his fellows' conception; that to use an essentially contested concept means to use it 'both aggressively and defensively.'[33]

For Gallie 'essential' means three things.[34] First, it indicates contestation-to-the-core of the concept: the concept is furnished with anomalies and disagreements

---

in Constitutional Interpretation?' (1995) 4 *Southern California Interdisciplinary Law Journal* 463, 479. Wright defines 'essential contestable concepts' as 'inherently approachable from conflicting perspectives.' Ibid.

27 H Dagan, 'The Distributive Foundation of Corrective Justice' (1999) 98 *Michigan Law Review* 138, 147-148. Radin also labels 'property' as an essentially contested concept. MJ Radin, 'The Liberal Conception of Property: Cross Currents in the Jurisprudence of Takings' (1988) 88 *Columbia Law Review* 1667, 1688.

28 Gallie (n 26 above) 171.

29 Ibid 171-172.

30 Ibid. Gallie also adds the obvious condition (iiia): 'Any essentially contested concept is liable initially to be ambiguous', otherwise contestability cannot be maintained. Ibid 172, n.1.

31 Ibid 172.

32 Ibid. Gallie also adds condition (iva) which holds that any such concept 'is *persistently* vague' simply because its use by one person would not guide all others to follow suit. Ibid 172, n.1.

33 Ibid 172. Reitan explains Gallie's formula in the following way: 'an essentially contested concept is, for Gallie, a positive appraisal of an achievement. In other words, there is a common value judgement that attaches to all objects that fall within the concept's extension: to be such an object is to have achieved something significant (consider the concept "art").' E Reitan. 'Rape as an Essentially Contested Concept' (2001) 16(2) *Hypatia* 43, 48. Garver, taking the example of violence, contends that the appraisal, which an essentially contested concept embodies, does not need to be positive. N Garver, 'Violence and Social Order', in *Philosophy of Law, Politics, and Sociology: Proceedings of the 12th International Wittgenstein Symposium* (Vienna: Holder-Pichler-Tempsky, 1988) 220, cited in Reitan, ibid.

34 See also J Waldron, 'Vagueness in Law and Language: Some Philosophical Issues' (1994) 82(3) *California Law Review* 509, 529-531 (hereinafter – 'Waldron 1994'). Here Waldron offers a useful interpretive guide to certain perplexing legal concepts, and clears up some confusion. He deals mainly with ambiguity, vagueness and contestability and examines the advantageous interplay between these concepts and the ways in which laws are applied and developed.

which generate conceptual patterns that stagger the very heart of the concept. Second, it requires contestedness to serve part of the very essence of the concept in question. And third, in the absence of the component 'essential', the concept may lack sufficient contestability and may lose its 'open' character. I will illustrate with an example from copyright. The European Database Directive shook the concept of database to the core. It has introduced a dual system for database protection: copyright and *sui generis*.[35] For person P_1, database definition D_1 in the European Directive is a 'monstrous caricature of true intellectual property laws'[36] while for P_2, for example, a private undertaking, D_2 means a novel step towards better protection for economic investments. This does not prevent P_3 from putting forward a D_3 and claim to have found a mid-way conception. But if P_3 says 'I do not understand why people find it difficult to understand the meaning of database protection in the Directive; after all there is one clear meaning of the concept', it indicates that he himself does not understand the inherent complexity recognised in the field of database protection, i.e., the implications from jurisdictional differences and the endless controversies concerning what copyright should *not* protect.[37]

Two additional conditions form the core of Gallie's articulated conceptual test: (vii) the availability of an original *exemplar* and (viii) sustainability and adaptability of the former by virtue of continuous competition between the contestant users of the concept.[38] An exemplar is a specific, concrete, template that serves as a single generally acknowledged tradition to follow. An example is a style of playing ice

---

35 Directive 96/9/EC of the European Parliament and of the Council on the Legal Protection of Databases (11 March 1996). For brief overview see G Tritton, *Intellectual Property in Europe* (London: Sweet & Maxwell 2nd ed., 2002) 356-364.

36 JH Reichman and P Samuelson, 'Intellectual Property Rights or Data?' (1997) 50 *Vanderbilt Law Review* 51, 164.

37 The ample scholarship written on the protection of databases in the European Union, whether from the perspective of economics, trade, or from the constitutional perspective, shows how contestable its nature is. See for example M Powell, 'The European Union's Database Directive: An International Antidote to the Side Effects of Feist?' (1997) 20 *Fordham International Law Journal* 1215; M Schneider, 'The European Union Database Directive' (1998) *Berkeley Technology Law Journal* 551; Y Benkler, 'Constitutional Bounds of Database Protection: the Role of Judicial Review in the Creation and Definition of Private Rights in Information' (2000) 15 *Berkeley Technology Law Review* 535; N Thakur, 'Database Protection in the European Union and the United States: The European Database Directive as an Optimum Global Model' (2001) 1 *Intellectual Property Quarterly* 100; J Wald, 'Legislating the Golden Rule: Achieving Comparable Protection Under the European Union Database Directive' (2002) 25 *Fordham International Law Journal* 987; R Lubens, 'Survey of Developments in European Database Protection' (2003) 18 *Berkeley Technology Law Journal* 447; MJ Davison and PB Hugenholtz, 'Football Fixtures, Horseraces and Spin Offs: The ECJ Domesticates the Database Right' (2005) 27(3) *European Intellectual Property Review* 113; S Corbett, 'A Human Rights Perspective on the Database Debate (2006) 28(2) *European Intellectual Property Review* 83.

38 Gallie illustrates using the concepts of art, democracy, social justice and religion. Gallie (n 26 above) 180-187.

hockey that established a tradition of ways to play the game but is recognised as the original template from which this tradition has evolved. Put simply, an exemplar requires that the specific method of playing ice hockey derive from a single, generally acknowledged exemplar. Yet, the 'open character' of the concept dictates that the application of the exemplar may differ from team to team.[39] This means that it would seem to be quite impossible to fix a general principle for deciding which of two teams plays best. In Gallie's words:

> [B]ecause of the internally complex and variously describable character of the exemplar's play, it is natural that different features in it should be differently weighted by different appraisers, and hence that our different teams should have come to hold their very different conceptions of how the game should be played. To this we should add that recognition or acceptance of the exemplar's achievement must have that 'open' character which we have ascribed to every essentially contested concept…To follow an exemplar is to exert oneself to revive its (or his) way of doing things, not only to the utmost of one's ability, but to the utmost that circumstances, favourable or unfavourable, will allow.[40]

Against Gallie, Waldron, examining the meaning of the 'Rule of Law', claims that an exemplar may not always be necessary.[41] Situations arise in which no exemplar exists, but just a problem with which our social and political institutions grappled for thousands of years (or a principle which scholars are constantly debating). And this problem renders the 'Rule of Law' 'a solution-concept rather than an achievement concept; it is the concept to a solution to a problem we're not sure how to solve; and rival conceptions are rival proposals for solving it or rival proposals for doing the best we can in this regard given that the problem is insoluble.'[42]

It appears that Waldron recognises two types of disputes: disputes that neatly conform to Gallie's thesis and disputes that do not. Waldron argues that 'reference back to an exemplar may be too narrow an account of what makes a contested concept nevertheless a shared concept.'[43] We should not *always* look for an exemplar which 'may emerge in the course of discussion...rather than as a foundation that makes the argument possible in the first place'[44] and the emergence of fruitful arguments 'are *signs* that a conceptual contestation is fruitful, rather than explanations of its

39 Ibid 177.

40 Ibid 176-177.

41 Waldron defines Gallie's idea as follows: 'the key to Gallie's idea of essential contestability seems to be a combination of *normativity* and *complexity*: only normative concepts with certain internal complexity are capable of being essentially contested.' Waldron 2002 (n 1 above) 150.

42 Ibid 158. Waldron raises another difficulty with Gallie's argument. For Gallie, essential contestability enriches our understanding of a given concept. Waldron claims that disputation can make things better regardless of whether people associate that with the idea of essential contestability. Ibid 163.

43 Waldron 1994 (n 34 above) 533.

44 Ibid.

fruitfulness.'[45] Gallie himself is aware of this criticism and remarks that it may sometimes be difficult to comply with the condition of exemplar. In his discussion on the concept of art he suggests that instead of insisting on a particular exemplar, 'it is fairly easy to see what particular artistic tradition or set of traditions is being regarded as the "exemplar term".'[46]

Art, Copyright and the Value of Essential Contestability

Art is one of the concepts Gallie uses to illustrate his conceptual paradigm.[47] He claims that the concept 'art' satisfies conditions (i)-(v) rather easily: its daily uses makes it appraisive; its achievements – works of art – are always internally complex; its achievements are controversial and invite an indefinite number of descriptions; every artistic achievement is always 'open in character' since it allows modifications but no one can predict which form of art will develop and in what direction; artists and their admirers agree that the concept 'art' is used both aggressively and defensively. Gallie, however, casts doubt on whether 'art' may satisfy the condition of exemplar, because there is not one artistic tradition that can apply to the general concept 'art.' He claims that there can be different traditions, each of which may satisfy an 'exemplar term.'[48] Moreover, given the eclectic nature of artistic activities, tastes and viewpoints, 'art' may easily satisfy the remaining condition of plausibility and sustainability.[49]

If Gallie finds the concept 'art' to satisfy conditions (i)-(viii), can this diagnosis apply to copyright? I contend that, just as Green argues that the concept 'good citizenship' is complex and contested,[50] the concept 'just copyright' constitutes a classic example of a concept that fully complies with Gallie's formula. From the theoretical discussion in the previous chapter, and the ongoing debate by scholars on which of the theories best ensures a better balance between public and private interests, there is no doubt that copyright is a contested concept which embraces many conflicting views of the proper balance in copyright. As for Gallie's conditions: (i) our daily use of the term 'just copyright', and the value we attach to copyrighted products make it appraisive – a value-concept; (ii) for the many different perceptions of copyright, it is an intrinsically complex discipline that produces and protects complex entities. For example, judging copyright is not as straightforward as arguing

45 Ibid.

46 Gallie (n 26 above) 182-183.

47 Ibid 181-183. See also Waldron 1994 (n 34 above) 530-531.

48 Ibid 182.

49 For Rushton, dealing with 'art' in this context is a 'problem' since the lack of one definition imposes barriers on an agreement of what art is and is not. He contends, that the courts may not be the right place to define 'art' and perhaps there is even no need for a definition. See M Rushton, 'An Economic Approach to Copyright in Works of Artistic Craftsmanship' (2001) 3 *Intellectual Property Quarterly* 255, 268.

50 L Green, *The Authority of the State* (Oxford: Clarendon Press, 1990) 195.

whether my shirt today is red or blue; (iii) it is variously describable in the sense that its evaluation refers to the respective contributions of its various elements; (iv) no one will dispute that it is constantly evolving and that it is amenable to resolutions and modifications, i.e., it is 'highly open in character'; (v) every person, whether an author or a user, recognises that his use of the concept is contested by others' conceptions and will use the term both defensively and aggressively. This disposes of Gallie's conditions (i)-(v).

There is something to be said about conditions (iii) and (iv). What parameters should we consider when we ask how to judge whether copyright is an internally complex concept and whether it is open and unpredictable in character? A definition of complexity is not necessary here simply because the vast discourse on how to approach copyright, whether from utility, desert or personality, and its many internal conflicts, such as exceptions to the right or its duration, testify to this concept's complexity and openness.[51] For example, the recent inclusion of intellectual property in the draft European Constitution introduces a new conception of copyright: copyright (and property) as a European constitutional guarantee.[52] Hence, copyright's complexity is anything but static. In fact, it was recently argued that if the European Union is an essentially contested concept than 'its Constitution represents the paradigm of contestability.'[53] This has a direct effect on the many new principles embedded in the Constitution, including intellectual property.

If the concept 'just copyright' satisfies Gallie's model, what can be identified as its exemplar? It is fairly easy to decide on a moment in the history of copyright which established a tradition followed by every common law jurisdiction. The Statute of Anne of 1709 constitutes an appropriate exemplar for copyright from which disputes, competing aspirations and reforms have emerged. Anglo-American

---

51 As Madison remarks: in copyright 'complexity considerations may be applied in a variety of ways. In fair use doctrine, for example, the factor-driven statutory framework is a helpful beginning, but it remains subject to being hijacked by arguments that "commercial" reuse is presumptively unfair. The so-called "transformative" use doctrine is a healthy tonic, but one that is liable to misapplication and overemphasis on its own terms. The scope of copyright in computer programs should likely be reconsidered, as well as such issues as the term of copyright, and the extent which copyright law should pre-empt equivalent rights under state law. Not all of these directly implicate the First Amendment itself, but they do play important roles in the shape and structure – the architecture – of copyright, and complexity lies within them as well as in fair use and the public domain.' MJ Madison, 'Complexity and Copyright in Contradiction' (2000) 18 *Cardozo Arts & Entertainment Law Journal* 125, 172-173.

52 Article II-17(2), *Draft Treaty Establishing a Constitution for Europe* (adopted by consensus by the European Convention on 13 June and 10 July 2003) 18 July 2003; *cf* Article 295 Treaty Establishing the European Community (ECT).

53 M Wilkinson, 'Constituting Europe: Flexibility or Finalité' (2002) 22 *Oxford Journal of Legal Studies* 177, 177-178. See also Z Bankowski and E Christodoulidis, 'The European Union as an Essentially Contested Project', in Z Bankowski and A Scott (eds.), *The European Union and its Order* (London: Blackwell, 2000) 17.

copyright law recognises the authority of the Statute of Anne as the first copyright law, and the original, specific, and concrete template to follow. Even French copyright law, recognised as the world's leading proponent of moral rights, is argued to be a reflection of the Statute of Anne. As Peeler remarks: 'The first French copyright law was enacted in 1793 and was likely modelled after England's Statute of Anne and the Copyright Act of May 1790, which was America's first copyright act.'[54] Although in early modern French copyright law moral rights predominate over the traditional economic approach to copyright, the ambiguous distinction between moral and economic reassures that it has envisioned copyright in similar terms to those of its Anglo-American predecessors, namely, securing economic incentives.[55]

The Act from 1709 reads: 'An Act for the Encouragement of Learning, by vesting the Copies of printed Books in the Authors, or Purchasers, of such Copies, during the Times therein mentioned.'[56] The English Act from 1988 follows the philosophical skeleton of the Statute of Anne and provides a limited in time property right for authors.[57] But more closely to the Statute of Anne, the US Constitution empowers Congress 'to promote the Progress of Science and useful Arts, by securing for limited

---

54 CD Peeler, 'From the Providence of Kings to Copyrighted Things (and French Moral Rights)' (1999) 9 *Indiana International and Comparative Law Review* 423, 429.

55 It is often claimed that Anglo-American copyright law and continental copyright law were inspired by different interests – that the former concentrates on instrumentalism while the latter on authors' natural rights. Ginsburg convincingly refutes the contrast between the two systems and argues that it is exaggerated. She finds that both systems view authorial ownership from the perspective of the public good and only to the extent that ownership patterns in artistic and authorial creations will inspire and promote the public good. JC Ginsburg, 'A Tale of Two Copyrights: Literary Property in Revolutionary France and America' in B Sherman and A Strowel (eds.), *Of Authors and Origins: Essays on Copyright Law* (Oxford: Clarendon Press, 1994) 131. Following recent legislative developments in Europe, the distinction seems to blur even more. See KJ Koleman, 'Copyright Law and Economics in the EU Copyright Directive: Is the Droit d'Auteur Passé?' (2004) 35(6) *International Review of Intellectual Property and Competition Law* 603.

56 The following examples confirm the place of the Statute of Anne as an exemplar – the moment from which conceptions of modern copyright have started to emerge. See H Ransom, *The First Copyright Statute: An Essay on the Act for the Encouragement of Learning, 1709* (Austin: University of Texas Press, 1956); HB Abrams, 'The Historic Foundations of American Copyright Law: Exploding the Myth of Common Law Copyright' (1983) *Wayne Law Review* 1119; J Litman 'Copyright, Compromise, and Legislative History' (1987) 72 *Cornell Law Review* 857; M Rose, *Authors and Owners: The Invention of Copyright* (Cambridge Mass.: Harvard University Press, 1993); B Sherman and L Bently, *The Making of Modern Intellectual Property* (Cambridge: Cambridge University Press, 1999); D Burkitt, 'Copyrighting Culture – The History and Cultural Specificity of the Western Model of Copyright' [2001] 2 *Intellectual Property Quarterly* 146; R Deazley, *On the Origin of the Right to Copy: Charting the Movement of Copyright in Eighteenth Century Britain* (Oxford: Hart Publishing, 2004).

57 Copyright, Designs and Patents Act 1988 (1988, c.48).

Times to Authors and Inventors the exclusive Right to their respective Writings and Discoveries.'[58]

Copyright's complexity is best defined by its obscure and competing philosophical, as well as doctrinal, confusion. Copyright is as an 'essentially contested concept', uniquely describable and universally acknowledged.[59] The exemplar's achievement – recognition of proprietary rights in authorial and artistic entities, is tied to another achievement: the need to strike a balance between private rights and public interests. The 'open character' of the concept 'copyright' dictates that application of the exemplar may, like the ice hockey game, differ from one philosopher (and jurisdiction) to another, just as philosophers' disagree on the balance to strike between private and public in copyright. The continuous competition between the various applications of the exemplar does not justify any claim, but ensures that the concept remains contested.

Attempts to harmonise copyright standards may raise the question whether we will ever reach an uncontested copyright system? Indeed, if all succumb to one vision, copyright would cease to exist as an essentially contested concept. A segment of copyright exemplar's legacy is the limited duration of the right. The European Term Directive, extending the protection to 70 years after the death of the author forced the US to come to terms with the new standard, if its nationals are to receive reciprocal treatment in Europe.[60] The Congress enacted the Copyright Term Extension Act of 1998 (CTEA) adding 20 more years for copyright protection period.[61] In the recent *Eldred v Ashcroft* case the American Supreme Court was asked to rule on the constitutionality of the Act.[62] Justice Ginsburg found that the Congress acted within its powers and that 'by extending the baseline United States copyright term to life plus 70 years, Congress sought to ensure that American authors would receive the same copyright protection in Europe as their European counterparts.'[63] In contrast, Justice Stevens was not persuaded that extension of the term was necessary and argues that extending terms for existing copyrights neither induced an author to create new works, nor did it support the public interest and the stability of the public domain.[64] This disagreement shows the contestable nature of copyright, and illustrates how the concept/conception paradigm operates in copyright practice: while there was

58 US Constitution Art 1 s 8 cl 8.

59 Gallie raises the interest in examining why a certain facet of an essentially contested concept has a stronger appeal than another. That would include, Gallie asserts, psychological, sociological and influences on a 'person's or group's background, to explain their present preferences and adherences.' Gallie (n 26 above) 192.

60 Council Directive 93/98/EEC Harmonising the Term of Protection of Copyright and Certain Related Rights (29 October 1993) Art 1(1).

61 See Sonny Bono Copyright Term Extension Act, Pub L No 105-298, 112 Stat 2827 (1998) (codified as amended at 17 USC, 108, 203(a)(2), 301(c), 302, 303-304 (2000).

62 *Eldred v Ashcroft* 537 US 183 (2003).

63 Ibid 204-208.

64 Ibid 240-241.

no dispute about that the concept copyright exists, there was a disagreement on the conception – how long should copyright last?

This attempt to harmonise the duration of copyright protection did not end debates about the future of the duration. For example, Lessig advocates a five-year renewable term[65] and Landes and Posner recently argued for 'indefinitely renewable copyright.'[66] This reaffirms that copyright is not only an essentially contested concept, but developments in the field of science and technology will perpetuate its character as an 'open concept.'[67] The sustainability of competing views of copyright ensures that copyright remains 'open in character' – an 'essentially contested concept.'

To recapitulate, a 'concept' provides the frame, such as justice, liberty, property or copyright, while a 'conception' refers to a particular specification within that 'concept.' Conceptual inventions in copyright maintain its diverse and open character. Copyright controversies are not resolvable, and it seems that scholars will not agree on any conception of copyright, bringing an end to the concept's contested nature. As a concept, 'copyright' is treated as the general legal standard entrusted in recognising protection for authors, artists, architects, craftsmen, lyricists and so on. Maintaining its open character and contestable nature will ensure future improvements of the concept of copyright and its capacity to meet unpredictable social and cultural challenges.

Reitan applies Gallie's formula to the concept 'rape' and remarks that '…we should expect that as our cultural appreciation of diverse perspectives evolves, the extension of the concept will expand to reflect the deepened understanding of the moral landscape that accompanies the introduction of new perspectives.'[68] Likewise, any moral advances we may make in the domain of intellectual property 'will depend on our capacity to admit alternative voices into the discussion'[69] of copyright. Meeting the challenge of copyright's conceptual matrix will greatly contribute to the dialogue and the evolution of its doctrinal principles. At the heart of Gallie's definition is

65 L Lessig, *The Future of Ideas: The Fate of the Commons in a Connected World* (New York: Vintage Books, 2002) 251-252.

66 WM Landes and RA Posner, 'Indefinitely Renewable Copyright' (2003) 70 *University of Chicago Law Review* 471. See also SL Clemens, 'Copyright in Perpetuity' (2002) 6 *Green Bag* 2d 109.

67 Indeed, international harmonisation of intellectual property standards fuels contestability. As Aoki observes: 'The discourse of globalization collides with the discourse of difference. Widely divergent concepts of property and ownership, originating in extremely diverse political, economic, and social circumstances, provide the fuel for *hotly contested and seemingly unresolvable disputes*.' K Aoki, 'Considering Multiple and Overlapping Sovereignties: Liberalism, Libertarianism, National Sovereignty, "Global" Intellectual Property, and the Internet' (1998) 5 *Indiana Journal of Global Legal Studies* 443, 462-463 (emphasis added).

68 Reitan (n 33 above) 21.

69 Ibid.

the belief that contestability can make the concept better.[70] Essential contestability allows multiple interpretations of a specific concept that together allow to see the broader conceptual reach of the concept. This has the capacity to make the concept a better concept. Contestability, as Gray remarks, intends to 'enrich intellectual life and to promote tolerance within it'[71] and highlight misconceptions and flaws that would otherwise be left untouched. In Gallie's words:

> Recognition of a given concept as essentially contested implies recognition of rival uses of it (such as oneself repudiates) as not only logically possible and humanly 'likely', but as of permanent critical value to one's own use or interpretation of the concept in question...One very desirable consequence of the required recognition in any proper instance of essential contestedness might therefore be expected to be a marked rising of the level of quality of arguments in the disputes of the contestant parties.[72]

Literature on copyright shows that copyright is a unified concept with a cluster of competing conceptions. However, it does not explicitly refer to or draw benefits from the conceptual game in copyright. Our tendency to search for the balance in copyright requires a clearer conceptual base if it is ever to find its way within copyright's definitional complexity. This book is an example of the interplay between copyright as a 'concept' and 'authorial constructionism' as a conception, that bring me to delve into the open character of copyright, recognise the authority of the exemplar and the importance of rethinking its effect on our understanding of copyright, and aggressively defend a new conception: a social constructionist approach to copyright.

The best way to make meaningful progress in the way we approach and think of copyright is by admitting into our discourse on copyright alternative approaches to ownership which emphasis the public interest and its contribution to the formation of copyrighted entities. In this way we will be able to protect the integrity of the

---

70 MacIntyre argues that certain legal institutions are not essentially contested. He writes: 'It is far from the case that all social concepts have the character of essential contestability. Indeed some social concepts are only able to function as they do and to have the range of application that they have because they lack essential contestability. A legal-cum-economic system, for example, normally cannot function unless there is a kind of agreement in definitions which precludes essential contestability. What counts as a contract, what counts as a bill of exchange or a check, what determines the rate of exchange between currencies must be fixed in a way that such concepts as those of political party or tragic drama or education are not.' MacIntyre (n 26 above) 9.

71 J Gray, 'On Liberty, Liberalism and Essential Contestability' (1978) 8 *British Journal of Political Science* 385, 389. See also by the same author, 'On the Essential Contestability of Some Social and Political Concepts' (1977) 5 *Political Theory* 331. Elsewhere he asks whether democracy and morality are really disputes about concepts: '[M]ight they not be just quarrels about the use of words?' He answers: 'perhaps what we have is indeed meaning-variance rather than competition in the use of a shared vocabulary.' Gray (n 26 above) 95.

72 Gallie (n 26 above) 193. Waldron supports this argument. Waldron 2002 (n 1 above) 151-152.

copyright discourse by ensuring that no single voice can exclude other voices, and allow sufficient conceptual flexibility to permit open discourse about the way we should approach and redefine the entitlement structure in copyright. In the next chapter I undertake an elaborate disquisition on the proprietary nature of entitlements copyright confers on authors. I examine specific principles embedded in copyright, which are responsible for its contested nature and triggered the arguments I defend in this book.

Chapter 3

What Copyright Is

A Bundle of Rights

Rights and Boundaries of Tangibility

'I have a copyright' is a challenge to the world. It denotes a *property* right against all other conflicting rights and interests.[1] It is superior to all non-rights. Like property, the strength of the copyright title secures excessive rights of use and exclusion. Lessons gleaned from what the right to property is,[2] are important to the future development and understanding of copyright.[3] In land law, for example, the extent of an owner's right is captured by the principle that he who owns the land owns everything 'up to the sky and down to the centre of the earth.'[4] This means that the owner also enjoys an exclusive right to the mines and minerals contained underground.[5] However, conceptual equivalents to mines and minerals are not necessarily part of the bundle of rights in copyright, where the terms 'exclusion' and 'use' have different connotations.

I argue that in order to properly analyse the entitlement structure in copyright, conceptual reorganisation is required. My criticism is directed at this structure, and in this chapter I will define what copyright comprises and establish that every allocation of a claim-right imposes duties on certain portions of society, which sometimes implies far-reaching consequences that can directly affect society as a whole. Copyright requires us to first understand the nature of the right, then study its implications in order to ascertain what copyright *is* and what it *should* be. One

---

1 CDPA 1988 s 1(1) provides that '[c]opyright is a *property* right…' (emphasis added). I shall use the term property as a generic term and take examples mainly from land law.

2 See for example, CM Rose, 'Property as the Keystone Right?' (1999) 71 *Notre Dame Law Review* 329.

3 It is arguable that the intellectual property system would not have been emerged if we did not have a legal and social history moulded by debates for and against the right to property. However, Harris remarks that '[w]hether intellectual property could have emerged in the absence of property over tangible resources constitutes an unanswerable counterfactual speculation.' JW Harris, *Property and Justice* (Oxford: Oxford University Press, 1996) 46.

4 This is known as the Latin phrase: '*cuius est solum eius est usque ad coelum et ad inferos*.' See *Corbett v Hill* (1870) LR 9 Eq 671, 673.

5 This rule is subject to exceptions and for example, it does not cover coal and gas found under land. These resources are now public property. See Petroleum (Production) Act 1934 s 1; Coal Industry Act 1994 s 9.

may argue that since copyright is a powerful, bounded, and protected right, and is a deeply ingrained and enduring one, the question 'what copyright is?' can be simply answered.[6] I will argue that although the entitlement structure reflected in copyright law almost perfectly mimics that of traditional property, its social nature should render it a lesser form of property. In practice, however, copyright is a strong form of property, enough to destabilise its delicate balance.[7]

Associating copyright with property is attractive for many reasons. In fact, 'those who started using the word property in connection with inventions had a very definite purpose in mind: they wanted to substitute a word with a respectable connotation, "property", for a word that had an unpleasant ring, "privilege".'[8] Similarly, a statement like 'copyright is property' has its roots in the attraction of a private right to control an object to the highest possible degree. As Blackstone once wrote: 'There is nothing which so generally strikes the imagination and engages the affections of mankind, as the right to property; or that sole and despotic dominion which one man claims and exercises over the external things of the world, in total exclusion of the right of any other individual in the universe.'[9]

The right to copyright is the right to control the social and economic agenda of an abstract entity, which implies its separation from a community of similar entities, from the public domain. In copyright, as in property, people are concerned with acquiring possessions and protecting mine and thine, preserving the rightholder's exclusive possessions from trespassers. Like private property, to have copyright is to have an exclusive title, which confers on its owner the right to use, the right to exclude all others both from use and possession, and the right to transmit use and possession to others. It means that a private individual has the right to determine

6 Libling argues that due to the differences between intangibles and tangibles, when we discuss the former, we are to be concerned only with the right to commercial exploitation. DF Libling, 'The Concept of Property: Property in Intangibles' (1978) 94 *Law Quarterly Review* 103, 104.

7 See C. Geiger, 'Copyright and Free Access to Information: For a Fair Balance of Interests in a Globalised World' (2006) 28(7) *European Intellectual Property Review* 366.

8 F Machlup and E Penrose, 'The Patent Controversy in the Nineteenth Century' (1950) 10 *Journal of Economic History* 1, 16.

9 Sir William Blackstone, *Commentaries on the Laws of England* (Butterworth and son, 16th ed. 1825) bk 2, 1 (emphasis added). The desire we show when we talk property is affected by the multi-faceted character of the property institution. This has brought some to argue that the concept 'property' has 'so many variations and specialized uses that its meaning has disintegrated.' TC Grey, 'The Disintegration of Property' in JR Pennock and JW Chapman (ed.), *Property*, Nomos, XXII, (New York: New York University Press, 1980) 85.

what will be done with an object.[10] It embraces what is not common to all, but controlled by a lesser number of people, whether one individual or more.[11]

In *Property and Justice* Harris argues that there is nothing like a full property right, in his favourite parlance – 'full-blooded ownership.'[12] For Harris, an object is capable of being property 'if either it is subject to specific trespassory protection or if it is separately transmissible as part of a person's private wealth.'[13] Harris treats the concept of trespassory rules as the defining characteristic of property. It 'encompasses all rules which, by reference to a resource, impose obligations (negative or positive) upon an open-ended range of persons, there being expected some privileged individual, group or agency.'[14] Trespassory rules are central for discussions of property and intellectual property.[15] Copyright laws are considered a means to prevent trespassers – copiers and free-riders – from violating the rights authors have in their protected works. As Woodmansee and Jaszi put it: 'So important to us is this vision of intellectual property into mine and thine that we have codified it in laws of copyright and authors' rights that enable us to prosecute trespassers.'[16]

---

10 Waldron defines property as 'the concept of a system of rules governing access to and control of material resources.' J Waldron, *The Right to Private Property* (Oxford: Oxford University Press, 1988) 31 (hereinafter – 'Waldron 1988').

Honoré attempts to provide a list of the rights one can have by virtue of being the owner of an object. He designs an argument comprising of eleven standard features, or *incidents* as he calls them, of the 'liberal concept of full individual ownership': 'The right to possess' ('the foundation on which the whole superstructure of ownership rests'); 'the right to use'; 'the right to manage'; 'the right to income'; 'the right to the capital'; 'the right to security'; 'the incident of transmissibility' (the heritability of the interest in the thing ad infinitum); 'the incidence of absence in term' (no interest in the thing beyond the expired time); two social limitations which are 'the duty to prevent harm' and 'liability to execution'; and 'residuary character' (a right to the reversion of the rights comprised by lesser interests in the thing upon the extinction of those interests). AM Honoré, 'Ownership', in *Making the Law Bind* (Oxford: Clarendon Press, 1987) 166-179. Note that he does not explicitly include the right to exclude in these incidents.

11 In the words of Reich: 'Property draws a circle around the activities of each private individual or organisation. Within that circle, the owner has a greater degree of freedom than without.' C Reich, 'The New Property' (1964) 73 *Yale Law Journal* 733, 771.

12 Harris (n 3 above) 29-32, 221-222, and 228-229.

13 Ibid 42 and 67-68.

14 Ibid 25. For Harris the institution of property is composed of 'the twin notions of trespassory rules and the ownership spectrum.' Ibid 5.

15 BeVier examines the relationship between copyright, property and trespassory rules and finds the latter useful for the resolution of disputes over conflicting claims of access to copyrighted works. See, LR BeView, 'Copyright, Trespass, and the First Amendment: An Institutional Perspective' (2004) *Social Philosophy and Policy* 104.

16 M Woodmansee and P Jaszi, 'Introduction', in M Woodmansee and P Jaszi (eds.), *The Construction of Authorship: Textual Appropriation in Law and Literature* (Durham and London: Duke University Press, 1994) 1, 2.

Trespassory rules provide the great advantage of legally enforceable physical and intangible boundaries. They are a powerful economic tool, and provide the connection between rights and rewards. Rules of trespass enforce the owner's strong right to exclude, which is complemented by, for example, the rules of contract law and conveyancing, which also safeguard the owner's right to transfer an object. The same applies to intellectual property: 'By instituting trespassory rules whose content restricts uses of the ideational entity, intellectual property law preserves to an individual or group of individuals an open-ended set of use-privileges and powers of control and transmission characteristic of ownership interests over tangible items.'[17]

As a property right, copyright is a relational right. It is not a right between a person and an object but a right between people with respect to objects.[18] That is, copyright, like property, is a matter of rights.[19] The right itself is intangible, even where the object is tangible. Individuals tend to lose track of the distinction between the physical relation between a person and an object and between the normative – moral or legal – nature of property that determines relationships between persons with respect to things, because the two concepts are frequently conflated in everyday life. This becomes, as Waldron puts it, our *conversational* habit.[20]

Consequently, we can identify two different, but complementary, senses of property. First, property as a set of legal relations. Second, in the conversational sense, property as a thing, *a res*, which usually implies an owner. A tenant may have a right to live in his rented apartment in a building but not the right to sell it or if the tenancy agreement so specifies, not to sublet it; the landlord may have the right to sell the building, but not necessarily freely or without notice to enter the tenant's apartment. Similarly, a flautist may play a new adaptation of Mozart's 'Jupiter' Symphony, but is not entitled to publicly perform the work or sell rights to it.

Possession of traditional property differs from that of intangible property. Copyright is a species of incorporeal property while traditional physical property can be 'touched.' Tangibility, however, as Carter contends, 'is an accident; not all that is created can be touched.'[21] True, copyright protects abstract entities, and its boundaries are not definable in physical terms, but, as Gordon asserts

---

17 Harris (n 3 above) 44.

18 In the words of Cohen '[p]rivate property is a relationship among human beings such that the so-called owner can exclude others from certain activities or permit others to engage in those activities and in either case secure the assistance of the law in carrying out his decision.' FS Cohen, 'Dialogue on Private Property' (1954) 9 *Rutgers Law Review* 357, 373. See also A Mossoff, 'What is Property: Putting the Pieces Back Together' (2003) 45 *Arizona Law Review* 371, 429, n 241.

19 Many questions may emerge from the idea of property as a species of rights. For example, whether we can now claim that all rights are property rights? See GF Gaus, 'Property, Rights and Freedom' (1994) 11 *Social Philosophy and Politics* 209, 211-216.

20 Waldron 1988 (n 10 above) 27-30.

21 SL Carter, 'Does it Matter Whether Intellectual Property Is Property?' (1993) 68(2) *Chicago-Kent Law Review* 715, 723.

> Copyright provides its own boundaries which, by and large, substitute well for physical boundaries, both in regard to promoting transactions and to keeping liability within tolerable limits...Inevitably, the boundaries of intangibles will be less precise than the metes and bounds of realty, and the courts must be vigilant in enforcing copyright's limits lest the public be 'chilled' in its proper use of the unprotected aspects of the work.[22]

The law invented ways to clarify the distinction between traditional property and copyright, proving that tangibility does not necessarily imply lack of boundaries or that lack of boundaries does not imply weaker protection of property. Tangibility, however, dictates a different set of trespassory rules. This can be illustrated by the idea/expression dichotomy, stipulating that copyright protects only the expression of ideas, not the ideas themselves.[23] Ideas, no matter how valuable or creative, are excluded from the scope of copyright protection. Their consumption is non-rivalrous and their benefits are non-excludable. This distinction, however, is not very clear.[24] Laddie refers to it as a pithy catchphrase that may lead to confusion,[25] and that 'philosophically speaking, there is no such dichotomy.'[26] Although there must be a line between what is protectable in copyright and what is not

---

22 W Gordon 'An Inquiry into the Merits of Copyright' (1989) 41 *Stanford Law Review* 1343, 1381-1383 (hereinafter – 'Gordon 1989').

23 In *Millar v Taylor*, Yates J puts the matter this way: 'Ideas are free. While the author confines them to his they are like birds in a cage, which none but he can have a right to let fly: for, till he thinks proper to emancipate them, they are under his own dominion.' *Millar v Taylor* (1769) 98 Eng Rep 201, 242. Similarly, Frankfurter J in *Marconi Wireless Co v US*, remarks that great inventions and copyrighted works 'have always been part of an evolution, the culmination at a particular moment of an antecedent process...the history of thought records striking coincidental discoveries showing that the new insight first declared to the world by a particular individual was in the air...' *Marconi Wireless Co v US* 320 US 1, 62 (1943) (Frankfurter J dissenting). True, the nature of an idea is that once 'let fly' it can be used infinitely. My goal is to claim for the public a similar right to that of the author in the expression.

24 Music, for example, more than any other form of modern culture, collapses the gap between what separates idea from expression. Is the string of six notes that initiates 'Happy Birthday to You' an idea, an expression, or both? Landes and Posner define a copyright work as 'the joint output of two types of input, only one of which is protected by copyright law.' WM Landes & RA Posner, 'An Economic Analysis of Copyright Law' (1989) 18 *Journal of Legal Studies* 325, 349.

For matters of argumentative clarity, it is of importance to note that by their nature expressions are also non-rivalrous. Copyright law secures an exclusive right in expressions notwithstanding that it is non-rivalrous, thereby creating *false* scarcity and rendering their benefits excludable. As Harris explained: 'society's law have been extended to include those trespassory rules which create artificial scarcity in unpublished and published ideas.' Harris (n 3 above) 46. See also Chapter 1 above, n 63.

25 Laddie et al, *The Modern Law of Copyright and Designs* (London: Butterworths, 3rd ed. 2000) 3.76.

26 Ibid 3.77.

[R]eferences to a supposed principle that copyright is confined to expression does not assist in drawing that line. One must discover some different principle in order to begin the task of drawing it…therefore: (a) the proposition that copyright protection is confined to form of expression is not to be found in any Act of Parliament; (b) it is, in its narrow sense, unjust and has not been the law for many years; but (c) is the narrow sense is jettisoned, what is left of the concept is no meaningful guide to action…'[27]

Rosen challenges the inability to draw a distinction between idea and expression. He advocates a distinction between a general idea and a specific idea. He contends that 'there is no intrinsically "right place" to draw the line between an idea and its expression. The distinction…is arbitrary…because it is conventional, and it is conventional because it exists only where and when we choose to employ it.'[28] Rosen recognises the role of the dichotomy to ensure that ideas remain in the public domain,[29] that there are no trespassory rules applicable to general ideas.[30] As Jacob J remarks: 'United Kingdom copyright cannot prevent the copying of a mere general idea but can protect the copying of a detailed "idea".'[31]

Despite the vagueness and difficulties in drawing a clear line between the protectable components and the non-protectable components in a copyrighted entity, it seems that there exists a division between what is capable of being protected and what is not. A general idea can still be separated from a more complex, detailed, and more developed idea. For example, Rodin's sculpture *The Kiss* (1901-4), as an idea, is no more than a work of two lovers kissing. But the actual work is not a general idea, it reduces the banal idea of two lovers kissing to a more detailed expressive idea.[32] Whether or not the line can be easily drawn it does not weaken the argument that trespassory rules in copyright are important to define as different from tangible property. Exclusivity in copyright has a different, more limited, meaning and does not cover general ideas.

---

27 Ibid 3.77.

28 A Rosen, 'Reconsidering the Idea/Expression Dichotomy' (1992) 26(2) *University of British Columbia Law Review* 263, 280.

29 Ibid 270.

30 Rosen claims that the social aim of the idea/expression dichotomy can be promoted by drawing a distinction between ideas and expression on the basis of (i) whether the given idea is in a general form and can be further developed in ways that are likely to benefit the public; and (ii) whether the given idea is already highly developed. Ibid 277. The danger in such a formula is in placing judges as final arbiters of where social development starts and where it ends. In Chapter 6 I further explore the subjectivity issue in that respect.

31 Jacob J in *Ibcos Computers Ltd v Barclays Mercantile Highland Finance Ltd* [1994] FSR 275, 302 (Ch).

32 Laddie explains: 'the law does not protect a general idea or concept which underlies the work, nor any one fact or piece of information contained therein. However, a more detailed *collection* of ideas, or pattern of incidents, or compilation of information' may amount to a copyrighted work. Laddie (n 25 above) 3.79. Laddie also highlights the fact that the detailed collection of ideas or information has to be reduced to writing or other material form in order to be susceptible of copyright protection. Ibid.

Furthermore, ideas are not scarce as tangibles,[33] and their benefits are non-excludable, or, as Waldron puts it, these objects are 'non-crowdable.'[34] An object is crowdable if 'one person's use of it is an obstacle to at least one other's use of it.'[35] For example, if I use the hoe to plant daffodils in my garden, the hoe can be used only by me at the time. If I pick an acorn and decide to crush it, I am the only person who could make this infinite use of the acorn. The hoe and the acorn are crowdable objects in the sense that the use I make of them precludes either temporary or absolute use by others. In the realm of ideas, the fact that the law does not afford protection to ideas, makes them non-crowdable in the sense that a person's use of an idea would never amount to an interference with the freedom of another person to use the same idea. While a poetry book or a painting are crowdable objects, the lyrics of a song contained in the book or the idea to portray sunrise not in yellow and red, are non-crowdable, as their use is no obstacle to anyone. These ideas are non-rivalrous and do not preclude others from using, utilizing or expressing them.

The Bundle

Copyright and property secure a bundle of rights for rightholders that, singly or collectively, define the relationship of an owner to a resource and between the owner and other individuals.[36] Ownership is often referred to as an 'abstract bundle of

---

33 As Baird remarks: 'We typically can reap only the wheat we sow on our own land, and how land becomes private property in the first place remains a mystery. In any event, wheat and information are fundamentally different from one another. It is the nature of wheat or land or any other tangible property that possession by one person precludes possession by anyone else. A court must decide that A should get the wheat or that B should get the wheat. It cannot decide that both get all of it. Many people, however, can use the same piece of information.' DG Baird, 'Common Law Intellectual Property and the Legacy of International News Services v Associated Press' (1983) 50 *University of Chicago Law Review* 411, 413.

34 J Waldron, 'From Authors to Copiers: Individual Rights and Social Values in Intellectual Property' (1992-1993) 68 *Chicago-Kent Law Review* 841, 870 (hereinafter – 'Waldron 1993')

35 Ibid 870-871.

36 Gray puts the matter this way: 'When I sell you a quantum of airspace the whole point is that – apart from molecules of thin air – there is absolutely nothing there. The key is, of course, that I have transferred to you not a thing but a "bundle of rights", and it is the "bundle of rights" that comprises the property.' K Gray, 'Property in Thin Air' (1991) 50 *Cambridge Law Journal* 252, 259.

Mossoff criticises the 'bundle' approach as applied to property and intellectual property for its lack to conceptually unify the concept 'property.' Mossoff (n 18 above) 373-374. Instead, he offers the integrated theory of property which, in general, ensembles together every constituent of the right to property in order to 'represent a conceptual unity that together serve to give full meaning to the concept of property.' Ibid 376. The integrated theory of property encompasses exclusive rights to acquisition, use and disposal. Ibid. I am not in dispute with Mossoff that fragmentation in property theory affects its conceptual tidiness, and in fact submit that copyright is a prime example of a highly fragmented discipline.

legal relations',[37] 'a cluster-right',[38] 'a complex aggregate of rights',[39] 'a range of ownership interests along the ownership spectrum',[40] 'complexes',[41] or just a label for a 'bundle of sticks.'[42] In Heller's words 'private property can be defined in terms of a core bundle of rights chosen from the infinite relations that may exist among people with respect to a scarce resource.'[43] The fact that property constitutes a bundle of rights does not mean that one can conclusively define it. As Penner remarks

> On this view, 'property is a bundle of rights' expresses the idea that 'property' is a concept that is not applied on the basis of some set of necessary and sufficient criteria; rather, in a particular case the various incidents or indicia of property may add up in some way, or show sufficient resemblance to a paradigm, such that 'property' is correctly applied to describe it. Here, then, 'property is a bundle of rights' asserts the claim that property is a concept without a definable 'essence'; different combinations of the bundle in different circumstances may all count as 'property' and no particular right or set of rights in the bundle is determinative. This I call the 'conceptual' version of the thesis...[44]

The bundle of rights in copyright is highly fragmented and covers many different entitlements that affect the delicate stability of the system.[45] As one commentator asserts: '[o]nce vested, the bundle of rights known collectively as "the copyright" gives the author the exclusive rights to reproduce, to adapt, to distribute, to perform

---

37 M Heller, 'Symposium: Critical Approaches to Property Institutions: Three Faces of Private Property' (2000) 79 *Oregon Law Review* 417, 430.

38 J Thomson, *The Realm of Rights* (Cambridge, Harvard University Press, 1992) 55-57.

39 WN Hohfeld, *Fundamental Legal Conceptions* (Yale University Press: 1919) 96 (hereinafter – 'Hohfeld 1919').

40 Harris (n 3 above) 86.

41 A Carter, *The Philosophical Foundations of Property Rights* (New York and London: Harvester Wheatsheaf, 1989) 129.

42 *Kaiser Aetna v United States* 444 US 164, 176 (1979). See also EL Rubin, 'Due Process and the Administrative State' (1984) 72 *California Law Review* 1044, 1086.

43 M Heller, 'The Tragedy of the Anticommons: Property in the Transition from Marx to Markets' (1998) 111 *Harvard Law Review* 621, 665.

44 JE Penner, 'The Bundle of Rights Picture of Property' (1996) 43 *UCLA Law Review* 711, 723.

45 Many intellectual property scholars define copyright by analogy to the 'bundle of rights' familiar to traditional property. See for example, ST Johnson, Note, 'Internet Domain Name and Trademark Disputes: Shifting Paradigms in Intellectual Property' (2001) 43 *Arizona Law Review* 465, 475; BR Poquette, 'Information Wants to be Free' (2000) 22 *Hamline Journal of Public Law and Policy* 175, 179-181; OG Hatch, 'Toward a Principled Approach to Copyright Legislation at the Turn of the Millennium' (1998) 59 *University of Pittsburgh Law Review* 719, 721; J Lipton, 'Information Property: Rights and Responsibilities' (2004) 56 *Florida Law Review* 135, 171-174.

Controlling the 'bundle' means that authors and artists can license 'less than her entire bundle of rights to a licensee under terms consistent with the copyright laws.' MA Lemley, 'Beyond Preemption: The Law and Policy of Intellectual Property Licensing' (1999) 97 *California Law Review* 111, 144.

publicly and to display publicly the copyrighted work.'[46] As such, in the words of Chafee: 'copyright is a bundle of distinct and specific monopolies' that suffers from the 'Wide Range Problem' of distinct monopolies.[47] These monopolies are defined in copyright laws as exclusive rights and entitlements.[48]

Exclusivity of the 'bundle' in copyright has two meanings stemming from two sets of rights: economic and moral.[49] The first set of rights includes rights to reproduction (to make copies of the work),[50] make derivative works (eg, adaptations, translations and arrangements),[51] public distribution,[52] public performance and display,[53] and the right to broadcast the work.[54] The second set of rights are moral rights that seek at least to protect the integrity of a work and the author's connection with it.[55] This set of rights includes the right to be identified as author or director,[56] and the right to object to derogatory treatment of the work and that the work, when performed

46 DS Ciolino, 'Why Copyrights are not Community Property' (1999) *Louisiana Law Review* 127, 133.

47 Z Chafee Jr, 'Reflections on the Law of Copyright: I' (1945) 45 *Columbia Law Review* 503, 522.

48 CDPA 1988 s 2(1).

49 It was not until 1988 that moral rights were given explicit legislative form in British law. See CDPA 1988, s 2(2)(a)-(c) and s 77-89. Pre-1988, copyright laws in England did not acknowledge such moral rights, and other branches of law facilitated the underlying principle of the moral right. Pre-1988 laws that facilitated the aim of a moral right were for example, the torts of defamation, see *Humphreys v Thompson* (1905-1910) Mac CC 148; and the law of passing-off. See *Samuelson v Producers Distributing* [1932] 1 Ch 201.

Interestingly, Vickers argues that the concept of moral rights are not at all a modern invention. He writes that '[i]n the sixteenth and seventeenth centuries the Stationers' Company protected the copyright of its members and adjudicated in many disputes. However, as in ancient Rome, writers vigorously asserted their moral rights to their own intellectual property, and despised plagiarism.' B Vickers, 'Abolishing the Author? Theory *versus* History' Appendix II in B Vickers, *Shakespeare, Co-Author* (Oxford: Oxford University Press, 2002) 506, 519. He also asserts that '[t]he fact that writers could identify the plagiarists' victim reinforces the dominant impression produced by this enquiry, that in sixteenth- and seventeenth- century England an author was regarded as having a moral right in his or her works, whether published or still in manuscript.' Ibid 525.

50 CDPA 1988 s 16(1)(a) and s 17.

51 CDPA 1988 s 16(1)(e) and s 21. See for example *Redwood Music Limited v Chappell & Co Ltd* [1982] RPC 109.

52 CDPA 1988 s 16(1)(b) and s 18. Public distribution includes the capacity to rent or lend the work to the public. Ibid s 16(1)(ba) and s 18A.

53 CDPA 1988 s 16(1)(c) and s 19.

54 CDPA 1988 s 16(1)(d) and s 20.

55 See generally G Dworkin, 'Moral rights in English Law – The Shape of Things to Come' (1986) *European Intellectual Property Review* 144; W Cornish, 'Moral Rights Under the 1988 Act' (1989) *European Intellectual Property Review* 449; D Vaver, 'Moral Rights Yesterday, Today and Tomorrow' (1999) 7(3) *International Journal of Law and Information Technology* 270.

56 CDPA s 77-79.

or publicly displayed, is not mutilated,[57] including the right to privacy of certain photographs and films.[58]

Copyright's bundle of rights protects works of authorship invested in different standards of creative manifestations. Classically, copyright works have been 'literary and artistic works' – the creations of authors, playwrights, composers, artists and film directors.[59] It also protects revolutionary works of authorship and modern art, computer programs and compilations of information such as a timetable index and listing of programmes to be broadcast,[60] trade catalogues,[61] business letters,[62] consignment notes,[63] street directories,[64] football fixture lists,[65] and a racing information service.[66]

However, the bundle of rights in copyright differs from traditional property in the way one comes to acquire rights. In property, as we know, rights do not necessarily require one to invest money, effort or distinct labour. One can acquire property by virtue of discovering an island or picking an acorn. In copyright, protection is not as automatic as in property, and any allocation of a right from the bundle of entitlements requires meeting certain conditions. The making of copyrighted entities can be viewed as a two-stage process. First, one acquires unowned properties such as ideas and facts, then elaborates and expresses them in a way that distinguishes them from prior works. In the seminal case of *University of London Press v University Tutorial Press*, dealing with examination papers, Peterson J defines 'literary work' in this way:

57 CDPA 1988 s 80-85.

58 CDPA 1988 s 85.

59 CDPA 1988 s 1(1) provides that copyright works are: '…(a) original literary, dramatic, musical or artistic works; (b) sound recordings, films, broadcasts or cable programme; and (c) the typographical arrangement of a published edition.' Literary work is defined in s 3(1) as 'any work, other than a dramatic or musical works, which is written, spoken or sung, and accordingly includes – (a) a table or compilation other than databases; (b) a computer program; (c) preparatory design material for a computer program; and (d) a database; 'dramatic work' includes a work of dance or mime; and 'musical work' means a work consisting of music, exclusive of any words or action intended to be sung, spoken or performed with the music.' Chapter 1 of the CDPA 1988 further takes the types of works that s 1 describes as constituting copyright works, and defines databases (s 3A), artistic works (s 4), sound recordings (s 5A), films (s 5B), broadcasts (s 6 and s 7, including satellite broadcasts), cable programmes (s 7) and published editions (s 8).

60 *Blacklock v Pearson* [1915] 2 Ch 376; *Independent Television Publications v Time Out* [1984] FSR 64.

61 *Collis v Carter* (1898) 78 LT 613; *Purefoy v Skyes Boxall* (1955) 72 RPC 89 (CA).

62 *British Oxygen Co Ltd v Liquid Air Ltd* [1925] Ch 383

63 *Van Oppen & Co Ltd v Van Oppen* (1903) 20 RPC 617.

64 *Kelly v Morris* (1866) LR 1 Eq 697.

65 *Football League v Littlewoods* [1959] Ch 637.

66 *Portway Press v Hague* [1957] RPC 426.

> Under the Act of 1842, which protected 'books', many things which had no pretensions to literary style acquired copyright; for example, a list of registered bills of sale, a list of foxhounds and hunting days, and trade catalogues; and I see no ground for coming to the conclusion that the present Act was intended to curtail the rights of authors. In my view the words 'literary work' cover work which is expressed in print or writing, irrespective of the question whether the quality or style is high. The word 'literary' seems to be used in a sense somewhat similar to the use of the word 'literature' in political or electioneering literature and refers to written or printed matter. Papers set by examiners are, in my opinion, 'literary work' within the meaning of the present Act.[67]

Protection is not granted automatically and 'skill judgement and labour'[68] is a requirement that operates as a proviso *de minimis*.[69] It is a condition that requires that there must be 'a relation of creation between the work and the author whatever this act of creation (sometimes only presentation) means.'[70] Accordingly, courts may refuse to recognise works as literary works in which the degree of literary composition is minimal.[71] Once skill and judgement are evident, the work has to

---

67 Peterson J, in *University of London Press v University Tutorial Press* [1916] 2 Ch 601, 608.

68 See for example, *Ladbrooke (Football) Ltd v William Hill (Football) Ltd* [1964] 1 All ER 465; *Redwood Music v Chappell* (n 51 above) 115; *Ibcos Computers v Barclays Mercantile* (n 31 above); *Bookmakers Afternoon Greyhound Services Ltd v Wilf Gilbert (Staffordshire) Ltd* [1994] FSR 723 (Ch); *Reject Shop Plc v Manners* [1995] FSR 870 (QB); *Cala Homes (South) Ltd v Alfred McAlpine Homes East Ltd (No 1)* [1995] FSR 818 (Ch); *Bowater Windows Ltd v Aspen Windows Ltd* [1999] FSR 759 (Ch); *IPC Magazines Ltd v MGN Ltd* [1998] FSR 431 (Ch); *Hi Tech Autoparts Ltd v Towergate Two Ltd (No 1)* [2002] FSR 15 (Patent County Court); *Beckingham v Hodgens* [2004] 6 ECDR 46 (CA). Or, as the Canadian Court once remarked: 'work, taste and discretion.' *Slumber-Magic Adjustable Bed Co v Sleep-King Adjustable Bed Co* (1984)3 CPR (3d)81 (BCSC) 84-85.

69 It was held, however, that where calculating racing forecasts is a routine repetitive task which involves feeding the relevant information into a computer, the activity does not involve sufficient skill, labour or judgement for the formula for calculating the racing forecasts to produce an original literary work each time. *Bookmakers' Afternoon Greyhound Services v Wilf Gilbert*, ibid.

70 A Dietz, 'The Artist's Right of Integrity Under Copyright Law – A Comparative Approach' (1994) 25 *International Review of Industrial Property and Copyright Law* 177, 182. This condition, the court held, cannot be defined in advance as it must be examined on a case-to-case basis. See *Biotrading & Financing OY v Biohit Industries Inc* [1989] AC 217.

71 See for example, *Kirk v Fleming* [1928-1935] Mac CC 44. In this case the court refused to grant copyright protection to an advertisement consisting of four commonplace sentences. See also *Rose v Information Services* [1987] FSR 254. In *Macmillan v Cooper*, concerned with copyright in textbooks containing excerpts from existing works with notes for students, Lord Atkinson redefines and highlights the centrality of the requirement of 'labour skill and capital': 'To secure copyright for this product it is necessary that labour, skill and capital should have been expended sufficiently to impart to the product some quality or character which the raw material did not possess, and which differentiates the product from the raw material.' *Macmillar & Co Ltd v Cooper* (1924) 40 TLR 186, 188.

qualify for the root requirement of originality,[72] not in the sense of producing a novel work but that the work has originated from its creator and was not copied from another source. Peterson J holds:

> The word 'original' does not in this connection mean that the work must be the expression of original or inventive thought. Copyright Acts are not concerned with the originality of ideas, but with the expression of thought, and, in the case of 'literary work', with the expression of thought in print or writing. The originality which is required relates to the expression of the thought. But the Act does not require that the expression must be in an original or novel form, but that the work must not be copied from another work – that it should originate from the author.[73]

In the recent case of *Sawkins v Hyperion Records Ltd*[74] the claimant, a musicologist recognised as a leading authority on the French baroque composer Lalande, sued a record company for infringement of copyright by virtue of recording four works by Lalande. The defendant used editions of the works prepared by the claimant. The claimant claimed royalties for reproduction and distribution of the recordings on CD. Patten J held:

> The amount of skill and labour necessary to establish a copyright is not very large and is often expressed in negative terms ('not insubstantial'). Nor need it involve inventive thought, although the use of inventive thought is obviously likely to confirm the originality of the work. What, however, the work need not be is unique, and therefore in the case of a musical, just like a literary work a rearrangement of an earlier work can easily give rise

---

72 CDPA 1988 s 1(1)(a). The requirement for a literary work to be 'original' was first added to the Copyright Act of 1911.

73 *University of London Press v University Tutorial Press* (n 67 above) 608. In the *Interlego* case the defendant was trying to convince the Privy Council that there must be an original creative input by the author and that the skill and labour is not that relevant. The Court of Appeal rejected this argument referring to Peterson's J remark. *Interlego AG v Tyco Industries Inc* [1989] AC 217, 259-260.

The inherent absurdity in the principle of originality is well illustrated by the *Redwood* case. In that case the plaintiff claims copyright in various adaptations and arrangements made by the defendant of an original song. A question arose as to the degree of skill and labour which the arranger had to show he exercised in order to establish copyright in the arrangement. Goff J accepted the defendant's submission that the degree of originality required means that the manner of expression in permanent form is such that it can be regarded as have being originated from the arranger rather than having being copied from the original, and subject to that, an arrangement could attract copyright notwithstanding that it is no more than a straightforward arrangement of a well known song. The *Redwood* case well illustrates how little originality is required for copyright to subsist. In other words, building on existing works and altering their arrangement is a basis for a valid claim of exclusive rights. *Redwood Music v Chappell* (n 51 above).

74 *Sawkins v Hyperion Records Ltd* [2004] 27 EMLR 542; [2005] RPC 4 (Ch); See also *Baigent v Random House Ltd* [2006] EWHC 719 (Ch. D).

to a copyright…The purpose of copyright is to protect from misappropriation the skill and labour of the author which is expended on the production of the original work.[75]

Award of any entitlement from the bundle of rights is dependent on whether the alleged work complies with the requirement of originality. Yet, this seems to be an easy task as originality is defined in the sense of 'originating from an author.'[76] This poses a conceptual problem. If I write a poem and did not copy it from another source, then the work does not only represent a thing that has been originated in me, but also, due to differences between people, it contains a modicum of originality in the sense of creating a *different* substance. The originality of the authorial creation and whether it can be attributed to a solitary achievement is another question that will occupy a great deal of discussion in subsequent chapters.

Copyright Entitlement Structure

The Role of Correlatives

A property right in respect of a given resource arms its owner, *inter alia*, with a bundle of legal rights. The primary rights considered here are three. Combined, these rights usually characterise the right to private property: the right to use; the right to exclude others from use and possession; and the power to transfer the owned object as a gift, by sale or bequest.[77]

---

75 Ibid 564-565.

76 In comparative terms, the concept of originality has gone through many changes in recent years. While English Courts remain steadfast on the original condition of skill, labour and judgement, and their US counterparts require a modicum of creativity, the Canadian Supreme Court made an attempt to provide a mid-way solution – labour and skill that is neither trivial nor mechanical in nature. Arguably, this formula looks closer to the requirement of modicum of creativity rather than a mid-way solution. See *Feist Publications Inc v Rural Telephone Service Co* 499 US 340 (1991); *CCH Canada Ltd v The Law Society of Upper Canada* [2004] 1 SCR 339. For further illustration see also *Interlego A/S v Exin-Lines Bros SA* (1989) 48(4) PD 133 (Israel); and *Telstra Corporation Ltd v Desktop Marketing Systems Pty Ltd* [2001] FCA 612 (Australia).

Making creativity a condition for copyright protection has attracted ample criticism. See for example, R VerSteeg, 'Sparks in the Tinderbox: Feist, 'Creativity', and The Legislative History of the 1976 Copyright Act' (1995) 56 *University of Pittsburgh Law Review* 549; G Pessach, 'The Legacy of *Fiest* Revisited: A Critical Analysis of the Creativity Requirement' 36 (2002) *Israel Law Review* 19; DJ Gervais, 'Feist Goes Global: A Comparative Analysis of the Notion of Originality in Copyright Law' (2002) 49 *Journal of the Copyright Society of the USA* 949; and by the same author, 'Canadian Copyright Law Post-CCH' (2004) 18 *Intellectual Property Journal* 131.

77 I shall use the term 'rights' to denote the legal relations that a property right imposes. The bundle of rights a property holder has includes more than those mentioned, but the three rights that I am dealing with are the most fundamental and powerful. For example see Honoré (n 10 above). *Cf*, Mossoff (n 18 above), in particular 413-427.

The right to exclude is the right that each of us has, for example, in respect to state-owned property like the use of the seashore and public parks. Once the right to exclude is combined with the right to use we get the right that we aim at – the right to use our own land. As the defining characteristic of private property, it is the right to exclude that chiefly attracts our imagination.[78] In the words of Cohen: the 'essence' of property 'is always the right to exclude others.'[79] The right to exclude then, is the right that transforms a right to an essentially *private* right. The right to transfer, is subject to the availability of the right to exclude, and cannot be independently realised. Only when an individual has a right to exclude others from access or use of an asset, can he enjoy the freedom to exercise the right to transfer his private property to others. Yet, the first two rights will continue until varied by the right to transfer[80]

The realisation of the three primary rights is affected by the intrinsic relational character of the institution of private property. Property rights are correlative in nature, since acquisition imposes duties on others.[81] Hohfeld attempts to provide

78 The right to exclude may, to some extent, bring one to remark that although property is about rights, there is still a certain form of relation between the owner and the resource. This idea is nicely captured by Honoré in the following passage: 'The idiom which directly couples the owner with the thing owned is far from pointless; where the right to exclude others exists, there is indeed (legally) a very special relation between the holder of the thing and the thing.' Honoré, ibid 106, 134.

79 M Cohen, 'Property and Sovereignty' (1928) 13 *Cornell Law Quarterly* 8, 12. Merrill also writes that 'to the extent one has the right to exclude, then one has property; conversely, to the extent one does not have exclusion rights, one does not have property.' TW Merrill, 'Property and the Right to Exclude' (1998) 77 *Nebraska Law Review* 730, 753. *Cf* Mossoff (n 18 above) 396. See also DL Callies and JD Breemer, 'The Right to Exclude Others from Private Property: A Fundamental Constitutional Right' (2000) 3 *Washington University Journal of Law and Policy* 39; and LS Underkuffler, *The Idea of Property: Its Meaning and Power* (Oxford: Oxford University Press, 2003) 137-161.

Justice McKenna in 1913 put the matter this way: 'The conception of property is exclusiveness, the rights of exclusive possession, enjoyment and disposition. Take away these rights and you take all that there is of property. Take away any of them, force a participation in any of them and you take property to that extent.' Justice J McKenna in *Pipe Line Cases*, 234 US 548, 571 (1913).

80 There are exceptions to this general assertion. For example one can transfer a right to use his land in the form of a positive easement such as right of way and there can be many with rights over a single resource. In copyright, one can transfer his property in the object but still retain the copyright, for example, when one writes a letter to a friend the friend have property in the physical object (the paper) but not the copyright, unless he was assigned the copyright. A thief will have neither; he would only have illegal possession.

81 In a well-known essay, Gibbard asserts: 'If a person owns a thing, his ownership enhances his liberty, but it does so at the expense of the liberty of others. Ownership of a thing gives a person the right to exclude others from its use, and that right, though it adds to the freedom of the owner, detracts from the freedom of those others.' A Gibbard, 'Natural Property Rights' in RM Stewart (ed.), *Readings in Social and Political Philosophy* (New

us with the tools to analyse and understand the meaning of having rights in terms of the correlative propositions about duty that they entail.[82] Hohfeld devises a comprehensive legal taxonomy, comprising the terms right, duty, privilege and power as categories of entitlements attached to private property.[83] His great achievement is that his analysis compels us to carefully calculate the spectrum of private ownership with respect to the benefits of the rightholder against the burdensome duties these benefits impose on non-owners.[84] Waldron explains this logic and asserts that:

> It is always tempting to take the perspective of the right-bearer, and show what a marvellous thing it is for him to have all these rights. They protect and promote his personality. They vindicate his right to the labour of his body. They reward his desert. They allow him to make plans, and to exercise his autonomy. The virtue of the Hohfeldian analysis is that it compels us to concentrate on the other side of the coin: the correlative duty.[85]

Hohfeld tells us that if an individual has a right over a certain resource, then there will always be a duty attached to that right on those who do not hold the right. A justified property right over a given resource is the calculation of the three primary rights and the duties they impose on others. For this calculation process, Hohfeld identifies eight basic legal relations, which he arranges in two tables of 'jural opposites' and 'jural correlatives'[86] and argues that proprietary interests

---

York: Oxford University Press, 1986) 237. In a later article, Gaus and Lomasky explain: 'Gibbard hereby points to a possible tension in a liberal case for private property. Once my right to X is established, then I enjoy options with respect to the use or disposition of X that I previously lacked. You, however, are now burdened by a correlative obligation to defer to my decisions concerning X.' GF Gaus and LE Lomasky, 'Are Property Rights Problematic?' (1990) 73(4) *The Monist* 483.

82 Hohfeld 1919 (n 39 above). See also Hohfeld's earlier article, 'Fundamental Legal Conceptions as Applied in Judicial Reasoning' (1913) 23 *Yale Law Journal* 16 (hereinafter – 'Hohfeld 1913').

83 For useful accounts on the Hohfeldian classification see J Waldron, 'Introduction' in J Waldron (ed.), *Theories of Rights* (Oxford: Oxford University Press, 1984) 1, 4-9; and D Knowles, *Political Philosophy* (London: Routledge, 2001) 138-154. Although Hohfeld did not mention the term 'bundle of rights', he is claimed to have brought new understanding of the term. See for example, CC Tedrowe, 'Conceptual Severance and Takings in the Federal Circuit' (2000) 85 *Cornell Law Review* 586, 589; TW Merrill and HE Smith, 'The Property/Contract Interface' (2001) 101 *Columbia Law Review* 773, 780-783; Penner (n 44 above) 724-725.

84 There are many questions and conflicting philosophies around the principle of ownership. Should ownership be recognised? What form of ownership should society prefer? The concept of ownership is ruled out by definition. Yet, 'the possibility that no specific form of ownership is justifiable, is a possibility to be taken seriously.' JO Grunebaum, *Private Ownership* (London: Routledge & Kegan Paul, 1987) 24.

85 Waldron 1993 (n 34 above) 844.

86 Hohfeld 1913 (n 82 above) 16. Hohfeld's construction attracted criticism from legions of commentators. See for example, J Singer, 'The Legal Right Debate in Analytical

must be decomposed into their constituent elements: rights, privileges, powers and immunities.[87]

The most important and powerful of these is the correlative right/duty. Hohfeld argues that 'even those who use the word [right] and the conception 'right' [or claim] in the broadest possible way are accustomed to thinking of 'duty' as the invariable correlative.'[88] In property, to have a Hohfeldian right means that there are at least two players in the game: the right-bearer and the duty-bearer. The entitlements of each are correlative: '...if X has a right against Y that he shall stay off the former's land, the correlative (and equivalent) is that Y is under a duty toward X to stay off the place.'[89] Thus, every question pertaining to private property is actually a question of restraints.

The *right* in the context of property is particularly attractive since it applies to a claim directed against the entire world. This is probably one of the first axioms introduced to the law student in any introductory course on property law. This right is known as right *in rem*, as opposed to right *in personam*, which is directed at a single person. A good example is the difference between a promise to an individual to provide him with my lecture notes, and the right I have 'against the world' that no-one will take my bag in order to secure the notes. Every non-owner of my property is under a duty not to use, damage or destroy it.

How do the four pairs of rights/correlatives operate in law? Consider the example of a plot of land. Prior to acquisition, we are all in the same situation. Each of us has a *privilege to use* the land. The fact that an individual has a *privilege* to perform a given act indicates that it has not been made the subject of a *duty* so far. Once the individual has exercised his privilege, he can perhaps claim to be an original owner. By using his *powers* to create this claim, the individual has transformed his privilege of use to an exclusive *right*, which excludes others from possession and use of the plot. The rightholder also enjoys *immunity* against other people altering his privileges and rights by exercising their powers, and protection against having unwanted goods foisted upon him. If the rightholder abandons the plot, we may return to the starting point in which everyone has the privilege to use the plot and the power to create rights over the land.[90]

Jurisprudence from Bentham to Hohfeld' (1982) *Wisconsin Law Review* 975, 986-95, 1049-1050; and Gordon 1989 (n 22 above).

I agree that Hohfeld's construction clarifies the difference between a right (or claim) and a privilege (or liberty) in a very useful way. Yet, no matter how articulate it is in helping us to understand the inevitable costs of entitlements, is it at all possible to confine legal rights to a conclusive list?

87 The four categories of rights and their correlatives are right(claim)/duty; privilege/no-right; power/liability; immunity/disability.

88 Hohfeld 1919 (n 39 above) 31.

89 Ibid.

90 Penner remarks that Hohfeld's system of correlatives, coupled with Honoré's ownership incidents, define the saying 'property is a bundle of rights.' Penner (n 44 above) 712.

Copyright laws specifically refer to the right to prevent others from copying the work and limit certain uses. First, the idea of copyright as an exclusive property right is as strong as the Hohfeldian right to exclude others from doing with the work what otherwise they would have been authorised to do. The right to authorise certain uses supplements this right to exclude. Second, the different methods of use resemble Hohfeldian privileges. The author has a privilege to use his work as the law specifies, and if an author has the right to authorise others to use his work in certain circumstances, the author has the power to transfer his set of entitlements in the work, and to alter the legal status of a given work.

Finally, an author also enjoys Hohfeldian immunity. An author has immunity against others imposing on him claims to use the work in certain ways without his permission. He also holds immunity against third parties using their powers to alter the rights and privileges he holds in his creation without his permission. In copyright terms, a musician has a right to exclude others from accessing or making adaptations of his composition, a privilege to make and use the adaptations, a power to authorise others to make adaptations and an immunity against others exercising their powers and affecting the legal status of the original work and adaptations.

Rights of Exclusion

As mentioned above, the right to exclude is what usually characterises and defines the true power of a private property right. In Hohfeldian and copyright terms: if X has a *right* against Y prohibiting Y from copying his screenplay, it means that Y has a *correlative duty* not to copy the screenplay. If X has a duty toward Y, Y holds a right against X. In terms of the right to exclude, the fact that X has a right to exclude *others* from copying the screenplay entails that others hold a duty to refrain from copying the screenplay without X's permission. The right to exclude is correlative to the duties that *others* – except the right-holder – undertake. The consequence of this is simple: now, the right-holder can exercise his right by requesting the government to compel the duty-holder to act in accordance with the duty.

The primary rights constitute the copyright-holder's core bundle of rights. As with tangible property, the most powerful right an author may have is the right to exclude others from access and use of his works. As Gordon remarks: 'Copyright's grant of exclusive rights thus most closely parallels landowners' "right to exclude", for patent law gives proprietors something more than a "right to exclude" and trademark and trade secret law give something less. Copyright gives authors only what trespass law gives landowners: Authors have the right to exclude others from what they own.'[91] That is, the right to exclude guarantees that copying an author's work without his permission amounts to an infringement of his copyright.

---

91 Gordon 1989 (n 22 above) 1370. See also by the same author, 'A Property Right in Self-Expression: Equality and Individualism in the Natural Law of Intellectual Property' (1993) 12 *Yale Law Journal* 1533, 1552-1554.

Violations of copyright may yield sanctions and remedies. A jazz adaptation of one of Vanessa Mae's violin ensembles or a public performance of the ensemble, requires her permission, otherwise the performer may find himself liable for damages, criminal penalties and other sanctions familiar to the property institution in general. However, since copyright controls rights in the intangible parts of a creation, one may correctly raise the issue that differences between tangibles and intangibles may yield different results once an infringement of the right to exclude is at stake. If I send a painting I painted to a friend, my friend owns the painting. However, unless expressly authorised by me, he is restricted from reproducing my work and distributing it amongst his friends. Similarly, if I sold my work to the Del Prado museum in Madrid but the museum did not purchase my copyright interest in the work, Del Prado is restricted from making reproductions or postcards carrying my work without my permission.[92]

One then may identify two senses of ownership protecting a painting, a sculpture or a phone directory. The first sense provides protection to the physical form of an artistic work as a tangible entity, while the copyrighted parts – the abstract entities, protectable under copyright laws – are the second sense.[93] Copyright law is designed to protect the right to *exclude* others from certain *uses* and *enjoyment* of the *abstract* entity of a copyrighted work; uses that sometimes may well have nothing to do with physicality. As Lord Chancellor Cottenham pointed out in an early case involving a defendant who was not authorised to publish a catalogue listing private etchings made by Queen Victoria and the Prince Consort: 'The matter or thing of which the party has obtained knowledge, being the exclusive property of the owner, he has a right to the interposition of this Court to prevent any use being made of it, that is to say, he is entitled to be protected in the exclusive *use and enjoyment* of that which is exclusively his.'[94] From a similar point of view, Gordon remarks that 'a copyright owner's rights largely operate independently of the rules governing physical ownership. Intellectual property is concerned not with entry or physical interference but with forbidding specific *uses* of the work that may be quite

92 For the same reasons a US court held that the owner of a Mark Twain manuscript is not entitled to publish it because physical ownership does not mean that the elements pertaining to copyright ownership were obtained. *Chamberlain v Feldman*, 300 NY 135, 89 NE 2d 863 (1949).

93 In other words, copyrights are 'quite distinct from any physical work which may embody them and, for example, the transfer of a manuscript does not amount to a transfer of the copyright in the work. Equally, an assignment of the copyright (or any of the other property rights) does not carry with it ownership of any physical article embodying the right…' Laddie (n 25 above) 22.2. See also *Re Dickens* [1935] Ch 267, CA; *Moorhouse v Angus & Robertson No 1 Pty Ltd* [1980] FSR 231.

94 Lord Cottenham LC in *Prince Albert v Strange* (1849) 1 Mac And G 25 (emphasis added).

independent of physical touching. Nevertheless, this right, like the right at the core of tangible property, can be viewed as a right of exclusion.'[95]

Although physicality is less relevant to the idea of having a copyright, encroachment into one's personal autonomy amounts to trespassing. Full realisation of an individual's expression of personality and his efforts necessitate exclusion rights similar in strength to those governing traditional property. Jurisdictions in which moral rights are more central to questions of copyright ownership, would probably argue that the physicality issue is moot, since we are not protecting a copyrighted *work* but rather an expression of a person's personal identity. This distinction between the corporeal and the incorporeal constituents of a copyrighted entity is captured in Kant's distinction between a 'real right' and a 'personal right.' In *What is a book?* Kant identifies this distinction and claims that the error in copyright is that we confuse a 'real right' with a 'personal right':

> The basic cause of an appearance of legality in something that is nevertheless, at the first inspection, such an injustice – as book piracy is – lies in this: that the book is, on the one hand, a corporeal product of art (*opus mechanicum*), which can be copied (by him, who finds himself in legal possession of an exemplar of this product) – consequently has a real right therein; on the other hand, however, a book is also merely an address of the publisher to the public, which this publisher, without having the authorization thereto of the author, may not publicly repeat (*praestatio operae*) – a personal right; and now the error consists in this, that the two are confused with each other.[96]

In other words a book is a corporeal object of art which I hold when I read. This denotes a 'real right.' A book is also the address by one person to another person. According to Kant, an author can authorise use to others, but can never alienate his personal right.[97] Palmer explains: '[a] copier, or infringer, offers to the public the thoughts of another. That is, he speaks in the author's name which he can properly do only with his permission. The author has given permission, however, only to his authorised publisher, who is wronged when a book edition is pirated.'[98]

---

95 Gordon 1989 (n 22 above) (emphasis added) 1368. It is arguable then that the right to exclude in copyright is best definable as a 'right of enjoyment', or 'the right to exclude others from enjoyment.' The above shows that in copyright, the right to exclude, is a mixture of the other two primary rights, and they should be read *in tandem*.

96 E Kant, Was ist ein Buch?', in *Die Metaphysik Die Sitten* (T Palmer trans., W Weischedel ed., 1977) 405, cited in TG Palmer, 'Are Patents and Copyrights Morally Justified? The Philosophy of Property Rights and Ideal Objects' (1990) 13 *Harvard Journal of Law and Public Policy* 817, 839-840.

97 I Kant, 'Von der Unrechtsmässigkeit des Büchernachdrucks' in *Copyrights and Patents for Inventions* (R MacFie ed. 1883) vol 2, 580, 582, cited in Palmer, ibid 839. 840-841. Of importance to note is that for Kant the key issue in copyright is speech. Thus, translations or derivative works cannot be prohibited because they do not amount to the very speech of the author albeit the thoughts might be similar. Palmer, ibid 840-841.

98 Ibid 839.

Privileges of Use

A privilege is a right of use.[99] The right to exclude others from using or interfering with my property is not the same as the right to *use* the property. The right to use a property is not a [claim] right simply because it does not in itself impose duties on others.[100] A privilege (or liberty) is defined as the opposite of a duty and its correlative is 'no-right.' A privilege to do an act amounts to the absence of a duty not to do that act. If X has the right that Y should not encroach onto his Blackacre, X himself has a privilege to enter; he is not under a duty to stay off the land and if he wishes, he has a privilege to build an amusement park on his land in the outskirts of his hometown. Once municipal authorities have approved the project, the privilege is crystallised, and other people have no right to prevent X from exercising his desire to build this park for the exclusive use of orphans.

Privileges are not unlimited and an owner has to take account of possible repercussions.[101] In addition, there are situations in which strangers/non-rightholders may have a right of passage in X's land in emergencies. 'I have a privilege' or 'it's my property' then, is no defence in all circumstances. It is possible to conclude then, that X's privilege to use his land is limited by *duties* the owner may have to the public. The term 'liberty' may further explain this: the right to use is correlative to a negative proposition in respect of the duties of the right-holder. Although X's privilege may also be accompanied by a duty on *others* not to interfere, that does not mean that every liberty that X may have will be supported by a right. Others may also have liberties that can exist simultaneously. In copyright, non-rightholders always retain a privilege to use the underlying idea of a given expression, and, as I shall argue, the law recognises principles such as fair dealing exceptions and the public interest defence, which make limitations and emergency situations in copyright disputes easier to inflict on rightholders.

I have already mentioned that in copyright the right to exclude is intertwined with the right to use. In this respect, another inherent difference between a privilege of use in tangibles and in copyright, should also be noted. A copyrighted work, once its terms of protection have expired, becomes part of the public domain. From that time, every member of the public, including the creator, the previous sole privilege-

---

99 That includes the privilege to *not* use.

100 'Second, A has an indefinite number of legal privileges of entering on the land, using the land, harming the land, etc., that is within the limits fixed by law on grounds of social and economic policy, he has privileges of doing on or to the land what he pleases; and correlative to all such legal privileges are the respective legal no-rights of other persons.' Hohfeld 1919 (n 39 above) 96.

101 If, for example, the land on which the amusement park is to be built is contaminated with asbestos, then a court may inquire into the proper use of the given piece of land and the eventual effects on those who are likely to use the facilities of the park. It might even inquire into the decision-making process of the municipal authority as to how this privilege was authorised without noticing the environmental and public health risks. Only when the land becomes his, the owner can exercise his right to exclude.

holder, share the same privilege of use. With tangibles, a lost or abandoned product can receive a new owner, while once a copyrighted work becomes part of the public domain, it remains there.[102] True, another creator can make it part of his new work, but he cannot exclude others from making the same use whether as a basis for new creations or mere enjoyment.

Powers of Transfer

In addition to having rights and privileges, owners have *powers*. A power denotes an owner's ability to alter legal relations and transfer his legal interest to another.[103] For example, an owner of a plot of land has the power to create rights [claims] over a given resource, and consequently to introduce duties to be respected by others. How can we, however, prevent a non-owner from using his powers to change the legal status of a resource owned by X? In order to answer this question Hohfeld introduces *immunities* as the last category of his rights.[104] Immunity is to be viewed in two ways: first, every person has immunity against other people imposing property claims on him without his permission. Second, every person has immunity against other people using their powers to alter the rights and privileges he has without his permission.

The right to transfer is a Hohfeldian power. As with tangible property, an author would be able to exercise his right to transfer only when he has a right to exclude others from a given work. Yet, the divisibility of copyrighted works complicates attainment of the right to transfer: a film, for example, is composed of the screenplay, the choreography, the sound track, etc. Treating a copyrighted work as an entity comprising different elements that are subject to separate copyright protection, widens the scope for possible manipulations of the right to exclude. At the same time, however, it introduces complexities that the law of copyright has to accommodate. Finally, in general terms, like traditional tangible property, in copyright, the right to use and the right to exclude continue, until varied by the right to transfer, abandoned

102 This situation should be distinguished from remote situations where people bequeath their property to the public, for example, making their home a public museum.

103 'Third, A has the legal power to alienate his legal interest to another, ie., to extinguish his complex aggregate of jural relations and create a new and similar aggregate in other person; also the legal power to create a life estate in another and concurrently to create a reversion in himself; also the legal power to create a privilege of entrance in any other person by giving "leave and license"; and so on indefinitely. Correlative to all such legal powers are the legal liabilities in other persons – this meaning that the latter are subject *nolens volens* to the changes of jural relations involved in the exercise of A's powers.' Hohfeld 1919 (n 39 above) 96.

104 'Fourth, A has an indefinite number of legal immunities, using the term in the very specific sense of non-liability or non-subjection to a power on the part of another person… Correlative to all these immunities are the respective legal disabilities of the persons in general.' Ibid 96-97.

or destroyed. Continuation of these rights, of course, is determined by the temporal nature of copyright protection.[105]

Copyright-Limitation Rules

Like every property system, copyright should be demarcated carefully. In addition to the bundle of rights, copyright laws claim to establish a solid bundle of limitations of the rights. These limitations provide rightholders civil and criminal remedies on the one hand, and designed to accommodate fundamental societal needs on the other hand. However, the question is whether the degree to which the 'bundle of limitations' incorporated in copyright law, adequately satisfies the concerns I expressed above about the uncontrollable dimension of private rights in copyright.

The idea of establishing a property right was not the only import from traditional property into copyright. Certain norms of justice, set in property laws and crafted by judicial decisions, continually shape copyright ownership patterns. However, the lack of a universally accepted definition of property – as opposed to the universal recognition of a person's right to own property[106] – or a universally accepted recognition of *one* definition of copyright,[107] dictates that jurisdictional differences

---

105 To clarify, I argue that rights can be *shared* with others, *against* others, or *from* others: while a privilege is *shared* with others whose correlative is no right. A right to exclude is *against* others whose correlative is a duty upon others. For example, before one expresses one's artistic ideas, the ideas form part of the common of all and each of us has a privilege to consume as many ideas as he wishes. The effort in expressing them in a tangible medium is what distinguishes between a privilege that all have and a right that only the right-holder has. From that moment the right to exclude is present, and the author enjoys a right to copy and reproduce the work which is a right enforceable *against* others. At the same time, the author enjoys a right *from* others, which means (i) the capacity to keep stable existing legal relations or to create new relations, and (ii) the capacity to stop anyone from imposing legal relations without permission. The right to transfer does not involve placing duties on others. It is not a right in the sense that the right to exclude is, and is dependent on the existence of the two preceding rights. However, whether a right *shared* with others – a common privilege to use and consume unprotectable artistic and authorial commodities – suffices for matters of copyright balance remains an open question.

106 See The Universal Declaration of Human Rights (1948) Article 17(1) and Article 17(2); The African Charter on Human and People's Rights (1981) Article 14; The American Convention on Human Rights (1969) Article 21(1); Not surprisingly, endless controversies resulted in non-inclusion of a right of property in the European Convention on Human Rights (Article 1 of Protocol 1 includes a right to peaceful enjoyment of possessions).

107 There are many international and regional agreements aiming to harmonise copyright. For example, the Berne Convention for the Protection of Literary and Artistic Works 1886 (Paris Act, 1971); The Universal Copyright Convention 1952 (Paris Act, 1971); WIPO Copyright Treaty 1996, and WIPO Performances and Phonograms Treaty 1996 (known together as 'WIPO Internet Treaties'). There are also regional arrangements such as the Directives of the European Union and the Inter-American copyright agreements; and trade arrangements such as the North American Free Trade Agreement (NAFTA) and the TRIPs

will continue to determine the fate of the right. There are, however, certain limitation rules that are universally attributed to private property and were adapted, with variations, to copyright.

A key limitation in common law systems, with a clear impact on the evolution of property limitation rules, is the tort of nuisance. The rule limits landowner's primary rights if their realisation causes certain unlawful harms to his neighbours.[108] A plaintiff, in order to invoke this rule will have to show 'not only that he has sustained damage, but that the defendant has caused it by going beyond what is necessary in order to enable him to have the natural use of his land.'[109] That is, 'if the user is reasonable, the defendant will not be liable for consequent harm to his neighbour's enjoyment of his land.'[110]

The principle of no-harm is well ingrained in copyright policy and affects both authors and users. It holds that for an author to part from his laborious efforts and elements of personality infused into the work created, or from the other side of the fence, to withhold from the public to do certain acts with protected copyrighted entities, amount to violation of the no-harm principle. The no-harm principle normally applies to individuals but it has a social function. For example, just as environmental conservation rules impose radical restrictions on the use of privately owned land in order to avoid harming the environment, which in turn secures collective benefits for society as a whole, so copyright aims to balance the no-harm for the public and the no-harm to the author. Although this may look as an irresolvable stalemate, this book is about challenging this argument, finding and defining a balance between the no-harm to the individual and the no-harm to the collective.

Examples of invocations of property-limitation rules illustrate prevailing trends in copyright protection. In two historic cases on property the House of Lords declines to recognise a person's 'right to light'[111] or to grant an injunction against obstruction

---

Agreement. In addition, there are international agreements regulating neighbouring rights. For a comprehensive overview of international copyright law and policy, see P Goldstein, *International Copyright: Principles, Law, and Practice* (Oxford: Oxford University Press 2001); GB Dinwoodie, WO Hennessey and S Perlmutter, *International Intellectual Property Law and Policy* (New York: M Bender, 2001); and S Ricketson and JC Ginsburg, *International Copyright and Neighbouring Rights*, Vol I-II (Oxford: Oxford University Press, 2nd ed., 2006).

108 This rule is known as *sic utere tuo ut alienum non laedas.*

109 Brett LJ in *West Cumberland Iron and Steel Company v Kenyon* [1879] 11 Ch D 782, 787.

110 Lord Goff in *Cambridge Water Co v Eastern Countries Leather Plc* [1994] 2 AC 264, 299. Further, according to the rule in *Rylands v Fletcher,* it is possible to deny an owner some use of his land if that use causes harm to his neighbours: 'the person who for his own purposes brings on his land and collects and keeps there anything likely to do mischief if it escapes must keep it at his peril.' Blackburn J in *Rylands v Fletcher* [1966] Exch 265, 279.

111 *Taplin v Jones* (1865) 11 HLC 290, 329, reversed in *Colls v Home & Colonial Stores Ltd* [1904] AC 179 (HL). In *Phipps v Pears* Lord Denning MR relied on *Taplin v Jones* and held that '[e]very man is entitled to pull down his house if he likes. If it exposes your house to

of water flow to waterworks, even when it was established that a malicious act was carried out in order to force the plaintiff to buy the land at a higher price: 'He prefers his own interest to the public good. He may be churlish, selfish, and grasping. His conduct may seem shocking to a moral philosopher. But where is the malice?'[112] Analogously, I shall argue that copyright laws also blatantly allow one to prefer his own interest over the public good. If the 'right to light' is comparable to a fundamental right to consume social and cultural wealth vested in copyrighted entities, then copyright laws decline to protect this right also by limiting the strength of limitation rules. A question which I shall leave open in this chapter is how much copyright laws should allow an author or an artist to be 'churlish, selfish, and grasping'?

Another example concerns the rights of members of the public to pass and repass a road dedicated as a highway, even though the highway is privately owned. The English Court of Appeal has limited this right to pass the highway and entitled the owner to an injunction to prevent a racing tout from walking up and down the highway in order to make notes about race horses being trained on the plaintiff's adjoining land. Romer LJ remarks that: 'The soil of the highway belonging to the plaintiff he has a right to ask for what purpose the defendant entered on to it, whether for the purpose of using it in the ordinary and reasonable way in which a highway may be used or for the purpose of doing that which amounted to an interference with the plaintiff's legal use of his own land.'[113] In copyright, passing and repassing have a different meaning, which lies at the heart of copyright. As an abstract commodity, a copyrighted work is different from 'the soil of the highway.' On the one hand, the distinction between protectable and non-protectable material allows non-owners to enter into rightholders' private realm. On the other hand, this distinction explains why it is more convenient to avoid the public interest and leave the public to enjoy the less valuable – non-protectable – elements.

There are several immediate, and unconditional limitations on a copyright: the idea/expression dichotomy; the non-substantial part principle; the fair dealing doctrine; and the duration of the right. The most important copyright limitation rule stems from the idea/expression dichotomy. Because of this distinction, literary, musical and dramatic works, choreography, graphic, audiovisual and pictorial works, motion pictures, sound recording and architectural works are protectable subject-matter. Systems, schemes, facts, concepts, methods, principles and ideas are not protected.[114] For example, ideas and facts relating to environmental disasters and large-scale atrocities in a bio-chemical war or a Civil War family besieged by the terrors and hardships of internecine conflict are not protectable under copyright.

the weather, that is your misfortune. It is no wrong on his part.' Lord Denning MR in *Phipps v Pears* [1965] 1 QB 76, 83.

112 Lord MacNaughten in *Mayor and Corporation of Bradford v Pickles* [1895] AC 587, 600-601.

113 Romer LJ in *Hickman v Maisey* [1900] 1 QB 752, 759.

114 As Lindley LJ once remarked: 'Copyright…does not extend to ideas, or schemes, or systems, or methods; it is confined to their expression, and if their expression is not copied the copyright is not infringed.' See for example, *Hollinrake v Truswell* (1894) 3 Ch 420, 427.

Similarly, the claim of a painter to own ideas to spread upon canvass stories from the Bible, or a poet who inspires students to write on how to instruct mankind to appreciate the beauty of nature, are beyond the scope of copyright's cluster of proprietary entitlements. Their expression in a book, film, street show or graffiti, are copyrightable. In other words, copyright transforms common conceptions and ideas into property, making it a right against the copying of a defined transformative form of ideational entities.

To the non-protectable nature of ideas one should also add the principle of non-substantial part, according to which a non-owner is allowed to copy non substantial parts from other works, make them part of his new creation and claim copyright over the whole work.[115] In this way the law guarantees that exercise of an author's bundle of rights is not absolute, or better put – is always open in character and vulnerable for use by fellow non-owners. The non-substantial part principle, like the idea/expression dichotomy, provides users an immediate right to acquire from a work aspects which the law does not protect.

The duration of the right, not only distinguishes copyright from tangible property for which perpetuity plays a significant role, but also limits maximisation of the enjoyment of the bundle of rights. This limitation has been the subject of great criticism and contention between partisans of perpetual rights and those who believe copyright systems should be abolished altogether.[116] Protection of the economic and

---

115 The fact that an author has added enough skill, labour and judgement to secure protection to his efforts does not settle the question whether he has infringed copyright or not. The issue is whether a substantial part of the plaintiff's work survives in the defendant's so as to appear to be a copy of it. See for example *Redwood Music v Chappell* (n 51 above); and *Designers Guild Ltd v Russell Williams Textiles Ltd* [2000] 1 WLR 2416 (HL).

The principle of substantial part is particularly difficult when applied to satire or music. For example in *Glyn v Weston Feature* a film burlesque of Elinor Glyn's novel, *Three Weeks*, was found not to infringe copyright since very little was taken from the novel and also in an incidental way. *Glyn v Weston Feature* [1916] 1 Ch 261. Another example is the *Joy Music* case in which it was held that one repeated phrase of a parodied song in pursuit of Prince Philip is not substantial enough to constitute substantial part and hence an infringement act. *Joy Music v Sunday Pictorial* [1960] 2 QB 60. See also *Newspaper Licensing Agency v Marks & Spencer plc* [2001] 3 WLR 290, 296-298; and *Rowling v Uitgeverij Byblos BV* [2004] ECDR 7 (the Netherlands).

See generally, M Gredley, 'Parody: A Fatal Attraction?' (1997) *European Intellectual Property Review* 339; M Spence, 'Intellectual Property and the Problem of Parody' 114 [1998] *Law Quarterly Review* 594; and A Bridy, 'Sheep in Goat's Clothing: Satire and Fair Use After Campbell v Acuff-Rose Music Inc.' (2004) 51 *Journal of the Copyright Society of the USA* 257.

116 Extending the duration of copyright protection, Vaidhyanathan remarks 'has jeopardized the idea/expression dichotomy, public domain, fair use, open access to information, and the ability to freely satirize, parody, or comment on an existing work…[the Congress] was finally willing to grant far more than… we need.' S Vaidhyanathan, *Copyrights and Copywrongs: The Rise of Intellectual Property and How it Threatens Creativity* (New York and London: New York University Press, 2001) 80.

moral rights in a copyrighted work lasts 70 years 'from the end of the calendar year in which the author dies.'[117] This rule ensures that works will eventually reside in the public domain.

A controversial category of immediate limitation imposed on copyright owners are the exceptions composing the fair dealing doctrine.[118] This doctrine is but a zero-price compulsory licence on copyrighted works for particular uses identified by the law, so that certain acts do not amount to an infringement of copyright even though the author's permission was not granted. These acts include *inter alia*, use for research or private study;[119] criticism, review and news reporting;[120] other different uses (preparation for instruction, playing or showing) for teaching and educational purposes;[121] use by libraries and archives;[122] and also incidental inclusion.[123] In Hohfeldian terms, in these situations the user has a complete privilege (correlative to a compulsory licence). Also, one could argue that a user has a temporary, and strictly defined, right to use, while the copyright owner has a duty to allow such use. These limitations are so central to the legitimacy of the copyright system as they seek to

---

Assuming there is a general understanding that authors should be protected during their lifetime and for a limited period after their death, the question remains, how long should the period of copyright protection last? The Whitford Committee criticised the duration of copyright for its arbitrary allocation of rights: 'The development of copyright law in this and other countries and the acceptance of obligations under international conventions has made it virtually impossible to deal with term on a logical basis.' Cmnd 6732, para. 41.

On the term protection see generally, SL Stanley, 'A Dangerous Step Toward the Over Protection of Intellectual Property: Rethinking Eldred v. Ashcroft' (2003) 26 *Hamline Law Review* 679; MP Schwartz and WM Treanor 'Eldred and Lochner: Copyright Term Extension and Intellectual Property as Constitutional Property' (2003) 112 *Yale Law Journal* 2331; C Seville, 'Copyright's Bargain – Defining Our Terms' [2003] 3 *Intellectual Property Quarterly* 312; M Jones, 'Eldred v Ashcroft: The Constitutionality of the Copyright Term Extension Act' (2004)19 *Berkeley Technology and Law Journal* 85; CW Dallon, 'Original Intent and the Copyright Clause: Eldred v Ashcroft Gets it Right' (2006) 50 *Saint Louise University Law Journal* 307.

117 CDPA 1988 s 12(2). Under CDPA 1988 s 86(2), moral rights will continue to exist so long as copyright subsists in the given work. This do not include a situation where the rights, pursuant to s 87, have been waived. To this rule there are certain exceptions. For example, CDPA 1988 s 86(2) provides that the right to false attribution recognised pursuant to s 84, will last 20 years after the person's death.

118 CDPA 1988 Chapter III 'Acts Permitted in Relation to Copyright Works.' Chapter III complies with the list of exceptions and limitations provided under Article 5 of Directive 2001/29/EC of the European Parliament and of the Council on the Harmonisation of Certain Aspects of Copyright and Related Rights in the Information Society (22 May 2001).

119 CDPA 1988 s 29.

120 CDPA 1988 s 30.

121 CDPA 1988 s 32-36A.

122 CDPA 1988 s 37-44.

123 CDPA 1988 s 31.

establish a proper balance between the legitimate rights of copyright owners and the legitimate public interests.

The fair dealing doctrine is an exhaustive list of limitations built into the law. It does not aid the public in certain *ad hoc* situations or emergencies. Most jurisdictions give the public privileges to act reasonably in emergency situations, despite the fact that exercising this privilege may cause intrusive harm to someone's private property. In other words, owners of a piece of land are not absolutely entitled to withhold others from causing unintentional and non-negligent harms to the land. In those situations, a stranger has a temporary power to alter the legal status of the owner's right over the land. The latter temporarily loses his right of exclusion, and consequently the stranger may enter the land. It is important to highlight that the stranger has the right to use the owner's land and to *only* temporarily limit the owner's right to exclude. Copyright law is not silent with regards to emergencies and recognises a common law defence of public interest,[124] which although incorporated into copyright law, is an independent defence that is not limited to copyright. Although severely limited in scope and application, it allows courts a wider interpretive space where codified laws cannot solve specific situations.[125]

Another set of limitation rules is expropriation rules. The functions served by these rules are diverse and they live up to the maxim that 'justice has inevitable costs.'[126] These rules govern situations in which an owner's rights can be taken away from him against his will. For example, in private law, one's property may be stripped away as a means of enforcing payment of debts in civil execution or through bankruptcy procedures. Criminal law provides sanctions by ways of fines and confiscation. Under the doctrine of proprietary estoppel, courts may divest owners of property in favour of those who have relied on expectations generated

---

124 CDPA 1988 s 171(3).

125 See for example, *Beloff v Pressdram* [1973] RPC 783; *Lion Laboratories v Evans* (1984) 2 All ER 417; *Hyde Park Residence Ltd v Yelland* [2000] 3 WLR 215.

Although the scope of the public interest defence is limited, in the *Ashdown* Case the Court criticised Aldous LJ's decision in *Hyde Park.* The case concerns a copyright claim in the minutes of a secret meeting held between the Prime Minister and the former leader of the Liberal Democratic Party, Paddy Ashdown. The Court of Appeal was asked to examine the fair dealing and common law public interest defences for infringement of copyright in light of the Human Rights Act 1998. The Court held: 'We do not consider that Aldous LJ was justified in circumscribing the public interest defence to breach of copyright as tightly as he did. We prefer the conclusion of Mance LJ that the circumstances in which public interest may override copyright are not capable of precise categorisation or definition. Now that the Human Rights Act is in force, there is the clearest public interest in giving effect to the right of freedom of expression in those rare cases where this right trumps the rights conferred by the Copyright Act. In such circumstances, we consider that section 171(3) of the Act permits the defence of public interest to be raised.' *Ashdown v Telegraph Group Ltd* [2002] Ch 149, 170; *Hyde Park*, ibid 238-9. See also J Griffiths, 'Copyright Law after *Ashdown* – Time to Deal Fairly with the Public' [2002] 3 *Intellectual Property Quarterly* 240.

126 Harris (n 3 above) 279.

by the owner's conduct. Finally, states exercise the power to tax money and other property owned by their citizens. Courts, however, have recognised that 'the taking of a person's land against his will is a serious invasion of his proprietary rights', and therefore 'the use of statutory authority for the destruction of those rights requires to be most carefully scrutinized...'[127]

This approach towards expropriation rules shape similar modes in copyright. A search order or injunction for the freezing or retention of assets, were designed primarily to help the plaintiff amass evidence of infringement. The Anton Piller Order, for example, is a procedure that enables the plaintiff to inspect the defendant's premises and to seize materials relevant to the alleged claim of infringement of copyright without notice.[128] In addition, copyright laws, subject to specified conditions, enable injunctions for the freezing or retention of assets. This interlocutory procedure is known as the Mareva injunction,[129] directed not for the discovery and preservation of 'fragile' evidence, but for the retention of assets that belong to the defendant. As a self-help remedy it is invaluable for the success of an action against infringement. Finally, other laws impose additional limitations on the ways one may use one's work. For example, defamation laws prohibit an author from publishing a story that maligns someone falsely, anti-pornography laws limit distribution of certain works, and limits are also placed for ways of disseminated copyrighted works over the media. The law also invalidates contracts regarding real and personal property should they counter public policy.

I have emphasised that copyright-limitation rules constitute tools designed to secure copyright's precarious balance between private and public welfare. It is clear that copyright is a form of property, and although it seems parasitic on prevailing principles of traditional property, copyright systems invented a distinct bundle of rights and fences which do not exist in the realm of traditional property. Yet, no matter how similar one may conclude traditional property and copyright rules to be, one may find scholars from time to time asking: 'does it matter whether intellectual property is property?'[130] For reasons already discussed and that will be explored later on in this book, the answer *must* be affirmative. It matters because copyright *is* property and *should* preserve incentives in the guise of proprietary entitlements; *but* it also matters, because copyright, despite its limited scope, *has* become an insensitive variant of traditional property.

In this chapter I explored how property rights can be burdensome to others. In the next chapters I argue that copyright laws have become nothing but powerful legal tools, which 'institutionally serve modern technology's tendency to colonize ever-greater spheres of social life by transforming its instruments into saleable

127 Watkins LJ in *Prest v Secretary of State for Wales* (1982) 81 LGR 193, 211.

128 *Anton Piller v Manufacturing Processes* [1976] Ch 55; [1976] RPC 719. Civil Procedure Act 1997, s 7.

129 See *CBS United Kingdom v Lambert* [1983] FSR 123 (CA).

130 Carter (n 21 above) 723.

commodities.'[131] Perhaps a definition of 'full-blooded ownership'[132] which eliminates 'unequal holdings of private wealth' embodies the proper balance of powers of control and privileges of use is acceptable. It may not be, however, an absolute right *per se*. In order to secure private rights for authors, yet *not* at the expense of the public interest, I shall next define what the public contributes to the process of copyright creation, then examine how this contribution should change ownership patterns dominating our idea of what copyright *is*.

131 LE Wolcher, 'The End of Technology: A Polemic' (2004) 79 *Washington Law Review* 331, 337.

132 Harris (n 3 above) 141.

Chapter 4

Authorial Collectivity

Authorship and the Limits of Original Appropriation

The "Isolated" Author

Works of authorship, whether the result of years of study and labour or sudden leaps of spontaneous insight, begin with what has been done in the past, and they go beyond the past in logical and understandable ways. It is possible to argue that the creative act is mere representation: 'x represents y if and only if x resembles y appreciably.'[1] I do not propose to follow this view in its totality. However, if one places the creative individual in historical context, that is, if one attempts to determine what the person knew, how he interpreted that knowledge and how he builds new knowledge, then one is able to understand the development of even most radical new works. The understanding of how intellectual property is built can warrant the design of a more appropriate ownership mechanism for copyrighted works, premised on the contribution of unrewarded sources.

Literature on copyright frequently refers to the "romantic author". We sometimes take this idea for granted, as part of the ordinary copyright lexicon. In fact, as Stillinger writes, the naturalness and inevitability of romantic ideas about authorship have become 'so widespread as to be nearly universal.'[2] The reason is grounded, as I shall argue, in the recognition of a fictitious conception of originality as the core principle of copyright protection, on which a system of rewards to authors and artists is premised. Courts are aggressively applying this principle, placing authors as almighty creators while denying the contributions of external sources and the rights and interests of the general public. Copyright laws allow disproportionate enclosures of portions of the public domain, of social symbols and cultural elements fundamental to the development of society and its members. Copyright laws deny the contribution of the general public to the formation of copyrighted entities.

Boyle advances a conception of "romantic authorship" which characterises and causes contemporary doctrinal problems in intellectual property.[3] His main concern is the uncontrollable expansion of intellectual property at the expense of

1 N Carroll, *Philosophy of Art: A Contemporary Introduction* (London & New York: Routledge, 1999) 34.

2 J Stillinger, *Multiple Authorship and the Myth of Solitary Genius* (New York: Oxford University Press, 1991) 183.

3 J Boyle, *Shamans, Software, and Spleens: Law and the Construction of the Information Society* (Cambridge MA.: Harvard University Press, 1996) 51-60.

the public interest and societal needs. Like Boyle, my reference to the "romantic author" is premised on the recognition of a rigid system of exclusive property rights in intellectual property. I argue that "romantic authorship" plays a significant role in copyright discourse, even if we do not expressly mention it. A claim that copyright laws sanctify romantic authorship does not require an argument that authors retain perpetual right in their creations, or that copyright laws protect *total* ownership.[4] Such a claim does not conflict with the fact that copyright scholars do not reject the sociality of the creative act. Such a claim means that we tend to consider authorial and artistic works more original than they are and that the reward systems we design to protect these works and their makers are unrealistic and ill-defined. As Coombe writes:

> [T]he writer is represented in Romantic terms as an autonomous individual who creates fictions with an imagination free of all constraint. For such an author, everything in the world must be made available and accessible as an "idea" that can be transformed into his "expression", which thus becomes his "work." Through his labor, he makes these "ideas" his own; his possession of the "work" is justified by his expressive activity. So long as the author does not copy another's expression, he is free to find his themes, plots, ideas, and characters anywhere he pleases, and to make these his own (this is also the model of authorship that dominates Anglo-American laws of copyright).[5]

Courts' decisions I examine in Chapter 3, legislation, the emergence of moral rights alongside economic rights, and case studies I evaluate in the present Chapter, all suggest that 'Romantic authorship and its connotations are deeply embedded in legal consciousness',[6] and that there is a well established practice of treating "the author" as an idealized figure, isolated creative entity, uncommonly wise, autonomous creator whose works are characterised as embodiments of personal qualities, rich subjectivity and distinct originality, a construct of the eighteenth century who creates original works, an original thinker.[7]

---

4 Ibid 35-36.

5 RJ Coombe, *The Cultural Life of Intellectual Properties: Authorship, Appropriation and the Law* (Durham and London: Duke University Press, 1998) 211, 219-220 (hereinafter – 'Coombe 1998'). See also RJ Coombe and J Cohen, 'The Law and Late Modern Culture: Reflections on Between Facts and Norms from the Perspective of Critical Cultural Legal Studies' (1999) 76 *Denver University Law Review* 1029, 1048.

On the romantic conception of authorship see for example, M Woodmansee and P Jaszi (eds.), *The Construction of Authorship* (Durham and London: Duke University Press, 1994); L Bently, 'Copyright and the Death of the Author in Literature and Law' (1994) 57 *Modern Law Review* 973; K Aoki, 'Authors, Inventors and Trademark Owners: Private Intellectual Property and the Public Domain (Part I)' (1994) 18 *Columbia Journal of Law & Arts* 1; Boyle (n 3 above).

6 P Jaszi, 'Towards a Theory of Copyright: The Metamorphoses of "Authorship"' (1991) *Duke Law Journal* 455, 501.

7 Durham remarks that recent critical literature on copyright and authorship has seen decreased emphasis on the author-genius and increased emphasis on the text. The reason is

Boyle claims that in today's state of affairs in copyright we 'play down the importance of external resources by emphasizing the unique genius of the author and the originality of the work.'[8] We have to treat copyrighted works as derivative works and recognise the contribution of external sources. Lemley criticises Boyle's conception of romantic authorship and claims that it 'cannot explain the changes that are taking place in intellectual property law in the modern world.'[9] He disputes the existence of a conception of romantic authorship in contemporary intellectual property laws: copyright laws impose limitations on authors' rights and recognise the public interest. The problem is 'that the rhetoric and economic theory of real property are increasingly dominating the discourse and conclusions of the very different world of intellectual property.'[10] Although Lemley favours a traditional economic explanation for the law of intellectual property, it seems that Boyle and Lemley share something in common: they criticise the idea of exclusivity and the dominating author-vision in copyright. While the former argues that 'authors tend to win',[11] the latter remarks that judges and policy makers support "the author".[12] Both would agree, I think, that copyright law has gone too far in overvaluing creators' originality and ignoring the public interest, and that we need to balance the complex, intertwined interests of authors and the public. That is, both criticise the hegemony of romantic conceptions of the author in contemporary copyright.

It is clear that '[r]omantic ideologies of authorship justify copyright protection and the commodification of cultural texts.'[13] Romantic authorship 'is alive and well'.[14] Denying the domination of the author-vision thesis in copyright may bring

---

that '[g]enius, personality, and effort may produce superior works, but it is the product that is important to society.' AL Durham, 'The Random Muse: Authorship and Indeterminacy' 44 (2002) *William & Mary Law Review* 569, 618.

Jaszi once wrote that copyright is, so to speak, 'the law of "texts"'. Ibid 458. The arguments I defend in this book address both authors and copyrighted products. I argue that any examination of the "authorship" concept requires simultaneous examination of authors and their works. If we want to fully understand the construction of authorship and how it has been mobilized in legal discourse, it would be wrong to separate the notion of author-genius in arguments on levels of creative activity and originality.

8 Boyle (n 3 above) 114. Similarly Coombe writes that romantic conceptions 'cannot capture the dangerous nuances of cultural appropriation in circumstances in which the very resources with which people express difference are the properties of others.' RJ Coombe, 'Critical Cultural Legal Studies' (1998) *Yale Journal of Law and the Humanities* 463, 480.

9 Lemley criticises Boyle's emphasis of romatic authorship as a dominating concept in copyright. MA Lemley, 'Romantic Authorship and the Rhetoric of Property' (1997) 75 *Texas Law Review* 873, 879. See also P Samuelson, 'The Quest for Enabling Metaphors for Law and Lawyering in the Information Age' (1996) 94 *Michigan Law Review* 2029.

10 Ibid 895.

11 Boyle (n 3 above) 116.

12 Lemley (n 9 above) 894.

13 Coombe 1998 (n 5 above) 283.

14 P Jaszi, 'On the Author Effect: Contemporary Copyright and Collective Creativity' in M Woodmansee and P Jaszi (n 5 above) 29, 38.

one to 'neglect the importance of the public domain. This neglect means that property rights for "authors" can actually *restrict* debate and slow down innovation.'[15] In fact, '[o]ur current definitional denial of these consequences merely makes them all the more likely.'[16] For these reasons we ought to realise what "romantic authorship" means and how it affects the development of copyright.

The perception of the author as a "creative genius" possessing the 'capacity to leap significantly beyond present knowledge and produce something new'[17] is problematic to those challenging existing copyright standards. True, some people possess certain abilities that enable them to see 'the relationship between facts or pieces of information in a new or unusual way' and to 'perceive the significance of new facts when others see them merely as anomalies that don't fit their set, their way of perceiving information.'[18] That is why some works find a lasting place in history while others do not. But these works, although they 'break the mould', combine knowledge, facts and information collectively produced and maintained by the collective. Treating an author as a 'genius' who expresses creativity via an extraordinary thinking process is unrealistic.[19] As Canaday remarks: 'There is a popular and absurd conception of the 'inspired' artist who works in a kind of hypnotic frenzy. His creations gush forth from some hidden reservoir of emotion without any effort on his part…This simply does not happen. Or if it does happen, what gushes forth is formless and chaotic and hence not art.'[20]

An author, the law specifies, is a title 'in relation to a work…the person who *creates* it.'[21] In the previous Chapter I showed how the interaction between legal rules and judicial decisions elevates authors to the status of sole creators of originals, as long as the works 'originate in a given author/s'.[22] What does 'originate in him'

---

15 Boyle (n 3 above) 155.

16 Ibid.

17 J Briggs, 'The Genius Mind' (1984) 92 *Science Digest* 74, 76.

18 Ibid.

19 Stillinger once wrote that in most works there are 'situations where someone other than the nominal author is essentially and inextricably a part of the authorship'. Stillinger (n 2 above) 20.

20 J Canaday, *What is Art? An Introduction to Painting, Sculpture and Architecture* (London: Hutchinson, 1980) 23.

21 CDPA 1988 s 9(1) (emphasis added).

22 The recent saga of copyright in the Dead Sea Scrolls illustrates the absurdity of our conception of originality and how it stretches the boundaries of the isolated author. In *Eisenman v Qimron* the Supreme Court of Israel granted copyright protection to Elisha Qimron in his decipher of one of the Dead Sea Scrolls discovered in Caves near the Dead Sea. C.A. 2790, 2811/93 *Eisenman v Qimron* 53(4) PD 817 (Israel). The discovery of the Scrolls is considered by many as the greatest archaeological achievement of the 20th Century. LH Schiffman, *Reclaiming the Dead Sea Scrolls* (Philadelphia: Jewish Publication Society, 1994).

Scholars reconstructed the text of the ancient Scrolls. They claimed copyright protection in their version. Copyright protection of the Scroll has far-reaching implications for the *sine qua non* of copyright, namely, the requirement of originality: who, in fact, is the author of

actually means? Can anything originate in one individual in the sense that he does not consciously depend on and copy others' works? What does the process of authorial creation – which brings a composer to think of a melody, a painter of a scene, a poet of a line or a linguistic of a phrase – involve? Is it a solitary activity in which the individual is isolated from the external world and creates totally unknown authorial and artistic commodities? If this is not the case, should we pay more attention to the contribution of collective sources when we think of how to design future patterns of copyright ownership?

In the law and literature on copyright, the individual author is recognised as the sole entity responsible for the initiation and execution of original expressions of art and authorship. Copyright scholarship refers to this tendency as the romantic vision of authorship. At the heart of this vision is the idea that authors create originals and therefore are entitled to the set of exclusive rights the law confers upon them. A key organising characteristic of such a vision is devaluing the contribution of external resources to the process of authorial creation. In the words of Boyle: 'the romantic vision of authorship plays down the importance of external sources by emphasizing the unique genius of the author and the originality of the work.'[23]

As a property right, exclusivity in copyright is determined according to and divided between the number of participants in a given creation, reflecting their respective efforts and contributions. These contributions are nurtured by interaction between individuals in society, which influences and inspires copyright creation. This interaction, however, is not only between copyright creators in their individual capacity, but also between them and the public at large, between them and the external social environment which is maintained by the public collectively. It is only in this way that a stable provision of social and cultural materials is guaranteed.

Authorial expressions are not inventions of a singular entity. It is a complex process. Creative thinking begins with what is already known. At the same time, however, the creative act involves unique subjective input by authors, reflective of the author's innate endowment, personality, plus objective, socially neutral, external and universal elements. Herein lies the problem. Joining together things already known with the subjective contribution on the part of the author is what usually takes authors *beyond* what is already known, and what should secure for them a proportional right to own the works they produce.[24] But how wide should this right

---

the original text? It is arguable that since Qimron's deciphered Scroll is just one of 800, he enjoyed the contribution of the scientific community and the other 799 archaeologists who deciphered other scrolls.

23 Boyle (n 3 above) 114.

24 The author can be looked at as borrowing from the public and investing the borrowed elements in a personal object. Wicklund analyses the causal way in which individuals can be said to borrow ideas from a group, implement them and eventually appropriate them. The group functions as the source. The group provides the potential appropriator the moral principles, values or creative thoughts – the raw materials for translating the idea for the 'personal operationalization'. The product cannot be said to exist due to direct group instructions, but rather as a result a 'person's actively borrowing and finally 'plagiarizing' the

be? Drahos writes that '[a]uthors, composers, musicians and scientists move in traditions and cultures which they react to or against' and the 'link between tradition and creativity suggests that, in the creative process, individuals play out another role, that of the borrower and the copier. When intellectual property rights are claimed, right holders often lose sight of the duality of roles they have occupied, preferring to think of themselves exclusively in terms of creator'.[25]

The central purpose of this book is to establish the public's authorial role for purposes of copyright ownership.[26] A book, a blueprint, a musical, a composition, and this book, are collective enterprises embodying collective properties that are the property of the general public. An obvious question is whether this combination creates rights on the part of the public? If it does, is the public an author by virtue of its input? A possible reaction to these questions is that the public contributes unprotectable elements such as ideas, and its contribution does not amount to authorial contribution. Another argument, recently advocated by Ginsburg, is that because authors are 'the constitutional subjects of copyright', authors should be the focus in debates on copyright.[27] For Ginsburg 'an author is (or should be) a human creator who, notwithstanding the constraints of her task, succeeds in exercising minimal personal autonomy in her fashioning the work.'[28] The public, on this account, cannot be an author. In order to reject these arguments it is pertinent to ask whether copyrighted entities are created in isolation from social and cultural forces, and whether collective ownership of these forces yields a collective or joint, as oppose to singular, entitlement in works of authorship? I shall argue that intellectual creation means that its products *always* represent the creative collectivity, and certain collective properties shall *never* be subject to exclusive ownership.

At present, copyright law stands in the way of the collective; preventing it from accomplishing its tasks of ensuring availability of cultural and social properties necessary for authors and their expressive abilities. Copyright law secures isolated, rigid and disproportionate autonomies for authors which impose non-negotiable duties on the part of the public. Copyright laws diminish the role of the collective, thereby institutionalising denial of its authorial contribution. Diminishing the role

---

group's ideas'. RA Wicklund, 'The Appropriation of Ideas' in PB Paulus (ed.), *Psychology of Group Influence* (New Jersey and London: Lawrence Erlbaum Associates Publishers 2ed, 1989) 393, 418-419.

25 P Drahos, *A Philosophy of Intellectual Property* (Dartmouth: Ashgate 1996) 62.

26 Yet, 'the public has no automatic entitlement to whatever they could receive in a world without intellectual property rights.' W Gordon, 'An Inquiry into the Merits of Copyright: The Challenges of Consistency, Consent, and Encouragement Theory' (1989) 41 *Stanford Law Review* 1343, 1465.

27 J Ginsburg 'The Concept of Authorship in Comparative Copyright Law' (2003) 52 *DePaul Law Review* 1063, 1068.

28 Ibid 1092. She supports her argument with Ricketson's view that the Berne Convention reserves authorship for human beings. S Ricketson, 'People or Machines? The Berne Convention and the Changing Concept of Authorship' (1991) *Columbia Journal of Law & the Arts* 16.

of the collective and restricting its ability to secure collective interests and renew itself for future creative activities lay the foundations for a no-purpose and empty, copyright regime.

I shall argue that an author is a transformative entity, and although it represents personal qualities and abilities such as talent and creativity, these can be realized and then vested in actual creative expressions only by the contribution of the public. This, I will later argue, amounts to authorial contribution on the part of the public, which secures an equal proprietary entitlement in copyrighted endeavours for the public. Presently, I define the nature of the public's contribution and defend the claim that copyright creation is in fact a collective social enterprise between authors and the public.

Original Appropriation: A Definitional Exercise

Copyright laws treat the individual author as an original proprietor of a newly created entity. The principle of original appropriation (OA) is a good point of departure from which to begin exploring the inequity in treating copyright works as works of original content rather than as manifestations of collective efforts. I will not enter into an elaborate examination of that principle. My aim here is rather modest: to draw benefits from a principle that is a key conceptual component in the skeletal definition of copyright.

OA is the appropriation of resources that are not already appropriated by someone else. It applies to things that are *nullius in bonis* (nobody's private property). OA theories hold that 'by hypothesis, there are no previous owners'[29] and 'an illegitimate original acquisition would similarly infect all subsequent transfers.'[30] OA is a term that comes to define a moment from which a given unowned resource has become the property of a given acquirer.[31] Copyright scholars do not explicitly refer to OA *per se*, but indirectly challenge its applicability to copyright. In a seminal article, Litman argues that works of authorship can never be labelled totally 'original'. Because the act of authorial creation is more akin to 'translation and recombination', an author cannot be the original proprietor of an entire resource.[32] In Litman's words:

---

29 D Schmidtz, 'When is Original Appropriation Required?' (1990) 73(4) *The Monist* 504, 506.

30 J Arthur, 'Resource Acquisition and Harm' (1987) 17 *Canadian Journal of Philosophy* 337-338.

31 Courts apply variations of the OA principle. See for example *Parker v British Airways Board* [1982] QB 1004, 1017 CA. The principle was also implicitly applied in the context of aboriginal rights in land and water according to traditional laws and customs. The High Court of Australia overturned the concept of *terra nullius* (a land belonging to no one) on which the tenure system in Australia had been based. *Mabo v State of Queensland* (No 2) (1992) 175 CLR 1 HC (Australia).

32 J Litman, 'The Public Domain' (1990) 39 *Emory Law Journal* 965, 966.

> To say that every new work is in some sense based on the works that preceded it, is such a truism that it has long been a cliché, invoked but not examined. But the very act of authorship in any medium is more akin to translation and recombination than it is to creating Aphrodite from the foam of the sea. Composers recombine sounds they have heard before; playwrights base their characters on bits and pieces drawn from real human beings and other playwrights' characters; novelists draw their plots from lives and other plots within their experience; software writers use the logic they find in other software; lawyers transform old arguments to fit new facts; cinematographers, actors, choreographers, architects, and sculptors all engage in the process of adapting, transforming, and recombining what is already 'out there' in some form. This is not paratisitism: it is the essence of authorship. And, in the absence of a vigorous public domain, much of it would be illegal.[33]

Scholarship on property often refers to the principle of OA.[34] Harris and Waldron refer to 'first occupancy'. According to Harris, the tendency is to 'clothe the law's reliance on first occupancy as a root of title with the dress of natural rights.'[35] Yet, the legal and social dimensions of the right 'must stipulate both what conduct is sufficient to constitute first occupancy' if at all, and 'also what perimeter of trespassory rules in respect of the thing occupied, going beyond' should be allowed.[36] In other words, while I might have a natural right in object O, it is a natural wrong for someone else to interfere with my right.[37]

---

33 Ibid.

34 Benson, for example, argues that this principle is the *only* way to justify private acquisition. P Benson, 'Philosophy of Property Law' in J Coleman and S Shapiro (eds.), *The Oxford Handbook of Jurisprudence and Philosophy of Law* (Oxford: Oxford University Press, 2002) 752, 760. See also R Epstein, 'Possession as the Root of Title' (1979) 13 *Georgia Law Review* 1221, 1228.

35 JW Harris, *Property and Justice* (Oxford: Oxford University Press, 1996) 214.

36 Ibid 214.

37 Interestingly, Harris distinguishes between first occupancy in respect of individuals and first occupancy in respect of communities. He views a community identity as stronger for a claim of first occupancy on the basis of natural law. He writes: 'It may be argued that artefacts closely identified with the cultural identity of a particular community, which were taken from it in the past, ought now to be restored and vested in some agency representing the community, on the ground that, whether or not the taking was warranted by positive law, it constituted a natural wrong to the community'. Ibid 217. For a discussion on the tension between group authorship and the current intellectual property system, see S Scafidi, 'Intellectual Property and Cultural Products' (2001) 81 *Boston University Law Review* 793.

The idea of group authorship and collective production of culture reflect recent discussions on rights of indigenous people. For example, in September 2000 WIPO established the Intergovernmental Committee on Intellectual Property and Genetic Resources, Traditional Knowledge and Folklore, in order to monitor and defend rights of communities over their traditional resources. See for example RJ Coombe, 'The Recognition of Indigenous Peoples' and Community Traditional Knowledge in International Law' (2001) 14 *St Thomas Law Review* 275.

For Waldron the concept of first occupancy relates to the relations between the first possessor of a recourse and subsequent rightholders: '[T]he first person to take possession of a resource does so, *ex hypothesi*, without pushing aside, and, unless he voluntarily relinquishes that possession, he is the one that must be pushed aside by second and subsequent occupiers.'[38] Similarly, Penner refers to the term 'first appropriation'[39] and defines OA as 'essentially concerns the kind of advantages any individual may get by his own actions, by appropriating unowned things without the consent of others...A right of *first* appropriation in these contexts is a notional right the exercise of which in a parable about the justice of property rights inevitably leads to, i.e., *creates*, the property system.'[40]

The conditions under which one can remove items that have no individual owner from the common, i.e., that are collectively owned, without the consent of the other commoners, is a related issue. John Locke poses this problem at the outset of his theory on property.[41] Locke argues that a person becomes an original owner of a commonly owned object by virtue of expending labour. However, the right is subject to several social conditions, of which the central one is that unless the person leaves in the common of all 'enough and as good' resources for latecomers he cannot appropriate. Locke's aim is to 'show how it is morally possible for private property in external things to arise...from a condition in which there is no such property at all.'[42] Locke's approach towards original appropriation is well ingrained in copyright policy and law. For originality to be established, an author is required to employ certain intellectual effort such as 'skill, judgement and labour'.[43] Once the work has qualified as an original work, the author is treated as an original appropriator

38 J Waldron, *The Right to Private Property* (Oxford: Oxford University Press, 1988) 285-287. Waldron rejects the principle of first occupancy because in the end, it means something like the following statement: 'the first person who *acts as though he is the owner* of a resource gets to *be* its owner', and such a view can only work 'if private property has already been argued for.' Ibid 286-287.

39 J Penner, *The Idea of Property in Law* (Oxford: Clarendon Press, 1997) 80-82.

40 Ibid 81 (emphasis added).

41 See above, Chapter 1, and below, Chapter 6.

42 AJ Simmons, 'Original Acquisition Justifications of Private Property' (1994) 11(2) *Social Philosophy and Policy* 63, 72. The question is whether a given justification is 'a morally *permissible* (or morally possible) arrangement, even without any demonstration of its moral optimality'. Ibid 70. With regards to OA, justification should be interpreted as concerning 'not the *first brute takings by human beings*, but rather the first *creation of property by persons*'. Ibid 76.

Many refute the applicability of Locke's theory for questions such as why should producers of social wealth impose obligations on non-producers, especially in the age of scarcity. For example, Gaus and Lomasky argue that it is 'terribly odd to look into some remote part to see if our system of property is justified'. To do so may amount a 'justificatory embarrassment.' GF Gaus and LE Lomasky, 'Are Property Rights Problematic?' (1990) 73(4) *The Monist* 494, 496. Mautner also denies the contemporary relevance of Locke and OA theories. T Mautner, 'Locke on Original Appropriation' (1982) 19 *American Philosophical Quarterly* 259.

43 See above, Chapter 3.

of something new that never existed and had no previous owner. Although the copyright system tries to provide mechanisms in the spirit of Locke's restrictions on the spectrum of the right, it treats the author as a sole creator of a new substance, thereby embracing a rigid variation of the OA principle. Furthermore, an author, in the course of preparing a creative work, is allowed to copy non-substantial parts from others' works. This proves that legislatures are not unaware of the fact that copyrighted creations are a merger between what is known and what is unknown and that new creations cannot be examined in isolation from already existing works. However, under copyright laws authorial and artistic entities are treated as original acquisitions of a given creator for the work originated in him and is his exclusive property, including parts owned by others or collectively owned by society.

OA theories were challenged on, amongst other, two main grounds. First, for Grunebaum, OA theories aim at justifying benefits associated with *private* ownership, and therefore, fail to acknowledge other, nonprivate, forms of acquisition, although they carry similar benefits for collective and social appropriations. Thus, OA arguments can only partially justify private property and do not adequately address the central dilemma.[44] They 'specify the conditions for taking unowned goods; but "unowned" can mean many things, depending on which conception of ownership is being assumed, OA theorists mean by "unowned", not "privately owned". And this simply begs the question against alternative possible forms of ownership".'[45] Second, Waldron argues that OA imposes unilateral obligations on people. For this reason, we should be wary and suspicious of this principle.[46] OA in copyright presupposes no ownership of the created work. It regards copyright as a creation *ex nihilo* and emphasises the author's private dominion. It establishes a rigid dichotomy between privately owned materials and unowned elements. It does not recognise a mid-way which would compensate collective contributions. As such, it refuses to acknowledge nonprivate ownership alternatives such as collective ownership of cultural properties. OA deliberately imposes obligations to respect the newly created private property on the public and allows, without the latter's consent, private enclosures of sources integral to its collective identity.

International law does recognise the inapplicability of OA to certain natural resources and regards them a part of mankind's collective property – as 'the common heritage of mankind'.[47] I accept arguments that copyright does recognise certain

---

44 J Grunebaum, 'Ownership as Theft' 73(4) *Monist* 544, 545-546; Simmons (n 42 above) 79-80.

45 Simmons, ibid 80, referring to J Grunebaum, *Private Ownership* (London: Routledge & Kegan Paul, 1987) 53, 74, 80-81, 84-85. Simmons rejects the objections raised by Grunebaum and Waldron. However, while he applies reservations to traditional private property, he distinguishes it from intellectual property such as proceeds from inventions. Ibid 84.

46 Waldron (n 38 above) 265-271; Simmons, ibid 81-84.

47 For example, the 1979 Moon Treaty and the 1970 UN Declaration of Principles Governing the Seabed and Ocean Floors stipulate that certain natural resources cannot be subject to national appropriation. UN Declaration of Principles Governing the Seabed and

nonproprietable elements as part of 'the common heritage of mankind' such as ideas, facts and expressions to which protection has expired. But, this is hampered by possible appropriation of ideas due to a lack of a coherent distinction between ideas and expressions and the duration of the right; thereby allowing disproportionate private enclosures of traditions and other collective properties. That is, our prevalent copyright system remotely qualifies for the so-called 'common heritage' principle.

If authorship cannot be examined in isolation from what is already in existence, can a copyrighted work ever represent an original manifestation of one (or more) individual's creative input? I examine this question and demonstrate that copyrighted works represent the creative collectivity and as such can only be original creations in the collective sense. That is to say that their defining features inevitably have a prior owner: the public. Consequently, they should be jointly owned between public and authors.

Authorship and Collective Intentionality

'Intent to be an Author'

What makes the public an entity capable of claiming a right in the authorial contribution it makes? This question is at the heart of the public authorship model. In order to answer this question, it is important to ask what – besides labour, efforts and investment of personality – makes a particular person an author? In dealing with this question, copyright scholars emphasise the intention to produce a work of authorship. Three conditions, Becker observes, may satisfy a test for when 'a thing may be said to have an author…(1) its causal history is traceable to the intentional states of an agent or agents; (2) those agents…are also creating and realizing their mental representations of it; (3) those representations either constitute the artifact itself, or play a substantial causal role in its production.'[48] Intention and causality, for Becker, are essential ingredients in the process of authorial creation. For causality to subsist and affect creative expressions, a history of relationship between collective and individual labour is necessary. According to these three conditions, causality in authorship is determined by an agent's intentions and their eventual mental representations. Can *the public*, as an indeterminate group of people, have an intentional capacity? Is it possible to classify *the public* as an intentional agent?

The grant of copyright protection to Elisha Qimron in his decipherment of one of the Dead Sea Scrolls discovered in caves near the Dead Sea,[49] brought Nimmer to question the very definition of author and authorship and to place at the forefront

---

Ocean Floor 1970, reiterated in Art. 136 and 137 of the 1982 Convention on the Law of the Sea; 1979 Moon Treaty Art. xi. For a brief overview see M Shaw, *International Law* (Cambridge: Cambridge University Press, 2004) 453-455.

48 LC Becker, 'Deserving to Own Intellectual Property', (1992-93) 68 *Chicago-Kent Law Review* 609, 613.

49 *Eisenman v Qimron* (n 22 above).

of current copyright dialogue the issue of 'intent to author'.[50] The Scrolls provide fresh evidence of the period in which Judaism was consolidated and Christianity was born. Scholars reconstructed the text of the ancient Scrolls. Although they were not the authors of the Scrolls they argued for copyright in their version because of the many educated guesses that the fallible process of reconstruction necessitated. Nimmer draws a distinction between the 'intent to create a work' and the 'intent to create a work of authorship'. Copyright should be available only when the latter is present. He writes:

> The legal definition of the author is windless, dry, and plain: the author is given rights to a cultural space over which he or she may range and work; all authors share the same cultural space; they are defined by their presence there as well as by their rights to it… let us not look to the law for the easy answer: the same law that defines the author is responsible for much of the confusion about what authors were and are.[51]

Nimmer argues that we have to ask what constitutes authorship and redefine the breadth of the definition of an author, or, in other words, to ask what makes a person an author of a particular work. Nimmer remarks:

> [C]opyright law is remarkably unconcerned with any theory at all about what constitutes authorship – with one single exception: intentionality. Copyright protection arises only for works that reflect an intent to produce something personal or subjective. By contrast, works that are objective, whether in fact or as presented, fail to qualify as works of "authorship" in the copyright sense.[52]

He then remarks that an author 'must intend to author in order for a copyright work to emerge. Intentionalism hereby creeps back as a *sine qua non* for copyright protection.'[53] Furthermore, in order to prove intent a plaintiff will have to show intent 'to imbue subjectivity into the mix.'[54] Although the single author, as an agent, cannot act alone and needs the contribution of the public and other fellow commoners, the

---

50 D Nimmer, 'Copyright in the Dead Sea Scrolls: Authorship and Originality' (2001) 38 *Houston Law Review* 1.

51 Ibid 199.

52 Ibid 159.

53 Ibid 205.

54 Ibid 209. Patterson supports Nimmer's argument and remarks: 'The Dead Sea Scrolls are an aberrant work in terms of copyright law. One will not find many 2000-year-old manuscripts at the centre of a copyright controversy, especially one of overwhelming importance to world religions and culture. When the intent test is applied to Qimron, it seems clear that in compiling and translating the fragments he did not intend to create a work of authorship. He intended to convey what the Teacher of Righteousness wrote; indeed, creativity on his part would have defiled his reputation as well as his purpose. The only creativity he could employ with integrity was creativity as to how to decipher the fragments. And however difficult and meritorious, that effort was sweat-of-the-brow.' LR Patterson, 'Nimmer's Copyright in the Dead Sea Scrolls: A Comment' (2001) 38 *Houston Law Review* 431,443. *Cf*, Ginsburg (n 27 above) 1085-1088.

issues we should address pertain not only to the contribution of the public but also include the question whether the public qualifies for the intent element which both Becker and Nimmer advocate, and which I accept.[55]

Many social scientists, as I shall shortly argue, believe that some groups and organisations have the capacity for intentional action. The question, however, is whether *the public* – an entity which comprises each and every one of us – can have similar intentional capacity to human agents. The public is a group of individuals composed of artisans, authors, peasants, politicians, salespersons, shoemakers, simple people we meet on our way to work, or more important people in our lives such as members of the board of directors in the company where we work. Can such a large group form collective intention? Does it matter whether the public is a social group? If it does, what features does it have that may qualify it as a superagent capable of intentional states?

Just as Becker and Nimmer argue that for a person to be an author, intention is required, social scientists often recognise intention as an essential feature of social groups. I doubt anyone would reject the idea that the general public is a social group, despite the fact that it is, to some extent, an abstract and indeterminate entity. If this is the case, can the public as such form a collective intention to author? This is not a simple question.[56] Since I argue that the public is a *joint* author of every copyrighted entity, the element of 'intent to author' has a special significance in the public authorship model, for intention is a condition for joint authorship.

Collective Intentionality and the Public

Individualising Collective Intention Certain social norms impose on us a collective joint commitment. This is why we create laws and rules and rebuke those who violate them. By virtue of our humanity, we share a collective commitment, a general will, to preserve our cultural and social realities, including their building blocs – elements that we, as a collective, create and nurture – and share and have access to certain items of social wealth which result from this collective commitment.

See also Elkin-Koren N., 'Of Scientific Claims and Proprietary Rights: Lessons from the Dead Sea Scrolls Case' (2001) 38 *Houston Law Review* 445; TH Lim, HL MacQueen and CM Carmichael (eds.), *On Scrolls, Artefacts and Intellectual Property* (Sheffield: Sheffield Academic Press, 2001).

55 This condition may, as Ginsburg observes, 'supply a means to sort out the equities of ownership in cases in which more than one contender is vying for authorship status.' Ginsburg (n 27 above) 1087. However, she rejects placing intent to author as a basic condition for assessment of authorship, except in cases of joint authorship. Ibid 1088.

56 As Searle once remarked: 'perhaps the hardest case of all is intention.' JR Searle, *Intentionality* (Cambridge: Cambridge University Press, 1983) 34.

It is a known practice to attribute responsibilities to small and large groups.[57] Even ardent individualists accept the argument that a poetry reading group, a football team, a corporation and even nations have intentions. As Tollefsen asserts:

> [T]here is a rich and complex practice of attributing moral and legal responsibility to groups. These attributions presupposes that groups intend to commit the actions for which they are held responsible…our everyday practice of holding groups responsible cannot be easily dismissed…The social and legal sanctions that groups incur are not metaphorical. They have very real social, economic, and political effects.[58]

The question is, however, if large groups accept collective responsibilities, can such responsibilities be attributed to the public at large? Can the public show intention to meet the challenges of these responsibilities? There are many examples in which the general public acts together, claims responsibilities and shares a commitment to take action. We collectively accept the importance of certain needs. We agree that we have to preserve water reservoirs, to limit the use of nuclear weapons, that air pollution triggers environmental disasters. We are collectively committed to ensure this does not happen.[59] Responsibilities can also be attributed to the general public in the collective sense. For example, the collective is responsible for the climate change and the collective is currently in the process of agreeing and ratifying international rules on that issue. In the very near future the collective may also find itself responsible for the collapse of African states for lack of access to certain medications and food. This means that indeterminate large groups can have the capacity to accept joint responsibilities and intend to collectively execute certain actions. On this basis, I propose that we think of the public at large as having a collective intention to retain a right in every copyrighted entity, by virtue of forming a collective intention to participate in the making process of authorship and intention to preserve the collective social and cultural realities. This claim is meant literally and not simply metaphorically.

Many arguments advocating collective intentionality analyse group intentional state in terms of the individual intentional states of group members. There are two versions of this approach: summative and nonsummative. Summative approaches hold that most members of a particular group have the attitude ascribed to the group. Accordingly, Group G believes in idea I if and only if all or some of its members

57 For a brief account on the different approaches to collective intentionality see, F Hindriks, 'Social Groups, Collective Intentionality and Anti-Hegelian Skepticism' in M Sintonen, P Ylikoski, and K Miller (eds.), *Realism in Action: Essays in Philosophy of the Social Sciences* (Dordrecht: Kluwer, 2003) 213. Hindriks advocates the importance of collective intentionality for any adequate analysis of social institutions.

58 D Perron Tollefsen, 'Collective Intentionality and the Social Sciences' (2002) 32(1) *Philosophy of the Social Sciences* 25, 27.

59 There will always be borderline cases and exceptions, and those who would reject these or other collective commitments. I believe these are marginal cases and do not have the power to destabilise the collective agreement we share to respect these commitments.

believe in I. This approach analyses group attitude in terms of the sum of individual attitudes, and the group attitude is always an indirect way of explaining the attitudes of its members.[60] Some say this view is too strong,[61] or maintain that collective intentions cannot be reduced to individual intentions.

A key work defending a contrasting non-summative approach is Searle's *The Construction of Social Reality.*[62] Searle attempts, *inter alia*, to explain collective intentionality and why it is irreducible to individual intentions. Imagine two scenarios. In scenario A, a group is walking on a pedestrian close to the university. Suddenly, it begins to rain and they all run to stand under the first building they see. Group A is composed of individuals who each have what Searle calls an 'I-intention': 'I intend to find shelter from the rain'. In scenario B, a film director organizes a group of actors to perform similar act to the group in scenario A. The difference between the two scenarios lies in the mental component. In scenario B the group acts collectively. For Searle, collective intentional states are in this way irreducible. They are a distinct form of intentional classification. As he remarks: 'The crucial element in collective intentionality is a sense of doing (wanting, believing, etc.) something together, and the individual intentionality that each person has is derived from the collective intentionality that they share.'[63] He argues that collective behaviour or collective intentionality cannot be analysed as the simple summation of individual behaviour or individual intentionality which he takes to be a biologically primitive capacity of individual brains.[64] That is, he attributes collective intentional states to individuals only where a single person can have in himself the collective intention

---

60 See A Quinton, 'Social Objects' (1975) 76 *Proceedings of the Aristotelian Society* 1.

61 See for example, M Gilbert, 'Modelling Collective Belief' (1987) 73 *Synthese* 186.

62 JR Searle, *The Construction of Social Reality* (New York: The Free Press, 1995) (hereinafter – 'Searle 1995). For critic of Searle's views see generally, J Hornsby, 'Collectives and Intentionality' (1997) 57(2) *Philosophy and Phenomenological Research* 429; D Fitzpatrick, 'Searle and Collective Intentionality: The Self-Defeating Nature of Intentionalism with Respect to Social Facts' (2003) 62(1) *American Journal of Economics and Sociology* 45; and LA Zaibert, 'Collective Intentions and Collective Intentionality' (2003) 62(1) *American Journal of Economics and Sociology* 210.

63 Searle 1995, ibid 25.

64 JR Searle, 'Collective Intentions and Actions', in P Cohen, J Morgan and ME Pollack (eds.), *Intentions in Communication* (Cambridge MA.: MIT Press, 1990) 401 (hereinafter – 'Searle 1990'). According to Searle, 'anything we say about collective intentionality must meet the following conditions of adequacy: (1) It must be consistent with the fact that society consists of nothing but individuals. Since society consists entirely of individuals, there cannot be a group mind or consciousness. All consciousness is in individual minds, in individual brains; (2) It must be consistent with the fact that the structure of any individual's intentionality has to be independent of the fact whether or not he is getting things right, whether or not he is radically right, whether or nor he is radically mistaken about what is actually occurring. And this constraint applies as much to collective intentionality as it does to individual intentionality. One way to put this constraint is to say that the account must be consistent with the fact that all intentionality, whether collective or individual, could be had by a brain in a vat or by sets of brains in vats.' Searle 1995 (n 62 above) 407.

"we intend to do X": 'The intentionality that exists in our individual heads has the [simple] form "we intend".'[65] As Meijers explains: Searle's 'solution is to conceive collective intentions as genuine we-intentions *inside* the brains of individuals. The mistake is to think that individuals can only have intentional *I* states, whereas, in Searle's view, these individuals can have intentional *we* states as well.'[66] Searle's approach is thus highly individualistic, and views society as nothing over and above the individuals that comprise it. He strives to show how collective intentions do not undermine individualism. The public, on his account could never collectively establish a "we-intention".

Collective intentionality for Searle is a crucial element in understanding social reality. It confers function on artifacts and changes them into social facts. A flower has the meaning of a flower because we create it through collective intentionality. Pieces of coloured paper function as money because we intend them to do so. Through intentionality Searle explains how do the various parts of the world relate to each other, and how does the mental relate to the physical. He approaches this task by formulating two principles: (i) the principle of constitution: according to which "*X* constitutes *Y* in context *C*"; and (ii) the principle of transfer: "*X* counts as *Y* in context *C*".[67] The former explains how high-order properties arise in both physical and biological systems. The latter refers to the fact that '[f]unctions of everyday objects – such as pencils, screwdrivers, or radios – exist, according to the analysis in *The Construction of Social Reality*, because they are *assigned* by beings that have intrinsic intentionality, where the assignment can be described in terms of "*X* counts as *Y* in context *C*."'[68] That is, collective intentionality creates social facts.

Searle's views have met with various criticisms. Are intentions merely determined by internal aspects? If intentions belong to individuals, and individuals do not have to possess similar intentions for collective intentions to exist, what do we exactly share in Searle's approach to collective intentionality? How is society socially constructed if collective intentionality is internal to the individual? Bratman argues that some form of *unified* agency is necessary.[69] That is, "we intend to do a joint action J" means that we share the intention to do joint action J: 'First, our shared intention to

---

Searle summarises his argument in the book as an attempt to show 'how a world of brute facts can give rise to intentional facts which in turn can give rise to social and institutional facts.' JR Searle, 'Précise of *The Construction of Social Reality*' (1997) 57(2) *Philosophy and Phenomenological Research* 427, 428. Or as he remarks in his book: 'how can there be an objective world of money, property, marriage, governments, elections, football games, cocktail parties and law courts in a world that consists entirely of physical particles in fields of force, and in which some of these particles are organized into systems that are conscious biological beasts, such as ourselves?' Searle 1995, ibid xi.

65 Searle 1995, ibid 26.

66 A Meijers, 'Can Collective Intentionality be Individualized' (2003) 62(1) *American Journal of Economics and Sociology* 167,181.

67 Ibid 168-169.

68 Ibid 169.

69 ME Bratman, 'Shared Intention' (1993) 104(1) *Ethics* 97.

paint together will help coordinate my activities with yours (and yours with mine)... Second, our shared intention will coordinate our actions...Third, our shared intention will tend to provide a background framework that structures relevant bargaining.'[70] In particular, Bratman emphasises coordination and interrelations.[71] For Bratman, 'a shared intention is not a single attitude, but a web of related and interlocking attitudes of the individual participants. Such an intention should lead to coordinated planning and unified activity by a group of agents, or, put the other way around, this planning and action should be explained by appealing to the shared intention.'[72] Like Searle's, Bratman's approach is also broadly individualistic in spirit since he argues that shared intentions are not the intention of a plural agent. Since an individual cannot have a shared intention, collective intentions consist primarily of attitudes of individuals and their interrelations. His emphasis on coordination and interrelations depends on the functioning of individual attitudes.

Searle and Bratman thus "individualize" collective intentions. While the former places "we-intention" as an innate primitive capacity of the individual, the latter avoids recognizing the plural agent, emphasizing that collective attitudes are a mix of individual attitudes with common content and their interrelations.[73] Both are concerned to avoid the specter of the collective mind. Intention is a mental state, and minds belong to individuals or persons. As Searle remarks: 'Talk of group of minds...[is] at best mysterious and at worst incoherent.'[74] And in Bratman's words: 'A shared intention is not an attitude in the mind of some superagent.'[75]

Many questions emerge from these accounts. One may wonder whether cognitive attitudes are enough to explain collective intentionality, whether they are sufficient to explain the sharing of intentionality. How can several different minds submit themselves to a single element? If Searle attempts to tell us something about the construction of *social* reality, ought he not emphasise the centrality of *social relations* in the process of forming and executing collective intentionality? Can collective intentions be reduced to the aggregate intentions of individuals composing a group? How can we *share* intention?[76] Do normative attitudes take part in the formulation of collective intentionality? Is there a plural agent to which we should ascribe collective intentionality?

---

70 Ibid 99.

71 Ibid 100-102.

72 Meijers (n 66 above) 175. See also, Bratman, ibid 108.

73 For criticism of these views see, JD Velleman, 'How to Share an Intention' (1997) 57(1) *Philosophy and Phenomenological Research* 29.

74 Searle 1990 (n 64 above) 404.

75 Bratman (n 69 above) 99.

76 As Velleman explains: '[S]hared intention is not supposed to be a matter of one person's deciding or planning the activities of a group; it's supposed to be a matter of shared intending, in which each member of the group participates equally in forming and maintaining the intention, fully recognizing the others as equal participants. What we are going to do is supposed to be determined by you and me jointly, in this case; and each of us is supposed to regard the issue as being thus jointly determined.' Velleman (n 73 above) 34.

The Sociality of Collective Intention Gilbert argues that there is a normativity involved in collective intentionality.[77] She claims that obligations and joint commitments are part of collective activities. Her account is less individualistic than that of Searle and Bratman.[78] Gilbert is willing to speak of a "plural subject" which involves two or more subjects that together create one subject. In the case of a goal, for example, she remarks that the goal is 'the goal of the plural subject, as opposed to the shared personal goal of the participants.'[79] Gilbert places the principle of joint commitment at the heart of her theory and remarks that:

> People have the concept of joint commitment and are constantly creating – and dissolving – such commitments. These joint commitments play a major role in organizing their behavior, including their reactions to one another. It follows that social scientists cannot afford to ignore the concept of a joint commitment for either interpretive or descriptive purposes. This concept is of fundamental importance for all who seek to understand human behavior in both *general* and particular circumstances.[80]

For Gilbert 'people become jointly committed by mutually expressing their willingness to be jointly committed, in conditions of common knowledge.'[81] Once these features are present, the members of a group will recognise themselves as a social group or a plural subject and acknowledge the rights and obligations that their joint commitment imposes on them.

Gilbert's account sounds close to talk of group minds or superagents. True, she makes frequent references to examples of small groups, for example, of two people walking together. However, she also recognises the principle of 'society-wide convention'[82] and provides a broad definition of 'plural subject': '*any set of jointly committed persons*, whatever the content of the particular joint commitment in question.'[83] In her definition she includes items such as unions and armies, but not only. She also refers to '*social rules* and *conventions*, *group languages*, *everyday agreements*, *collective beliefs* and *values*, and *genuinely collective emotions*.'[84] Arguably, her ideal of "plural subject" – an entity formed when individuals unite

---

77 M Gilbert, 'Walking Together: A Paradigmatic Social Phenomenon' (1990) 15 *Midwest Studies in Philosophy* (1990) 1. And by the same author *On Social Facts* (Princeton: Princeton University Press,1989).

78 See also K Miller, 'Commitments' in M Sintonen, P Ylikoski, and K Miller (eds.), *Realism in Action: Essays in Philosophy of the Social Sciences* 169, 172.

79 M Gilbert, *Living Together, Rationality, Sociality, and Obligation* (New York: Rowman & Littlefield, 1996) 187 (hereinafter – 'Gilbert 1996').

80 M Gilbert, 'The Structure of the Social Atom: Joint Commitment as the Foundation of Human Social Behavior' in FF Schmitt (ed.), *Socializing Metaphysics: The Nature of Social Reality'* (Lanham, MD: Rowman and Littlefield, 2003) 39, 41 (emphasis added) (hereinafter – 'Gilbert 2003').

81 Gilbert 1996 (n 79 above) 349.

82 Gilbert 2003 (n 80 above) 43.

83 Ibid 55.

84 Ibid.

in a particular way – can apply at a more general level, suggesting the existence of superagents. Gilbert asserts:

> [T]here is no reason in principle why larger populations may not create joint commitments for themselves. Here the parties will express their readiness to be jointly committed with certain others described in general terms, such as "people living on this island," "women," and so on. As long as there can be common knowledge of the openness of these expressions, the conditions for the creation of a joint commitment can be fulfilled. Hence the parties to a given joint commitment need not know each other or even know of each other as individuals.[85]

Gilbert thus emphasises the sociality of intention and joint commitments. Her argument admits various interpretations of which one suggests the existence of superagents. On this view, we may say the general public is a plural subject which unites individuals and creates a bond between them to perform certain acts as would a single individual. It does not necessarily mean that we all have to "walk together" in a given act. As long as we commit ourselves to the preservation of some peace, social stability and cultural development, we can create a commitment that binds us all. If we, for example, collectively create language and certain cultural and social symbols, we work as a plural subject. As members of the public we share a commitment, we are part of a body of joint commitments. These are irreducible to aggregate individual commitments. Since our commitments are interrelated, unless every member of the public rescinds, the joint commitment continues.[86]

Although Gilbert requires that people express their willingness to submit to the commitment, there are social activities that do not require express agreement. We share a "collective will" – a general will to preserve certain social norms. This line of reasoning is advocated by Tuomela who explains group collective intentionality by reference to an authority system – a group-will formation system. For collective intention we have to believe in one common will: '"Groupness" means the existence of "one will", as it were, and it is shared group-intentions that make one will out of many wills.'[87] There exists the capacity 'of "pooling the individual wills into a group will"', and this allows us to move from a multitude of "I's" to a "we".[88] In this way an authority system is created and individuals transfer their wills to the group. But transference of will is not enough.

Tuomela emphasises the centrality of the principle of acceptance. Collective intentionality presupposes acceptance of social norms, rules, and institutions (for

---

85 Ibid.

86 This permits coercion in certain circumstances and rebuking those who violate social rules.

87 R Tuomela, *The Importance of Us: A Philosophical Study of Basic Social Notions* (Stanford: Stanford University Press, 1995) 175 (hereinafter – 'Tuomela 1995'). See also by the same author, 'We Will Do It: An Analysis of Group-Intentions' (1991) 51(2) *Philosophy and Phenomenological Research* 249.

88 Tuomela 1995, ibid 177.

example, money and law): '[A]n institution is created and, especially, maintained by our collective acceptance…'[89] For example, we share a "collective will" – "one will" – to regulate ownership of authorial and artistic endeavours. Otherwise we would allow exclusive propertization of every idea, general principles of culture, art and creativity. Even if we have different views on how to regulate ownership of these endeavours, there exists a "we-intention" in the very idea of regulating them. For this matter, we collectively accept the need for an enforceable regulation and accept the institution of copyright as the means to regulate the spectrum of ownership of authorial and artistic endeavours.

We accept social and cultural institutions by virtue of expressing our collective will through democratic processes. These wills become part of our community, and their results bind us collectively. Because of these wills nations adopt certain political policies as a result of economic or civil instability, and democratic systems do not permit limitless private enclosures of culture, language and other types of social institutions through intellectual property laws. We cannot refer to these examples by simply referring to individual intentional states.

So, can the public have intentions? Can we view the public as a party to a joint commitment? Take for example Gilbert's definition: 'Persons *A* and *B collectively intend* to do *X* if an only if *A* and *B* are jointly committed to intend to do *X*.'[90] I propose that this applies to the relationship between authors and the public. When X is the preservation of the public domain and our cultural environment, it would be difficult to reject the proposition that authors and the general public collectively intend to do X and are jointly committed to intending to do X. This conclusion is derived from our joint commitment to do X. This commitment means that we '"act as a body" in a specified way, where "acting" is taken in a broad sense.'[91] This commitment is a common knowledge between authors and the general public.[92] This common knowledge implicitly exists in virtue of our social nature. This is analogous to Gilbert's principle of background understanding, according to which 'many people develop expectations that the joint activity in which they are participating will reach an appropriate conclusion' and these expectations create reliance between the participants.[93]

There are certain patterns of social behaviour one will find difficult to explain if one recourses only to individual intentional states. This is especially important when discussing collective commitments and social obligations. Tollefsen examines the interplay between rational choice theory and collective intention. She argues that

89 R Tuomela, 'Collective Acceptance, Social Institutions, and Social Reality' (2003) 62(1) *American Journal of Economics and Sociology* 123, 146. See also Tuomela 1995, ibid 314-316.

90 Gilbert 2003 (n 80 above) 46.

91 Ibid 51.

92 If we decline to accept and fulfil our joint commitment we may create a situation where we will share 'collective moral responsibility or – in the negative form – collective moral guilt.' Ibid 57.

93 Ibid 45-46.

groups and organizations can, under certain conditions, form a rational point of view. Elster, for example, applies rational choice theory to nations. Although he does not explicitly defend group intentions, he uses this theory to argue that nations, rather than individuals, have the capacity to determine the rational way of making choices. Elster writes: 'On the basis of pure self-interest, reinforced by moral reasoning, a nation that has not already acquired nuclear weapons should abstain from nuclear power, so as not to have to hand down to later generations a potential for starting or precipitating a nuclear war.'[94] It seems that by applying rational choice theory to nations, Elster implicitly defends collective intentional states. Tollefsen develops this approach and argues that groups and organizations have a capacity to make rational choices, independent of individual decisions. She writes:

> Our interpretations of organizational acts in terms of the intentional states of the organization presupposes a certain level of rationality. But the rationality presupposed is not merely a property of individual participants in the organizations; the structure of the organization provides for a unified perspective, a rational point of view, from which organizational members can deliberate…rationality is embodied in the structure of the organization, not just in its members.[95]

It is the group, rather than the individuals comprising it, that is 'subject to norms of rationality and form a distinct locus of power and responsibility.'[96] It seems that groups, and the public, share something with individuals: they can, under certain circumstances, form a rational point of view. A problem that Tollefsen addresses is that groups and organizations, let alone the general public, lack consciousness and self-awareness. It would be wrong, she rightly asserts, to judge collective intentions by applying rigid conceptions of subjective intention. Although consciousness and self-awareness are properties important for the formation of individual intention, '[b]ecause groups do not have these properties, the conclusion one should draw is that groups do not have the features necessary for *individual* subjecthood…Groups are *not* individual subjects, they are groups.'[97] The same is applicable to large populations and the general public. The fact that we, as a collective, agree on certain rules and the power of certain norms and make rational choices in light of these, must not be examined with parameters applicable to individual intentional states.

Intention and the Public as a Plural Subject I propose to follow Gilbert, and regard public and authors as forming a plural subject which has a general goal which is 'the goal of the plural subject, as opposed to the shared personal goal of the participants.'[98] On this basis we may see the public *literally* as an intentional

94 J Elster, *Explaining Technical Change* (Cambridge: Cambridge University Press, 1983) 220.

95 Tollefsen (n 58 above) 34.

96 Ibid.

97 Ibid 44.

98 Gilbert (n 79 above).

agent, capable of intending to author. The agreement we share in society to commit ourselves to the maintenance of social and cultural stability is apparent in the many ways we regulate ownership of different kinds, including intellectual property. The rapid evolution of international copyright laws – for example, the 'invention' of WIPO's Internet Treaties, and global strategies to protect the intellectual property of indigenous communities – shows that the general public has a goal and act as an intentional agent. Just as nations and large populations can make rational choices and show their intention to do so, so can the general public, through the international copyright community, makes rational choices pertaining to the protection of its common culture. This view supports the collective's standpoint and is not reducible to "I-intentions".

It is not necessary that the agreement and commitments we collectively share are made explicit. As Meijers argues: '[m]any social activities are based on prior explicit or implicit agreements. Such agreements bind the subsequent participants in various ways and are an explanatory factor in the subsequent collective actions. The agreement is constitutive of both the collective intentions and the collective agent.'[99] Although this remark was made with respect to relatively small groups it no less applicable to larger ones. It would be difficult to reject the idea that certain social activities carry an implicit agreement on members of the public by virtue of our collective attitude *not* to do certain acts. I already mentioned some of these acts such as our commitment to preserve the environment and our culture. Intellectual property laws ensure that, for example, if I think of a unique word combination a Trademark Office may refuse its registration if it is offensive or not sufficiently distinctive. In this way the Office ensures that private disproportionate linguistic and cultural enclosures do not take place. Copyright laws also secure limited enclosures, but just as with trademarks which are created by the public, in the public domain,[100] there is no recognition to the public's contribution, its implicit, yet undisputable, intention to participate in the making process of authorship through its continuous provision of fundamental materials to this process, its intention to ensure stable cultural polity, and its intention to retain a right in its contribution.

It is arguable that the public shows its intention through social relations between its members and between them and the collective. Meijers advocates an externalist conception of collective intentionality that incorporates social relations:

> It conceives of collective intentional states as states of related individuals. The bonds between these individuals are the social relations formed in their speaking and acting. Agreeing is an act that creates such social relations as claim and obligation between the participants. It is constitutive of many forms of collective intentionality. Like Searle's approach, the relational approach avoids the false dilemma sketched above. It is neither reductive, nor does it allow for super minds "floating over individual minds". It is not compatible, however, with Searle's version of methodological individualism, which

99 Meijers (n 66 above) 177.

100 See S Wilf, 'Who Authors Trademarks?' (1999) 17 *Cardozo Arts & Entertainment Law Journal* 1.

claims that all social phenomena can be fully accounted for in terms of the intentions, beliefs, and desires of individuals (whether collective or not). Social reality requires a radical relational approach.[101]

I do not claim that the public possesses a super mind. I also do not metaphorically claim that there exists a public artificial mind. I argue only that the public is a social group, a non-human agent that exists independently of human agency and sometimes controls the actions of individuals. As members of the public we form a collective with a capacity to intentional states that determines certain ways that we, the collective, follow, and certain ways that we, the collective, reject. We share intention. I reach this conclusion by virtue of our tacit agreement to preserve our human nature which necessitates preservation of our cultural and social reality. This tacit agreement confers on us a shared commitment to preserve these elements. This commitment operates on a more abstract level than a commitment between two or four people to go to the Opera or between the twelve directors of a corporation to adopt a new marketing strategy. The fact that this commitment operates on a higher level of abstraction means that it allows deviations and disagreements which are less possible in small groups. These, however, do not affect the existence of the public's collective intention.

Becker's strategy for individual authorship is composed of three steps.[102] The first step is intention. Having shown that the public is an agent capable of intentional states, we can now move to the second and the third steps: (2) the agent is also creating and realizing its mental representations of its intention, and (3) those representations either constitute the artifact itself, or play a substantial causal role in its production. Following Tollefsen, we should not examine collective intention through the prism of individual intentional states. Therefore, despite the fact that the public does not have mental capacities, consciousness or self-awareness, acknowledging the independence of collective representations and general social facts – which means acknowledging their irreducibility to facts about individuals – would qualify the public for Becker's second step. In *Sociology and Philosophy* Durkheim writes:

> If there is nothing extraordinary in the fact that individual representations, produced by the action and reaction between neural elements, are not inherent in these elements, there is nothing surprising in the fact that collective representations, produced by the action and reaction between individual minds that for the society, do not derive directly from the latter and consequently surpass them. The conception of relationship which unites the social substratum and the social life is at every point analogous to that which undeniably exists between the psychological substratum and psychic life of individuals...The independence, the relative externality of social facts in relation to individuals, is even more immediately apparent than is that of mental facts in relation to cerebal cells...[103]

101 Ibid 181.

102 Becker (n 48 above).

103 E Durkheim, *Sociology and Philosophy* (Glencoe, Illinois: The Free Press, trans. DF Pocock, 1953).

In essence, Durkheim argues that 'social facts are in a sense independent of individuals and exterior to individual minds'[104] and that 'collective representations are exterior to individual minds…they do not derive from them as such but from the association of minds…No doubt in the making of the whole each contributes his part, but private sentiments do not become social except by combination under the action of the *sui generis* forces developed in association.'[105] He continues and remarks: 'From society derive all the essentials of our mental life...'[106] I refer to Durkheim to emphasise that collective representations exist and they are independent. The lack of the constituent 'mental' – which Becker includes in his test – does not negate their existence.

This conclusion is supported by Tollefsen's account of collective intentionality, on which I largely base the argument that the public in its collective sense is capable of intentional states. The public is a non-human, or superhuman agent that exists independently of human individuals and controls the actions of individuals. The public is responsible for the creation of certain mental properties and social relations that are reducible to physical entities. That is how copyrighted entities are born. Although the public does not have a human mind or a biological brain, our collective commitment and responsibility for the preservation of the cultural and social realities constitute collective intentional state to author.

Ascription of intentional states to the public provides us with a rich explanatory resource. For the reasons discussed, it would be wrong to reject the idea behind attributing moral and legal responsibilities to the collective. We make rational choices, decisions that affect the collective, and show intention to commit to certain actions which represent the collective interest. As long as we collectively accept certain concepts as dominating features of our collective reality, we may say that we share an intention to maintain the stability of these concepts. This does not in any measure confirm the superiority of "I-intentions" but simply reinforces the existence of collective intention that cannot be reduced to individual intentions.

Authors are limited to what the social stock has to offer. As I argue, they improve it and add of their own personalities, but they initially create in an environment that comes furnished with certain social and cultural facts and processes. If I decide to be a good author, a decision that I take autonomously, I create in a given social and cultural reality and have to take into account the collectivity of my audience. I should avoid offensive remarks and violations of normatively accepted social forces and legal rules. I have to guide my actions and choices by the collectivity that surrounds me.

We share a common interest and a joint obligation to preserve the Amazon basin, not to deplete the Ocean of its natural resources, not to plant a nuclear power station on planet Mars, and not to privatize our cultural reality in ways that restrict our daily access and use of it. Copyright laws, in effect, promote the expansion of the

104 Ibid 24.
105 Ibid 25-26.
106 Ibid 73.

private at the expense of the public. Even if we do not expressly announce our joint obligation to preserve the cultural and social collectivity we have an intention to participate in the making of authorship and through this intention to jointly form a social commitment, by virtue of our humanity, to respect this obligation.

The fact that the public can have implicit intentional states means that its contribution is not involuntary. It supports my argument that solitary authorship is a fiction. There is, as I argue, only one form of authorship: the joint authorship between public and authors. The public is not indifferent to its contribution. Its contribution amounts to investment of collective efforts and labour. The public is an active contributor whose efforts and labour are mixed with that of the individual author. Labouring is an intentional act. Otherwise the public's contribution could be defined as either mere causal relations or as a natural resource. That the public's contribution amounts to labour is an argument I explore and defend in the following sections and in Chapters 5, 6 and 7. This contribution is part of the bundle of the defining components of our collective commitment. In the reminder of this Chapter I apply Becker's third step and show how collective representations create, and are deeply embedded in, every copyrighted enterprise.

The Authorial Role of the Public

The Question Posed

Those involved in copyright scholarship tend to ignore issues such as the source of copyright endeavours when they deal with the future of the copyright regime or critique its existing form. In the words of Madison: 'How do 'creative' works of authorship come about? We care about the copyright system because we care about the answers to these questions, yet the questions are rarely asked in a formal way in connection with copyright debates.'[107] I posit this question at the core of this study and claim that before we allow the copyright system to 'erode the creative community's ability to renew itself'[108] we ought to recognise that the ability to create copyrighted entities is not innate. Unless we truly agree on an answer to the question just asked, we are unlikely to reach an acceptable resolution for how much balance there ought to be between private and public in copyright.

I began this Chapter with the observation that the romantic vision of the author is a fiction, which falsely embraces OA theories as its justificatory baseline. I raised objections to this fiction and argued that copyright creation is a process to which contribution is received from sources other than the individual author. Birnhack views copyright as a process of knowledge accumulation and maintains that we must 'have a conception of how knowledge is created, otherwise [copyright law] is

---

107 MJ Madison, 'Comment: Where Does Creativity Come From? And Other Stories of Copyright' (2003) 53 *Case Western Reserve Law Review* 747, 759-760.

108 WJ Gordon, 'Authors, Publishers, and Public Goods: Trading Gold for Dross' (2002) 36 *Loyola of Los Angeles Law Review* 159.

meaningless.'[109] In other words, copyright is a knowledge-based legal phenomenon and 'in order to identify a form of knowledge…we must seek the conditions which make the emergence of this knowledge possible.'[110] Understanding the origin and role of creative knowledge may well resolve some subtle questions in copyright policy.[111]

That authorial manifestations and artistic endeavours are social products is axiomatic. They represent individuals' experiences of the external reality through socially shared categories and 'a set of public standards to which community members appeal in critical discursive interaction.'[112] The larger community owns and nurtures these shared categories and standards without which the creative act would be stunted.[113] That is, the sociality of copyright creations requires us to reward sources that contribute to the realization of the creative ability. Although no one is likely to deny that copyrighted works are social entities, many would doubt whether the public's social contribution amounts to a *de facto* authorial contribution which

---

109 MD Birnhack, 'The Idea of Progress in Copyright Law' (2001) 1 *Buffalo Intellectual Property Law Journal* 3, 57.

110 P Macherey, *A Theory of Literary Production* (London: Routledge, Geoffrey Wall trans., 1978) 8.

111 The case law is perhaps the best source from which to draw examples to that a copyright product involves either musical, artistic, graphic, comics, mathematic, aesthetic and other forms of knowledge. In fact, '[t]he simple notion that human knowledge is the subject-matter of intellectual property law may be illustrated by reference to the various regimes.' W Van Caenegen, 'The Public Domain: Scientia Nullius?' [2002] 6 *European Intellectual Property Review* 324, 326.

The editors of a recently published collection of articles find 'knowledge' to represent the common ground to every arm of the intellectual property regime. They claim that the shape of our artistic and scientific future depends on the ways the 'knowledge society' decides to follow. R Dreyfuss, LD Zimmerman and H First (eds.), *Expanding the Boundaries of Intellectual Property: Innovation Policy for the Knowledge Society* (Oxford: Oxford University Press, 2001) ix-x. See also M Häyrinen-Alestalo, 'Is Knowledge-Based Society a Relevant Strategy for Civil Society?' (2001) 49(4) *Current Sociology* 203, 206.

Some would argue that certain areas of intellectual property are more knowledge-based than others. See W Powell, 'Networks of Learning in Biotechnology: Opportunities and Constraints Associated with Relational Contracting in a Knowledge-Intensive Field' in Dreyfuss, Zimmerman and First, ibid 252-266.

112 H Longino, *The Fate of Knowledge* (Princeton and Oxford: Princeton University Press, 2002) 148.

113 As a singular entity, society designs standards that are applicable to and consumable by all communities such as that sexual intercourse requires consent, that contaminating rivers with industrial chemicals is a criminal offence under environmental laws, that excavations on one's land is prohibited unless authorised by the owner, or that copying a composition, a soundtrack or a poem without their owner's permission is prohibited. That is, the knowledge authors possess has been fashioned by (i) being members of society (the public at large); and (ii) being a member of a more defined community (e.g., composers, writers, lyricists, and illustrators).

justifies the imposition of further limitations on copyright ownership. As a way to approach this controversy, I will first show how copyright works represent the authorial collectivity.[114] A defence of public entitlement to these works is reserved for Chapter 5, 6 and 7.

Wallas' Four-Step Test

A test offered by Wallas best illustrates the on-going reliance of authors on the public and the external environment while engaging in creative activities.[115] Wallas was first to clearly formulate the demarcation of the cognitive steps involved in the production of novelty. He argues for a cumulative test, composed of four complementary stages, common to all creative activity: preparation, incubation, illumination and verification. The first stage, preparation, involves a long period of intense conscious work, without any obvious milestones. During that period, after ideas are generated and considered, the issue is put aside and not consciously dwelt upon. At this time the second stage, incubation, commences. In the incubation stage the ideas on which the creator thought consciously take new shape and meaning, as they are combined in new ways in the unconscious. Once conceptual incubation is completed, illumination, the third step, comes into play. Illumination does not provide the creator with the ultimate answer or solution but rather a glimmer of what it is likely to be, while the solution often comes with the final fourth stage, verification.[116]

This four-step test demonstrates the social dependence and causal relation between each segment of the chain of creative activity. Each step builds and relies on preceding steps and each, in turn feeds the steps ahead. In fact, Weisberg tells us, 'most of the artists and poets reported that Wallas's four-step process…described their work. They said that an idea for a painting or a poem was not worked on immediately, but was first "carried around" for a period of time.'[117]

114 For the sake of clarity I refer to authorial collectivity as a generic term that covers the entire spectrum of copyrighted works.

115 G Wallas, *The Art of Thought* (New York: Harcourt Brace, 1926) referred to in R Weisberg, *Creativity: Beyond the Myth of Genius* (New York: WH Freeman, 1993) 47-48.

116 Another step 'intuition' was claimed to be a relevant hidden link in Wallas's four-step test. It is a step that could come between incubation and illumination since it concerns 'vague anticipatory perception that orients creative work in a promising direction.' E Policastro, 'Creative Intuition: An Integrated Review' (1995) 8 *Creativity Research Journal* 99. See also JE Eindhoven and WE Vinacke, 'Creative Processes in Painting' (1952) 47 *The Journal of General Psychology* 139, 139-140; and Weisberg, ibid 27-68.

117 Weisberg, ibid 47.

The Test in Reality: Collective Authorship, Social Dependence and Causality

Social Dependence and Causality In a fascinating study, Shapin argues that we should '*take for granted* that science is a historically situated and social activity and that it is to be understood in relation to the *contexts* in which it occurs.'[118] From Galileo's observation of sunspots, Boyle's water pump, Descartes' scheme for explaining reflex actions, to Kepler's temple of astronomy and Hooke's microscopic magnification of the eyes of a common fly, Shapin places revolutionary scientific products in their historical-social context and claims that the task is 'to display knowledge making and knowledge holding as *social processes.*'[119] Shapin does not deny that science could not develop unless from time to time it was shaken by revolutions, but he leaves us with the question of how *revolutionary* can a scientific revolution be?

In patent law, for example, the level of 'revolution' is determined by meeting certain conditions showing that scientific knowledge is acquired only in a causal way and is not socially independent. Patent laws protect inventions that are not already known and present some degree of novelty and inventiveness in them.[120] In essence, patent law requires advance over prior knowledge. It requires an inventive step. This requirement presupposes reliance and a causal connection between prior scientific steps and newly created inventions. The question about novelty, whether a hayraking machine,[121] a ball-point pen[122] or a chemical compound,[123] is whether the invention was anticipated – whether the same invention had already been made public? Whether it was for practical purposes obvious to the skilled person, familiar with all needed information and common general knowledge, to arrive at the patent proposed?[124] In other words, a *relatively new* knowledge has to be produced, but its success can only be measured in relation to prior inventions.

In contrast, copyright law considers authorial and artistic works as original creations; not a new step; not an advance over prior art. Copyright law considers authorial creation as an independent act of creation *ex nihilo*. It rejects the ultimate truth that 'novel knowledge', as Stehr remarks, 'results from endogenous social

118 S Shapin, *The Scientific Revolution* (Chicago: Chicago university Press, 1996) 9.

119 Ibid. Shapin explains his idea of what amounts to social processes. He gives the example of 'the use of metaphors from the economy in the development of scientific knowledge'. Ibid. He then concludes that '[t]here is as much society inside the scientist's laboratory, and internal to the development of scientific knowledge, as there is outside.' Ibid 10.

120 PA 1977 s 1-4; EPC Arts 52-57.

121 *Van der Lely v Bamford* [1963] RPC 61 (HL).

122 *Fomento v Mentmore* [1956] RPC 87 (CA).

123 *Opinion: Availability to the Public, Enlarged BA* [1993] OJ EPO 277.

124 The inventiveness test was articulated by Oliver LJ in *Windsurfing International v Tabur Marine* [1985] RPC 59. For the common general knowledge test see also *Taylor v Ishida (Europe) Ltd* [2000] FSR 224.

processes. It does not fall from the sky or appear by accident on the scene.'[125] The social nature of knowledge production and knowledge accumulation play no significant role in copyright law, and one of the results is a growing gap between perceived benefits and social costs. Perhaps the substantive part test in copyright is a modified version of the common knowledge principle in patent law. The fact that within copyright law, non-substantial parts can be copied indicates that the law recognises reliance on the pubic domain. The idea/expression dichotomy also shows that an individual is in need of publicly owned raw materials such as ideas, concepts and facts. There is nothing, however, in copyright law that recognises the dependence of ideas on publicly shared and produced concepts and other cultural properties, for matters of ownership. We tend to not only classify these items as insignificant raw materials but even to assume that they are not necessary: there is no requirement for a prior idea in order for an expression to attract copyright protection. Perhaps we are taking it for granted. But, if one refers to raw materials as common property or common knowledge, while common knowledge is unprotected in patent law, in copyright the vague distinction between ideas and expressions guarantees that common can become private and that enclosure of portions of the public domain is not too difficult. In addition, while the life of a patent is normally restricted to two decades, copyright permits protection to last over a century.

An author's ability to translate common knowledge into copyrighted entities is influenced by many factors such as creativity, and visions of taste and aesthetics. Research on creativity is burdened with the question whether the creative act is a creature of social dependence and causality or not.[126] In copyright terms, the question is whether there exists 'truth in the stereotypes of the introverted and moody artist, or the absent-minded yet brilliant professor'[127] that will be strong enough to allow romantic conceptions of the author to determine ownership in copyright? As I argue, copyright law does not concern itself with this question. In fact it perpetuates the place of the Romantic author as one of its defining principles.

True, principles of social dependence and causality are implicit in copyright debates. Copyright laws recognise their role in, for example, debates on the scope of copyright ownership, the notions of improvement on existing works, transformative

---

125 N Stehr, 'The Social and Political Control of Knowledge in Modern Societies' (2003) 55(4) *International Social Science Journal* 643, 650.

126 See generally, JD Roslansky (ed.), *Creativity* (Amsterdam and London: North-Holland Publishing Co., 1970); PE Vernon (ed.), *Creativity* (Penguin Books, 1970); R Sternberg (ed.), *The Nature of Creativity: Contemporary Psychological Perspectives* (Cambridge: Cambridge University Press, 1987); M Boden, *The Creative Mind: Myths and Mechanisms* (New York: Basic Books, 1992) and by the same author, *Dimensions of Creativity* (Boston: MIT Press, 1994); Weisberg (n 115 above); SM Smith, TB Ward and RA Finke (eds.), *The Creative Cognitive Approach* (Cambridge Mass.: MIT Press, 1995); T Amabile, *Creativity in Context* (Boulder: Westview Press, 1996); M Csikszentmihalyi, *Creativity: Flow and the Psychology of Discovery and Invention* (New York: HarperPerennial, 1996).

127 U Wolfradt and JE Pretz, 'Individual Differences in Creativity: Personality, Story Writing, and Hobbies' (2001) 15 *European Journal of Personality* 297, 298.

authorship and transformative uses (certain uses that add new material in a way that reflects critically on the original work), fair dealing and the rights of second generation creators.[128] They allow creators 'to utilize raw materials without incurring liability for infringement.'[129] In this way copyright laws hope to strike a balance between the rights of first and second generation creators. For example, 'copyright law does not extend protection to factual information because such information is the core raw material that other need to use to further progress.'[130]

The origin of authorial knowledge is yet to be fully explored in debates about the proper balance between private and public in copyright despite the fact that every item protected under copyright laws is a mixture of prior art and new substances. The reason for the lack of sufficient attention to the role of social dependence, causality and knowledge in copyright lays perhaps in that what interests philosophers 'can be ignored by lawyers.'[131] A lawyer would reject the contention that the origin of authorial knowledge and creativity is in communal interchange. But, art is shaped within a given social context. Its success is conditioned on use of collectively produced categories of cultural and social elements.[132] This social connection creates authorial dependence on social experiences and constant need for collectively produced properties.

Interactive Factors Many factors interact in the process of copyright creation. The interdependence between art, culture and society renders causality a key feature in the creation of copyrightable material. In general, inputs can be divided into two categories: (i) factors that depend on past experiences; on social and cultural traditions; and on the availability of collective properties; and (ii) factors that form part of a person's innate endowment. Neither of these categories alone is sufficient for generating creative activity. The two categories interact and in this way copyright generation and its expressive entities are realized.

---

128 MA Lemley, 'The Economics of Improvement in Intellectual Property Law' (1997) 75 *Texas Law Review* 989, 1027-1029.

129 MA O'Rourke, 'Beyond Microsoft: Antitrust, Technology, and Intellectual Property' (2001) 16 *Berkeley Technology Law Journal* 561, 584.

130 Ibid.

131 R Bagshaw, 'Legal Proof of Knowledge' in P Mirfield and R Smith (eds.), *Essays for Colin Tapper* (Lexis Nexis: Butterworths, 2003) 73.

132 Although relatively new to debates on the reach of the entitlement spectrum in copyright, the sociality of knowledge is not a new argument. Philosophical arguments on the sociology of knowledge are fascinating and are relevant to inquiries on copyright law. Longino summarises the main arguments and deals with Haack, Goldman, Kitcher, Hesse, Fuller and many others. She makes a distinction between the different school of thoughts and reaches a conclusion on who is more individualistic and who is less so. See Longino (n 112 above) 42-68. I use the 'knowledge as social' argument to justify limits to copyright ownership. In general terms, I do not only take the production of individual knowledge but also the production of collective knowledge by the public.

Coombe, for example, introduces the concept "recoding" into copyright theory and argues that the creative process is a complex one that requires the availability of publicly accessible symbols. The interaction between collective production of these symbols and individual consumption make the creative act possible. She writes: 'the consumption of commodified representational forms is productive activity in which people engage in meaning-making to adapt signs, texts, and images to their own agendas.'[133] Meaning-making is not an internal process. People are *engaged* in meaning-making, they do not create from nothing and the availability of external objects which the individual absorbs and modifies determines the success of the creative act. Meaning-making is an activity determined and shaped by many factors. A brief insight into three factors that play a pivotal role in the copyright creation process is useful as an illustration of the contribution of the public to the meaning-making process and for my argument for shared public/private entitlement to authorial and artistic works: the thinking process, intelligence and personality.

Thinking is a preliminary step and a core factor in the making process of copyright works. It is considered an 'internal process which brings the organization laid down by *past experience* and *learning* to bear upon responses to current situations, and which shapes their responses in keeping with inner needs.'[134] Thought is dependent on external objects. It is fuelled by consumption of shared symbols, images and other structured relations, social processes and cultural events. The human mind and its creative functioning, then, depend on past experiences and, to a great extent, on the chance occurrence of certain events. Thought is a process of conceptualisation whereby man's world is symbolized or schematized. Copyrighted works reduce the abstract conceptualisation to the way an author associates his ideas with existing objects, identifies and 'tangibly' expresses his ideal reflection of the world.

A and B can create by employing two opposite modes of thought: *convergent* and *divergent*. The former involves 'solving well-defined, rational problems that have one correct answer',[135] and the latter is more akin to 'originality in picking unusual associations of ideas.'[136] Authors would normally be recognised for their divergent thinking. The author who possesses the ability to create copyrightable works, has a capacity to combine internal and external resources to create an unanticipated result – the ability to create ABZ from A and B. He asks 'why' or 'how', interprets, defines, composes and actualises existing elements, creates derivatives, merges diverse elements to one operative figure and produces unique materials. He has a greater openness to experience.[137] Weisberg adds to this list other characteristics shared by

---

133 RJ Coombe, 'Objects of Property and Subjects of Politics: Intellectual Property Laws and Democratic Dialogue' (1991) 69 *Texas Law Review* 1853, 1863.

134 W Vinacke, *The Psychology of School Selection* (1952), cited in G Shouksmith, *Intelligence, Creativity and Cognitive Style* (London: Batsford, 1970) 22 (emphasis added).

135 Csikszentmihalyi (n 126 above) 60.

136 Ibid. On the distinction between convergence and divergence and their relation to creativity, see also L Hudson, 'The Question of Creativity' in Vernon (n 126 above) 217-234.

137 An individual's openness to experience is considered crucial for the development of the creative personality and for benefiting from the causal process. For example, McCrae found

all creative individuals: broad interests, independence of judgement, self-confidence, intuition, and a firm sense of the self as a 'creative' being.[138] However, the degree to which authors possess these attributes varies between authors A and B. This is how we come to have Dostoyevsky's tragedies; the story of Proteus who, in book IV of the *Odyssey*, turns into a lion and a snake, a panther and a boar, a stream and a great tree in leaf; Dickens's 'Great Expectations'; one who caricatures different events and political figures and another who poeticises them.

Imagination is an example for a factor that is an integral part of the thinking process and was argued to amount to a constitutional guarantee necessary for copyright. Rubenfeld claims that imagination makes people 'go beyond' what they know to be present.[139] He discusses the interplay between imagination and copyright and argues that the current interpretation of the US Copyright Act conflicts with the human freedom of imagination enshrined in the First Amendment. Imagination ought to be free. He remarks:

---

that openness to experience and divergent thinking interact and make creative production real. RR McCrae, 'Creativity, Divergent Thinking, and Openness to Experience' (1987) 52 *Journal of Personality and Social Psychology* 1258; and by the same author, 'Openness to Experience as a Basic Dimension of Personality' (1993) 13 *Imagination, Cognition and Personality* 39. *Cf* C Martindale and A Dailey, 'Creativity, Primary Process Cognition and Personality' (1996) 20(4) *Personality and Individual Differences* 409.

138 Weisberg (n 115 above) 73. Mackinnon, for example, applies these qualities and finds that creative architects differ significantly from their noncreative counterparts. He concludes his research with finding that what characterises a creative architect is his 'high level of effective intelligence, his openness to experience, his freedom from petty restraints and impoverishing inhibitions, his aesthetic sensitivity…and his unceasing striving for creative solutions to the ever more difficult architectural problems…' DW MacKinnon, 'The Personality Correlates of Creativity: A Study of American Architects' In GS Nielsen (ed.), *Proceedings of the 14th International Congress of Applied Psychology* (Copenhagen: Munksgaard, 1962) Vol 2, 11-39, cited in Vernon (n 126 above) 289-311. MacKinnon later remarks that he expects creative people to be more introverted and argues that architects were less socially inclined, having a 'desire not to be included in the activities of others nor to include them in their' activities. DW MacKinnon, 'IPAR's Contribution to the Conceptualization and Study of Creativity' in IA Taylor and JW Getzels (eds.), *Perspectives in Creativity* (Aldine: Chicago IL, 1975) 60-89. Whether architects choose to be excluded from the activities of others they cannot ignore them, they cannot ignore the social reality and its architectural needs, and they cannot deny the daily benefit they get from the external architectural landscape.

Architectural designs are protected under copyright law. In *Jones v Tower Hamlets LBC* the Court held that the design was entitled to copyright protection since it represented not merely a visually significant aspect of the design of the relevant houses but also a *singular solution to the problem* of a restricted interior. Given that the design was unique, the Court held, it was to be inferred that THLBC had copied it. *Jones v Tower Hamlets LBC (No.2)* [2001] RPC 23 Ch. The Court's decision reflects MacKinnon's view that the creative architect is 'unceasing striving for creative solutions to the ever more difficult architectural problems'. Ibid.

139 J Rubenfeld, 'The Freedom of Imagination: Copyright's Constitutionality' (2002) 112 *Yale Law Journal* 1.

> This should be First Amendment bedrock: No one may be penalized for what he dares to imagine. What a person can imagine, he may imagine. But what is imagination, and what is its relationship to speech? … Imagination comes in many forms: intellectual, visual, emotional, musical, and so on. There are probably as many forms of imagination as there are forms of apprehending the world. To define is to confine, and imagination resists confinement. But if we want to unite the various forms of imagination under one heading, we might begin by saying that to imagine is to conceive *what isn't there.* To imagine is to form an idea that goes beyond – that *introduces something new* to – what the mind has heretofore seen, heard, thought, or otherwise sensed. Imagination is the faculty by which the mind presents to itself what isn't actually present and what has never been actually present to it.[140]

I agree that imagination involves distinct mental and emotional processes unique to the individual. They take part in the creation of something that isn't there – something new. But imagination alone cannot trigger creative expressions. If imagination is to be taken into account in the copyright making process, then it should not be distinguished from any other transformative quality. The capacity to imagine is perhaps innate, but its developed and actual expression which transforms the capacity into an actual talent that takes part in the copyright making process, is a social creature that depends on collective cultural and social properties.

Innate endowment plays a role in my argument. Although copyrighted endeavours are a joint enterprise between authors and public, the law should maintain a scheme of private rights in copyright. Intelligence, for example, is used by people in different ways to build up a storehouse of concepts, skills and faculties, and to interpret and cope with the world. It is considered an innate principle. It holds the key to the innate capacity of the individual which is perhaps the only 'full-blooded'[141] ownership one may claim to have. A useful point of illustration is the distinction drawn between innate and developed intelligence. Hebb's two definitions of intelligence explain this distinction:[142] 'Intelligence A' is the capacity for development a person has and is a wholly innate property 'that amounts to the possession of a good brain and a good neural metabolism'.[143] 'Intelligence B' is 'the functioning of a brain in which development has already gone on'.[144] The latter determines 'the average level of performance or comprehension by the partly grown or mature person.'[145]

Finally, the manner in which one can own the authorial fruits of one's self-developed personality is an issue that affects the success of the meaning-making activity to which Coombe refers, and lies at the heart of my argument on authorial collectivity. While it is true that all creations have something that come from the creator's personality, the creative personality itself is a different form of personality.

---

140 Ibid 37 (emphasis added).

141 Harris (n 35 above) 29, 228.

142 D Hebb, *A Textbook of Psychology* (2nd ed., 1966) in G Shouksmith, *Intelligence, Creativity and Cognitive Style* (London: BT Batsford Ltd, 1970) 70.

143 Ibid.

144 Ibid.

145 Ibid.

Creative individuals possess a unique set of characteristics.[146] They infuse their internal code, composed of inborn and adaptive capacities, into an external object.[147] As such, expression of personality is not static.[148] Expressions of personality represent the author's ability, style, novelty, flexibility of mind, willingness to consider unusual possibilities, ability to attack greater or more difficult problems, dedication to a quest for ultimate meanings, and other related elements.[149] Only exposure to social realities and absorption of collective properties promote attainment and actualisation of these traits.

There are different creative personalities and each applies creativity in a different manner. Painters, for example, may have a great capacity to process and store visual information. Their visual imagination allows them to anticipate the impact of putting paint on canvas in a certain way. On the one hand, they have a highly developed sensitivity to colour, a high degree of hand-eye coordination and control over small-motor movements. On the other hand, they might not possess the respective qualities necessary to become the next Hayden or Tolstoy. The creative impulse, whether of an author, a composer or an architect, defines what kind of a person X is. Others may lack the personality traits to become any of these. The ability of the law to tailor a coherent model which identifies and ranks various levels of creative personalities can be called into question. But if it can, two issues must be raised. First, does infusion of more personality into a copyright work mean more property? And second, should certain categories of copyrighted works that do not employ sufficient degree of personality receive any protection at all? In other words, should a different set of moral rights be assigned to works that involve a lesser degree of their creator's personality? Is a poem more personality-based than a computer program for language learning? What are the parameters to decide on personality?

---

146 The Buss and Mansfield study, for example, found that scientists possess a stronger sense of the aesthetic, as they prefer asymmetrical and complex works. TV Buss and RS Mansfield,'The Blooming of Creative Scientists: Early, Late and Otherwise' (1981) *Gifted Child Quarterly* 63. For further analysis see by the same authors, *The Psychology of Creativity and Discovery* (Chicago: Nelson Hall, 1981).

147 In the words of Hegel: '[a]ttainments, eruditions, talents and so forth, are, of course, owned by free mind and are something internal and not external to it, but even so, by expressing them it may embody them in something external and alienate to them'. GWF Hegel, *Philosophy of Right* (1821) (Oxford: Oxford University Press, TM Knox trans., 1967) 43.

148 See generally Weisberg (n 115 above) 69-89.

149 For example, Feist's meta-analysis finds creative people to be more 'autonomous, introverted, open to new experiences, norm-doubting, self-confident, self-accepting, driven, ambitious, dominant, hostile and impulsive.' GJ Feist, 'A Meta-Analysis of Personality in Scientific and Artistic Creativity' (1998) 2 *Personality and Social Psychology Review* 290, 299.

Sternberg argues that a good deal of toleration of ambiguity is an asset of the creative personality. RJ Sternberg, 'A Three-Facet Model of Creativity' in Sternberg (n 126 above) 125, 143. And Eysenck argues that preference for complexity over simplicity characterises the creative achiever. HJ Eysenck, 'Creativity and Personality: Suggestions for a Theory' (1993) 4 *Psychological Inquiry* 147.

The law does not leave us without an answer to these questions and provides that, while some works have no sense of personality, other works employ 'the personal reaction of an individual upon nature.'[150] In the words of Hughes: while '[s]ome categories of intellectual property seem to be receptacles for personality; others seem as if they do not manifest any 'personality' of their creators. Poems, stories, novels, and musical works are clearly receptacles for personality. The same can be said for sculpture, painting, and prints…'[151] True, different categories of copyrighted works employ different styles of personality, some, the law tells us, are less receptacle for personality.[152] However, even the negligible employment of personality in the production of authorial or artistic materials reflects the causal relations between individuals and between them and the general public.

Interactive Results I do not suggest that collective social dependence or causal factors alone create copyright, and I am certainly not of the opinion that the public alone initiates the creative impulse and its eventual creative expressions. I believe that authorial knowledge and creativity are definable on two complementary grounds: collective and subjective. The latter relates to the use of innate qualities, common sense and reaction, in making judgements and inferences concerning aspects of experience that matter to us. The former relates to the contribution from the public. Interaction between the collective and the subjective is what makes copyright production real: innate capacities are transformed into actual abilities by experiencing, interpreting and enclosing collectively produced and owned properties. It's a game of managing contribution from two sources for the sake of control and power. However, in the current state of affairs in copyright, only one source, namely – the author, realizes that sense of control and reward.

In this study, I have no intention of denying the subjective dimension in copyright. Internalisation and subjective interpretations of collective social and cultural properties define the creative spark and take it in new and unexpected directions. What I was aiming at is to expose the fallacy in establishing principles of copyright protection on the claim that what authors' create, is their '*own intellectual* creation'

150 Justice Holmes in *Bleistein v Donaldson Lithographing Co* 188 US 239, 250 (1903).

151 J Hughes, 'The Philosophy of Intellectual Property' (1988) 77 *Georgetown Law Journal* 287, 340.

152 Computer generated works are a good example for copyrighted entities where there is no identifiable human author and with the widespread use of programming 'tools and automated processes for collecting, processing and compiling data, it is likely that an increased number of works, including computer programs and databases, will have no identifiable author or authors.' C Reed and J Angel (ed.), *Computer Law* (Oxford: Oxford University Press 5th ed., 2003) 196. See also *Express Newspapers Plc v Liverpool Daily Post & Echo Plc* [1985] 1 FSR 306; *Apple Computers Inc v Franklin Computer Corp* 714 F 2d 1240, 1253 (3rd Cir 1983). In the Whitford Report it was said that a computer used for the creation of a copyrighted work is a tool just as a paintbrush is a tool. See *Copyright and Design Law: Report of the Committee to Consider the Law on Copyright and Designs* (Cmnd 7632) (HMSO 1977) para 514. See also CDPA 1988 s 9(3), 12(7), 79(2)(c), 81(2) and 178.

– a language favoured in contemporary European copyright laws.[153] Authors, artists, composers and dramatists, including historic path-breaking figures such as Galileo, Dostoyevsky, Darwin, Gauguin, Newton, Einstein or Freud, are individuals whose expressive knowledge and creative labour depend on traditions and consumption of collectively produced and owned social and cultural properties vested in distinctive authorial and other representations. None can establish a claim for an exclusive property right based on the argument that he created something that represents his '*own* intellectual creation'.

Before examining incidents of copyright it is useful to look at a related example that illustrates the collective role: celebrities' right. Arguments about celebrity magnetism vary from considering it being a public property and part of popular culture to an exclusive property of the persona. Hughes argues that '[p]roperty rights in the persona give the individual the economic value derived most directly from one's personality. As long as an individual identifies with his personal image, he will have a personality stake in that image.'[154] Madow rejects this view and contends that,

> A celebrity…does not make her public image, her meaning for others, in anything like the way a carpenter makes a chair from a block of wood. She is not the sole and sovereign "author" of what she means for others…a celebrity like Madonna cannot say of her public image what the carpenter can say of his chair: "I made it." And because she cannot say this of her public image, she cannot lay a convincing moral claim to the exclusive ownership or control of the economic values that attach to it.[155]

Coombe takes this approach one step further and argues that the celebrity's 'successful image is frequently a form of cultural bricolage that improvises with a

---

153 This ideal has recently become a principle of contemporary European copyright protection and illustrates the inherent danger in adhering after it. Three EC directives provide for a definition of originality as 'the author's own intellectual creation'. See respectively Computer Programs Directive 91/250/EEC, Art 1(3); Term Directive 93/98/EEC Art 6; and Database Directive 96/9/EC Art 3(1).

The danger in adhering to the principle of 'own intellectual creation' and grounding it in legal documents, is expansion of the denial of the public interest thereby further institutionalising the ideal of romantic authorship; losing track of the latter's possible future implications; and wrongly assuming that it may reflect copyright creation enough to make it the optimal threshold for copyright protection. For example, Sterling suggests to 'obtain a consensus that the 'author's own intellectual creation' criterion' will be adopted in a future international copyright code. See JAL Sterling, 'International Codification of Copyright Law: Possibilities and Imperatives' (2000) 33 *International Review of Industrial Property and Copyright Law* (IIC) 270, 289.

154 Hughes (n 151 above) 340-341.

155 M Madow 'Private Ownership of Public Image: Popular Culture and Publicity Rights' (1993) 81 *California Law Review* 127, 195-196, n.338.

social history of symbolic forms.'[156] A 'celebrity is authored in a multiplicity of sites of discursive practice, and that in the process, unauthorized identities are produced, both for the celebrity and for her diverse authors.'[157] In another article Coombe asserts that '[p]ublicity rights arguably enable celebrities, their assignees, and their estates to control the meaning of the celebrity image in a fashion that deprives us of access to our collective cultural heritage…'[158] Next I will show how copyrighted commodities are 'authored in a multiplicity of sites of discursive practice' and represent 'our collective cultural heritage.' I shall take several examples of key authors and artists who have had an undeniable impact on our culture.

The examples I shall take clarify the argument that the public has a right in every copyrighted work. It also clarifies who the public *is* for purposes of the public authorship model. I shall refer to 'the public' as an entity comprising: (i) other individual contributors, *except* the principal author, who do not show *individual* intention to share the property in the work created and do not participate in the very creation of the particular copyrighted work; and (ii) the general public by virtue of its collective authorial contribution, provision of social and cultural properties, and collective intention.

I will progress chronologically, and show that there is no difference between figures whose original works were not protected under copyright laws, and others whose works represent living examples of the flaws in our copyright regime. I shall discuss Shakespeare, Mozart, Picasso, chance creations and indeterminate works of Dadaist artists and conclude that recognition of the public authorial contribution, if less relevant in pre-copyright laws periods, will ensure equity in modern copyright and secure society's social structure and collective cultural identity in today's copyright regime.

Incidents of Authorship and Continuity

'Shakespeare, the Co-Author'

A title such as, *Shakespeare, Co-Author*,[159] almost says it all. In his book, Vickers challenges the view that authorial and artistic creativity is an expression of a solitary creative outburst. Shakespeare's works predate the Statute of Anne of 1709.[160] That means, neither Shakespeare, nor his heirs, could have imagined the benefits

---

156 RJ Coombe, 'Author/izing the Celebrity: Publicity Rights, Postmodern Politics, and Unauthorized Genders' (1992) 10 *Cardozo Arts & Entertainment Law Journal* 365, 370. On this issue see generally, H Carty, 'Advertising, Publicity Rights and English Law' [2004] 3 *Intellectual Property Quarterly* 209.

157 Coombe, ibid 365.

158 Coombe (n 133 above) 1876.

159 B Vickers, *Shakespeare, Co-Author: A Historical Study of Five Collaborative Plays* (Oxford: Oxford University Press, 2002).

160 W Shakespeare (1564-1616).

of copyright protection. As Vaver remarks: 'Were Shakespeare still in copyright, his heirs could prevent the publication of Charles and Mary Lamb's Tales from Shakespeare (1807) for children, and other reductions such as the half-hour version of Macbeth mounted in 1994 by the Waterside Theatre Company of Stratford.'[161] However, a 'fresh translation of Shakespeare or Voltaire has full copyright protection for the translator's life' plus 70 years 'whether the source work is that of a living author or not.'[162]

In *Shakespeare, Co-Author* Vickers asks 'how much do we know about Shakespeare's collaboration with other dramatists?'[163] He examines five plays and finds each to be co-authored with another person.[164] For example, Fletcher's substantial contributions to *Henry VIII* and *The Two Nobel Kinsmen*, Peele's co-authorship of *Titus Andronicus* and the evidence amassed for Middleton's unquestionably substantial share in *Timon of Athens*. The test Vickers employs is composed of several components, for example: the verse style; parallel passages; the vocabulary used; linguistic choices; and function words used to convey special meanings.[165] In *Titus Andronicus* Vickers finds 'typical' authorial style by George Peele despite the fact that Shakespeare 'seems to exclude acknowledging the presence of another author'[166] in the play. The play was entered in the Stationers' Register on 1594 as 'a book instituted a Nobel Roman Historye of Titus Andronicus'.

Scholars have found similarities between *Titus*, *Hamlet* and *King Lear,* pointing to Shakespearean development in tragedy. In contrast, Vickers finds a strong case for co-authorship in *Titus* between Shakespeare and Peele. He examines three things: (i) comparison between *Titus* and a play by Peele of comparable subject-matter, *The Battle of Alcazar*;[167] (ii) the use of alliteration;[168] and (iii) the number of vocatives.[169]

---

161 D Vaver, 'Abridgements and Abstracts: Copyright Implications' (1995) 17(5) *European Intellectual Property Review* 225, 232.

162 D Vaver, 'Translation and Copyright: A Canadian Focus' (1994) 16(4) *European Intellectual Property Review* 159, 160-161. However, the basic depiction of a character is not subject to copyright protection. This may be illustrated by Learned Hand J decision in the case of *Nichols v Universal Pictures* where he uses the example that if Shakespeare's Twelfth Night was subject to copyright, then the creation of a character who was 'a riotous knight who kept wassail to the discomfort of the household' would not be enough to infringe copyright, and 'the less developed the character, the less they can be copyrighted.' *Nichols v Universal Pictures* 45F 2d 119, 121 (2d Circ 1930).

163 Vickers (n 159 above) vii. The fact that collaborative authorship was a standard practice in Elizabethan, Jacobean, and Caroline drama convinces Vickers that we can find clear traces of co-authorship in Shakespeare's plays. Ibid 137-147.

164 *Titus Adronicus*, ibid 148; *Timon of Athens*, ibid 244; *Pericles*, ibid 291; *Henry VIII*, ibid 333; and *The Two Noble Kinsmen*, ibid 402.

165 Ibid 44-134. See also, ibid 433-500, where Vickers discusses problems in identifying and monitoring co-authors.

166 Ibid 162.

167 Ibid 219-220.

168 Ibid 220-226.

169 Ibid 226.

He concludes that 'Peele was no doubt a useful co-author for Shakespeare, with his longer theatrical experience and greater knowledge of the classical world.'[170] His contribution to *Titus* is 'enough to gain Peele recognition as co-author.'[171] He reaches similar conclusions with regards to Wilkins' contribution to *Pericles* and Fletcher's contribution to *Henry VIII*[172] and *The Two Noble Kinsmen*.[173] In respect of Shakespeare's tragedy, *Timon of Athens*, Vickers takes his view on co-authorship even further and argues that all the methods employed to test the originality of the play 'agree in assigning Middleton a *substantial* part of *Timon*, and Shakespearians who continue to deny this point risk forfeiting their scholarly credibility.'[174]

The influence of Shakespeare on the evolution of legal reasoning is an interesting phenomenon in itself. For example, one commentator complains about the limited use courts make of Shakespearean quotations. Some references quote him as an authority that led to a certain activity of life and others go further and use him as an authority to establish the meaning of contemporary legal terms.[175] If we want to make references to Shakespeare in legal discourses, should we not learn a lesson from Shakespeare's mode of collaboration when we develop standards of copyright protection? Scholarship on copyright is attentive to the collaborative nature of Shakespeare's works. In a leading source on the evolution of copyright, Rose challenges the 'unoriginal' nature of Shakespeare's plays. Rose remarks:

> As a member of the King's Men and a shareholder in the Globe Theatre, Shakespeare participated in a collaborative and traditional enterprise of cultural production. Almost none of Shakespeare's stories were original with him…It would not be wholly inappropriate, I

---

170 Ibid 243.

171 Ibid.

172 Ibid 402.

173 Ibid 432.

174 Ibid 290. There are even claims that William Shakespeare was not the Author of the plays for which he is known as their author. The name 'Shakespeare' itself is alleged to have been borrowed. See for example, JP Stevens, 'The Shakespeare Canon of Statutory Construction' (1992) 140 *University of Pennsylvania Law Review* 1373.

175 J Gleicher, 'The Bard at the Bar: Some Citations of Shakespeare by the United States Supreme Court' (2001) 26 *Oklahoma City University Law Review* 327. See also JK Joyner, 'Future Technology Clauses: Would Their Lack of Compensation Have Discouraged Shakespeare's Creativity and Denied Society's Access to His Works in New Media?' (2002) 31 *Southwestern University Law Review* 575.

Moreover, Shakespeare, as one commentator argues, must have basic legal knowledge. T Regnier, 'Could Shakespeare Think Like a Lawyer? How Inheritance Law Issues in Hamlet May Shed Light on the Authorship Question' (2003) 57 *University of Miami Law Review* 377, 427-428. Ironically, could it be that the person who wrote Shakespeare was a lawyer, and still demands 'let's kill all the lawyers.' W Shakespeare, The Second Part of King Henry the Sixth, act 2, sc. 2.

> think, to characterize Shakespeare the playwright, though not Shakespeare the author of the sonnets and poems, in a quasi-medieval manner as a reteller of tales.[176]

And Madison questions Shakespeare's originality in the context of authorship:

> In Shakespeare in Love, the screenwriter, Tom Stoppard (with collaborator Marc Norman) uses 'Romeo and Ethel, the Pirate's Daughter' as the working title of the play that becomes 'Romeo and Juliet', not only to mock the notion that Shakespeare composed his plays as a sole "romantic" author but to remind us of the sometimes messy, unplanned, accidental, idiosyncratic nature of creativity and creation. It has been long recognized that Shakespeare borrowed shamelessly, from contemporaries, fellow actors, Anglo-Saxon literature, and Roman historians and playwrights. What we do not know is how purposive or fortuitous this process was. Likewise, in connection with copyright, we do not often ask whether the notion of authorship matters. We know…that authorship shapes the character of copyright law. But does authorship shape what copyright law cares about – the creative work of authorship? [177]

In the definition of 'the public' I include both previous generations of creative geniuses, collaboration with other fellow artists, except the principal creator, and the general public. That is, authors and artists do not create in a social vacuum. They are influenced by special circumstances, collective and personal social and cultural experiences, and other endless untraceable processes. For example, Norwich examines the close relationship between Shakespeare's plays, societal events and characters dominating his period.[178] Likewise, Vickers did not only refer to the individualistic contribution by Shakespeare's fellow dramatists but to the contribution from a community of dramatists and the public at large. He asserts that 'language change has a social dimension…The key point is that linguistic innovations are mostly made by an educated class, responsive to *outside influences and to social change*.'[179] And that examination of authorial collaboration 'allows us to trace the development of knowledge, as each generation of scholars builds on their predecessors' work, correcting and extending it.'[180] There are two parts in this statement, attesting to the unavoidable interplay between the collective and subjective sublimes in copyright creation: first, every dramatist's knowledge is dependent on the contribution of other dramatists and the contribution of the *public* by virtue of being a member of a given social structure; second, the individual dramatist uses the acquired knowledge 'correcting and extending' it in a way that makes *him* eligible to claim recognition of his own authorial contribution.

---

176 M Rose, *Authors and Owners: The Invention of Copyright* (Cambridge Mass.: Harvard University Press, 1993) 25-26. To this Rose mentions two exceptions: the epilogue to *2 Henry IV* and the epilogue to *Henry V*. Ibid. See also ibid 122-123.

177 Madison (n 107 above) 760.

178 JJ Norwich, *Shakespeare's Kings: The Great Plays and the History of England in the Middle Ages: 1337-1485* (London: Scribner, 1999).

179 Vickers (n 159 above) 119 (emphasis added).

180 Ibid 147.

Compositional Ingenuity and Mozart

Contrary to the claim of the romantic composers that their works suddenly sprung whole into consciousness, compositions only gradually take their final form, not without the aid of the collective. It was found that there is a significant correlation between optimal experience and the creative output of student compositions.[181] Mozart was a student in many senses. He, who most of us would consider the ultimate example of a musical genius, was influenced by experiences and his works owe much to other composers.[182]

Mozart's musical 'inventions' were influenced and triggered by many external factors. Besides his extensive travels and ordinary life experiences, masterpieces composed by Mozart are based on musical achievements of others. For example, his three E-flat concertos for French horn were modelled on horn concertos by Antoni Rosetti. His early symphonies written in London (1764-5) mimic the style of Johann Christian Bach.[183] Objective evidence indicates that his compositions did not come to Mozart complete. They are so un-romantic to even bring musicologists who have studied 'Mozart's letter' to conclude that his compositional style is a forgery.[184]

I do not intend to accuse Mozart of unoriginal compositional input, but I certainly believe that his dependence on other sources would prove legitimate to curtail copyright ownership even in today's music industry. Although from a more individualistic approach, Becker takes the example of Mozart and reaffirms that a creative musical composition is a mix of what is already known and resides in the public domain and the subjective contribution of the composer:

> Think of trying to give a complete, transitive casual account of the composition of Mozart's *Don Giovanni* that makes Mozart himself simply an intermediate link. Every note, voicing, key change, or tempo would have to be explained by events 'outside' Mozart. We certainly cannot give such an explanation, and we commonly think none exists – while we can find

181 C Byrne, R MacDonald and L Carlton, 'Assessing Creativity in Musical Compositions: Flow as an Assessment Tool' (2003) 20(3) *British Journal of Music Education* 277. They define 'flow' as 'the effortless involvement with everyday life and may occur when a person is engaged in absorbing and enjoyable activities.' Ibid 279. See also S O'Neill, 'Flow Theory and the Development of Musical Performance Skills' (1999) 141 *Bulletin of the Council for Research in Music Education* 129.

182 E Hertzman, 'Mozart's Creative Process', in PH Lang (ed.), *The Creative World of Mozart* (New York: Norton, 1991) 17.

183 See also Weisberg (n 115 above) 221-230.

184 Ibid 46. The composer Bach is another good example that composition necessitates reliance on others' works and resources. On Bach, Carrell wrote a work entitled *Bach the Borrower*. N Carrell, *Bach the Borrower* (London: George Allen & Unwin, 1967). Borrowing allows the making of variations on existing musical templates, and there are many examples for successful borrowing. For example, Brahms's *Variations on a Theme by Haydn* and Beethoven's *Diabelli Variations*. Weisberg , ibid 230.

> evidence of influences, tendencies, exigencies outside the composer that are part of a full explanation, another substantial part simply begins with Mozart's creative activity.[185]

Artists, composers, poets, all possess the great mastery of artistic, musical or poetic phraseology. They have in themselves the ability to contribute of their own. A composer, for example, 'continues to work exercises in imitation of his models will be surprised to finds that along with the thousand subtleties of technique he will absorb from his masters, he will discover the personal materials of his own art.'[186] As Mozart relates about himself in one of his letters, while rejecting the ideal of originality: 'When I proceed to write down my ideas, I take out of the bag of my memory…But why my productions take from my hand that particular form and style that makes them *Mozartish*, and different from the works of other composers, is probably owing to the same cause which renders my nose so large or so aquiline, or, in short, makes it Mozart's, and different from those of other people. For I really not study or aim at any originality.'[187]

The same method of musical composition holds for different contemporary music styles. For example, composing blues music is complex and relies, to a large extent, on collectively produced social and cultural properties, tradition, and borrowing from others' works. As Vaidhyanathan observes: 'the blues compositional ethic is complex and synergistic, relying on simultaneously exploring and extending the common elements of the tradition. Blues artists are rewarded for punctuation with collaboration, distinction within community, and an ability to touch a body of signs shared among all members of an audience.'[188]

Picasso's Les Demoiselles d'Avignon and Guernica

Picasso's works, as opposed to Shakespeare and Mozart, are protected under the CDPA 1988 until 2043.[189] Two of Picasso's artistic achievements: the paintings *Les Demoiselles d'Avignon* and *Guernica*, are considered by the artistic community, art historians and those who study the psychology of the creative act, to represent a radical departure in art and prime examples of the transcendence of creative thinking in the arts.

---

185 Becker (n 48 above) 614.

186 H Shapero, 'The Music Mind' *Modern Music*, Winter 1946, cited in B Ghiselin (ed.), *The Creative Process: Reflections on Invention in the Arts and Sciences* (Berkeley: University of California Press, 1952) 44.

187 E Holmes, *Life of Mozart* (London: JM Dent Ltd, and New York: EP Dutton, 1912) cited in Ghiselin, ibid 35.

188 S Vaidhynathan, *Copyrights and Copywrongs: The Rise of Intellectual Property and How it Threatens Creativity* (New York and London: New York University Press, 2001) 121.

189 P Picasso (1881-1973).

Picasso painted *Les Demoiselles d'Avignon* in 1907.[190] The grotesque appearance and sexual poses of the five women in the painting (originally part of seven; two men were omitted from the final version) are intended to repel the viewer and perhaps to provide him with some hidden insights into Picasso's sexual life. The women are prostitutes and the setting is the parlour of a brothel in Avignon Street in Barcelona's red-light district. The final painting, which looks totally original, was discovered to embody existing artistic patterns and motifs. X-ray analysis of earlier sketches reveals that two cycles of painting were undertaken.

Picasso's work is still considered radical. The asymmetric faces and bodies of the women were new and unfamiliar to those equipped to evaluate beauty and culture in paintings. The inspiration for the women's oval-shaped faces, with large lozenge-shaped eyes, large scrolled ears, and flat nose came from an exhibition of antique Iberian reliefs held at the Louvre museum in Paris in the spring of 1906 and 'had led him to a greater emancipation from objective appearances.'[191] Two features that particularly struck the attention of the art community were the women's large ears and the flat nose of two demoiselles that stand in the centre of the painting. The source of the ears is two antique statues that Picasso acquired in 1907. The nose, as Picasso himself tells us, was taken from a painting by Henri Matisse which he also obtained in 1907.

The Iberian phase of the painting was reflected in the first cycle. In the second cycle, Picasso modified his work extensively after his visit to an ethnographic museum that displayed works of primitive art. Picasso's *Les Demoiselles d'Avignon* also incorporates features from other artists' paintings and African art and is conceived by art historians as a response to other styles evident at that time.[192] For example, a flat nose was already to be found in Matisse's *Portrait of Marquerite* and distorted bodies were to be found in works by Cézanne and Matisse.[193] A year prior to the completion of *Les Demoiselles d'Avignon*, Matisse painted the *Le Bonheur de Vivre (The Joy of Life)*, the scene is not less sexual than Picasso's brothel. Some consider *Les Demoiselles d'Avignon* to be a negative response to Matisse's painting that portrayed a tranquil scene.

Thirty years after painting *Les Demoiselles d'Avignon*, Picasso painted *Guernica* – 'a cherished museum piece.'[194] The bombing of the Spanish City of Guernica during the Civil War in Spain was the trigger for the painting. This work has become a symbol of the sufferings of the Spanish people under the former dictator, Francisco

190 This case study is discussed in Weisberg (n 115 above) 193-209. See also T Hilton, *Picasso* (London: Thames and Hudson, 1975) 60-93. P Daix, *Picasso: The Cubist Years 1907-1916* (London: Thames and Hudson, 1979) 11-36.

191 Daix, ibid 30.

192 Hilton (n 190 above).

193 So influential were Cézanne and African art on Picasso that six or seven years after completing *Les Demoiselles d'Avignon* he concentrated on Cézanne and African art. Daix (n 190 above) 30.

194 H Marcuse, *Technology, War and Fascism* (London: Routledge, D Kellner ed., 1998) 201. See generally Weisberg (n 115 above) 202-209.

Franco. The symbolic importance of the work was enhanced by Picasso's decision to loan it to the Museum of Modern Art in New York until the time that democracy was restored in Spain. *Guernica* was returned to Spain after forty years in exile and eight years after Picasso's death. The final *Guernica* embodies artistic methods and features from other artists of the time. It has benefited from Picasso's experience of the war and was also influenced by the Spanish artist, Francisco de Goya. This influence is evident from examination of several preliminary sketches of the painting. Furthermore, a research by Fisch affirms that Picasso, in 1937, used a woodcut by Hans Baldung Grien, *The Bewitched Stable-Lad*, as a model for *Guernica* which came to his attention from a catalogue on Fantastic Art Dada Surrealism from the Museum of Modern Art in New York.[195]

A key feature in the copyright making process is continuity between old and new ideas: 'In order to be realistic, creative ideas need to be structured, and that structure needs to have evolved from previously established ideas and principles.'[196] Continuity in Picasso's *Guernica*, Finke observes, is a good example that 'even when a new idea consists of extensive transformations of previous ideas, one should still be able to discover a connective path that links the structures.'[197] Thus, the operation in two cycles of *Les Demoiselles d'Avignon* and the social history of painting *Guernica*, raise the question whether the artist was 'inspired' by the other works or 'copied' them:

> There is a thin dividing line between the meaning of the words 'inspired by' and 'copied from'. Sometimes an artistic work will be said to be the inspiration for a reproduction of that artistic work in for example a film. By virtue of the electronic techniques available these days to activate a picture or bring it alive, sometimes an artistic work is reproduced in such a way that, although it is clear that there has been a reproduction of an artistic work there has also been original contribution from the designer of the film and the argument propounded by the reproducer is that the film was only inspired by, for example, a Picasso painting.[198]

To base this thin line between being 'inspired' by or 'copied' on the availability of techniques is to devalue the role of the public in making and defining such a line. Coombe, for example, also refers to Picasso, but does not emphasise the obvious – the contribution of techniques. She shows that collectively produced entities –

---

195 E Fisch, *Guernica by Picasso* (London and Toronto: Associated University Press, 1988) 103.

196 RA Finke, 'Creative Realism' in Smith, Ward and Finke (n 126 above) 303-326, 304. Gifford, discussing movements in artistic development, writes: 'Despite the evolution of artistic subject matter, the broad-based movements themselves are best understood as a continuous progression of developmental stages reflecting back on earlier periods.' DJ Gifford, 'Innovation and Creativity in the Fine Arts: The Relevance and Irrelevance of Copyright' (2000) 18 *Cardozo Arts & Entertainment Law Journal* 569, 581-582.

197 Finke, ibid 304.

198 R Innocent, 'Copyright Problems as Experienced by Visual Artists' (1988) 10(7) *European Intellectual Property Review* 203, 204.

such as cultural elements produced for social reasons were borrowed by Picasso, and found their way to his paintings and became part of his personality: 'When a primitive statue, produced in a collectivity for social reasons, makes its way into a Picasso painting, the statue itself may still embody the identity of the culture from which it sprang, but any reproduction of it is legally recognized as the embodiment of Picasso's authorial personality.'[199] But, should legal recognition entail exclusive rights in cultural products? Ignoring the contribution of collective properties for the creation of art, by the copyright community, borders on absurdity: the law isolates the person from the social and cultural context and rewards it for giving the world an original object.

There is a story about Picasso who was interviewed in his maturity and asked why did he spend so much time on imitating the style of great masters of art: 'If I had not imitated them' he answered 'I would have to spend the rest of my life imitating myself.'[200] In another interview he remarks that '[a]t the beginning of each picture there is someone who works with me. Towards the *end* I have the impression of having worked without a collaborator.'[201] Picasso undoubtedly ventured beyond the works of his predecessors 'but even he recognised that without mastering the best achievements of a domain, one is left only with one's naked talents, having to reinvent the wheel without tools'.[202]

Chance Creations and Indeterminate Art

A still open question is whether 'chance creations' or randomly-generated works are subject to the critique I presented above. Our artistic traditions are reflective of a broad spectrum of tastes and attitudes towards art and what it should be. English copyright law does not embrace a qualitative test for authorship and leaves the question whether a given work constitutes art, or whether it is sufficiently creative to merit copyright protection, to the audience. It is beyond the scope of the present book to discuss whether the quantification of creative content should become a threshold for copyright protection. But an intriguing question that deserves some attention is whether anyone can claim an indeterminate work to negate the argument on social dependence and lack significant causal connection to collectively produced and owned properties?

199 Coombe 1998 (n 5 above) 225.

200 From 'Conversation avec Picasso' by C Zevros in *Cahiers d'Art*, 1935, in Ghiselin (n 186 above) 50.

201 Ibid.

202 Csikszentmihalyi (n 126 above) 421-422.

Arp and Duchamp are noted Dadaist artists.[203] Arp is known for collages arranged by the 'law of chance'.[204] He attempts to create *without-sense* – a 'flight into the Romantic or mystical model which functions as an alternative, as a utopia promising a release from the unstable and unsatisfactory present.'[205] Being unsatisfied with his inability to produce a drawing to his liking, Arp tore paper into small pieces allowing them to fall onto canvas and attaching them where they fall. He then saw the composition he wanted to draw in the chance arrangement of the scraps. He also composed poems by the principle of chance. He randomly chose words and phrases mainly taken from newspapers. Duchamp, like Arp, is famous for his 'chance operations'. Duchamp 'use[s] the confusion of modernity as a way of sweeping away the old structures'.[206] In one instance he allowed dust to settle on the glass for several months, and after being photographed, was wiped off everywhere but the cone areas where it was affixed with glue and made part of the work.[207]

Arp and Duchamp created collages by the principle of chance, which 'allows itself to be easily combined with the Dada concern with everyday life and media, creating an art of chaotic juxtapositions.'[208] Indubitably, the chaotic collages made by Arp and Duchamp went beyond what was already known. But, is there any noticeable role for collectively produced social and cultural properties in collages made by the principle of chance? Pegrum observes that the Dada style is a postmodern reaction to modernity. Duchamp, for example, 'challenges utilitarianism via his ready-mades such as the bicycle wheel, which represents a very old and very basic machine, now transposed into the aesthetic sphere and thus rendered completely useless in terms of its original purpose.'[209] Although it looks as if Dadaists are purely pro-chaos in the name of liberty, Arp 'accepts chaos but at the locus of a higher order and meaning, which effectively amounts to a rejection of the unstructured and meaningless nature of that chaos.'[210] That does not mean that the Dadaist reaction is created in isolation from the contribution of the collective.

Pegrum observes that there is an unavoidable link between postmodernism and Romanticism and the former may even seem an extension of the Romantic cultural stream. If this is so, '[i]s postmodernism in effect a radicalised version of the

203 See generally FM Naumann, *Making Mischief: Dada Invades New York* (Whitney Museum of Art: Harry N Abrams, 1996); and MA Pegrum, *Challenging Modernity: Dada Between Modern and Postmodern* (New York and Oxford: Berghahn Books, 2000). For a brief definition of the Dada art see Pegrum, ibid 309-311. See also Durham (n 7 above) 596-608.

204 Pegrum, ibid 245-249. See also J Hancock, 'Arp's Chance Collages', in SC Foster (ed.) *Dada/Dimensions* (Ann Arbor, MI: UMI Research Press, 1985) cited in Durham, ibid 597.

205 Pegrum, ibid 35, 39.

206 Ibid 100.

207 Durham (n 7 above) 599; Pegrum, ibid 246.

208 Pegrum (n 203 above) 246.

209 Ibid. 98.

210 Ibid 99.

Romantic assault on modernity? And what of Dada's relation to Romanticism?'[211] Pegrum, believes that the Dadaist is a 'daffier version of the lonely romantic rebel'.[212] That is, the reaction to the external culture and social reality define the creative act in both streams. Arp does not negate the beauty of accidental art but remarks that even in the case of accidental art, the artist has still to be attentive to external influences: 'accidents alone could not produce art; art required the imprint of human aspirations.'[213]

Arp and Duchamp, unquestionably express their personalities through their revolutionary works and display a high degree of imagination. That is, even if indeterminate works created in a random fashion – the kind of works that the courts may seem most reluctant to consider original – they can never be created in isolation from the contribution of the collective. They react against certain attitudes of the public and as such the raw materials they use are but collectively produced symbols and character and other cultural and social properties. One may even raise the objection, that a chaotic reaction against the status quo fails to satisfy the requirement of skill and labour, let alone creativity, where this is required. However, as Durham remarks, 'the random element serves as a counterpart, in many aspects, to the personal element contributed by an author's imagination.'[214]

Weisberg asserts that, 'for a product to be called creative, it must be the novel result of goal-directed activity; novelty brought about by accident would not qualify as creative, no matter how valuable the outcome'.[215] English copyright law does not require creativity or a goal-orientation. It allows accidental art to flourish and permits wide discretion in defining what art is, as long as the given work has authorial origins. Under English copyright law the works of Arp and Duchamp can be protected, irrespective of artistic quality, if each qualifies as, for example, a collage.[216] The addition of 'collage' to the CDPA 1988, Kearns asserts, 'accommodates non-motional visual art that may contain *pre-created material* by another but is so *originally arranged* as to gain its own copyright protection'.[217] Arguably, if a chance creation resulted in a collage which by any means is a complex artistic work, the work seems either more dependent on multiple, seemingly unrelated, sources, and thus more vulnerable to my arguments on the dependence on the public, or an extraordinary achievement. Either way, the works originated in an author and probably involves artistic skill, labour and judgement. In fact, the many reproductions made of the

---

211 Ibid 100.

212 Ibid, citing F Busi, *Dada and the "Trial" of Maurice Barrès* (1975) 64.

213 Durham (n 7 above) 597, n 168.

214 Ibid 633.

215 Weisberg (n 115 above) 244-245. He then offers 'assessment by members of the field.' Ibid 246.

216 CDPA 1988 s 4(1)(a).

217 P Kearns, *The Legal Concept of Art* (Oxford: Hart Publishing, 1998) 78.

works by Arp and Duchamp, revive the truth in Peterson's J maxim that 'what is worth copying is worth protecting.'[218]

Chance creations may satisfy the condition of originality, but how much can we stretch the condition? Take the example of photographs taken by sheer happenstance, but which have an incredible historic and social value. Photographs taken by Kampler of the late Prime Minister Rabin in late 1995 at the peace demonstration prior to his assassination, or by Zapruder of the assassination of the late President Kennedy, are still protected under copyright. The latter case was tested in Court.[219] Zapruder, a Dallas dress manufacturer and amateur photographer, was present by 'sheer happenstance' at the scene of the assassination of President Kennedy, and filmed it with his camera. For the same reason that the photo of Oscar Wilde was found entirely representative of the photographer's 'original mental conception',[220] Zapruder's work is still protected under copyright.[221] Zapruder had no idea prior to filming the event.[222] However, positioning the camera can be constructed as a 'mental conception' just as randomly choosing materials for a collage or accidentally choosing keys on a music dice game. In the case of Zapruder there is almost absolute reliance on the public whether by virtue of possessing photographic skills or merely the event itself and its surroundings. This is a dramatic example of copyright protection in the category of nonartistic and noncreative works that receives protection, an example that illustrates that sometimes nothing, except minimal manual labour, is sufficient for copyright protection. Whether happenstance and serendipity, judgement of merits, or a quality-based test, none negates the sociality of the copyright creation process or discredits its dependence on collectively produced cultural and social properties.

'Revision' as a Label

Many terms might be possible candidates for a more suitable label to characterise copyright creation: for example, 'imitation' or 'repetition'.[223] In *Revision and*

218 *University of London Press v University Tutorial Press* [1916] 2 Ch 601, 608. Durham holds the view that the works of Arp and Duchamp qualify for the post-Feist definition of originality, ie, they represent a modicum of creativity. Durham (n 7 above) 638.

219 *Time Inc v Bernard Geis Associates* 293 F Supp 130 (SDNY 1968).

220 *Burrow-Giles Lithographic Co v Sarony* 111 US 53, 60 (1884).

221 Arguable a post-*Feist* Zapruder might not qualify to the now discredited 'sweat of the brow' principle.

222 Zapruder and Kampler would enjoy protection under the CDPA. See CDPA 1988 s 4(1)(a) and s 4(2).

223 One repeats his predecessors, but in a way that adds a new dimension and hence results in a new work. In his criticism on the notion of creativity Osborne remarks that works of art involve repetition. Not repetition of the same activity, same object or specific theme, not repetition just for seeking an answer to something but of locating, deepening, embellishing a *problem*: 'in painting Chardin's repeated focusing on a few grapes, Giorgio Morandi's endless little bottles arranged and re-arranged on a shelf…' T Osborne, 'Against 'Creativity': A

Romantic Authorship Leader strongly rejects the romantic notions of authors and poets as solitary geniuses.[224] Leader takes the revision rather than the original drafting of authorial works as the organising principle of his work. He claims that 'the writings of the Romantic period (*as of all periods*) is a product of a network of literary and social relations, one in which the nominal author's contribution and authority are dominant but not exclusive. Even when fiercely professing independence, the author typically draws on a range of personal and institutional collaborators, including family, friends, publishers, reviewers and readers.'[225] Although Leader does not take the initial creative process as the paradigm of his analysis, he rejects any romantic understanding of subsequent revisions as a solitary artistic expression and questions the credibility of the romantic view of poetry as the result of a spontaneous and illogical process.[226] In defence of his argument, Leader uses examples of prose and poetry by Wordsworth, Byron and Coleridge, Shelley's novel *Frankestein*, and John Clare's poems revised by his publisher John Taylor, the poet Keats and others.

Leader does not randomly choose Coleridge as a case study. Coleridge had a clear conception of authorship, which excludes external stimuli or social contributions. Many contemporary authors would identify themselves with this view and get the support of copyright law in enforcing it. Hofkosh observes that Coleridge held a decidedly subjective view of authorship and authorial rights: 'the rationale regarding the author's natural right to own and to profit from his literary labour registers the stake the writer has in choosing "what an author means" for himself.'[227] Hofkosh continues by remarking that

> [A]uthorship in Coleridge's ideal description enacts a self-fulfilling economy, an organic circulation, in which value accrues to individuality within a naturally closed system without substantial change or exchange: no risk, no excess, nothing for which the author cannot himself account. Literary property is in this way crucially distinguished from "all other property" and the author from "ribbon-weavers, calico-printers, cabinet-makers and china-manufacturers" insofar as *what the author produces is the inalienable stuff of his own subjectivity*.[228]

Philistine Rant' (2003) 32(4) *Economy and Society* 507, 520. He rejects the idea of creativity and suggests that in order to liberate us from the 'potentially moronic consequences of the doctrine of creativity' a 'replacement by the more general…idea of inventiveness' is needed. Ibid 507, 523. He justifies his view with interestingly placing inventiveness as a 'more anonymous, more collective, more processual than the rather heroizing, romanticist notion of creativity'. Ibid 520.

224 Z Leader, *Revision and Romantic Authorship* (Oxford: Clarendon Press, 1996).

225 Ibid 15 (emphasis added).

226 Arguably, chance creations and indeterminate works might not qualify for Leader's label. However, they, in other words, revise what they have experienced, and in this way go beyond what is already known.

227 S Hofkosh, *Sexual Politics and the Romantic Author* (Cambridge: Cambridge University Press, 1998)15.

228 Ibid (emphasise added). Stillinger argues that Coleridge's concept of a stable text by his continuous revising suggests that 'the perfect poem was a chimera and that authority itself

For Leader 'the prose method itself implies the impossibility of ever controlling one's words, or freeing oneself from others' words, an impossibility that helps account for Coleridge's obsessive revisions.'[229] He observes a 'distinction between internally imposed revisions, whether a product of unconscious compulsions or matters of conscious convictions, and revisions of external origin, in involving the writer's personal and institutional affiliations…Wordsworth and Coleridge revised in *response to external as well as internal pressures*, as did Keats and Clare.'[230] Elsewhere in the work, he forcefully asserts that, Coleridge's poems 'directly question the autonomy of the self, language, 'possession' (that is, 'owning' or authorship of one's writing).'[231]

Leader closes his work with this revealing statement: 'What studying such revisions reveals is the inadequacy or incompleteness of the Romantic view: none of the writers discussed in this book fits the stereotype most of them helped construct. The spontaneous, extemporizing, otherworldly, autonomous author, the Romantic author, is a fiction much in need of revision…'[232] Throughout his study he never devalues the fact that a vital source of poetic inspiration is external stimuli, social and cultural ideals and collectively created and owned properties, and reminds us that even authorial revision, is not a solitary activity. It 'derives in part from external sources, is a 'collaborative' enterprise involving not only friends and publishers… but the *public* itself…'[233]

was therefore a fiction. He may, that is to say, have been…a deconstructionist'. Stillinger (n 2 above) 138, 146. See also Weisberg (n 115 above) 46.

229 Leader (n 224 above) 136.

230 Ibid 16 (emphasis added).

231 Ibid 137.

232 Ibid 315.

233 Ibid 263 (emphasis added).

Chapter 5

Subjects of Copyright and Social Construction

The Social Construction of 'Whats'

The Argument

A statement like 'copyright is a social construction' follows from the thesis of the authorial collectivity. This statement, however, sounds trivial or banal. No one would possibly deny that the institution of copyright is premised on centuries of legal, social, and historical events, as well as artistic attitudes, cultural traditions and conflicting economic aspirations. If indeed all agree on the social and historical construction of the institution of copyright, is there any reason to discuss this statement? It depends on how it is interpreted.

Although no copyright scholar would deny that copyright, as a legal institution, is a creature of historical events and social and cultural processes, some would, as law and literature show, deny that the subjects of copyright, for example authors as a species of person and original works of authorship and the arts as a classification of entities, are social constructs. When we refer to the romantic vision of copyright, we refer precisely to this kind of denial: 'I am the author. I created something new, almost equivalent to ex nihilo creation; independent of social conditions, and I therefore deserve an exclusive right to control the whole product created.' I have already argued that it is not enough to recognise the sociality of the copyright creation act. Mere recognition amounts to rejection of the many implications of copyright's social nature. The danger inherent in this tendency dominates our copyright landscape.

Social constructionists hold that items we had thought were inevitable are social products. Because of its many admirers, the social construction talk is open to scepticism and criticism.[1] Social construction was once considered as a 'liberating

1 The social construction debate is applied to many different fields: from race and ethnic identity to scientific facts, from oral history to reality and Zulu nationalism, knowledge, statistics, serial homicide, satellite systems and authorship. See for example, P Berger and T Luckmann, *The Social Construction of Reality: A Treatise in the Sociology of Knowledge* (New York: Anchor Books, 1966); J Coulter, *The Social Construction of Mind* (London and Basingstoke: Macmillan, 1979); D Golan, *Inventing Shaka: Using History in the Construction of Zulu Nationalism* (Boulder: L Rienner 1994); J Ferrante-Wallace and Brown P, *The Social Construction of Race and Ethnicity in the United States* (New York: Longman, 1998); M Woodmansee and P Jaszi (eds.), *The Construction of Authorship* (Durham and London: Duke

idea'[2] – almost a 'code';[3] but it has become a banal statement of social conditions and obvious facts.[4] This has become the norm in discussions of copyright and authorship: accepting, without qualification, that our institution of copyright is the product of historical events and social processes. So, what could possibly account for the excitement in contending that copyright is socially constructed? This is the answer. Because intellectual property laws control our social and cultural realities, an examination of the interrelationships between intellectual properties and the social environment is a way of approaching questions about the scope of property in works protected under intellectual property laws and exploring the influence of those laws upon the social environment which they control.[5]

In copyright, as in any other legal institution, there are many elements that can be said to be socially constructed. In fact, there can be almost an endless list of entities to which the question 'what is socially constructed' may apply. As Hacking puts it: '"the social construction of what?" need not have a single answer. That causes a lot of problems in constructionist debates. People talk at cross purposes because they have different "whats" in mind. Yet it is precisely the interaction between different "whats"

University Press, 1994); F Wilmer, *Social Construction of Man, the State and War* (Taylor & Francis Books Ltd Routledge, 2002).

2 Social constructionism is defined as: 'Analysis of 'knowledge' or 'reality' or both as contingent upon social relations, and as made out of continuing human practices, by process such as reification, sedimentation, habitualization', in T Honderich (ed.), *The Oxford Companion to Philosophy* (Oxford: Oxford University Press, 1995) 829.

3 I Hacking, *The Social Construction of What?* (Cambridge Mass.: Harvard University Press, 1999) vii.

4 From having an 'excellent shock value…it has become tired.' Ibid 35. Hacking concludes that he is not very much in favour of the language of social construction. Ibid 122.

Restating social conditions is not what social constructionism is about. For example, Gumperz argues that the basis of every possible intellectual achievement – literacy, is socially constructed. She merely advocates a social perspective on literacy and its acquisition and reaches the conclusion that literacy is a social process of demonstrating knowledgability. See J Cook-Gumperz (ed.), *The Social Construction of Literacy* (Cambridge University Press, 1986). Hacking criticises the book as representing a mere 'social perspective 'on an aspect of literacy.' Ibid 35.

5 Social construction, if interpreted and viewed properly, can add to our armoury against the current state of affairs in copyright. Indeed, as Hacking writes, '[o]ne of the attractions of 'construction' has been the association with radical political attitudes, stretching from bemused irony and angry unmasking up to reform, rebellion, and revolution. The use of the word declares what side one is on.' Hacking (n 3 above) 35. Hacking also mentions the possible division between left and right-wing politics in the context of constructionism. Although he finds it confusing, he remarks that 'constructionists are properly put on the left. Their political attitude is nevertheless very much not in harmony with those scientists who see themselves as allies of the oppressed, but also feel like the special guardians of the most important truths about the world, the true bastions of objectivity.' Ibid 95.

that makes the topic interesting…And confusing…'[6] The 'whats' I examined in the above discussion of authorial collectivity are two main items: the author as a kind of a person and original works of authorship and art as a classification of entities. My main argument holds that only if original works were *not* socially constructed could there be any good argument for assigning their authors exclusive rights in them.

A preliminary question is whether universal social constructionism is coherent. Haslanger notes that one occasionally encounters the claim that everything is socially constructed 'all the way down.'[7] In that respect Hacking observes that most constructionism is not universal: 'The authors who contribute books for my alphabetical list of topics, from authorship to Zulu nationalism, were making specific and local claims. What would be the point of arguing that danger, or the woman refugee, is socially constructed, if you thought that everything is socially constructed?'[8] That is the spirit in which we should interpret social constructionism in copyright, for instance, among those who find it important enough to *explicitly* reiterate that copyright is 'socially constructed and historically contingent'[9] or that the law 'like a novel or a poem, has an author and hence is just a social construction.'[10]

There is a tacit agreement that artists and authors build on traditions developed by and efforts of those who came before us; on collectively produced and owned social and cultural properties. In one of her recent works, Gordon reminds us what copyright scholars such as, Drahos, Jaszi, Woodmansee, Litman, Rose, Boyle, Netanel, Coombe, herself and many others, have argued for many years: that copyright norms in today's legal environment under-value the 'gift all artists receive, namely, a tradition and world they have not made.'[11] However, it is one thing to examine how a given entity is constructed and another to analyse the implications arising from this examination.

Social constructionism is therefore an invaluable explanatory tool in copyright's present state of affairs, because prevailing theories and approaches to intellectual

---

6 Hacking (n 3 above) 28. Yet 'what is confused is sometimes more useful that what has been clarified.' Ibid 29.

7 S Haslanger, 'Ontology and Social Construction' (1995) 23 *Philosophical Topics* 127, 128.

8 Hacking (n 3 above) 24. Hacking rejects universal constructionism in many different junctures of his book. He also writes that '[a]n all-encompassing constructionist approach has become rather dull – in both senses of the word, boring and blunted.' Ibid 35. Similarly, Gergen and Gergen contend that the 'anything goes' argument in social constructionism is wrong and based on 'misunderstanding or ignorance of constructionist ideas.' M Gergen and KJ Gergen, (eds.), *Social Construction: A Reader* (London: Sage Publications, 2003) 228. See also the discussion on 'Constructionism in Question.' Ibid 227-254.

9 J Boyle, *Shamans, Software and Spleens* (Cambridge Mass.: Harvard University Press, 1996) 114.

10 S Ghosh, 'Copyright as Privatization: The Case of Model Codes' (2004) 78 *Tulane Law Review* 653, 657.

11 WJ Gordon, 'Render Copyright unto Caesar: On Taking Incentives Seriously' (2004) 71(1) *The University of Chicago Law Review* 75, 77.

property do not yet fully address how and why the role of the authorial collectivity is consistently denied in the copyright realm. In previous chapters I provided examples from law and literature which show that copyrighted entities are manifestations of the authorial collectivity and support the conclusion that authors and copyrighted entities are socially constructed. Here my attempt is to posit the ramifications and consequences of my discussion of authorial collectivity within the matrix of the social construction debate.

Hacking's Formula

In *The Social Construction of What?* Hacking examines when and why we should refer to social constructionism.[12] He offers a schema for evaluating different social constructionist claims. Socially constructed entities are products of historical events, social forces and ideology.[13] Thus, 'by *constructionism* (or social constructionism if we need, on occasion, to emphasize the social) I shall mean various sociological, historical, and philosophical projects that aim at displaying or analysing actual, historically situated, social interactions or casual routes that led to, or were involved in, the coming into being or establishing of some present entity or fact.'[14]

In general, the social constructionist attempts to criticise the status quo. He may examine 'the social construction of idea *X*, of *X*, of the experience of being *X*, and so on, and how these interact with each other.'[15] Hacking's test of social constructionism is composed of four steps: one precondition and three primary conditions. The precondition stipulates that '[p]eople begin to argue that *X* is socially constructed precisely when they find that: (0) In the present state of affairs *X* is taken for granted, *X* appears to be inevitable.'[16] According to Hacking, precondition (0) would not hold for the institution of copyright, because 'institutions are the result of historical events and social processes.'[17] It is obvious that our prevalent copyright regime was *not* inevitable: it is the contingent upshot of historical events and social processes. On this account, copyright – the legal institution, fails to satisfy precondition (0). The precondition, however, does hold for certain ideas of *subjects* of copyright, such as authors and original works of art and authorship, since ideas, Hacking argues, 'with many of their connotations, seem inevitable.'[18] From court decisions to academic writings and daily practice, authors and original works are taken for granted. They appear to be inevitable, when in fact they are not. Once these ideas are found to be taken as inevitable the social constructionist can move to examine the three primary conditions. These conditions explain the very essence of Hacking's formula:

12 Hacking (n 3 above).
13 Ibid 2.
14 Ibid 48.
15 Ibid 123.
16 Ibid 12.
17 Ibid.
18 Ibid 14.

Social construction work, in other words, is critical of the status quo. Social constructionists about *X* tend to hold that

> *(1)* *X* need not have existed, or need not be at all as it is. *X*, or *X* as it is at present, is not determined by the nature of things; it is not inevitable.
>
> Very often [constructionists] go further, and urge that
>
> *(2)* *X* is quite bad as it is.
> (3) We would be much better off if *X* were done away with, or at least radically transformed.
>
> A thesis of type (1) is the starting point: the existence or character of *X* is not determined by the nature of things. *X* is not inevitable. *X* was brought into existence or shaped by social events, forces, history, all of which could well have been different. Many social construction theses at once advance to (2) and (3), but they need not do so. One may realise that something, which seems inevitable in the present state of things, was not inevitable, and yet is not thereby a bad thing. But most people who use the social construction idea enthusiastically want to criticise, change or destroy some *X* that they dislike in the established order of things. [19]

For Hacking, *X* ranges over many different kinds of things. In order to avoid confusion he suggests that we distinguish between *ideas* (eg, concepts, beliefs, theories, and classifications)[20] and *objects* (eg, people (children), states (childhood), institutions, quarks, and child viewer).[21] Common to all these items, is that the *X* need not have been 'at all as it is.' *X* is a creature of causation, social and historical processes. After all, as Hacking remarks, all 'construction stories are histories.'[22]

In order to assess the reason for applying a social constructionist approach to *X*, it is crucial to ask how obvious is the claim that '*X* is a social construct.' Hacking says that if it is utterly obvious to everyone that *X* satisfies proposition (1), then we should not bother using the language of social construction. On this account, battered women, for example, are considered social constructions. When *X* = battered women, steps (1), (2) and (3) are utterly obvious: they are the result of social forces such as domestic violence and a weak legal system; they are not determined by the nature of things; no one, except maybe ancient barbarian societies, would deny that a battered woman is a 'bad thing'; society would be better off if violence against women was totally outlawed and abandoned. Similarly, when *X* = authors, we can see that *X* satisfies proposition (1). Authors are not determined by the nature of things, i.e., when *X* = authors, *X* need not have been 'at all as it is'; social constructionists would argue that authors are wrongly perceived as almighty creators; and *X* has to be redefined and transformed.

19 Ibid 6-7.
20 Ibid 22.
21 Ibid 21-22.
22 Ibid 37, 48.

The same argument holds for institutions. For example, when *X* = the institution of copyright, propositions (1), (2) and (3) are painfully obvious. I doubt anyone would reject the argument that copyright is highly contingent; a 'bad thing' as it stands today (either from the point of view of authors and entertainment industries ('we want more control') or from the perspective of the public interest ('copyright went too far')); [23] and it should, as I will argue, not be abolished, but radically transformed. If it is utterly obvious that authors, and the institution of copyright are socially constructed, that they are 'the contingent upshot of social arrangements',[24] what is the added-value in discussing the social construction of authors or copyright? Hacking's reply to this question is that we ought to be attentive to the context.[25] According to his account, it is not the author or the institution of copyright that are socially constructed, but rather the classifications of what copyright, the system, protects. Then, *X* in copyright (for purposes of the present analysis) = (i) *authors* as a specific *kind* of a person; and (ii) *original works of art and authorship*; or as Hacking might say, the *ideas* of (i) and (ii).[26]

Hacking asserts that '[w]hat is socially constructed is not, in the first instance, the individual people',[27] for example, authors. It is the classification 'authors': 'The classification itself, and the matrix within which the classification works.'[28] An author, as a specific *kind* of person, is what matters for social construction discourse. We should not understand *X* to mean every individual, but the individual falling under the idea –individual qua 'author' of a work is a social construction. Classifying a given work as original, or a person as an author, is a product of social events and historical processes, cultural traditions and conflicts, artistic revolutions, and legislative developments that have and continue to shape the nature of art, authorship and their makers. The *X* in copyright – authors and original works, is changed by being so classified. Without this *X*, copyright would have become an

23 Here I should be more careful and accept the fact that some people may agree with proposition (2) claiming, for example, that the existing copyright system provides a coherent balance between the rights of authors and the public interest. They may point to the fact that we do not have perpetual copyright or an open-ended list of exclusive rights. However, I was hard put to find committed partisans of the status quo. Why does copyright attract so much academic interest? Why does almost every layman have a take on copyright? The reason is because we do not agree on proposition (2): the majority of us would agree that it is a bad thing, whether from the perspective of the author and the industry or the general public interest.

24 Hacking (n 3 above) 12.

25 Ibid 9.

26 Ibid 10-11. Hacking uses authorship as an item relevant to the social construction talk and refers to authors as kinds of people. Ibid 33-34, 58.

27 Ibid 9-10.

28 Ibid 11.

empty statement; a meaningless legal principle.[29] That is, we have to know what we want to ask:

> Think what the category of genius did to those Romantics who saw themselves as geniuses, and what their behavior did in turn to the category of genius itself…If someone talks about the social construction of genius…they are likely talking about the idea, the individuals falling under the idea, the interaction between the idea and the people, and the manifold of social practices and institutions that these interactions involve: the matrix, in short.[30]

Hacking contends that we can incorporate social construction talk into our daily discourse on a variety of issues, but not wholesale.[31] It would be banal to write a book entitled *The Social Construction of the European Trade Mark Office in Alicante* which is an institution developed from social and political changes in Europe; from the growing commercial sentiment to brand names and sources and from developments in consumer preferences; and recently changed due to the enlargement of the Union. This title would not satisfy precondition (0). But we can imagine a startling title on *The Social Construction of Trade Marks* addressing the question 'who authors trademarks?' emphasising that trademarks are linguistic inventions produced in the marketplace, by consumers, and examining the consumer as a kind of person.

Hacking distinguishes between idea-construction and object-construction. Although any such distinction between ideas and objects seems vague, it may help

29 Hacking's thesis can be clarified by his explanation of process and products. Hacking writes: 'Construction stories are histories, but to insist on only that angle is to miss the point. Constructionists about *X* usually hold that *X* need not have existed, or need not be at all like it is. Some urge that *X* is quite bad, as it is, and even that we would be better if *X* were done away with, or at least radically transformed. *X*, the product, is the focus of attention, although, as I have explained, it is usually not *X*, the thing teenage pregnancy, but the idea of *X*, the idea of teenage pregnancy, and the matrices in which the idea has life. If we overhear someone say, "And I am a social construction", we know that it is the person as product who is in question, a person who has been constructed by a social process, that person's life history. Process and products are both part of arguments about construction. The constructionist argues that the product is not inevitable by showing how it came into being (historical process), and noting the purely contingent historical determinants of that process.' Ibid 37-38.

30 Ibid 34.

31 A good example of Hacking's application of social constructionism pertains to science. He argues that on the one hand, the 'constructionist holds that explanations for the stability of scientific belief involve, at least in part, elements that are external to the professed content of the science. These elements typically include social factors, interests, networks, or however they be described.' Ibid 92.

On the other hand 'opponents hold that whatever be the context of discovery, the explanation of stability is internal to the science itself.' Ibid. The latter regards scientists as a special social stratum; as discoverers and proprietors of ultimate truths; as 'the deep probers of the inner constitution of things.' Ibid 95. In light of the discussion on the authorial collectivity, authors, artists, dramatists and choreographers are not different from scientists.

determine when we should use the language of social construction.[32] Some objects, on Hacking's account, are socially constructed, while others are not. In particular, Hacking is concerned with certain kinds. For example, women refugees and child viewer. A main feature in his argument is the concept of 'interactive kinds.'[33] An author is an interactive kind. An author interacts with similar kinds, for example, authors and artists, with individuals falling under other categories and with the different categories themselves.[34] Hacking gives as an example the difference between quarks and children. The former is an indifferent kind.[35] Quarks are the building blocks of the universe: 'Quarks are not aware that they are quarks and are not altered simply by being classified as quarks.'[36] An interactive kind is aware of its classification and through this awareness he maintains its identity as a member of this classification. This awareness 'may be personal, but more commonly is an awareness shared and developed within a group of people, embedded in practices and institutions to which they are assigned in virtue of the way in which they are

32 Ibid 102. 'When someone speaks of the social construction of *X*, you have to ask, *X*= what? A first move is to distinguish between objects, ideas, and the items' names by elevator words such as "fact", "truth", and "reality".' Ibid 68. See also ibid 10-11, 14, 21-22, 28-30. 'Elevator words' are words such as fact, truth, reality, and knowledge. 'These words are used to say something about the world, or about what we say or think about the world.' Ibid 23. Following his rejection of universal social constructionism Hacking criticises discussions on the social construction of 'elevator words.' For example, with regards to reality he remarks that the social construction of reality 'sound like the social construction of everything.' Ibid 24.

33 Ibid 32, 102-105.

34 Hacking terms this the 'looping effect.' It occurs when people, such as authors and artists, interact with the systems of classification they fall under. In Hacking's words: 'People classified in a certain way tend to conform to or grow into the ways that they are described; but they also evolve in their own ways so that the classifications and descriptions have to be constantly revised.' I Hacking, *Rewriting the Soul: Multiple Personality and the Sciences of Memory* (Princeton: Princeton University Press, 1995) 21. See also by the same author, 'The Looping Effects of Human Kinds' in D Sperber (ed.), *Causal Cognition* (New York: Clarendon Press, 1995).

In this way Hacking explains the social evolution of knowledge of human kinds. He writes that looping effects mark 'a cardinal difference between the traditional natural and social sciences' because 'the targets of natural sciences are stationary' while 'the targets of the social sciences are on the move.' Hacking (n 3 above) 108.

35 Ibid 104-106.

36 Ibid 32. Can quarks be socially constructed? Hacking asserts that: 'Perhaps it is the idea of quarks, rather than quarks, which is the social construction. Both the process of discovering quarks and the product, the concept of the quark and its physical applications, interest historians of science…All these ideas have histories, as does any idea, and they have different types of history, including social histories. But quarks, the objects themselves, are not constructs, are not social, and are not historical.' Ibid 30, 68-70. Indeed, in *What is History*, one of Carr's main themes is that every idea has a history. History, he asserts, cannot be examined in isolation from the past, and from the social forces that influence and shape its inner structure and value. EH Carr, *What is History* (New York: Vintage Books 1961).

classified.'[37] It is an awareness that operates within a 'larger matrix of institutions and practices surrounding this classification.'[38] So, the classification or idea of 'authors' takes place within a matrix of social institutions that shape and control the future evolution of individual authors and artists. In this way, the author, as a certain kind of person, is socially constructed.[39] Hacking takes the example of authorship and argues that it is built around kinds of people, such as authors:

> People of these kinds can become aware that they are classified as such. They can make tacit or even explicit choices, adapt or adopt ways of living so as to fit or get away from the very classification that may be applied to them. These very choices, adaptations or adoptions have consequences for the very group, for the kind of people that is invoked. The result may be particularly strong interactions. What is known about people of a kind may become false because people of that kind have changed in virtue of what they believe about themselves.[40]

Authors and artists may become aware that they are classified as such. They work and create within a matrix of social and political institutions that affect the very essence of the classification. They make artistic choices, and copyright law accommodates these choices. These artistic choices have consequences for the very group. Strong interactions between people of this kind are inevitable. Artistic and authorial activities are dependent on interaction. Despite her criticism of the limited applicability of Hacking's formula, Haslanger writes that 'ideas and objects interact in complex ways and transform each other over time. Broadly speaking, social construction is about this complex interaction...it may appear that social construction is all about causation...'[41] Copyright is a prime example of an institution in which the very existence of its subjects, authors and original works, are dependent on complex interaction and causation.[42] The discussion of the authorial collectivity reaffirms that interaction between authors, artists and the influences of the matrix in which they

---

37 Hacking, ibid 104.

38 Ibid 21-32, 103.

39 Ibid 11.

40 Ibid 34.

41 S Haslanger, 'Social Construction: The "Debunking" Project', in FF Schmitt (ed.), *Socializing Metaphysics: The Nature of Social Reality* (Lanham, MD: Rowman and Littlefield, 2003) 301, 315.

42 Social constructionists claim many social conditions to be crucial for our creative make-up and affect our ability to interact in society. Language is one of these items. Gergen and Gergen write: 'If we favour constructionist view of social life, we are immediately drawn to the importance of language. It is through language that we create the sense of the real and the good, that we create our histories and our destinies.' Gergen and Gergen (n 8 above). Another item is meaning. Gergen does not object to the idea that a person can have his own meaning of certain words and events but viewing meaning as a pure individualistic trait presents a riddle: if 'ultimate meanings' are private, how can we ever know what others mean? Gergen finds the answer in that meanings emerge from social practice and hence are socially constructed. KJ Gergen, 'Meaning in Relationship' in Gergen and Gergen, ibid 148-155.

create, define the creative act and determine the success of its results. Copyright law embraces concepts like originality and creativity, which were and still are created via false beliefs about what authors and artists can really do. As I argue in Chapters 1 and 4, authors and artists, supported by the Courts and policy makers, believe they create in a social vacuum, without the contribution of the public. They do not acknowledge the matrix. In this way, false beliefs about authorship are nurtured and eventually find their way as dominant features in our copyright culture. If we want to see a change in copyright we have to understand the classification of authors and artists and what it consists of.

The institution of copyright fails precondition (0). No one would possibly deny that it is not inevitable. However, contemporary classifications and ideas of the author and the original works he creates will not arise but for the existence of certain objects, including the institution. So, can we claim that because the object is an obvious social construct the ideas it generates are *ipso facto* obvious social constructs and thus fail precondition (0)? Would that not negate the applicability of Hacking's formula to copyright in general? Would anyone deny that we build on works of our predecessors; that we live in a social context which affects our sense of aesthetics and taste; that we paint because painting is accepted as an artistic activity invented by social and cultural developments. Despite my doubts that anyone would deny that authors and the ideal of solitary authorship are *obvious* social constructs, many, at the same time, forcefully adhere to these romantic ideals, and treat them as inevitable when they need not be so. We may at least agree that authors and ideas of original works are *constructs* of some sort; they are not born from thin air. But if not *socially* constructed, how else?[43]

Even if we all agree that the institution of copyright is socially constructed we may not, and often still do not, understand the full implications of this. We perpetuate conceptions of the lone author and his entitlement to exclusive property rights in his creations. We accept the public interest as a guiding principle to determine how much property we should give authors. But, at the same time, the public interest is not sufficiently reflected in our copyright regime and authors' rights are constantly strengthened. Perhaps a universal agreement that *X* is socially constructed may debunk the lore behind the social construction talk. But this argument, I think, is not compelling enough to seep into every legal institution. When the thesis is present, but at the same time ignored, it nurtures ill-defined conceptions and principles. An obvious case of social construction should not always be a reason to dismiss the need for social construction dialogue. To equate copyright to other traditional institutions is to miss the point. Copyright is a mechanism for control of intangibles, of commodities with distinct social content that are collectively produced and should be jointly owned by public and authors. It is not the European Trademark Office, the Federal Bank, the Ministry of Education and not the Monarchy.

To recapitulate, I believe social constructionism may be illuminating even with respect to institutions and objects that are obviously social constructions. Many

---

43 Hacking (n 3 above) 39-40.

scholars mention the construction of authorship and the idea of copyright, but they do not take any radical steps to truly realise what are the implications of copyright's social construction. I agree with Hacking's formula. If we all think of the institution of copyright as a social construct, it is instructive to deal with the ideas, objects and classifications comprising it. But not only that. The formula is valuable in reminding us to seek more clarity when we use the vernacular of copyright and social construction. However, as Hacking remarks, '[t]alk of construction tends to undermine the authority of knowledge and categorization. It challenges complacent assumptions about the inevitability of what we have found out or present ways of doing things.'[44] Hence, we have to be careful not to restrict the use we make of social constructionism. If '[c]onstructionists are greatly concerned with questions of power and control',[45] restricting social constructionism, something that might be suitable for certain facts of the world and discoveries (but not their ideas), runs the risk of leaving great parts of the present copyright system as they are today. In copyright, that is, social constructionism should apply to the institution, authors as a specific kind of person and original works of art and authorship.

Constructing Stages and Assembling

Hacking remarks that causal routes lead to and are involved in 'the coming into being or establishing of some present entity or fact'[46] and he argues that we take more seriously the idea that a construction is a kind of 'building, or assembling from parts.'[47] How should we define the act of composing from different parts a copyrighted entity? This question is closely related to my criticism of the romantic author and the discussion of the authorial collectivity. It has other parallels in philosophers' articulations of the relation between the social environment and who we are. For example, social relations and causality are not absent from John Locke's philosophy of knowledge and his insistence on the role of experience, and our ability to assemble (rather than create) is well ingrained in his 'workmanship model.' Locke argues that individuals are not makers or creators of products ex nihilo. For the most part, they tend to mix their labour with commonly owned objects.[48]

Whether viewed from the standpoint of interaction, social relations, social dependence or causality,[49] copyright creation is, in other words, a process of putting

44 Ibid 58.

45 Ibid.

46 Hacking (n 3 above) 48.

47 Ibid 49.

48 See below, Chapter 6.

49 Interaction depends on social relations. It creates causal relations. It creates derivatives. We are dependent on interaction if we, for example, want to understand the world around us; to understand different approaches to art or modern adaptations of Baroque music. In *The Social Construction of Reality* Berger and Luckmann provide a sociological analysis of everyday life and knowledge that guides conduct in everyday life. They do not claim that everything is socially constructed nor do they advocate universal constructionism. They begin with the

together – 'building or assembling from parts.' Hacking advocates a definition of building which should be followed by all social constructionists. Building for Hacking is 'always more than the sum of their parts.'[50] For Hacking, '[a]nything worth calling a construction was or is constructed in quite definite stages, where the later stages are built upon, or out of, the product of earlier stages. Anything worth calling a construction has a history. But not just any history. It has to be a history of building.'[51] We can never claim to have created something that has no history and no causal relations to existing templates. This is 'because there is something of a historical step-by-step building of specific techniques, institutions, and problems, each using previous steps, and assembled to form a further stage in the production of later techniques, institutions, and problems.'[52]

An original copyright work is an example of a socially constructed entity that has 'a history of building.' The same is true for authors. Copyrighted works and authors represent the authorial collectivity and are dependent on predecessors' efforts and works. At the same time a copyright work is not merely the sum of these efforts; it generates some unique added-value which makes it worthy of protection. An author, a socially constructed kind of a person, can only be said to build copyrighted entities; not to create. Authors and artists assemble together different entities. But they do not merely connect 'the dots to complete a picture. They had to put in the dots.'[53] In this way, they take already-existing works and templates in new directions and make their efforts eligible for copyright protection. That is, copyright creation is a continuous activity; a process of absorbing, assembling, translating, adding, then expressing.

Defending Radical Constructionism

Copyright is neither a natural resource nor a fact the world comes wrapped up with.[54] Its equivalent is not the DNA double helix or the Second law of Thermodynamics.

---

reality of everyday life and argue that it is premised on social relations and material objects. Berger and Luckmann (n 1 above) 19-34. A person's 'natural attitude to this world corresponds to the natural attitude of others.' Ibid 23. Every person is a member of society and 'participate in its dialectic', internalises its social elements and uses them in his daily reality. Ibid 129. Participation and interaction renders the products of these activities derivative. Berger and Luckmann also argue, that social reality has both objective and subjective dimensions. Ibid 47-183. This is another way of explaining why copyrighted entities are neither public nor private, but a joint enterprise that takes authors and artists *beyond* what is already known.

50 Hacking (n 3 above) 50.

51 Ibid 50.

52 Ibid 53.

53 Ibid 76.

54 Yet, that does not mean that scientific discoveries are not social. In the sciences we tend to cling to the myth of sudden illuminations that engender life-changing inventions. For example, Newton's well known formulation of the universal law of gravity was a synthesis of ideas proposed by thinkers such as Ptolemy, Copernicus, Kepler, Galileo, and Hooke.

If one thinks normal science progresses in an inevitable way, one has to realise that copyright is not scientific. If copyright were to be science, an anti-constructionist philosopher would claim that it is *false* to think that 'people in pursuit of certain ends could, in their interactions with the world, have gone more that one way.'[55] Then he would argue that existing patterns dominating the institution of copyright – the romantic vision of authorship and originality, the limited scope of fair dealing exceptions and the seemingly constant extension of the duration to almost perpetuity – when combined, define the only way to go. In copyright nothing determines that one ought to go the way one did. Interactions, social reliance and causality dominate the landscape of copyright creation. The danger in copyright is that once one insists on only one way, one is able to transform it to an almost irresistible factual ingredient of our social reality.

When it comes to copyright, radical constructionism is plausible, for almost everything in copyright is socially constructed all the way down, including both the institution and subjects of copyright. How radical this view is can be interestingly assessed with a test Hacking proposes, involving three 'sticking points': contingency, nominalism and external explanations of stability.[56] On this account: (i) there is no indication that one ought to go the way one did; (ii) entity *X* has no inherent structure. For the nominalist the world is not bundled with facts. Facts are akin to consequences of the different ways in which we represent the world. The nominalist aims 'to be

The Wright Brother's invention of the first airplane was not created in isolation from earlier attempts, for instance, Lilienthal's invention of the flying glider. On Watt's model of a steam engine it said that it is about time to reject 'the still current popular fallacy that James Watt "invented" the steam engine.' L Rolt and J Allen, *The Steam Engine of Thomas Newcomen* (New York: Science History Publications, 1977) 12.

Watson's and Crick's discovery of the structure of the DNA double helix, is not different. Watson and Crick were not working in a vacuum – neither intellectual nor a social vacuum. 'The work of producing a structural description of the DNA molecule was social, both collaborative and competitive.' H Longino, *The Fate of Knowledge* (Princeton and Oxford: Princeton University Press, 2002) 193. Crick himself remarks that a few days following his arrival to the laboratory he 'knew what to do: imitate Linus Pauling and beat him at his own game.' J Watson, *The Double Helix* (New York: Signet, 1968) 31-32.

For an interesting discussion on the social construction of scientific facts see B Latour and S Woolgar, *Laboratory Life: The Social Construction of Scientific Facts* (Beverly Hills: Sage, 1979). In the second edition of their book they delete the word 'social' from the title. They assert that: 'By demonstrating its pervasive applicability, the social study of science has rendered 'social' devoid of any meaning.' B Latour and S Woolgar, *Laboratory Life: The Construction of Scientific Facts* (Princeton: Princeton University Press, 1986) 281, referred to in Hacking (n 3 above) 40. I should state that I am not interested in finding the ancestors of the first creative work or the steam engine but rather to show how creativity, whether in sciences or the arts, cannot be conceived or produced without relying on the public.

55 Hacking, ibid 98.

56 Ibid 63-99.

true to experience and interaction';[57] and (iii) that the ultimate explanation for the stability of scientific beliefs to some extent, depends on their relations to external factors. That is, the answer to the question of whether the origin of idea *X* is based on how the world is – is no. While opponents of constructionism would argue that the world has an inherent structure, the constructionist would argue that there can be no predetermination of the results of *X*, it cannot be determined 'by how the world is';[58] we, and the social relations governing history, are dependent on interaction which produces these relations.

The approach presented in this book is 'a species of nominalism.'[59] In copyright, there is a key role for interaction, social dependence and causal relations: they define authorship and make ideals of the author possible. In Hacking's test one can score fifteen points maximum: five for each of the three sticking points. What one can score on contingency must be examined in light of the authorial collectivity. As I argued in Chapter 4, an author comes wired with some innate endowment that is a feature which also participates in the process of 'choosing the direction.' That is, the claim that in copyright nothing determined that one ought to go the way one did, is partly inaccurate. Probably, no one would object to the argument that our original constitution has an impact on what we favour or the paths we choose to follow, unless of course, one argues against innateness altogether or that every segment of our original constitution is only social construction.

Reconstructing the 'Copyright Moment'

Contrasting 'Moments'

What are the implications for the definition of copyright of the above discussion? And how do we to translate them into our daily copyright reality? The main implication is the transformation of the 'copyright moment', that is, the the moment in which the copyright entity is born; the moment after which the author is entitled to claim a property right in a given creation. In the present state of affairs, the 'copyright moment' is defined as the moment when one or more individuals collect ideas from the public domain and express them in a tangible medium. It is the union of collectively owned, but unprotected, entities, and the author's personal contribution. As Landes and Posner remark: 'the joint output of two types of input, only one of which is protected by copyright law.'[60] The 'copyright moment', as presently interpreted, assumes the creation of an independently created new entity of social

57 Ibid 84. The nominalist believes that 'the world does not come tidily sorted into facts. People constitute facts in a social process of interaction with the world and intervening in its affairs.' Ibid 174.

58 Ibid 73.

59 Ibid 33.

60 WM Landes and RA Posner, 'An Economic Analysis of Copyright Law' (1989) 18 *Journal of Legal Studies* 325, 349.

wealth and allows the individual to enclose the whole object and exclusively add it to his private dominion. This moment does not accommodate fundamental concerns with which I dealt in the course of my discussion on the authorial collectivity and social constructionism. It posits the individual as the entity responsible for making copyrighted materials; isolating him from the social matrix in which he creates. It denies the contribution the public makes.

Every individual has the desire, and deserves, to obtain recognition for his creative expressions. However, being dependent on the contribution of the public means that one is unable to produce without this contribution. 'Who owns this contribution?' is a question which we have begun to address. It is the public in its collective capacity that creates, nurtures and maintains this contribution. Some form of ownership of this contribution is imperative for the preservation of peace and order. As Harris remarks, 'peace and order required that most things should be in someone's ownership.'[61] But that does not entail that private ownership is the only preferred form. Collective ownership is also possible.

Understanding the combination of contribution from two sources, authors and the public, changes the essence of the 'copyright moment' – the moment in which person P becomes the original owner of object O. There is no moment in which a wholly original copyright work can be declared. Yet, there is a moment in which actual copyrighted works are born.[62] It starts when the individual interacts in society; the moment when the collective contribution is assembled and merged with the individual's contribution into an inseparable unitary whole, capable of ownership. It cannot be the sole moment of the public or the individual; it is either jointly constructed and realised or it does not exist at all. This moment is a moment

61 JW Harris, *Property and Justice* (Oxford: Oxford University Press, 1996) 215.

62 It is possible to interpret this 'moment' as the moment in which a *derivative work* is born. Along this study I mention that copyrighted works are not original in the sense of being new creations produced by a single individual. In other words, all copyrighted entities are derivative. Copyright laws protect derivative works. This means, as Bently and Sherman explain, that 'authors can copy (or use) pre-existing materials and still get copyright protection in the resulting work as long as they bring about a *material change* to the raw material…In so doing the law ensures that any copyright that is acquired in a derivative work is distinct from the original work that is incorportaed into it. The difficult question is deciding where to draw the line between legitimate borrowing from exisiting sources and illegitimate copying.' L Bently and B Sherman, *Intellectual Property Law* (Oxford: Oxford University Press, 2001) 86.

In that respect, the Court in *MacMillan v Cooper* remarks: the labour, skill and capital of the work must have imparted to the product created 'some quality or character which the raw material did not possess, and which differentiates the product from the raw material.' *MacMillan v Cooper* (1924) 40 TLR 186, 188.

I argue that authors are capable of bringing about a change to the raw materials they use; to create 'quality or character which the raw material did not possess.' However, the public's decisive authorial contribution is inseparable from that of the single author and the change should be attributed to both public and authors. Consequently, the resulted copyrighted entity can only be jointly owned between them.

of collaboration between authors and the public – an unavoidable consequence of the role of authorial collectivity and the nature of authors and original copyrighted entities as social constructions.[63]

By defending this conclusion I do not mean to announce the 'death of the author', but emphasise how original appropriation theories have no relevance to discussions on copyright. Without the public domain, without collectively owned social and cultural properties, copyrighted works are impossible. The basic assumption can be formulated in the negative: there is no support for the rule that copyright works are their creator's novel and sole expressions and hence they should not be treated as exclusive private property.

Where is the Public Domain? Refuting a Misconception

The public domain is a basic ingredient in the formulation of the 'copyright moment.' It 'is a subject that divides legislators, corporate and individual participants in creative endeavours, practicing lawyers, and intellectual property scholars in ways that, I suspect, would astonish their counterparts even twenty five or fifty years ago.'[64] It has a place of honour in almost every discourse on copyright.[65] Litman took up the

---

63 Although there are cases in which the dependence on the public is stronger, say, for example, in the case of parodies and satire where the public serves as an undeniable active source of inspiration and meaning-making, it does not mean that the public contributes less to other works.

Take for example the case of *University of London Press v University Tutorial Press* [1916] 2 Ch 601. Can Professor Lodge and Mr. Jackson – the examiners, be rewarded with exclusive rights over the copyright work they produced? The examiners drew the examination paper from knowledge that cannot, in any way, belong to them exclusively. They drew the questions 'upon the stock of knowledge common to all mathematicians…' Ibid 609. The examiners also enjoyed the general contribution of the public, and the contribution of students by the questions and comments they made during the course. Here the 'copyright moment is the moment in which the examiners joined their labour and knowledge to the knowledge common to all mathematicians.' The Court in this case remarks that 'if an author, for purposes of copyright, must not draw on the stock of knowledge which is common to himself and others who are students of the same branch of learning, only those historians who discovered fresh historical facts could acquire copyright for their works.' Ibid. I do not claim that an author does not add to our existing stock of knowledge, but rather that the right one can have in one's creative expressions cannot be exclusive. As socially constructed entities, in copyright terms, no author can discover 'fresh historical *facts*' but merely conjoin his contribution to that of the public.

64 DL Zimmerman, 'Is There a Right to have Something to Say? One View of the Public Domain' (2004) 73 *Fordham Law Review* 297, 301.

65 The concept 'public domain' differs from 'public interest.' Public domain secures public interests. Dreier recently remarked that these concepts are difficult to define: 'While the term 'public interest ' is often cited, there is a certain vagueness inherent in it. Who is, and who represents, the 'public'? In some instances, the reference is to the 'general' public, ie, to society as a whole. In other instances, the reference is to the interest of a certain

great challenge of defining the public domain. She argues that '[t]he public domain should be understood not as the realm of material that is undeserving of protection, but as a device that permits the rest of the system to work by leaving raw material of authorship available for authors to use.'[66] Similarly, Gordon defines the public domain as a source of rights that is 'largely filled with creations whose period of protection has expired, works which have been abandoned, or works for which no protection existed *ab initio*.'[67] In a later article she criticises the prevailing definition of the public domain and observes that:

> An artist's relationship to her tradition sometimes involves quotation and imitation in ways that implicate copyright law. That law insufficiently recognises that, because predecessors also built on tradition, the claims that they can rightfully assert against the makers of later art should be limited. Current copyright law understates those limits, largely because the law conceives of the 'public domain' as an area free of obligations. Under current law, anyone can copy from the public domain, and claim copyright in what he has added, regardless of whether doing so will impair others' use of the underlying domain that all inherited together.[68]

---

subgroup of society: for example, end-users, who are viewed as in opposition to the interests of rightholders. Furthermore, the label 'public' is sometimes used to mask private – often commercial – interests; by the same token, denial of a 'public interest' can be a mask for unfettered individualistic interests.' T Dreier, 'Balancing Proprietary and Public Domain Interests: Inside or Outside of Proprietary Rights?', in R Dreyfuss, LD Zimmerman and H First (eds.), *Expanding the Boundaries of intellectual Property: Innovation Policy for the Knowledge Society* (Oxford: Oxford University Press, 2001) 295, 297. I refer to the 'public' in the collective sense: the public at large. When reference is made to individuals as representatives of the public, I elucidate this point. Placing individuals or even subgroups for matters of defining the *general* public interest contradicts my vision of copyright as it blurs the boundaries between public and private and between the individual and the collective.

Van Caenegen asks whether we should allow private propertisation of every type of knowledge and argues that we have to devise a different perception of the public domain when we deal with indigenous people. W van Caenegen, 'The Public Domain: Scientia Nullius?' [2002] 6 *European Intellectual Property Review* 324.

66 J Litman, 'The Public Domain' 39 *Emory Law Journal* (1990) 965, 968.

67 W Gordon, 'Property in Self-Expression: Equality and Individualism in the Natural Law of Copyright' (1993) 102 *Yale Law Journal* 1533, 1558. On the public domain see generally, D Lange, 'Recognizing the Public Domain' (1981) 44 *Law & Contemporary Problems* 147; J Boyle, 'A Theory of Law and Information: Copyrights, Spleens, Blackmail, and Insider Trading' (1992) 80 *California Law Review* 1415; K Aoki, 'Authors, Inventors and Trademark Owners: Private Intellectual Property and the Public Domain (Part I)' (1994) 18 *Columbia Journal of Law & Arts* 1; Y Benkler, 'Free as the Air to Common Use: First Amendment Constraints on Enclosure of the Public Domain' (1999) 74 *New York University Law Review* 354; and by the same author 'Through the Looking Glass: Alice and the Constitutional Foundations of the Public Domain' (2003) *Law & Contemporary Problems* 173.

68 Gordon (n 11 above) 78.

Across the chasm, defenders of a robust public domain advocate its importance for the workability and stability of the intellectual property regime. Securing authors a steady flow of raw materials in the public domain is a key feature in Litman's argument for a stronger domain. She argues that not only authors and artists can be said to create something that is totally original, but that they must not enclose raw materials that belong to the common. Viewing raw materials as belonging to the public domain, but then excluding the public from accessing them once fixed in a copyrighted entity, is to simply maintain the status quo of the denial of the authorial collectivity. To this one should add the difficulties in separating unprotectable raw materials (for example, ideas and facts) from protectable materials. Litman recognises the danger in failing to appreciate the true meaning of the public domain:

> Because copyright's paradigm of authorship credits the author with bringing something wholly new into the world, it sometimes fails to account for the raw material that all authors use. This tendency can distort our understanding of the interaction between copyright law and authorship. Specifically, it can lead us to give short shrift to the public domain by failing to appreciate that the public domain is the law's primary safeguard of the raw material that makes authorship possible.[69]

Should we take raw materials as the essence of the public domain? A crucial feature in my argument is the fundamental need to preserve not only raw materials but end products as well. The evolved social reality should be saved for other members of the public to consume and make use of. It seems that for Litman and Gordon raw materials might suffice.[70] Litman mentions the term 'raw material' ten times in her article and recognises that raw materials are value-laden and remarks that 'when the author mines the raw material for her next work, significant portions of it will be the stuff of the outside world mediated by her experience. It is unsurprising, then, that parts of her work will echo the works of others.'[71] Her argument supports my claim that copyright scholars, although not explicitly, are aware of the sociality of copyright, that subjects of copyright are dependent on the authorial collectivity and that they are social constructions; that every idea 'that is debated, assessed, applied and developed' is 'situated in a social setting'[72] and that the same holds for the object.

Litman's assertion that 'the term "public domain" has fallen out of fashion' and that this is 'the public's price for the grant of copyright' is a main cause for concern.[73] Her definition of the public domain has had a pioneering effect, but her concentration on the availability of raw materials is misleading. In view of my examination of the authorial collectivity and subjects of copyright as social constructs, we should reject the notion that the rights of the public pertain to the preservation of raw

69 Litman (n 66 above) 966.

70 Ibid.

71 Ibid 1011.

72 Hacking (n 3 above) 125.

73 Litman (n 66 above) 1013.

materials and unprotectable elements. As opposed to Litman, I argue that raw materials of authorship do not only cover ideas and concepts, but also copyrightable expressions.

Even a recent attempt to redefine the public domain leaves the status quo practically unchanged. Zimmerman advocates a 'mandatory public domain' in which the main theme is that 'what goes into [the public domain] must stay there.'[74] True, she highlights many of the greatest flaws in the current copyright reality. For example, the revival of works now residing in the public domain, is possible. She recognises the criticism that her view may generate: 'Some will find the theory here an insufficiently radical view of the public domain because, although it captures much of our common sense intuition about how the free availability of speech goods intersects with our ability to communicate, it does not necessarily guarantee us a "perfect" public domain from their policy perspective. Others may find it radical because of the idea that there is an absolute limit on what can be subjected to intellectual property regimes.'[75] However, it seems that Zimmerman merely favours elevating the status of the term 'public domain' to that of a constitutional guarantee.[76] She does not address the wrong in treating the public as a graveyard for unprotectable materials, or a warehouse for unwanted goods.

The public domain is us. It can be found in *every* copyrighted entity. In fact, the entity is unattainable unless the public domain contributes to its formation. The public domain is the initiator of copyrighted endeavours. It is the treasury of elements which together trigger the creative impulse.[77] It is also a social construction, as it is constantly being reinvented and enhanced by historical events and social processes.

There is no public domain for copyright works only. It is a fiction to devise a domain in which only unusable copyrighted entities reside. The public domain in copyright cannot exist independent of the larger social domain. For the most part, it is definable as a sub-category within the larger social public domain, an entity that accommodates the specific needs of artists, authors and the like. Viewing the public domain as such does not deny authors' rights,[78] rather highlights the truth of the

---

74 Zimmerman (n 64 above).

75 Ibid 373.

76 Zimmerman writes: 'If a constitutional basis for recognizing some form of "mandatory public domain", particularly one that reaches both federal and state activity, is plausible, its recognition will bring order to sprawl in intellectual property rights, and stabilize the balance between incentives and access along more intelligible lines.' Ibid 311-312.

77 In the words of one commentator: the public domain should be first defined as a sensory stimuli and only then as a sort of intellectual commons. AS Oddi, 'The Tragicomedy of the Public Domain in Intellectual Property Law' (2002) 25 *Hastings Communications & Entertainment Law Journal* 1. Merges follows a similar line of reasoning and claims that the public has a 'self correcting' power and that legislation is not the only way to secure a dynamic public domain. RP Merges, 'A New Dynamism in the Public Domain' (2004) 71(1) *University of Chicago Law Review* 185.

78 Author's rights, as Gordon asserts, are a matter of corrective justice. And although they are conditional and defensible, they should be available as a reward for investment of

construction of authorship and copyright creation and avoids denial of the public interest and its contribution.

Boyle suggests that we 'need to invent the public domain in order to call into being the coalition that might protect it.'[79] The public domain as a concept and as an entity is already here. It is well ingrained in discourses on copyright. The coalition is us. Before we devise a way to reinvent the public domain, or make it mandatory,[80] we have to modify our one-way attitude towards what an author is and how works of authorship and art are created. Only then we can understand the implications of the dependence on the authorial collectivity and the social construction paradigm, and form the coalition that will truly protect the public domain. Moreover, if 'every viable society must develop procedures of reality-maintenance'[81] then our copyright law ought to promote a robust public domain and preserve the collective nature of its properties. The alternative is facing the end of the public domain.

Authors as Collaborators

The conceptual wrong in individualistic collaboration In *The Construction of Authorship*, Jaszi and Woodmansee invite readers to realise the true meaning of authorial creation. They argue that '[m]ost writing today – in business, government, industry, the law, the sciences and social sciences – is collaborative, yet it is still being taught as if it were solitary, originary activity.'[82] While Woodmansee examines the evolution of 'authorship' as a concept,[83] Jaszi argues that as the authorial creative process becomes increasingly collaborative and collective, traditional copyright laws become ineffective because the vigorous extension of laws detrimentally affect the attainment of the social objective of copyright. In particular, the notion of romantic authorship becomes more insistent and is likely to mislead rather then provide guidance.[84] This is where Woodmansee and Jaszi and I agree. Their attempt

---

efforts. W Gordon, 'On Owning Information: Intellectual Property and the Restitutionary Impulse' (1992) 78 *Virginia Law Review* 149.

79 J Boyle, 'A Politics of Intellectual Property: Environmentalism for the Net' (1997) 47 *Duke Law Journal* 87, 113.

80 Zimmerman (n 64 above) 370-374.

81 Berger and Luckman (n 1 above) 147.

82 Woodmansee and Jaszi (n 1 above) 9, 25.

83 M Woodmansee, 'The Genius and the Copyright: Economic and Legal Conditions of the Emergence of the "Author"' (1984) 17 *Eighteenth-Century Studies* 425; and by the same author 'On the Author Effect: Recovering Collectivity' in Woodmansee and Jaszi, ibid 15.

84 P Jaszi, 'On the Author Effect: Contemporary Copyright and Collective Creativity', in Woodmansee and Jaszi, ibid 29, 56. See also by the same author 'Towards a Theory of Copyright: The Metamorphoses of Authorship' (1991) *Duke Law Journal* 455. On the deconstruction of the Romantic author see also K Aoki, '(Intellectual) Property and Sovereignty: Notes Toward a Cultural Geography of Authorship' (1996) 48 *Stanford Law Review* 1293; and R Littrell, Note, 'Towards a Stricter Originality Standard for Copyright' (2001) 43 *Boston College Law Review* 193. See also above, Chapter 4.

to reconstruct authors and authorship is imperative for every discussion on copyright. It is, however, somewhat individualistic, as it deals with collaboration between individuals and not between individuals and the public at large.[85] Collaborative authorship can be viewed as either individualistic or collective but in copyright they operate simultaneously.

Although Woodmansee and Jaszi successfully explain the anatomy of authorship and consider fundamental limits to authorial rights for a stronger public domain, they still place individual authors at the vanguard. They consider collaboration to be the paradigm of relations between an author and other fellow authors or partners in their individual capacity. They embrace the argument that '[a]ny frank appraisal of authorship must conclude that each author's work contains both the author's original creations and material drawn from other authors.'[86] But what about the reliance on the public? It would be wrong to accuse Woodmansee and Jaszi of neglecting the role of the public domain in the copyright creation process. However, their emphasis on collaboration between individuals is misleading. In other words, while they enquire into the construction of authorship and authorial works, I examine the *social* construction of them.

Believing in the author Woodmansee informs us that the definition of the author and of authorship has been the subject of transformation and synthesis for centuries. For example, in the thirteenth century, there were four ways of making a book, none of which correspond to any notion of sole authorship. And [i]n the Renaissance…the author was an unstable marriage of two distinct concepts. He was first and foremost a craftsman' and inspired by the muses.[87] She claims that the idea that 'the writer is a special participant in the production process – the only worthy of attention – is of recent provenience. It is a by-product of the Romantic notion that significant writers break altogether with tradition or create something utterly new, unique – in a word, "original".'[88] Similarly, Rose examines the idea of the author and originality in its historical context and writes that 'copyright – the practice of securing marketable rights in texts that are treated as commodities – is a specifically modern institution, the creature of the printing press, the individualization of authorship in the late Middle Ages and early Renaissance, and the development of the advanced marketplace

85 A similar approach to collaboration was also advocated by Kaplan. He remarks that most 'intellectual work including the distinctively imaginative is now being done by teams, a practice apt to continue and grow' and that 'may diffuse and diminish emotions of original discovery and exclusive ownership.' B Kaplan, An Unhurried View of Copyright (New York: Columbia University Press, 1967) 117.

86 A Yen, 'The Interdisciplinary Future of Copyright Theory' in Woodmansee and Jaszi (n 1 above) 159, 166. See also Litman (n 66 above) 1010-1011.

87 M Woodmansee, *The Author, Art, and the Market: Rereading the History of Aesthetics* (New York: Columbia University Press 1994) 36. See in particular 34-56.

88 Woodmansee, 'On the Author Effect' (n 83 above) 16.

society in the seventeenth and eighteenth centuries.'[89] What Woodmansee and Rose implicitly tell us is, that they would accept Hacking's argument that the author as a kind of person is a social construction – a contingent upshot of historical events and social processes. Like many others, however, they do not fully explain, how to make use of this insight to change existing ownership patterns in copyright.

Although a social construction, an author exercises subjective judgement and breathes life into new ideas embedded in eventual products.[90] He shares with the world his exclusive property in elements that constitute his original make-up; elements without which the authorial act would not have existed. The individual is essentially the proprietor of his own person and capacities and he therefore has a valid claim for ownership over authorial products he creates. The author uses his qualities and capacities to comprehend, then translate and modify collectively owned cultural and social properties. But, if authorial products were premised on the author's contribution or subjective experiences only 'it would be impossible either to have a direct intercourse with the work or to know it.'[91]

Foucault's famous answer to the question 'What is an author?' supports the social construction argument.[92] He informs us that an author is an ideological figure and that it is 'worth examining how the author became individualized in a culture like ours.'[93] Foucault erodes the concept of the individual writer by referring to 'the author-function' and claims this is a historical variable. He then denies that author is the originator of a text having its own meaning and value and considers the author to be a social construct: 'the author function does not develop spontaneously as the attribution of a discourse to an individual. It is, rather, the result of a complex operation which constructs a certain rational being we call "author".'[94] The author – 'this intelligible being'[95] – gets its realistic form from *us*: 'these aspects of an

---

89 M Rose, *Authors and Owners: The Invention of Copyright* (Cambridge Mass.: Harvard University Press, 1993) 3. See also E Eisenstein, *The Printing Press as an Agent of Change* (Cambridge: Cambridge University Press, 1980).

90 For Ginsburg, an author 'succeeds in exercising minimal personal autonomy in her fashioning of the work.' JC Ginsburg, 'The Concept of Authorship in Comparative Copyright Law' (2003) 52 *DePaul Law Review* 1063, 1064 (emphasis added). The act of authorial creation is a process in which no player can act alone. Products resulting from this activity signify exercise of 'minimal personal autonomy' only. The law does not consider the level of autonomy exercised for matters of copyright entitlement. In fact, the law substitutes 'minimal' with 'optimal' and considers authors as creators of wholly new substances.

91 R Ingarden, *The Cognition of the Literary Work of Art* (Evanston, Ill: Northwestern University Press, 1973) 13-14 cited in TG Palmer, 'Are Patents and Copyrights Morally Justified? The Philosophy of Property Rights and Ideal Objects' (1990) 13 *Harvard Journal of Law & Public Policy* 817, 845.

92 M Foucault, 'What is an Author?' in P Rainbow (ed.), *The Foucault Reader* (New York: Pantheon Books, 1984) 101.

93 Ibid 101.

94 Ibid 110.

95 Ibid.

individual which *we* designate as making him an author are only a projection, in more or less psychologizing terms, of the operations that *we* force texts to undergo, the connections that *we* make, the traits that *we* establish as pertinent, the continuities that *we* recognize, or the exclusions that *we* practice.'[96] And although terms change, and conceptions take different directions at different times 'we can find through the ages certain constants in the rules of author construction.'[97]

Barthes announces the 'Death of the Author' and, like Foucault, rips from author certain powers and identity. Romantic authorship stipulates that a literary work or a work of art has a single true interpretation that its author conveys. Barthes challenges this idea: 'We now know that a text is not a line of words releasing a single 'theological meaning' but a multidimensional space in which a variety of writings, none of them original, blend and clash.'[98] As Durham explains: 'Authorship, according to this "un-romantic" point of view, is less a manifestation of the author's personal vision, created *ex nihilo*, than it is a synthesis of prior texts and cultural influences.'[99] Although many copyright scholars would support similar views, there is still a need for a wider understanding of Foucault, or similar approaches. As Woodmansee and Jaszi assert:

> However enthusiastically legal scholars may have thrown themselves into 'deconstructing' other bodies of legal doctrine, copyright has remained untouched by the implications of the Derridean proposition that the inherent instability of meaning derives not from authorial subjectivity but from intertextuality. Above all, the questions posed by Michel Foucault in 'What Is an Author?' about the causes and consequences of the persistent, overdetermined power of the author construct – with their immediate significance for law – have gone largely unattended by theorists of copyright law, to say nothing of practitioners or, most critically, judges and legislators.[100]

I distance my approach from Foucault and Barthes,[101] and position myself somewhere between their approaches and that of the scholars I just mentioned. For the former, the copyright moment is a fiction; for the latter it should be modified but not necessarily in a radical manner. Neither side portray the conception of authorship that I envision. I fully support applying social constructionism to authors and their

96 Ibid (emphasis added).

97 Ibid.

98 R Barthes, 'The Death of the Author', in R Barthes, *Image-Music-Text* in S Heath trans. (ed.) (London: Fontana, 1977) 142, 146.

99 A Durham, 'The Random Muse: Authorship and Indeterminacy' (2002) 44 *William and Mary Law Review* 569, 616.

100 Woodmansee and Jaszi (n 1 above) 8-9.

101 Burke argues that Barthes and Foucault did not succeed in constructing a coherent argument. In one of the opening paragraphs to 'What is an Author?' Foucault asks 'What does it matter who is speaking?' Foucault (n 92 above) 101. Burke argues that in subsequent writings Foucault relies on the concept of author and provides examples of why it does matter. S Burke, *The Death and Return of the Author: Criticism and Subjectivity in Bathes, Foucault and Derrida* (Edinburgh: Edinburgh University Press, 2nd enlarged ed., 1998) 93.

creative expressions, but I do not strip them of their contribution. For the same reasons that a copyrighted work cannot be created without the public's contribution, it cannot be realised without the individual's input. This is why we should endorse reconstruction of the 'copyright moment'; a moment in which the public and author join together and create an enterprise of social wealth for which both deserve a reward.

Chapter 6

Lockean Copyright Re-Imagined

Challenging Copyright-Lockeans

The Argument

John Locke's natural right theory of property has been so insistently applied to copyright philosophy, that it would be perverse to ignore it. Two main factors consolidated the hegemony of Locke's philosophy in copyright discourse. First, Locke's main theme of property ownership is based on a person's natural entitlement to the products of his labour, and as discussed in Chapter 3, labour is a key requirement for copyright. Second, scholars find Locke's theory of property, and the limits he sets on what a labourer can come to exclusively own and control, as a solid argument on which to solve contemporary problems in copyright.

There are three additional reasons why Locke merits detailed attention: (i) there are many misconceptions of how to interpret Locke when we discuss copyright; (ii) copyright scholars ignore Locke's *explicit* discussion of copyright and then invoke his general theory of property to justify the status quo; and, (iii) Locke's epistemology and philosophy of mind display important social constructionist overtones. Locke's view strengthens the argument for authorial collectivity and the social construction of authors and their creative works. It guarantees authorial rights but also acknowledges the public's contribution and, when read together with several other of his writings, supports a plausible vision of what copyright *should* be.

Two Fatal Flaws

Modern copyright-Lockeans repeatedly invoke Locke's natural right philosophy of property in discussions on copyright. This is an interesting phenomenon on its own.[1]

---

1 See most recently, L Zemer, 'The Making of a New Copyright Lockean' (2006) 29(3) *Harvard Journal of Law & Public Policy* 891; J Tehranian, 'ET TU, Fair Use? The Triumph of Natural-Law Copyright' (2005) 38 *U C Davis Law Review* 465; WJ Gordon, 'Render Copyright unto Caesar: On Taking Incentives Seriously' (2004) 71(1) *The University of Chicago Law Review* 75 (hereinafter – 'Gordon 2004'); and by the same author, 'Intellectual Property Law' in P Crane and M Tushnet (eds.), *Oxford Handbook of Legal Studies* (Oxford: Oxford University Press, 2003) 167; J Lipton, 'Information Property: Rights and Responsibilities' (2004) 56 *Florida Law Review* 135, 177-181; A Drassinower, 'A Right-Based View of the Idea/Expression Dichotomy in Copyright Law' (2003) 16 *Canadian Journal of Law and Jurisprudence* 3; BG Damstedt, 'Limiting Locke: A Natural Law Justification for the Fair

However, it is not at all necessary to map the differences between scholars in the way they invoke Lockean justifications because one common problem affects the strength and coherency of their arguments. They base their analysis and vindication of copyright solely on the twenty-six sections of Chapter V 'Of Property' of the *Second Treatise of Government*.[2] They not only confine their arguments to Chapter V,

---

Use Doctrine' (2003) 112 *Yale Law Journal* 1179; RA Spinello, 'The Future of Intellectual Property' (2003) 5 *Ethics and Information Technology* 1; CJ Craig, 'Locke, Labour and Limiting the Author's Right: A Warning Against a Lockean Approach to Copyright Law' (2002) 28 *Queens Law Journal* 1.

See also, SV Shiffrin, 'Lockean Arguments for Private Intellectual Property' in S Munzer (ed.), *New Essays in the Legal and Political Theory of Property* (Cambridge: Cambridge University Press, 2001) 138; W Fisher, 'Theories of Intellectual Property', in S Munzer, ibid 168; AD Moore, 'Towards a Lockean Theory of Intellectual Property' in AD Moore (ed.), *Intellectual Property: Moral, Legal and International Dimensions* (New York and Oxford: Rowman & Littlefield, 2001) 81; S Wilf, 'Who Authors Trademarks?' (1999) 17 *Cardozo Arts & Entertainment Law Journal* 1; AD Moore, 'Intangible Property: Privacy, Power, and Information Control' (1998) 35 *American Philosophical Quarterly* 365; LL Weinreb, 'Copyright for Functional Expression' (1998) 111 *Harvard Law Review* 1150; AD Moore, 'A Lockean Theory of Intellectual Property' (1997) 21 *Hamline Law Review* 65; SE Sterk, 'Rhetoric and Reality in Copyright Law' (1996) 94 *Michigan Law Review* 1197; P Drahos, *A Philosophy of Intellectual Property* (Dartmouth: Ashgate 1996) 41-72; RA Reese, Note, 'Reflections on the Intellectual Commons: Two Perspectives on Copyright Duration and Reversion (1995) 47 *Stanford Law Review* 707; B Friedman, Note, 'From Deontology to Dialogue: The Cultural Consequences of Copyright' (1994) 13 *Cardozo Arts & Entertainment Law Journal* 157; WJ Gordon, 'A Property Right in Self-Expression: Equality and Individualism in the Natural Law of Intellectual Property' (1993) 12 *Yale Law Journal* 1533 (hereinafter – 'Gordon 1993'); LC Becker, 'Deserving to Own Intellectual Property' (1992-1993) 68 *Chicago-Kent Law Review* 609; J Waldron, 'From Authors to Copiers: Individual Rights and Social Values in Intellectual Property' (1992-1993) 68 *Chicago-Kent Law Review* 841 (hereinafter – 'Waldron 1992-1993'); WJ Gordon, 'On Owning Information: Intellectual Property and the Restitutionary Impulse' (1992) 78 *Virginia Law Review* 149 (hereinafter – 'Gordon 1992'); WJ Gordon, 'The Norms of Copyright and the Problem of Private Censorship' (1990) 57 *The University of Chicago Law Review* 1009; TG Palmer, 'Are Patents and Copyrights Morally Justified? The Philosophy of Property Rights and Ideal Objects' (1990) 13 *Harvard Journal of Law & Public Policy* 817; DA Nance, 'Owning Ideas' (1990) 113 *Harvard Journal of Law and Public Policy* 757; AC Yen, 'Restoring the Natural Law: Copyright as Labour and Possessions' (1990) 51 *Ohio State Law Journal* 517; EC Hettinger, 'Justifying Intellectual Property' (1989) 18 *Philosophy & Public Affairs* 31; HM Spector, 'An Outline of a Theory Justifying Intellectual Property Rights' [1989] 8 *European Intellectual Property Review* 270; LJ Lacey, 'Of Bread and Roses and Copyrights' (1989) *Duke Law Journal* 1532; J Hughes, 'The Philosophy of Intellectual Property'(1988) 77 *Georgetown Law Journal* 287. This is not an exhaustive list.

2 J Locke, *Two Treatises of Government* (published 1689) edited with an Introduction and Notes by P Laslett (Cambridge: Cambridge University Press, 2nd ed., 1988) 134-428. All subsequent references to the *Second Treatise*, and in particular to Chapter V, 'Of Property', are simply by book and section, e.g. (2nd T: i 7) (hereinafter – 'Chapter V', '*Second Treatise*'). References to Locke's *First Treatise of Government*, follow similar format.

but also claim that Locke does not, either in the *Two Treatises* or elsewhere, address the issues of intellectual commons, intellectual property in general, or copyright in particular. In reaction, other scholars criticise their adherence to Locke because he is believed to have nothing to say about intellectual property and that Chapter V justifies strong private rights which we should avoid in copyright. This perception is erroneous, but it is a perception on which a well-established contemporary history of copyright theory is premised. Let me illustrate and then explain.

Because statutory and doctrinal innovations place private property rights at the forefront of our intellectual property system, it seems plausible to use Locke's property theory to justify copyright. This is particularly true since the main focus of his theory is 'the reconciliation of strong private property rights with a common of materials available to all.'[3] At the same time, Chapter V is applicable to intellectual property just as it is applicable, for example, to environmental and ecological regulation.[4] The problem in basing copyright justifications solely on Chapter V is that it presents Locke as the undisputed champion of exclusive private property, legitimising inequalities at the expense of public good.[5] I shall show that any argument based solely on commonly cited twenty-six sections of Chapter V is incomplete.

In two landmark articles, Hughes[6] and Gordon[7] introduced us to the lore behind Locke's property theory for matters of copyright discourse. They were subsequently followed by legions of commentators. Yet, they all confined their discussion to Chapter V of the *Second Treatise*. For example, Damstedt uses a Lockean justification to devise a cultural fair use doctrine.[8] He rightly claims that 'revising Locke for a theory of intellectual property has become vital'[9] but again, confines the analysis to Chapter V. Apart from two minor clear exceptions,[10] all other academic writings dealing with Locke and the justification for property rights in copyrighted materials follow suit.

3 Damstedt (n 1 above) 1181.

4 See BM Haddad, 'Property Rights, Ecosystem Management, and John Locke's Labour Theory of Ownership' (2003) 46 *Ecological Economics* 19.

5 This has brought Craig to claim that 'the normative force of labour-acquisition theory simply does not lie in the protection or furtherance of public interest.' Craig (n 1 above) 56.

6 Hughes (n 1 above).

7 Gordon 1993 (n 1 above).

8 Damstedt (n 1 above) 1207.

9 Ibid 1180.

10 I have found two clear exceptions to this general observation. The first is an article written by Wilf in which he considers both Chapter V and Locke's *Essay Concerning Human Understanding* for the justification of a community wide right in trademarks. Wilf (n 1 above). The second exception is an article by Shiffrin in which she discusses, apart from Chapter V, Locke's minor essay entitled 'Liberty of the Press.' Shiffrin (n 1 above). It should also be noted that Rosen applies Locke's definition of language in the *Essay* for purposes of drawing a distinction between ideas and expressions. A Rosen, 'Reconsidering the Idea/Expression Dichotomy' (1992) 26(2) *University of British Columbia Law Review* 263, 270-273.

This selective reading of Locke has sometimes lead to unfavourable judgements of his theory. Gordon, for example, argues that 'the common explicitly discussed in the *Two Treatises* was the physical realm'[11] and then asserts that 'Locke's labor theory of property and allied approaches have been used so frequently as a justification for creators' ownership rights that Locke's *Two Treatises* have been erroneously credited with having developed an explicit defense of intellectual property.'[12] Drahos argues that 'when Locke wrote on property…it was the ownership of physical rather than abstract objects that occupied his attention.'[13] Reese remarks that Locke's tangible property 'might not simply apply *mutatis mutandis* to intangible intellectual property.'[14] Craig claims that 'Locke's labour theory is so commonly invoked in examinations of copyright doctrine that one might be forgiven for believing that he explicitly defended intellectual property rights.'[15] More recently, Epstein asserts: '[t]o be sure, Locke did not offer any explicit treatment one way or the other of intellectual property rights, which adds to his charm.'[16] As we shall see, these claims are misleading.

The second problem is raised in a question posed and challenged by Craig: whether 'Lockean property theory can be re-imagined to shape a copyright system that furthers…maximum creation and dissemination of intellectual works.'[17] Craig is concerned with the social and cultural aspects of our copyright regime and whether they can be accommodated in a copyright law drafted close to a robust property rights system. She does not believe that Locke's theory can be refashioned in this manner, because Locke's property theory clearly 'carries the same threat of copyright expansionism.'[18] I shall argue that her conclusion is partially incorrect. It is indeed difficult to re-imagine Locke within the confines of the *Second Treatise* because in this work he was certainly concerned primarily with the individual. I agree that Locke was wrong to subject every type of property to the principle of exclusive ownership as envisioned in Chapter V of the *Second Treatise*, albeit acknowledging the difference between traditional property and intellectual and cultural property. However, Locke's ideals of property and copyright should be re-examined in light of his other works, particularly the philosophy of knowledge and his idea of authors' rights. Such scrutiny will reveal that it is wrong to associate Locke solely with exclusivity and individualism. Indeed, I shall defend a collectivist and social approach to copyright, based on Lockean principles of ownership and knowledge

11 Gordon 1993 (n 1 above) 1558.

12 Ibid 1540.

13 Drahos (n 1 above) 47.

14 Reese (n 1 above) 708.

15 Craig (n 1 above) 21.

16 RA Epstein, 'Liberty versus Property? Cracks in the Foundations of Copyright Law', *Chicago John M Olin Law & Economics Working Paper* No 204 (2d Series) (April 2004) 28.

17 Craig (n 1 above) 54.

18 Ibid 55.

creation which support the view of authorial collectivity and the social construction of authors and their works.[19]

I shall argue that Locke's theory of property can in fact be re-imagined in three ways. First, Locke presents a clear vision of a system of authors' rights in which he balances private rights against public interest. Second, Chapter V actually deals with property in general, and applies to intellectual property. Third, Locke's theory of knowledge in his *Essay Concerning Human Understanding*[20] has a social constructionist dimension.

Indisputable Lockean Copyright

In a letter entitled 'Liberty of the Press', Locke writes in 1694 that he was aware of the dilemmas and tensions inherent in any copyright regime.[21] In particular he is sensitive to the social and economic impact that a long term right will have on authors as well as on ordinary members of the community. The letter is the first time Locke makes an attempt to reconcile the connection between self-constitution and property ownership. It is also the first time he explicitly refers to authorial entities, and the first time he introduces his readers to his vision of the limits a property institution must recognise in the field of authorial creations.

---

19 Scholars sharply disagree on how to read and interpret Locke. For example, Tully advocates a collectivist Locke, while Macpherson asserts that Locke designs his theory to justify class-based social wealth and it should serve as an ideological basis for modern capitalism. J Tully, *A Discourse on Property: John Locke and His Adversaries* (Cambridge: Cambridge University Press, 1980); CB Macpherson, *The Political Theory of Possessive Individualism: Hobbes to Locke* (London: Oxford University Press, 1972). See also J Waldron, *God, Locke, and Equality: Christian Foundations in Locke's Political Thought* (Cambridge: Cambridge University Press, 2002) 172-175 (hereinafter – 'Waldron 2002').

Finding arguments pertaining to the sociality of copyright in Locke's philosophy may attract criticism from many scholars. But the charm in Locke's writings is undisputable. As Chappell writes: 'It is however, one of the attractions of Locke's work for contemporary philosopher-scholars that credible answers to philosophical questions he himself never considered can often be drawn from his text, even when they are not obviously present there.' V Chappell, 'Locke's Theory of Ideas' in V Chappell (ed.), *The Cambridge Companion to Locke* (Cambridge: Cambridge University Press, 1994) 26, 55. As I will demonstrate, Locke's contribution to copyright is comprised of a mixture of clear and unambiguous references to authors' rights.

20 J Locke, *An Essay Concerning Human Understanding* (first published 1690) edited with an Introduction by PH Nidditch (Oxford: Clarendon Press, 1971). All subsequent references to the *Essay* are by book, chapter and section (e.g., E Bk vi xvi 2) (hereinafter – the '*Essay*').

21 J Locke, 'Liberty of the Press' (published 1694-1695) in M Goldie (ed.), *John Locke: Political Essays* (Cambridge: Cambridge University Press, 1997) 329. See also in ES De Beer (ed.), *The Correspondence of John Locke* (Oxford: Clarendon Press 1979) Appendix, Vol 5, 785-795; and in Lord King, *The Life and Letters of John Locke* [1884] (New York: Burt Franklin repr. 1972) 202-209. I refer to Goldie's version.

'Liberty of the Press' is a letter opposing the renewal of the Licensing Act of 1662. The Act is a punitive instrument for controlling printing and printing-presses.[22] It restricts the number of printing presses and revives the pre-Civil War practice in which all publications had to be approved by a Licensor. The Licensing Act, in the words of Macaulay, 'is condemned, not as a thing essentially evil, but on account of the petty grievances, the exactions, the jobs, the commercial restrictions, the domiciliary visits, which were incidental to it.'[23] The Act lapsed in 1679, was renewed in 1685 for seven years, and renewed in 1692 and 1693 for an additional year. In November 1694, the House of Commons appointed a Committee entrusted with reviewing laws due to expire. In January 1695 the Committee recommended renewal of the Licensing Act. In February 1695, the House took a step back and appointed a Committee to prepare a new Bill.

Locke was able to influence the government's initiative through friends such as John Freke and Edward Clarke who were members of the 'College', a private club founded by Locke as a forum to discuss political affairs. Clarke, who was a member of the Bill's Committee, introduced the proposed Bill in March 1695. A copy of the Bill was sent to Locke, inviting his comments. Clarke informed Locke that despite the title of the Bill 'for regulating the press', it was 'so contrived that there is an absolute liberty for the printing everything that 'tis lawful to speak.'[24] Locke was satisfied that Clarke was entrusted with introducing the Bill, and in a comment he sent on March 1695 he articulates his support and suggests amendments designed to defend the rights and interests of authors, scholars and other users.

Neither the Bill nor the renewal of the Licensing Act made any progress.[25] The result was that pre-publication censorship disappeared in Britain in 1695. And, as Lord Macaulay asserts, with the expiration of the Licensing Act 'English literature

22 The Act entered into force in 10 June 1662 and was entitled 'Act for preventing abuses in printing seditious, treasonable and unlicensed books and pamphlets, and for regulating of printing and printing-presses.' Under the Act: 'Legislative authority was given to the Rules and Ordinances of the Stationers' Company whereby the activities of printers, booksellers, and bookbinders were controlled. Sanction was afforded the ancient custom of the Company whereby the entrance of a book or copy in the Register was deemed to vest a perpetual copyright in the stationer who entered it; and protection was provided for the printing privileges of the two universities and the monopolies granted by royal letters patent to the Company or to individuals.' R Astbury, 'The Renewal of the Licensing Act in 1693 and Its Lapse in 1695' (1978) 33 *The Library* (5th Series) 296, 297. On the 1662 Act, and methods of control and enforcement see generally, FS Siebert, *Freedom of the Press in England 1476-1776: The Rise and Decline of Government Control* (Urbana: University of Illinois Press, 1965) 237-302.

23 TB Macaulay, *History of England from the Accession of James II*, in CH Firth (ed.), (London: Macmillan, 1913) Vol V, 2480, 2482.

24 Goldie (n 21 above) 329. Locke's influence on the Bill is undeniable. Siebert tells us that Locke's comments had a great impact on the House of Commons who 'followed Locke's reasoning if not his exact words by emphasizing the commercial restraints contained in the Act.' Siebert (n 22 above) 261.

25 Macaulay (n 23 above).

was emancipated, and emancipated for ever, from the control of the government.'[26] These words of satisfaction, and especially the term 'emancipation', well characterise Locke's agenda. He elaborates the reasons for abolishing the Company's monopoly enabling readers free access to literature and scholarship, and encouraging study and dissemination of information. He also puts forth his view about the kinds of authorial rights that should be granted, and distinguishes between these rights and the general right to property.

'Liberty of the Press' is composed of three papers: Locke's criticism of the Licensing Act of 1662; a draft Bill for Regulating Printing;[27] and Locke's comments on the Bill.[28] Locke's critique of the 1662 Act is an attack on the monopoly of the 'dull wretches'[29] Stationers' Company, and on pre-publication censorship and licensing policy. In his letter, Locke combines arguments for freedom of expression and social exchange, economic equality, common equity and recognition of authors' rights. As Astbury explains:

> In his *Memorandum*, though Locke spelt out in detail the ill-effects on the book trade, and on authors and readers, of the monopoly system and the powers, and the abuse of power, of the Stationers' Company, most of his complaints reveal directly or by implication his concern for the intellectual, economic, and social freedoms of the individual...and he linked [his statement] to an implied defence of the right to communicate new philosophical and scientific truths...[30]

Explicitly referring to authorial freedom and criticising pre-printing censorship Locke remarks: 'I know not why a man should not have liberty to print whatever he would speak.'[31] Locke himself had a personal interest in scrapping the 1662 Act. His project to publish a new edition of *Aesop's Fables* as a Latin–English Primer was rejected by the Company. The project was not published until 1703, although Locke worked on it during 1691.[32] In fact, if Locke had published his edition six years later, the year the Statute of Anne entered into force, his project would have been protected for at least fourteen years, renewable for another fourteen years.

The idea of a limited-in-time property right in authorial works has a central part in Locke's vision of authorial rights. In his critique of the 1662 Act he rejects the

---

26 Ibid 2483.

27 Goldie (n 21 above) 329.

28 For a brief commentary see Goldie, ibid 329-330; De Beer (n 21 above) 785, 791; and Astbury (n 22 above). It is important to note that 'Liberty of the Press' predated the first Copyright Act of 1709, known as the Statute of Anne and entitled: 'An Act for the Encouragement of Learning, by Vesting the Copies of printed Books in the Authors, or Purchasers, of such Copies, during the Times therein mentioned.' Locke, as I shall show, had a clear view on the underlying ideals behind the Statute of Anne, for example with regards to encouraging learning and controlling duration of authorial rights.

29 Goldie, ibid 333.

30 Astbury (n 22 above) 308.

31 Goldie (n 21 above) 331.

32 Ibid 332. See also Astbury (n 22 above) 304.

perpetual right the Stationers' Company enjoyed, and remarks: 'Upon occasion of this instance of the classic authors I demand whether if another Act for printing should be made it be not reasonable that nobody should have any peculiar right in any book which has been in print fifty years, but any one as well as another might have the liberty to print it, for by such titles as these which lies dormant and hinder others many good books come quite to be lost.'[33] He continues and concludes:

> That any person or company should have patents for the sole printing of ancient authors is very unreasonable and injurious to learning. And for those who purchase copies from authors that now live and write it may be reasonable to limit their property to a certain number of years after the death of the author of the first printing of the book as suppose 50 or 70 year. This I am sure, 'tis very absurd and ridiculous that anyone now living should pretend to have a property in or a power to dispose of the property of any copies or writings of authors who lived before printing was known and used in Europe.[34]

In these letters there are two main lines of argument: an economic one and a social one. Since his letter was mainly an attack on the monopolistic power of the Stationers' Company, Locke makes many remarks pertaining to the economic side of his argument. For example, he declares that 'the Company of Stationers have a monopoly of all the classic authors and scholars cannot but at excessive rates have the fair and correct editions of these books and comments…';[35] or that 'whatever money by virtue of this clause they have levied…I am apt to believe not one farthing of it has ever been accounted for the king or brought into the Exchequer…';[36] and that the Act creates a situation in which '[t]he nation loses' since 'our books are so dear and ill printed that they have very little vent amongst foreigners.'[37]

As an author himself, Locke was sensitive to securing 'the author's property right in his copy, or to whom he has transferred it.'[38] He 'complained about the Act as a scholar and book buyer.'[39] In his amendments to the draft Bill he states that 'no printer shall print the name of any person as author or publisher of any book, pamphlet, portraiture, or paper without authority giving in writing…'[40] A modern copyright lawyer might associate this statement with the right of reproduction as well as with the moral right of attribution. However, Locke clearly refers to the 'penalty of forfeiting the sum' of money that should reach the actual rightholder, be

33 Goldie, ibid 333.

34 Ibid 337; Astbury (n 24 above) 309.

35 Goldie, ibid 332. Elsewhere Locke writes that this is the 'great oppression on scholars.' J Locke, 'Locke to Clarke', 2nd January 1692 in B Rand (ed.), *The Correspondence of John Locke and Edward Clarke* (Cambridge Mass.: Harvard University Press 1927) 366-367.

36 Goldie, Ibid 333. Locke also advocates 'common equity' for people to establish a trade and claims the Act contradicts such equity. Ibid 334.

37 Ibid 335.

38 Ibid 338.

39 Astbury (n 22 above) 304.

40 Goldie (n 21 above) 338.

it the author or the publisher.[41] To make sure that his commentary on the Bill is not misunderstood, and that the property of the author is assured, the letter ends with the assertion that there exists 'a privilege in the author of the said book his executors, administrators, and assigns, of solely reprinting and publishing the said book for [blank] years from the first edition thereof, with a power to seize on all copies of the said book reprinted by any other person which by virtue of this Act shall be forfeited to the said author, his executors, administrators and assigns.'[42]

The social aspect is demonstrated by Locke's observation that the 'patent' (copyright-like) clauses in the 1662 Act cause a loss to *everyone*. Locke identifies a triangle of beneficiaries: (i) the government and its peers[43] or the private enterprise that enjoys exclusive powers; (ii) scholars and authors; and (iii) the public at large. He remarks that '[b]y this Act, England loses in general, scholars in particular are ground [down] and nobody gets [anything] but a lazy ignorant Company of Stationers...'[44] Here Locke identifies the nation, the Company, scholars, authors and the public. He contends that the monopoly and excessive powers of the Company adversely affect the dissemination of knowledge and availability of classic authorial works, a policy that brings one to 'starve for printing Dr. Bury's case or the history of Tom Thumb.'[45] The latter is further evidence that Locke was sensitive to the general public good: *Tom Thumb* was a popular 'penny merriment', illustrated for the non-literate.

The fact that Locke's arguments have a social dimension is decisively demonstrated by his concern over two other issues: encouraging learning and limits to authorial rights. Under s 17 of the 1662 Act '[t]hree copies of every book are to be reserved, whereof two to be sent to the universities [Oxford and Cambridge] by the master of the Stationers' Company.'[46] Locke is very sceptical about the application of this requirement, and writes:

> This clause upon examination I suppose will be found to be mightily if not wholly neglected, as all things that are good in this Act, the Company of Stationers minding nothing in it but what makes for their monopoly. I believe that if the public libraries of both universities be looked into (which this will give a fit occasion to do) there will not be found in them half, perhaps not one in ten, of the copies of books printed since this Act.[47]

For Locke, encouraging education and dissemination of knowledge is fundamental. He asserts that copies should be available '[f]or the use of public libraries and

41 Ibid 338.

42 Ibid 339.

43 Locke launched a great attack on the peers whose houses have in 'every corner and cofer in them, under pretence of unlicensed books, a mark of slavery which I think their ancestors would never have submitted to.' Ibid 335-336.

44 Ibid.

45 Ibid 336. Dr Bury who published Oxford's *The Naked Gospel* (1690) was charged with heresy, condemned and burnt by the University. Ibid.

46 Ibid.

47 Ibid.

universities',[48] and for the advancement of education.[49] Locke also views limiting the duration of an author's right as vital. Locke claims that the 1662 Act violates the three basic rights of 'trade, liberty, and property',[50] because a perpetual right vested in the Company denies the author his property rights and violates the liberty to exchange and trade with his property. In response Locke suggests a limited in time property right.[51] As Astbury explains:

> Locke was especially concerned about authors' rights and he advocated the inclusion of a clause which stipulated either that anyone who printed an author's name on a publication without his permission should be liable to forfeit to the author all the copies he had printed, or that when copies of new books were delivered to the libraries, the King's librarian and the Vice-Chancellors of the universities should issue certificates which in effect vested in the authors the sole right to reprint these books for a certain number of years after the publication of the first edition. In making this recommendation that authors should have the power to control the publication of reprints Locke anticipated the terms of the Copyright Act of 1709.[52]

As I observed in the introductory chapter of this book, when one reads 'Liberty of the Press' one is tempted to crown Locke 'the Boyle of copyright.' Scholars have praised Locke for being forward-looking and appreciating 'that the world was changing.'[53] Shapiro, for example, remarks that when reading Locke, we may come to have a better understanding of the world in which we live today: Locke's works 'are remarkable historical documents addressed to the turbulent political conflicts of Locke's day, yet at the same time they transcend that and many another particular context to which they have been deemed relevant.'[54] Copyright is a clear evidence that these remarks are accurate.

Locke's ideal of a limited authorial right addresses the public interest, property and economic ambitions of authors and private undertakings, generally mirrors the social and moral dimensions enshrined in contemporary copyright laws, which limit the right for educational purposes and research, and resembles contemporary remedies allowing seizure of infringing copies.[55] Perhaps the most striking point is

---

48 Ibid 338.

49 Ibid.

50 Ibid 336.

51 Ibid 339.

52 Astbury (n 22 above) 313.

53 G Schocet, '"Guards and Fences": Property and Obligation in Locke's Political Thought' (2000) 21(3) *History of Political Thought* 365, 388.

54 I Shapiro 'Introduction' in I Shapiro (ed.), J Locke, *Two Treatises of Government and A Letter Concerning Tolerance* (New Haven: Yale University Press, 2003) ix.

55 An author's property right in his copy includes not only the right for remuneration but also the 'power to seize copies' reprinted by others. Goldie (n 21 above) 339; and Astbury (n 22 above) 296-297, 308-309. This resembles remedies available for copyright owners under the Anton Pillar Order and the Mareva Injunction. These remedies were also available under the 1662 Act. See also above, Chapter 3.

that in 1694 Locke predicted what, allowing for some differences, over 300 years later has become the formula and the internationally accepted standard for the duration of copyright. Locke remarks that 'nobody should have any peculiar right in any book which has been in print fifty years'[56] and extends this recommendation and supports a term of year copyright followed by a lapse into the public domain because it would be reasonable to restrict authors' 'property to a certain number of years *after* the death of the author *or* the first printing of the book as suppose 50 or 70 years.'[57] Currently copyright lasts 70 years *after* the death of the author. Locke provides two alternatives: either fifty years after publication or 50-70 years post mortem. Although it has sometimes been said that Locke is 'not a philosopher noted for his consistency',[58] not a 'tidy thinker',[59] his conception of copyright is striking,[60] clear and certainly consistent with his general view on property and its limits. Locke is attentive to the danger in perpetual copyright and offers an alternative to the present copyright duration, which can extend over a century. Defenders of a weaker form of copyright should re-read Locke because he advocates a more reasonable timeframe for copyright and directs us to think where we should stop extending copyright duration and reviving works to which protection has lapsed. That was the first, and most obvious, way in which Locke's theory can be re-imagined.

Natural Rights, Labour and Copyright

Definitions

Locke's ideal of copyright should be read and examined not only in light of the *Second Treatise*, but also in relation to his *Essay Concerning Human Understanding* which preceded it. It would also be wrong to separate his property theory from his ideal of copyright because in the *Second Treatise* he does refer to intellectual property, albeit somewhat vaguely. The proximity between publication of the *Second Treatise* and 'Liberty of the Press' clears the way for arguing that for Locke the terms 'property' and 'labour' do not refer solely to tangibles or the physical realm.

'Property' Although copyright scholars tend to take Locke's definition of 'property' to mean physical possessions, the issue is not that straightforward. Locke has several

56 Goldie, ibid 333.

57 Ibid 337.

58 J Waldron, *The Right to Private Property* (Oxford: Oxford University Press, 1988) 213 (hereinafter – 'Waldron 1988').

59 R Singh, 'John Locke and the Theory of Natural Law' (1961) 9 *Political Studies* 105.

60 Given the fact that the duration of copyright has been only recently extended and was 50 years after the death of the author attests to the coherency of Locke's ideal of authors' rights. In fact, in Canada the duration of copyright is still 50 years after the death of the author. Canadian Copyright Act 1985, s 6.

definitions of property.[61] Many of them are organised in trios. For example, he refers to 'Lives, Liberties and Possessions';[62] and 'Lives, Liberties and Estates, which I call by the general Name, Property.'[63] These trinities appear in the *Second Treatise*, the *Essay*, and other sources. Each of these works has its own agenda. The *Second Treatise* discusses the establishment of a stable political order. The *Essay*, on the other hand, focuses on Locke's theory of knowledge and philosophy of mind. The fact that Locke refers to property at different junctures in his political philosophy indicates that there may be more than one Lockean definition of property, or that Locke had in mind a general conception of property referring to a bunch of rights which includes both physical and intangible assets. In fact, Locke's reference to lives and liberties in Chapter V reaffirms the general application of his definition of property, which includes, in that sense, various rights and privileges.

In the *Second Treatise* Locke provides many examples of conventional property, such as: fields, acorns and apples[64] and moss and leaves[65] 'gathered from the Trees in the Wood';[66] timber cut in the wood;[67] water drawn from a fountain[68] or drunk from a river;[69] deer killed;[70] fish caught in the ocean;[71] land that is cultivated;[72] bread, wine, cloth, bricks, masts, ropes and tar that people make;[73] and shells, sparkling pebbles, and diamonds that people pick up.[74] Yet, he then remarks that this does not represent the entire institution of property. For example, property is '*all* the Materials made use of in the Ship that brought any of the Commodities made use of by any of the Workmen to *any* part of the Work.'[75] Accordingly, Schocet remarks:

> What appears to tie [Locke's] differing usages is that property refers to personal ownership that either comprehends or emanates from the self, be it the necessary goods, land – especially land – and money of the state of nature of the life, liberty and estate of

61 There is some support in literature for the idea that Locke had a "conventional" meaning to property. Cherno, for example, suggests that in Chapter V 'we may take Locke to mean "property" as we ordinarily use the term.' M Cherno, 'Locke on Property: A Reappraisal' (1957) 68 *Ethics* 51.

62 E Bk II xxviii 9.

63 2nd T: ix 123.

64 2nd T: v 46.

65 2nd T: v 42.

66 2nd T: v 28, 31, 46.

67 2nd T: v 43.

68 2nd T: v 29.

69 2nd T: v 38.

70 2nd T: v 37.

71 2nd T: v 30.

72 2nd T: v 32, 37-38, 42-43.

73 2nd T: v 42-43.

74 2nd T: v 46.

75 2nd T: v 43 (emphasis added).

civil society. As Locke said: 'By Property I must be Understood here, as in other places, to mean that Property which Men have in their Persons as well as Goods.' (2nd T: 173)[76]

Locke's remark that property encompasses what 'Men have in their Persons as well as Goods'[77] provide some support for the claim that intellectual expressions are not clearly excluded from his vision of what the concept property covers. In Chapter V, Locke seems to draw a distinction between persons in the natural, or biological sense, and an evolving person that includes the self. This is illustrated in his remark that 'every Man has a *Property* in his own *Person*. This no Body has any Right to but Himself.'[78] A copyright work, as we all know, is an item of goods but is also a manifestation of the *person* – of one's self.

Property, then, in the *Second Treatise*, should be read as a general term regulating ownership and control of different kinds of things, not necessarily confined to the physical realm. Further support for this conclusion is provided by Locke's frequent references to the term 'property' in the *Essay.*[79] As a document that deals with man's post innate constitution and the accumulation of knowledge, these references testify to the fact that Locke did not merely associate commodities with tangibility but also with their social context and in relation to ownership of language and knowledge.

'Labour' In the jurisprudence of rights, the assumption that one has the right to the produce of one's creative labour is probably the most intuitive basis for arguing in favour of a natural private property right.[80] But what did Locke have in mind with regards to 'labour' when he wrote on property in the *Second Treatise*?

---

76 Schocet (n 53 above) 379. See especially, 376-381.

77 2nd T: xv 173.

78 2nd T: v 27. See also 2nd T: v 44. These remarks by Locke brought scholars to claim that in Chapter V Locke has subscribed to a personality theory. See Hughes (n 1 above) 329. Olivercona supports this view and writes: 'The acorn becomes the property of the collector when he picks it from the ground. This is the moment when something of his personality is infused into the acorn.' K Olivercona, 'Appropriation in the State of Nature: Locke on the Origin of Property' (1974) 35 *Journal of the History of Ideas* 211, 225. Hamilton also asserts that: 'Locke never disassociates property from the personality of which it is an expression; because it is the creation of man it has the sacredness which he attaches to human life itself.' WH Hamilton, 'Property – According to Locke' (1932) 41 *Yale Law Journal* 864, 868. See also M Rose, *Authors and Owners: The Invention of Copyright* (Boston: Harvard University Press, 1994) 114.

79 E Bk II xxxi 6; E Bk III vi 50; E Bk III ix 17; E Bk IV iii 18; E Bk iv iii 10.

80 Courts apply 'labour' to signify intellectual efforts, creative input, personal contribution and personal judgement. For example, in *Sayre v Moore* Lord Mansfield remarks that 'men of ability, who have employed their time for the service of the community, may not be deprived of their just merits, and the reward of their ingenuity and labour.' *Sayre v Moore* (1785) 1 East 361. Moreover, in a recent copyright saga, the Federal Court of Canada explicitly refers to Locke's labour theory. See *CCH Canadian Ltd v Law Society of Upper Canada* [2004] 1 SCR 339. See also above, Chapters 1 and 3.

Published only a year before 'Liberty of the Press' and five years after the *Second Treatise*, Locke's essay 'Labour' strengthens the argument that when he uses the term 'property' in Chapter V he is well aware of intellectual property.[81] Here, Locke highlights the advantages of labour, its moral value, and its importance for human happiness, good health and the better use of power and control. The key issue is directing the distribution of labour in the world for the sake of 'more knowledge, peace, health and plenty.'[82]

In his attempt to reaffirm his great support for a property right to the laborious and industrious, Locke explicitly refers to 'labour in useful and mechanical art'[83] and draws a clear distinction between manual labour performed by the 'country man', 'the working artisan' and the 'man of manual labour' and intellectual labour carried by the 'gentlemen and scholar.'[84] For Locke, man should be engaged in labour for twelve hours a day.[85] However, his ideal of 'honest labour' differs for a manual labourer and the scholar. Locke provides guidelines for a favourable distribution of labour in the day and remarks that six hours of study for 'improvement of his mind' should suffice the scholar.[86] He then modifies his stand, writing: 'If this distribution of the twelve hours seem not fair nor sufficiently to keep up the distinction that ought to be in the ranks of men let us change it a little. Let the gentlemen and scholar employ nine of the twelve on his mind in thought and reading and the other three in some honest labour. And the man of manual labour nine in work and three in knowledge.'[87]

The concept 'labour' in Locke's language then, is not reserved for physical labour only or associated merely with tangibles. Locke's reference to the labour of the 'gentlemen and scholar', the scholar's work of mind in 'thought and reading', and study for matters of 'improvement of his mind',[88] all support the view that for Locke, labour is also an activity associated with accumulation and expression of knowledge by scholars and artists, and intellectual products were not segregated from other commodities when he wrote his property theory.

'Conveniences of Life' In 'Labour' Locke makes several references to the 'conveniences of life.'[89] The term appears also in s 44 of Chapter V, where Locke writes:

---

81 J Locke, 'Labour' (published 1693), in Goldie (n 21 above) 326-328.

82 Ibid 328.

83 Ibid 326.

84 Ibid 327-328.

85 Locke asserts: 'Half the day employed in useful labour would supply the inhabitants of the earth with the necessities and conveniences of life, in full plenty.' Ibid 326.

86 Ibid 327.

87 Ibid 328.

88 Ibid 327.

89 Ibid 326, 328.

> From all which it is evident, that though the things of Nature are given in common, yet Man (by being Master of himself, and *Proprietor of his own person*, and the Actions or *Labour* of it) had still in himself *the great Foundation of Property*; and that which made up the great part of what he applied to the Support or Comfort of his being, *when Invention and Arts had improved the conveniences of Life*, was perfectly his own, and did not belong in common to others.[90]

Many analogies can be drawn between s 44 and 'Labour' which signify the generality and flexibility of the way Locke understands the term 'property.' For example 'support and comfort' and 'conveniences of life' in Chapter V can be analogised with Locke's references in 'Labour' to 'necessaries and conveniences of life', to books and 'pleasures', and 'arts and instruments of luxury.'[91] In addition, in the *Essay* Locke also refers to 'Conveniences of Life' including in the context of useful arts.[92] Although when Locke refers to the terms 'invention' and 'arts' in the *Essay* he often means natural faculties, the many combinations he makes of the terms and the many uses he makes of other terms that relate to 'invention and arts', suggest that when writing Chapter V, Locke refers to 'invention and arts' to denote not only employment of natural faculties and abilities in the making of traditional properties, but also laborious intellectual achievements capable of private title, as long as they advance the 'conveniences of life.'

When read together with his remarks in the *Essay*, with his note 'Labour', and coupled with his approach to property as a general concept, s 44 highlights the fact that Locke did think of intellectual property when he wrote Chapter V. This also highlights the mistake ingrained in scholarship on copyright claiming that Locke did not think of intellectual property. Perhaps Locke's reference to intellectual property in the *Second Treatise* is not very clear or explicit. Yet, *his* mistake was that he did not distinguish between physical and cultural property. In other words, his mistake is in his belief that even when '*Invention and Arts had improved the conveniences of Life*' it is perfectly admissible to treat all kinds of works as the exclusive private property of an individual creator, because such works now do 'not belong in common to others.'[93] However, a few years later, he compensates in 'Liberty of the Press' and clearly defines the limits of exclusive ownership when works of authorship are at stake.

A Natural Right Justification

Collective and individual rights through labour-mixing Locke's attitude towards authorial rights is based on his understanding of the very idea of property as emanating from a person's right to his labour. His philosophy regarding both property

90 2nd T: v 44 (emphasis added).

91 Goldie (n 21 above) 328.

92 See for example, E Bk IV xii 11.

93 2nd T: v 44.

and authorial rights, illustrates how his ideal of ownership opposes dogmatic justifications for the classic political status quo.

In Chapter V of the *Second Treatise* he crafts a theory of original appropriation to justify private enclosure of commonly owned objects, and in doing so provides the framework for any property argument, including intellectual properties. Chapter V is a 'skilful bit of dialectic'[94] permitting private enclosures through mixing labour with commonly owned properties and guarantees a natural private property right in an original object.[95] Through the expenditure of laborious efforts the labourer, be it a peasant, a hunter or an author, secures himself a private dominion embedded with properties of many kinds. Locke does not include in this formula Kings or their agents,[96] which, in light of 'Liberty of the Press', includes the Stationers' Company.

The setting in Chapter V is that of the state of nature – the pre-political state of mankind in which '*everyone has the Executive Power* of the Law of Nature',[97] a '*State of Liberty*, yet it is not a *State of Licence*, though Man in that State have an uncontrollable Liberty, to dispose of his Person or Possessions…'[98] Our copyright regime is embedded with conceptual elements from the state of nature. Copyright law stipulates that ideas are not protected; they are allegedly infinitely inexhaustible: ideas are free as the air for all to use and not in risk of depletion. The only rule that regulates their consumption is that there is no limit to the amount of ideas one can use. Copyright laws, however, distinguish ideas from their expression, circling the latter with fences that prohibit others from using and consuming what is not their own.

The Lockean labour theory can be regarded as the union of two basic theses that complement each other. The first is that everyone has a natural property right in the labour of his body – the famous metaphor of labour mixture. The second thesis argues that a property right is limited by specific social norms. In Locke's words:

> Though the Earth, and all inferior Creatures be common to all Men, yet every Man has a *Property* in his own *Person*. This no Body has any Right to but him. The *Labour* of his Body and the *Work* of his Hands, we may say, are properly his. Whatsoever, then, he removes from out of the State that Nature hath provided, and left it in, he hath mixed his *Labour* with, and joined to it something that is his own, and thereby makes it his *Property*. It being by him removed from the common state Nature placed it in, it hath by this *labour* something annexed to it, that excludes the common right of other Men. For this *Labour* being the unquestionable Property of the Labourer, no Man but he can have a right to

94 Hamilton (n 78 above) 867.

95 In *Millar v Taylor* the court applies a natural law theory to copyright alongside the economic approach taken by the Statute of Anne. *Millar v Taylor* (1769) 98 Eng Rep 201, 252. The court's decision was overruled by the House of Lords in *Donaldson v Beckett* (1774) 1 Eng Rep 837.

96 See generally R Ashcraft, 'Locke's Political Philosophy', in Chappell (n 19 above) 226.

97 2nd T: ii 13.

98 2nd T: ii 6.

what that is once joyned to, at least where there is enough, and as good left in common for others.[99]

Locke introduces labour as a tool to overcome the consent difficulty. He rejects the theory of universal compact as a necessary condition of legitimate appropriation, as held by Grotius and Pufendorf.[100] He writes that if commoners were not able to enclose common properties via labour, appropriation would require a worldwide compact: man would starve 'notwithstanding the Plenty God had given him.'[101] In order to overcome this, Locke shows 'how *labour* could make Men distinct titles to several parcels of it, for their private uses'[102] and that 'Man (by being Master of himself, and *Proprietor of his own person*, and the Actions or *Labour* of it) has in himself "*the great Foundation of Property*".'[103] Once a property right has been established in an item, the item cannot be taken from its owner without consent.[104]

By the mixing of labour with a commonly owned object, the labourer becomes the owner of the object.[105] He has annexed something to it 'more than Nature, the common Mother of all, had done.'[106] Labour justifies the integration of a physical object into the labourer's realm, the *suum*,[107] and the result is ownership[108] – the deer that the Indian has killed is his in the sense that it is a part of himself, and a completed plan for a tulip garden in the centre of Brussels is the planner's own, as it now constitutes part of himself.[109]

---

99 2nd T: v 27.

100 On that issue see, S Buckle, *Natural Law and the Theory of Property: Grotius to Hume* (Oxford: Clarendon Press, 1999) 125-190.

101 2nd T: v 28.

102 2nd T: v 39. As Laslett states: 'it is through the theory of property that man can proceed from the abstract world of liberty and equality based on their relationship with God and natural law, to the concrete world of political liberty guaranteed by political arrangements.' P Laslett, 'Introduction' (n 2 above) 102. Gobetti also remarks that Locke invokes 'inequality, because he is convinced that equality is a source of conflict, as the transformation of the state of nature into a state of war shows.' D Gobetti, *Private and Public: Individuals, Households, and Body Politic in Locke and Hutcheson* (London and New York: Routledge, 1992) 97.

103 2nd T: v 44.

104 2nd T: 138, 140, 193. For further analysis of the compact theory as applied to Locke see J Simmons, *The Lockean Theory of Rights* (Princeton, Oxford: Princeton University Press, 1992) 236-241.

105 2nd T: v 34, 45.

106 2nd T: v 28.

107 The *suum* means – what belongs to a person is what is one's own. For a brief explanation of the term 'suum' see Olivercona (n 78 above); and Buckle (n 100 above) 169-173.

108 Day challenges the idea of ownership through labour and argues that one cannot talk of 'owning labour' because labour is an activity that can be performed, but cannot be owned. See also JP Day, 'Locke on Property' (1966) 16 *Philosophical Quarterly* 207, 212.

109 Denicola argues that 'the act of aggregating isolated pieces of information' should be a ground for copyright protection in part because of considerations of 'natural right to the

In the introduction to this chapter, I accepted Craig's criticism of Lockean approaches to copyright for their lack of appreciating that Locke's theory of property may expand the boundaries of copyright control.[110] In light of the discussion of authorial collectivity, when a copyright work is at stake, two entities are entitled to say 'I own it.' There are two labourers: public and author. Both labour on making the creation and both therefore deserve a property right in it. In the words of Hettinger: 'Given this vital dependence of a person's thoughts on the idea of those who came before her, intellectual products are fundamentally social products. Thus, even if one assumes that the value of these products is entirely the result of human labour, this value is not entirely attributed to *any particular labourer* (or small group of labourers).'[111]

If, according to Locke, only labour justifies entitlement to property, then, on the argument for authorial collectivity, the public's collective contribution must satisfy the requirement of labour for purposes of ownership. Labour, as I show in Chapter 3 is a core element in the assessment of copyright subsistence. It has been broadly interpreted by the Court and does not mean physical labour only. That is, laborious contribution is not limited to the contribution of the person 'who pushed the pen' onto paper.[112] In Chapter 4 I show how the contribution of the public amounts to collective labour. It includes physical contribution of members of the public, and general social and cultural input. Locke forcefully advocates that any violation of the individual's right amounts to unlawful intrusion into the individual's realm. The same should hold for the public: any violation of the collective right by virtue of disproportionate enclosures of cultural and social portions of the public domain, violates the public's property right in its labour. As Gordon most poignantly remarks: 'Natural rights theory…is necessarily concerned with the rights of the public as well as with the rights of those whose labors create intellectual products.'[113] Locke did not account for the public's labour and here lies one the greatest difficulties in applying Chapter V to intellectual property. Before I critique Lockean approaches to copyright I examine whether Locke treated the public interest in Chapter V the way he treated it in 'Liberty of the Press.'

The no-harm principle The concept of ownership should be distinguished from the moral justifiability of owning a particular thing. It is one thing to ask what powers over X are normally connoted by the statement that 'A owns X', but quite another thing to ask under what conditions A is morally entitled to exercise these powers and to be regarded as the owner of X. Locke's strategy is to argue that under certain

---

fruits of one's labour' and unjust enrichment. R Denicola, 'Copyright in Collections of Facts: A Theory for the Protection of Nonfiction Literary Works' (1981) 81 *Columbia Law Review* 516, 519-520, 528, 530; See also Gordon 1992 (n 1 above) 166-167, 266-273.

110 Craig (n 1 above).

111 Hettinger (n 1 above) 38 (emphasis added).

112 *Cala Homes (South) Ltd v Alfred McAlpine Homes East Ltd* [1995] FSR 818, 835 (per Laddie J). I further emphasise this point in Chapter 7.

113 Gordon 1993 (n 1 above) 1535.

conditions individual acquisition does not violate anyone's right to property in the common. However, if a person has within himself the '*Foundation of Property*'[114] and, if labour creates property entitlement, what limits a person's right to appropriate from the common? Locke invokes the no-harm principle to address this issue. This principle ensures that a person's natural property right is protected only once it is balanced against and regulated by certain social norms, so that it does not conflict with the 'common good.'[115] As Gordon explains:

> The essential logic is simple: Labor is mine and when I appropriate objects from the common I join my labor to them. If you take the objects I have gathered you have also taken my labor, since I have attached my labor to the objects in question. This harms me, and you should not harm me. You therefore have a duty to leave these objects alone. Therefore I have property in the objects. Similarly, if I use the public domain to create a new intangible work of authorship or invention, you should not harm me by copying it and interfering with my plans for it. I therefore have property in the intangible as well.[116]

Locke's no-harm principle as envisioned in Chapter V is composed of two immediate conditions set upon private property and an additional condition securing minimum sustenance in extreme circumstances. First, Locke argues that the labourer may appropriate only the amount that he can come to use – 'Nothing was made by God for Man to spoil or destroy.'[117] I refer to this as 'the no-spoliation Proviso.' Second is the 'enough and as good Proviso' holding that a man has a right to appropriate from the common as long as there is 'enough, and as good left in common for others.'[118] In addition, Locke articulates a charity principle by which in extreme circumstances commoners have a right to take and consume of others' private resources.[119]

---

114 2nd T: v 44.

115 In that respect Zuckert writes that there are limitations on what human beings may do, for example 'they may not indirectly harm each other through taking more than their fair share of goods of the external world.' P Zuckert, 'Do Natural Rights Derive from Natural Law?' (1997) 3 *Harvard Journal of Law & Public Policy* 695, 724.

Interestingly, Article 43 of the Irish Constitution recognises property rights as natural rights, but one's natural property rights will be protected *as long as* they are balanced and regulated by the principles of 'social justice' and do not conflict with the 'common good.' This is a powerful statement of two crucial propositions. First, there is an inherently social dimension to private property. Second, where conflicts between individual self-interest and the public good exist, the public good has priority. The open-textured language of such provisions highlights the fundamental nature of social obligations. Yet, the social balance these provisions aim to protect is dependent on the way they are interpreted.

116 Gordon 1993 (n 1 above) 1544-1545. See also Gordon 2004 (n 1 above) 80-81.

117 2nd T: v 31.

118 2nd T: v 27. Gordon even names this Proviso the '[no-harm] Proviso.' Gordon 1993 (n 1 above) 1581.

119 1st T: iv 42. Locke's theory, in other words, informs Harris's definition of natural rights: 'Natural rights are such rights as follow from the interaction between the formal and substantive requirements of *just treatment* and the *fact of the world*.' JW Harris, *Property and Justice* (Oxford: Oxford University Press, 1996) 183, 213 (emphasis added).

It will facilitate my analysis if I recall the Hohfeldian terms:[120] every commoner has a privilege – liberty – to use the common; no one has, in Locke's state of nature, a right (or claim) to the common. After a commoner has exercised the privilege which others also have, by labouring on a commonly owned object, he deserves a reward for his efforts and he may become the owner of that object. Once the labourer has complied with the two Provisos, he has become the owner of the object and he has a right to that object, while every other commoner has the correlative duty to refrain from interfering with his right. In other words, labour and compliance with the Provisos transform a commoner's privilege to a duty and a labourer's privilege to a right. A labourer that does not leave 'enough and as good' for others remains a commoner-privilege-holder and not a labourer-right-holder. His right to the produce of his labour did not mature.[121]

The idea/expression dichotomy dictates that in copyright the labour and the no-harm principle bear different meanings. For example, if I surreptitiously waxed your car, I own neither the car, not the wax. Similarly, when I labour on an idea to film a documentary movie on the atrocities in the Second World War, I own neither the idea nor the expression of it, if it was expressed by someone else. As Drassinower argues: '[a]ll that is copyrightable originates in the author's labour, but not everything originating in the author's labour is subject to copyright protection.'[122] Although, under Locke's account, encroachment into another's realm might lead to injury, copyright law justifies such an injury in order to account for the public interest. It creates moral injury under the idea/expression dichotomy, and in the form of the various fair dealing exceptions and public policy defence. These 'injuries' can, however, be looked at as a benefit for authors and artists. As Gordon explains: 'Some limitations on authors' rights may benefit the consuming public without harming authors. Since authors are part of the public – and in fact may constitute the part of

---

Harris suggests a three step principle applicable to Locke's entitlement paradigm, which he calls the 'creation-without-wrong' argument for a natural property right: 'If a person (a) creates a new item of social wealth, and (b) wrongs no-one in doing so, it follows that (c) he ought to be accorded ownership of that new item.' Ibid 197. Harris strongly criticises the validity of Locke's property theory to tangibles and intangibles alike. Ibid, 182-212.

120 See above, Chapter 3.

121 It can be argued that Locke distinguishes between *de jure* property and *de facto* property. A labourer will never become a *de facto* owner of a previously commonly owned object unless he complies with certain social limitation. He will always be *de jure* owner of the object because the labour he expended on it is his 'unquestionable Property' (2nd T: v 27), but a *de facto* ownership is dependent upon compliance with the relevant conditions. Viewed in this way, it might be that a Lockean labourer would have to comply with the conditions in a set time. The fact that he has a *de jure* property right will secure for him the first-in-time right, as long as he meets the conditions in time.

122 Drassinower (n 1 above) 18. In that respect Simmons writes, that 'mixing labour is not a way of losing labour…Our labour extends our selves into the natural world. Our purposive activities are inseparable from our selves.' AJ Simmons, 'Makers' Rights' (1998) 2 *The Journal of Ethics* 197, 211.

the public most in need of using prior works as bricks when building new works – it is likely that some privileges to copy will aid authors more than harm them.'[123] In fact, in 'Liberty of the Press' Locke justifies the imposition of involuntary harm on authors' property rights for matters of public interest and advocates a weaker version of a natural right for authors – limited in time and available for purposes of education and learning.[124]

Copyright and the no-spoliation proviso Locke maintains that a labourer who is too keen and, for instance, appropriates more apples than he can come to use and allows them to perish commits an injury against others and violates the 'the common Law of Nature' and is 'liable to be punished; he invaded his Neighbour's share, for he had *no Right, farther than his* Use called for any of them.'[125] It is an absolute condition set on appropriation and ensures that '*Nothing*' was made by God to spoil or destroy.[126]

Copyright scholars disagree on the relevancy of the no-spoliation Proviso as it pertains to intellectual property. Gordon hardly mentions it. Hughes does not think it is a key element and argues that it is absent in intellectual property systems.[127] Craig provides a thorough criticism,[128] and Damstedt advocates its fundamental importance. The latter defines spoliation as occurring 'where a unit of a product of labor is not put to any use',[129] and claims, *inter alia*, that nonuse violates the condition, and that the Proviso therefore justifies the claim underlying the fair use doctrine: 'justified taking can be seen as a natural way to police the waste prohibition.'[130]

It is mistaken to ignore the no-spoliation condition when discussing copyright. We may easily see that the no-spoliation Proviso leaves the allocation of strong private copyrights intact. In and of themselves, ideas are non-rivalrous, they do not perish, and the law allows us to consume as many ideas as we wish to. Even if we consume more than we can use, we cannot prevent anyone else from doing the same – ideas are free as the air. The success of this argument is dependent, however, on the following two issues: the ability of our judges to separate ideas from their expressions, and the spoliation of the latter.

Scholars connect the Proviso to copyright in a perplexing way. Drahos for example observes that 'ideas can spoil in the sense that, once appropriated, their time span of useful application in many cases is limited. Those who appropriate ideas

---

123 WJ Gordon 'An Inquiry into the Merits of Copyright' (1989) 41 *Stanford Law Review* 1343, 1461.

124 Shiffrin (n 1 above) 155.

125 2nd T: v 37, 31.

126 2nd T: v 31.

127 Perhaps a requirement of publication for copyright subsistence could have manifested a strong Proviso in intellectual property. Hughes (n 1 above) 328-329. *Cf* Hettinger (n 1 above) 44-45, and Damstedt (n 1 above).

128 Gordon 1993 (n 1 above) 1543, 1551; Craig (n 1 above) 31-34.

129 Damstedt (n 1 above) 1182.

130 Ibid 1196.

with a view to do nothing with them arguably infringe Locke's spoilage Proviso.'[131] Craig illustrates a situation where 'the intellectual property owner wasted the idea by preventing its communication and development.'[132] How can copyright owners violate the Proviso if ideas are not protected and 'they almost always retain future value'?[133] Moreover, in a society that sanctifies principles of freedom and democratic discourse, can we force people to talk? Can I, after a discussion with my friend, force him to communicate the ideas we discussed to other people? No matter how socially valuable these ideas are, I cannot force him to either communicate them or develop them in any possible way. It seems that the connection between violation of the Proviso and copyright, and Craig's example, depends on a viable separation of an idea from its expression. The distinction between ideas and expressions is blurred, based on instinct and subjective interpretations.[134] Ideas intermingle with expressions and enclosures of 'universal truths or transcendent essence that cannot and should not be captured or controlled by one artist' become subject to copyright.[135] Due to the inability to successfully separate the two constituents of a copyright work – ideas from their expressions – current copyright laws not only deplete the common of its cultural and social elements but permit virtually uncontrollable appropriation of ideas. This may trigger severe violation of the no-spoliation condition. As Drahos writes: '[a]s abstract objects ideas cannot spoil, but the opportunities that they confer may.'[136] That is why we must ensure that the separation of ideas from their expression

131 Drahos (n 1 above) 51.

132 Craig (n 1 above) 33.

133 Hughes (n 1 above) 328.

134 As Cohen writes: 'There may be no way for the new artist to extract the "idea" without the "expression".' It is simply a subjective test. AB Cohen, 'Copyright Law and the Myth of Objectivity: The Idea-Expression Dichotomy and the Inevitability of Artistic Value Judgements' (1990) 66 *Indiana Law Journal* 175, 231. On this point see also Chapter 3.1(1) above.

The distinction is so ridiculously subjective that Lord Hoffmann in the *Designers Guild* case ironically remarks that 'copyright law protects foxes better than hedgehogs.' *Designers Guild Ltd v Russell Williams Textiles Ltd* [2000] 1 WLR 2416, 2423 (HL). In a later case, Lewison J adds to the confusion and remarks: '[I]t is sometimes said that there is no copyright in ideas; only in the expression of ideas. Like many beguilingly simple propositions, this one needs to be treated with caution.' J Lewison in *Ultra Marketing (UK), Thomas Alexander Scott v Universal Components Ltd* [2004] EWHC 468 Ch.

The risk is that, '[o]n the one hand, if courts adopt a narrow view of idea and a broad view of expression, more and more similarities will be similarities of expression and will therefore support claims of infringement. In turn, this implies a broad scope of copyright. Conversely, if courts adopt a broad view of idea and a narrow view of expression, few similarities will qualify as similarities of expression. This will result in a relatively limited scope of copyright.' AC Yen, 'A First Amendment Perspective on the Idea/Expression Dichotomy and Copyright in a Work's 'Total Concept and Feel' (1989) 38 *Emory Law Journal* 393, 400, in particular 398-407.

135 Cohen, ibid 231.

136 Drahos (n 1 above) 51.

is viable, if we want to maintain some social sense of copyright, namely that ideas are not protectable and cannot be appropriated as private property.

Intellectual goods are perishable,[137] but the Proviso becomes relevant only once an idea has been expressed and attracts copyright protection.[138] Hughes distinguishes between spoilage in the 'social context' and for the 'individual organism.'[139] Access to the social value is dependent on the duration of the right. In many cases, once protection has expired, the work no longer has the same social value and therefore has been 'spoiled', even if it surprises us with a sudden revival and yields value at a later date. Novels become 'old', architectural styles fall in and out of fashion, and computer programs lose their social value and become obsolete, sometimes long before expiration of the right.[140] Furthermore, Hughes is mistaken to assume that there is no loss to the 'individual organism' because, for the owner the internal value remains constant. The 'individual organism' clearly loses by virtue of not communicating and sharing the creation with others: the owner deprives himself of the true value of the creation, for example, that another will generate a derivative idea and he would develop his initial creation even further.[141]

Locke applies a tacit no-spoliation Proviso in 'Liberty of the Press.' He is aware that in situations of perpetual copyright, spoilage of social value is inevitable. His copyright ideal proves that any system of authors' rights must incorporate the no-spoliation condition as part of its moral applicability. His suggestion of a limited-in-time property right given to authors and the requirement of public access to authorial works for educational and learning purposes, limit the possible violations of the Proviso. That is, Locke's ideal of a system of authorial rights respects that some items have 'certain natural and proper uses, such that it would be perverse to use them otherwise',[142] and prohibiting proper use violates the Proviso.

Copyright and the 'enough and as good' Proviso Every labourer is under an obligation to leave in the common 'enough and as good' for other commoners to appropriate.[143] The credibility of Locke's property theory depends on the realization of this Proviso.[144] It appears both before and after the no-spoliation condition, and

137 Hughes (n 1 above) 328.

138 According to Hughes, due to the absent of a publication requirement, the Proviso is less relevant for intellectual property. Ibid.

139 Ibid 327.

140 Ibid 328. *Cf* Craig (n 1 above) 31-32.

141 This is one of the reasons why, as Damstedt argues, we should invoke a fair use right against an owner of an intellectual property who is letting the good spoil and waste. Damstedt (n 1 above).

142 A Ryan, *Property and Political Theory* (Oxford: Blackwell, 1984) 37.

143 2nd T: v 27, 33, 34.

144 Waldron challenges those who insist on the Proviso's importance. He is concerned with the operation of the Proviso in the age of scarcity and claims that the '"enough and as good" requirement is merely a fact about appropriation in the age of abundance.' J Waldron, 'Enough and as Good Left for Others' (1979) 29 *Philosophical Quarterly* 319, 322; and

before the introduction of the money economy. Its prevalence can lead one to believe that Locke intends the Proviso to affect every scenario of appropriation. As Gordon puts it, '[i]t is the Proviso therefore that gives Locke's theory much of its moral force.'[145]

This Proviso is attractive for several reasons. Morally, it respects the right of every fellow commoner to appropriate from the common. Practically, it does not require the consent of all commoners prior to appropriation. At the same time, it ensures that the common is not devalued and provides the public with a moral right to encroach into their members' private dominion. In intellectual property terms, it ensures that a 'grant of property does no harm to other persons' equal abilities to create or to draw upon the preexisting cultural matrix and scientific heritage'[146] since it restricts the ownership of intellectual creations and widens the doorway to new creators.

Some scholars take the view that this Proviso applies seamlessly to intellectual property. For example, Hughes observes that '[i]ntellectual property systems… do seem to accord with Locke's labor condition and the "enough and as good" requirement. In fact, the "enough and as good" condition seems to hold true only in intellectual property. That may mean that Locke's unique theoretical edifice finds its firmest bedrock in the common of ideas.'[147] Similarly Moore remarks that '[t]he individual who takes a good drink from a river does as much as to take nothing

---

Waldron 1988 (n 58 above) 209-218, 280-283; Waldron 2002 (n 19 above) 172. Waldron then concludes that the Proviso indicates that 'men would have a general right to private property, in the sense that they would have a right, enforceable against others, not to be left in a situation where appropriation was impossible for them.' Waldron 1988, ibid 218. For criticism of Waldron's approach see G Sreenivasan, *The Limits of Lockean Rights in Property* (New York: Oxford University Press, 1995) 37-41, 47-58.

Waldron also rejects Nozick's argument for a 'weak Lockean Proviso.' For Nozick the 'crucial point is whether appropriation of an unowned object worsens the situation of others.' R Nozick, *Anarchy, State and Utopia* (Oxford: Basic Books, 1974) 175. This means that 'someone whose appropriation otherwise would violate the Proviso still may appropriate provided he compensates the others so that their situation is not thereby worsened.' Ibid 178. See also Sreenivasan, ibid 123. Waldron asserts in reaction that Nozick's formula 'is too weak for Locke; it does not even live up to the demands of the minimal Lockean requirement of charity.' Waldron 1988, ibid 216. The problem and the danger are, as Bogart argues, that in scarcity situations 'every acquisition worsens the lot of others – and worsens their lot in relevant ways.' JH Bogart, 'Lockean Provisos and the State of Nature' (1984-1985) 95 *Ethics* 828, 834.

Sanders offers an alternative interpretation according to which we should drop the 'leaving' constituent of the Proviso. However, '[s]ince this part is the very heart of Locke's Proviso, it seems plain that the Proviso should…simply be abandoned.' JT Sanders, 'Projects and Property' in D Schmidtz (ed.), *Robert Nozick* (Cambridge: Cambridge University Press, 2002) 34, 39-41.

145 Gordon 1993 (n 1 above) 1565.

146 Ibid 1562.

147 Hughes (n 1 bove) 329.

at all. The same may be said of those who acquire intellectual property…[T]he case for Locke's water-drinker and the author or inventor are quite alike.'[148] These statements use Locke's Provisos in order to reinforce the status quo: the Proviso is easily satisfied because ideas are non-rivalrous and infinitely consumable, hence 'enough and as good' ideas are always available.

Two questions pertaining to copyright and the 'enough and as good' Proviso must be addressed. First, for whom must 'enough and as good' be left? Whose condition the Proviso intends to affect? It is evident that Locke sought the public good, remarking that everything is done for the public good, for 'the good of every particular member of that society…'[149] Gordon observes that in introducing the Proviso Locke intended to defend the welfare of everyone, in particular the non-propertied.[150] This is also evident in the way Locke advocates limits to authors' rights in 'Liberty of the Press.' In fact, he mentions that man should not 'starve for printing' of classic books.[151] It shows that for Locke basic sustenance cannot start and end with conventional properties but include elements necessary for the stable evolution of the self. To

---

148 Moore (n 1 above) 98.

149 1st T: iv 92. The inclusion of the charity principle in Locke's political philosophy grounds further support for its moral force and that Locke thought of the public good. Locke applies the principle for situations where there is 'extream want.' Locke considers charity a matter of natural right, not of supererogation. However, the right to charity should be carefully demarcated because 'for, upon a very modest computation, it may be concluded that above one half of those who receive relief from the parishes are able to get their livelihood.' J Locke, 'A Report on the Board of Trade to the Lords Justices 1697, Respecting Relief and Unemployment of the Poor', in HR Fox Bourne, *The Life of John Locke* (London: Henry S King, 1876) vol 2, 378. See also JC Winfrey, 'Charity Versus Justice in Locke's Theory of Property' (1981) 42(3) *Journal of the History of Ideas* 436.

Waldron emphasises the centrality of the charity principle and observes that: '[a] man in need has "a right" to another's surplus goods: indeed Locke twice talks of his having "a title" in a way that suggests that this too is to be regarded as a property entitlement.' Waldron 2002 (n 19 above) 180.

Gordon examines the charity principle in the context of intellectual property. She distinguishes 'unearned rights' from other rights. The latter relates to rights that are 'fundamental human entitlements.' They are defined as such since we posses them by 'virtue of our humanity.' Gordon 1993 (n 1 above) 1543. According to Gordon, a labourer does not have an absolute right to the product of his labour when he faces others in great need. The right to charity then, is an 'unearned' right. Gordon rightly argues that in copyright terms, this implies that one has a restricted right to the creative expressions of one's labour if the public or a specific user are 'in need.' Ibid.

150 Ibid 1570. Gordon also asserts that 'although the natural-rights approach is usually thought to be inconsistent with a public-benefits approach to intellectual property, it in fact supports a demand that significant components of intellectual property law be crafted to serve the public benefit.' Ibid 1609. *Cf* Hundret who argues that Locke and his successors: 'sought their own rather than the public interest.' EJ Hundret, 'Market, Society and Meaning in Locke's Political Philosophy' (1977) 15 *Journal of the History of Ideas* 15, 44.

151 Goldie (n 21 above) 336.

claim that Locke did not intend the public good is to discredit the social pattern enshrined in his ideals of property and authors' rights and to deny his concern for the social condition of the general public and its members.[152]

The second question to ask is this: is Locke's Proviso what is needed in copyright? Comprehension of the difficulty inherent in applying Locke's 'enough and as good' Proviso to intellectual property constitutes a first step in answering this question. Locke applies the Proviso specifically to raw materials and excludes its applicability to the products which result from mixing raw materials and labour. Fisher observes that there are seven categories of raw materials with which a Lockean labourer would mix his labour: the universe of facts; languages; elements of our cultural heritage that 'we "share" and that gives our culture meaning and coherence'; ideas apprehended by at least one person but owned by anyone; ideas apprehended by at least one person; the set of 'all "reachable" ideas'; and 'the set of all "possible ideas" – that is, all ideas that someone might think of.'[153] Fisher finds anomalies in these categories as, for example, certain components of our cultural heritage, which should remain accessible to all, are brought under copyright protection (eg, Mickey Mouse).[154] The danger, as Drahos observes, is the following:

> [E]ven where the stock of abstract objects is infinite, the human capacity to exploit that stock at any given moment is conditioned by the state of cultural and scientific knowledge which exists at that historical moment...The set of usable abstract objects may also be further reduced because some ideas or knowledge may be necessary gateways to others... Contrary to the view that societies are awash with information, it may be that, at various points in history, societies may face a shortage of supply of abstract objects. Under such conditions of shortage, those who claim property rights in abstract objects may well fail to leave enough and as good for others.[155]

Denial of the fact that we are worse off because of our strong copyright regime 'is to ignore the nature of cultural development and the human drive to participate in the social conversation.'[156] It ignores the implications of the authorial collectivity, detrimentally affects our ability to build on our predecessors, and impedes our ability to preserve cultural dialogue, collective identity, and social realities. A situation where there is left not 'enough and as good' runs the risk of stripping the common of materials necessary for the maintenance of the creative society, a situation which would ultimately lead to an empty copyright regime.

Another problem engendered by Locke's theory of property is his claim that the mixing of labour with collectively owned objects entitles the owner to the *whole* product. Locke fails to explain why an individual labourer should retain rights to

---

152 For example, Locke asserts that one who injures another has 'declared War against all Mankind, and therefore may be destroyed as a *Lyon* or a *Tyger*...' 2nd T: ii 11.

153 Fisher (n 1 above) 186.

154 Ibid.

155 Drahos (n 1 above) 51. See also Craig (n 1 above) 23-31.

156 Craig, ibid 27.

the whole product. As Spector remarks: '[i]f the labour employed by a person does not offer an explanation for the total value of a commodity – and only explains the added value – then Locke's theory does not justify ownership over the whole commodity.'[157] In the case of authorial collectivity, even if isolating the added-value is possible, it is still not the sole creation of the individual labourer. True, a creator deserves property-reward since the fruits of his labour add to social wealth. However, difficulties may arise when culturally and socially constructed properties are at stake. Why does a labourer come to own the whole object? Locke is often thought to hold a desert-based labour theory. Labour warrants appropriation because it creates social value.[158] This is evident in his assertion that it is '*Labour* indeed that *puts the difference of value* on every thing…'[159] The labourer's right, then, is based on the principle of 'public reciprocation':[160] he introduces public benefit and deserves 'a fitting and proportional benefit from the public for doing so.'[161]

Hughes claims that the value-added constitutes a contribution that warrants the conferment of property rights.[162] Does that mean that every piece of intellectual property created should receive the full market value it generates?[163] Coombe distinguishes publicity rights from rights granted under copyright, patent and trademark laws as 'none of these laws provides a degree of protection against unauthorised appropriation equal to that afforded to celebrities.'[164] Coombe claims that the Lockean argument is inadequate to justify full realisation of the value created where a celebrity's image is concerned:

> A Lockean labor theory justifying property rights in the celebrity image is inadequate to establish a right to receive the full market value of the star persona or to establish exclusive rights to control its circulation and reproduction in society…Liberal values

---

157 Spector (n 1 above) 272.

158 As Buckle observes: for some 'the doctrine of the origin of labour will not properly be understood if it will not be recognized that Locke thinks of labour as a rational (or purposeful), value-created activity.' Buckle (n 100 above) 151.

159 2nd T: v 40.

160 Becker (n 1 above) 624. Becker observes that the value the labourer creates and the reward he claims should be determined by the principle of proportionality. However, there is a difficulty: the vagueness of 'proportionality' is a potential stumbling block. Ibid 625-26.

In that respect Waldron writes that 'Locke makes no assumption about the proportions in which goods will exchange in the market place, and indeed his views about the arbitrariness and conventionality of exchange indicate a scepticism about the possibility of any quantitative theory in this area.' Waldron 1988 (n 58 above) 192.

161 Becker, ibid, 624.

162 Hughes (n 1 above) 305-310.

163 See JW Child, 'The Moral Foundation of Intangible Property' (1990) 73(4) *The Monist* 578, 580.

164 R Coombe, *The Cultural Life of Intellectual Properties: Authorship, Appropriation and the Law* (Durham and London: Duke University Press, 1998) 99. Coombe writes that publicity rights can only be 'loosely analogized to rights granted by copyright, patent, and trademark laws.' Ibid.

> protecting individual freedom guarantees the possession and personal use of the product of one's labors only insofar as the exercise of this right does not harm the rights of others. As Wendy Gordon argues, deprivation of public domain and loss of access to cultural heritage are forms of harm that might be contemplated. Moreover, rights to possess and personally use the fruits of one's labor do not necessarily entail the imposition of full property rights to perpetually garner the full profits that such a product would yield in the market.[165]

Existing intellectual property systems, Gordon argues, 'give rights in excess of what a Lockean model would justify…copyright law gives authors rights over the "derivative works" that others make by building on their creations…the public is owed compensation if courts or legislatures violate the Proviso by creating private rights that impair the public's access to the common.'[166] Therefore copyright, 'at least in its present form, does not appear to leave enough and as good.'[167] What, then, would be an ideal Proviso for copyright?

Taken literally, the Proviso is unworkable.[168] If I throw three containers of white paint to a river to celebrate the success of the 'Addidas three-stripes' design, does that mean I own the river or that I lost the colour and with it the labour I mixed with throwing the paint?[169] The Proviso eliminates such an absurd hypothesis. Propertising the river's water violates the Proviso. Literal reading of the Proviso directs me to ask whether Locke thought that everyone is entitled to exactly the same.[170] Considering the limited amount of resources we have, does that mean that the Proviso is unable to accommodate more than one generation?[171] This depends on the way the Proviso is interpreted.

---

165 Ibid.

166 Gordon 1993 (n 1 above) 1608.

167 Craig (n 1 above) 30. Gordon suggests that where one fails to satisfy the Proviso he 'would be entitled to a lesser degree of control, such as a right to a monetary benefit.' Gordon, ibid 1575.

168 As Sartorius remarks: 'Understood as an original limitation on the right to appropriate natural resources, the condition…could not of course be literally satisfied by any system of private property right.' R Sartorius, 'Persons and Property' in RG Frey (ed.), *Utility and Rights* (Minneapolis, MN: University of Minnesota Press, 1984) 196, 210.

169 As Nozick's famous example demonstrates: 'If I own a can of tomato juice and spill it in the sea so that its molecules mingle evenly throughout the sea, do I thereby come to own the sea, or have I foolishly dissipated my tomato juice?' Nozick (n 144 above) 175. See also Waldron 1988 (n 58 above) 188; Waldron 2002 (n 19 above) 159; and Gordon 1993 (n 1 above) 1565.

170 Sanders argues that if the Proviso requires us to leave 'enough and as good' for all future generations 'then it is hard to imagine that the Proviso would allow you to mix your labour with much more than an infinitesimal slice of land.' JT Sanders, 'Justice and the Initial Acquisition of Private Property' (1987) 10 *Harvard Journal of Law and Public Policy* 367, 377.

171 Harris asks: 'What possible application could it have today in an over populated and under-resourced world?' Harris (n 119 above) 200.

If I pick strawberries from a wild field, it is obvious that the amount of strawberries available for others has been reduced, and no one will be able to pick *exactly* the same strawberry. In the next season there will be more strawberries because I did not destroy the field. In this way I avoided violating the Proviso, as others have the potential to use exactly the same resource, but not the same amount at the same time.[172] I may even pick up all the strawberries in that particular field, but unless I uproot the strawberry bushes and leave no potential for future growth, I did not violate the condition. In fact, 'leaving goods in the commons fails to satisfy the Proviso' since it 'ensures their ruin.'[173] Temporary violation of the Proviso is justified as a matter of necessity in everyday life, and as such, a basic right of every commoner. Gordon observes that '[p]ersons whose rights in the common are not adversely affected by the creator's property right would have no grounds for complaint, and the creator could assert property rights against them unimpeded.'[174] To argue that by picking strawberries I adversely worsen the situation of other generations is a mistake. It renders the Proviso totally unworkable – something Locke did not intend.[175] The question now is whether such examples are applicable to intellectual property.

I argue that an author-labourer must leave enough *and* as good in the common. First, as I already stated, many believe that in respect of ideas the Proviso is satisfied and leaves other commoners no ground for complaint. That is, the Proviso ensures that, since ideas are an infinite resource the same quantity (enough) and quality (and as good) is always left for others. Thus regarded, the 'consumability' of ideas is potentially infinite. They are not scarce in the sense that a tangible entity can be.[176] But this interpretation is somewhat hypothetical: due to the vague distinction

172 In the words of Rose: 'To be sure, any appropriation diminishes to some tiny degree the amount of a resource that is available to others. But up to some point, it just doesn't matter – no one is damaged in any way that she or anyone else can perceive or care about…At some point, however, the appropriation of resources from a common pool will begin to matter. If appropriation goes on long enough and if the pool is not replenished, the diminution of opportunities for others becomes important or perceptible to them.' CM Rose, '"Enough and as Good" of What?' (1987) 81 *Northwestern University Law Review* 429, 426.

173 D Schmidtz , 'When is Original Appropriation Required' (1990) 73(4) *The Monist* 504, 508. Schmitz articulates a use-Proviso: 'It is not true that appropriation of land inevitably decreases the amount of land available to others. It only inevitably decreases what is available for original appropriation by others, which is not the same thing at all. Thus, appropriation…is not only required…but is also permitted by the Proviso.' Ibid 512.

174 Gordon 1993 (n 1 above) 1564.

175 In the words of Waldron: 'after all, Locke could not possibly have meant that no one should appropriate any resources if there were not enough for everyone' and therefore 'the sufficiency Proviso is better understood as a sufficient condition…highlighting the point that there is certainly no difficulty with unilateral acquisition in circumstances of plenty, but leaving open the possibility that some other basis might have to be found to regulate acquisition in circumstances of scarcity.' Waldron 2002 (n 19 above) 172.

176 Waldron divides objects of property into two classes: 'crowdable objects' and 'non-crowdable objects.' 'An object is "crowdable" if one person's use of it is an obstacle to at least one other's use of it.' Ideas, then, are 'non-crowdable.' Waldron 1992-1993 (n 1 above) 871.

between ideas and expressions, our copyright system cannot fully absorb the benefit of the Proviso.

Therefore, granting an unconditional monopoly-type right for one's copyright works resembles a situation where one destroys the strawberry field. The exclusive ownership of a copyright work, be it a computer program, a parody or a picture, is synonymous with uprooting a strawberry bush. It will have a prohibitive effect on the possibility of making derivative works. It is not enough to allow only the copying of the idea behind the work.[177] This is also a natural consequence of the social construction theory and the role of the authorial collectivity. That is, withholding public access to copyrighted materials always adversely affects the public interest. For example, if a particular work is 'out there' and I, as a member of the public, contributed to its formation, restricting my access to that creation amounts to a violation of the no-harm principle. Furthermore, if the public is restricted from use and consumption of items of social and cultural wealth to which it has contributed, the risk to the integrity of the collective and to the cultural identity of the public is vast.

For example, Waldron takes the Mickey Mouse image and argues that once a cultural object is 'thrust out into the cultural world to impinge on the consciousness of all of us'[178] we cannot ignore it, 'it has become part of our lives.' [179] Hence, it should be treated as now part of the public domain.[180] Gordon concurs with this position and argues that the grant of a patent for a food additive enzyme violates Locke's 'enough and as good' Proviso:

> [O]nce a creator exposes her intellectual product to the public, and that product influences the stream of culture and events, excluding the public from access to it can harm…Thus… the mere presence of abundant raw materials would not suffice to give A a right to exclude B and other strangers from the enzyme or from learning how it can be made…This is essentially a reliance argument: having changed people's position, the inventor cannot then refuse them the tools they need for surviving under their new condition.[181]

In a later essay Gordon further develops this reasoning and advocates a self-help remedy under the Proviso: the Proviso empowers authors to use prior works by a 'self-defense privilege based on a kind of reliance.'[182] A generous interpretation of

---

177 *Cf* RA Spinello, 'The Future of Intellectual Property' (2003) 5 *Ethics and Information Technology* 1, 10-11.

178 Waldron 1992-1993 (n 1 above) 883.

179 Ibid.

180 This issue is further complicated by the fact that even subconscious copying may lead to an infringement suit. If the defendant denies any intention to copy, the court may or may not believe him. The test the court will apply is composed of several elements such as the 'degree of familiarity with the plaintiff's work, the character of the work, particularly its qualities of impressing the mind and memory, the objective similarity…' and more. Wilberforce J in *Francis Day v Bron* [1963] Ch 587, 614.

181 Gordon 1993 (n 1 above) 1567-1568.

182 Gordon 2004 (n 1 above) 83.

the Proviso guarantees that in such cases where the components of our cultural and social realities are at risk of being propertised, members of the public will have a right to the creation. Abundance of raw materials will not suffice. Thus, when we talk copyright, the Proviso is to be interpreted literally: an author has to leave *exactly* 'enough and as good.'

Locke thought of the public good, and I think that he was aware that property must be limited in order to maintain a stable social order, that an author is not like any other labourer, and that authorial rights should be carefully scrutinised and balanced against certain social norms. I am also in agreement with Gordon that 'what is true for private property should be true for public property as well.'[183] I believe that Locke directs readers of the *Second Treatise* to reach a conclusion not too different from Gordon's observation. It is wrong to portray Locke as a defender of a robust system of natural property right, unencroachable by norms of equality and public good. Copyright scholars cannot ignore 'Liberty of the Press' as evidence of Locke's commitment to the public interest. He does not only advocate strictly limiting the duration of authorial rights, but also raises the fundamentality of encouraging learning and dissemination of information. That does not mean that 'Liberty of the Press' presents a clear utilitarian argument and transgresses the outer boundary of natural law. It provides for authorial rights based on labour and subjects them to restrictions similar to those Locke recognises in the *Second Treatise*.

Indeed, Locke's remarks in 'Liberty of the Press', as Shiffrin observes, are not easily reconciled with the view that Locke's theory endorses strong natural rights to intellectual property. In this essay he 'contends that there is no "reason in *nature*" to preclude a freer system of use…'[184] For Locke, a natural right does not require perpetuity, and in certain situations, such as where authorial entities are concerned, perpetuity violates the Provisos he introduces in the *Second Treatise* as limits to every property right; it may violate the laws of nature. It is now clear that a natural right for Locke is a dynamic rather than static guarantee, changing to meet the needs of the particular situation. This is the second way in which Locke's property theory can be re-imagined.

Still, I do not think that Locke's labour or authors' right theories can adequately accommodate all of the concerns identified in the discussion of authorial collectivity and the social construction of authors and their creative works. Remarkably, however, Locke's *Essay Concerning Human Understanding* does address these concerns. I shall now discuss the third way in which Locke's property theory can be re-imagined.

183 Gordon 1993 (n 1 above) 1608.

184 Shiffrin (n 1 above) 155.

Locke and Social Construction

The Argument

In Chapters 4 and 5 I argue that the concept of original authorship is a fiction. Every copyright work starts with preexisting materials. That is the nature of collectively produced and socially constructed entities. Locke's *Essay* holds promise for defending the role of the authorial collectivity and the social construction. The *Essay*, in which Locke examines the nature of knowledge and the ability of man to absorb and understand it, is considered his masterpiece.[185] In the *Essay*'s four books Locke argues that realising the extent of human understanding will enable people to make better use of their powers.[186] At the heart of Locke's epistemology is the definition and role of ideas for the formation of knowledge.

Although no copyright scholar would argue that a musical composition is an original work only if it is inborn in its composer, there are, as I already showed, scholars, authors and artists who advocate a robust copyright system, who embrace the notion of authorial originality associated with the notion of the Romantic author, and who do not recognise the public's authorial role. It appears that they support the idea that an author is an entity capable of creating something which is almost equivalent to creation *ex nihilo.* For example, Child writes on patents:

> The most interesting thing about my friend's ideas as property – indeed, I consider it amazing – is that he created them *ex nihilo*. Property was created out of nothing but mental labour. He didn't even need raw materials – as the farmer needs land and seed, or the potter needs clay. Of course, he needed a pencil, paper, a drafting board, and a slide rule…But these are more like tools. He needed no 'stuff' with which to mix his labour.[187]

Although new *value* can certainly be created, it does not follow that it can be created in a vacuum, without any mental or intellectual raw materials. In copyright, while an author can write a new poem or artist initiate a new artistic style, these are not original creations *ex nihilo*; they are not entirely new nor have they exclusively originated with them. Authors merely mix their labour with preexisting ideas and collectively owned objects. If some authors and artists, as well as the law as it stands today, favour the idea of the Romantic author and ignore the contribution of the public, then their argument would *require* something close to *innateness*. Locke forcefully rejects the idea of innateness and with it that no one can create something *ex nihilo*. We can only improve what we already know.

---

185 E Bk I i 1.

186 E Bk I i 5.

187 Child (n 163 above) 588.

Labourer or Creator?

Philosophers devote considerable attention to the question of whether Locke's metaphor of labour mixing means that a labourer merely mixes his labour or does he create something totally new. This question, Tully remarks, is 'a common theme uniting the *Essay* and the *Second Treatise*.'[188] Tully introduces the workmanship model which regards God as a maker and man as his workmanship.[189] Simmons explains:

> Locke would be claiming that God's dominion over the earth and man's property in the products of his labour have no common foundation. God's dominion is based in God's self-evident right of creation; man's property is based in man's mixing of his labour with unowned nature. God's property is based on his having created new things; man's property is based on extending his property in his person by acts of labour, which may or may not 'make' new things, but which never make them in a way sufficiently like God's *ex nihilo* creations to bring the two kinds of 'making' under a common principle.[190]

The thrust of Tully's model is that '[d]ue to the analogy between God and man as makers, anything true of one will be, *ceteris paribus*, true of the other. Since [the doctrine of maker's right] is the explanation of God's dominion over man and of why man is God's property, it also explains man's dominion over and property in the products of his making.'[191] On this account, making is an activity associated with bringing something into being *ex nihilo* and a labourer possesses God-like rights – absolute rights.[192]

Waldron criticises Tully's model and remarks that there are serious difficulties with the latter's interpretation of property rights as creators' rights because the conclusion 'is far too strong.'[193] He rejects the workmanship model and observes that it would be difficult to defend the two Provisos if property rights are absolute.[194] Indeed, in Locke's writings we are lead to assume that only God has the ability to

---

188 Tully (n 19 above) 4.

189 Ibid 35-50; Waldron 1988 (n 58 above) 198-201; Sreenivasan (n 144 above) 59-92; and Simmons (n 122 above). See also Ryan (n 142 above) 14-48. Shapiro for example, names the model the 'workmanship ideal' and argues that it concerns man's ownership over his productive capacities and the subsequent right to own that he produces. I Shapiro, *The Evolution of Rights in Liberal Theory* (Cambridge: Cambridge University Press, 1986) 96; and by the same author, 'Resources, Capacities, and Ownership: The Workmanship Ideal and Distributive Justice' (1991) 19 (1) *Political Theory* 47.

190 Simmons, ibid 200-201.

191 Tully (n 19 above) 37.

192 Ibid 97.

193 Waldron 1988 (n 58 above) 198.

194 Ibid 199. Simmons also rejects Tully's model and claims that it is too broad in scope. He calls it the 'full workmanship model' and advocates his own version of a 'minimal workmanship model.' Simmons (n 122 above) 199-201.

create and that men are his workmanship.[195] But that does not mean that man can have divine powers of creation. A labourer cannot create something totally new; he cannot bring into being something *ex nihilo*. As Locke asserts: 'The Dominion of Man…in the great World of visible things…however managed by Art and Skill, reaches no farther, than to compound and divide the Materials, that are made to his Hand; but can do nothing towards the making the least Particle of new Matter, or destroying one Atom of what is already in being.'[196] Indeed, '[n]owhere does Locke say or imply that labor grounds property because by our labor we make new things.'[197] Is this inconsistent with Locke's view of how ideas are formed? Locke argues that complex ideas come into being in three ways:

> 1. By Experience and *Observation* of things themselves. Thus, by seeing two Men wrestle or fence, we get the *Idea* of wrestling or fencing. 2. By *Invention*, or voluntary putting together of several simple Ideas in our own Minds: So he that first invented Printing or Etching, had an *Idea* of it in his Mind before it ever existed. 3. Which is the most usual way, by *explaining the names* of Actions we never saw, or Notions we cannot see; and by enumerating, and thereby, as it were, setting before our Imaginations all those *Ideas* which go to the making them up, and are the constituent parts of them.[198]

In Chapter V Locke refers to 'mixture' and 'annexation', in the *Essay* he talks about 'experience' and 'putting together' but also mentions 'first invented.' Although Locke's wording – 'he that *first invented* Printing or Etching, had an Idea of it in his Mind before it ever existed'[199] – raises the question whether he thinks a given person can be the first to invent, the phrase is qualified by the assertion that any 'first inventor' *must* have a prior idea. Only the combination of pre-existing ideas and templates makes a person the '*first* inventor.'

Therefore, the labourer cannot be said to create something *ex nihilo* or totally original though he can be said to improve that which God gave us in common.[200] Waldron is right to reject Tully's argument and argue that '[n]owhere does Locke give any indication that he wants to connect this labour theory of use-value with any doctrine of creator's entitlement'[201] because if he could, one would assume that the powers of God mirror the abilities of a labourer.[202] How then, can a labourer become an original owner? Sreenivasan explains

---

195 See for example 2nd T: ii 6; E Bk II xxviii 8; and E Bk iv iii 18. See also Essays IV and VI of Locke's *Essays on the Law of Nature* in Goldie (n 21 above) 79, 100, 116.

196 E Bk II ii 2.

197 Simmons (n 122 above) 203.

198 E Bk II xxii 9.

199 Ibid (emphasis added).

200 See Buckle (n 100 above) 151.

201 Waldron 1988 (n 58 above) 200.

202 Support for this we can also find in Locke's statement that '[t]he original and foundation of all law is dependence. A dependent intelligent being is under the power and direction and dominion of him on whom he depends…If man were independent he could have no law but his own will…He would be a God to himself…' J Locke, 'Law', in Goldie (n 21

> [E]ven though [man] cannot create, man as a maker can still bring new things into being and is therefore entitled to property in them. Still, there will be an important difference in the logic of the entitlement in the two cases. This difference reflects the fact that making, in the technical sense, always begins from pre-existing materials. For with making, unlike with creation, there is always a prior question concerning the maker's entitlement to the materials from which she begins.[203]

The Formation of Ideas and Authorial Knowledge

In Book I of the *Essay* Locke launches his attack on the notion of innateness and claims that knowledge can never be innate or find its origin in divine imprinting. Ideas, without exception, are based on experience, and 'all that we know about the world, is what the world cares to tell us.'[204] The dismissal of innate ideas and principles from epistemology and the philosophy of mind is one of the most dramatic features of Locke's theories.[205] According to Locke, the only features that one has, and are 'native', are his natural faculties. Since the human mind at birth is a blank slate, experience dominates the ability to think, and to create ideas.[206] In the words of Locke:

> Let us then suppose the Mind to be, as we say, white Paper, void of all Characters, without any *Ideas*; How comes it to be furnished? Whence comes it by that vast store, which the busy and boundless Fancy of Man has painted on it with an almost endless variety? Whence has it all the materials of Reason and Knowledge? To this I answer, in one word, From *Experience*; In that all our Knowledge is founded, and from that it ultimately derives itself. Our Observation, employ'd either about *external, sensible Objects, or about the internal Operations of our Minds, perceived and reflected on by ourselves, it that which*

---

above) 328. Therefore in order to maintain a stable order, man cannot attract to himself God-like powers or character.

203 Sreenivasan (n 144 above) 75. He also makes useful distinction between natural and artificial things (things that are 'made' in the technical sense). We can come to own things from the latter category. Ibid 85.

204 'Empiricism', in *Oxford Companion to Philosophy* (Oxford: Oxford University Press, T Honderich (ed.), 1995). Aarsleff explains empiricism in this way: 'Empiricism is also a mode of philosophy that thrives on communication and discussion, does not expect that truth will come in a flash (if it ever comes), and has a low estimate of the claims of isolated genius and of a speculative brooding on deep matters.' H Aarsleff, 'Locke's Influence' in Chappell (n 19 above) 252, 261.

205 Even the idea of God, according to Locke, is not innate. E I iv 8. On Locke's philosophy of ideas see generally JW Yolton, 'Ideas and Knowledge in Seventeenth-Century Philosophy' (1975) 13 *Journal of the History of Philosophy* 145; SJ Winchester, 'Locke and the Innatists' (1985) 2 *History of Philosophy Quarterly* 411; G Wall, 'Locke's Attack on Innate Knowledge' (1974) 49 *Philosophy* 414; and H Kim, 'Locke on Innatism' (2003) 3 *Locke Studies* 15.

206 Stich contends that '[a]dvocates of the doctrine of innate ideas and innate knowledge commonly take the notion of innateness itself to be unproblematic. They explain it with a few near synonyms, "inborn" or "unlearned"…' SP Stich, 'Introduction' in SP Stich (ed.), *Innate Ideas* (Berkeley California: University of California Press, 1975) 1.

> *supplies our Understanding with all the materials of thinking*. These two are the Fountains of Knowledge, from whence all the *Ideas* we have, or can naturally have, do spring.[207]

Many philosophers disagree with Locke's emphasis on experience. A core disagreement in the innatist-empiricist controversy is that between Locke and Descartes. The former holds that none of our ideas is innate, while the latter holds that ideas are part of our original constitution: 'all our ideas are innate in us in the sense that we are born, not with the capacity to receive them from outside, but with a power to form each of them without receiving them from outside.'[208] Another disagreement is between Locke and Leibniz. Hacking posits this dispute in the context of social constructionism and remarks that 'you can even cast historical debates between, for example, Locke and Leibniz in terms of external and internal. Leibniz thinks that the reasons underlying truths are internal to those truths, while Locke holds that (our confidence) in truths about the world is always external, never grounded in more than our experience.'[209]

In the chapter on 'No Innate Practical Principles' Locke does not deny that we possess natural inclinations as 'there are natural tendencies imprinted on the Minds of Men...But this makes nothing for innate Characters on the Mind, which are to be the Principles of Knowledge, regulating our Practice.'[210] But, as Waldron remarks, in order to be guided by innate inclinations there is a need for 'some assurance that it guides us as we ought to be guided, and that assurance can only come from

---

207 E Bk II i 2. Yet, in a draft version of the *Essay* Locke claims that there is knowledge that does not derive from experience. See R Woolhouse, 'Locke's Theory of Knowledge' in Chappell (n 19 above) 146, 148-149.

208 RM Adams, 'Where Do Our Ideas Come From? – Descrates vs. Locke' in Stich (n 206 above) 71, 78. See also GAJ Rogers, 'Innate Ideas and the Infinite: The Case of Locke and Descrates' (1995) 26 *The Locke Newsletter* 49. Lowde also claims that there is knowledge, which is innate or 'imprinted.' J Lowde, *A Discourse Concerning the Nature of Man* (London, 1694) 57, cited in Woolhouse, ibid 150.

209 I Hacking, *The Social Construction of What?* (Cambridge Mass.: Harvard University Press, 1999) 91. For further discussion see RM Adams, 'The Locke-Leibniz Debate' in Stich, ibid 37; and J Harris, 'Leibniz and Locke on Innate Ideas' (1974) 16 *Ratio* 226.

In a recent attack on the 'blank slate theory' Pinker follows the line of Leibniz and claims that the problem with blank slates is that they do nothing. He remarks: 'As long as people had only the haziest concept of what a mind was or how it might work, the metaphor of a blank slate inscribed by the environment did not seem too outrageous. But as soon as one starts to think seriously about what kind of computation enables a system to see, think, speak and plan, the problem with blank slates becomes all too obvious: they don't do anything.' S Pinker, *The Blank Slate: The Modern Denial of Human Nature* (New York: Penguin Books, 2003) 34. Pinker also argues that the blank slate theory can no longer be valid because science proves that 'the brain's basic architecture develops under genetic control' and that 'brain systems show signs of innate specialization and cannot arbitrarily substitute for one another.' Ibid 102.

210 E Bk I iii 3.

the exercise of our *intellect*.'[211] There can be no exercise of the intellect without experience. Greenlee also asserts that Locke 'allows that there are innate capacities to know'[212] and it is innate 'in the sense of being something that can be developed.'[213] However, Locke forcefully rejects any idea that we have an innate capacity to knowledge because 'if the Capacity of knowing be the natural Impression contended for, all the Truths a Man ever comes to know will, by this Account, be, every one of them, innate: and this great Point will amount to no more, but only to a very improper way of speaking...'[214] The implication for copyright is that a person has innate inclinations capable of being transformed into ideas and knowledge which are subsequently developed into an ability to create authorial and artistic works. This conclusion emphasises the collective nature of the copyright creation process: the social dependence on the collective, and the combination of contributions coming from the individual author and the general public.

In order to bolster his empiricism, in Book II of the *Essay*, Locke launches into an account of ideas and the ways in which the mind acquires them. Locke differentiates between simple ideas and complex ideas and holds the latter category to ultimately operate on experience, to be mentally constructible out of simple ideas. Ideas are 'the materials of reason and knowledge.'[215] Locke confirms this in a later note where he writes: 'The extent of knowledge cannot exceed the extent of our ideas.'[216] Working out the connections between those ideas produces knowledge. It is a product of reason, and without reason, all that we have is a belief, not knowledge.[217] A simple idea is an indefinable and unanalysable idea, which cannot be created by us. It is an idea that is 'being each in it self uncompounded, contains in it nothing but *one uniform Appearance*, or Conception in the Mind, and is not distinguishable into different *Ideas*.'[218] Locke's examples of simple ideas include description of the physical attributes for objects: '*Yellow, White, Heat, Cold, Soft, Hard, Bitter, Sweet*…'[219] In short, every simple idea, Locke says, owes its existence to experience. In the words of Locke:

---

211 Waldron 2002 (n 19 above) 161.

212 D Greenlee, 'Locke and the Controversy Over Innate Ideas' (1972) 33(2) *Journal of the History of Ideas* 251, 257. Greenlee then contends that Locke is not a true empiricist: 'It would be a mistake to see the Lockean attack on innateness as an expression of Locke's empiricism…It is, instead, correct to ascribe to Locke a concern with a method of discovery, which, as characterised above, is designed to yield new knowledge rather than to buttress old beliefs long accepted as knowledge.' Ibid 262.

213 Ibid 256.

214 E Bk I ii 5.

215 E Bk II i 2.

216 J Locke, 'Some Thoughts Concerning Reading and Study for a Gentleman' (published 1703) in Goldie (n 21 above) 348, 349.

217 E Bk IV xix 14.

218 E Bk II ii 1.

219 E Bk II i 3. Locke continues and sub-divides the category of simple ideas into: (i) ideas of sensation (ideas conveyed into the mind via bodily senses) (ii) ideas of reflection

> These *simple Ideas*, when offered to the mind, *the Understanding can* no more refuse to have, nor alter when they are imprinted, nor blot them out and make new ones itself, than a mirror can refuse, alter, or obliterate the Images or *Ideas,* which, the objects set before it, do therein produce. As the Bodies that surround us, do diversely affect our organs, the mind is forced to receive the impressions; and cannot avoid the Perception of those *Ideas* that are annexed to them.[220]

Complex ideas comprise Locke's second category of ideas. These ideas are compounds of two or more simple ideas. Locke includes in this category ideas which, although not created *ex nihilo* in the mind, are new. The potential to create new ideas lends further support for a claim for property in authorial works. Chappell explains:

> But in addition to complex ideas of this kind, which experience imposes on our minds, Locke recognizes others, which the mind itself creates. It does not create them *ex nihilo*, of course. What it does, Locke claims, is join together ideas that are already in its possession separately, so as to make a single new idea out of them: the former serve as raw material or data for the latter…In this process of creating new complex ideas, the mind is no longer merely passive. Instead it actively exerts itself, operating upon the ideas it has to make the new ones. Furthermore, its action is voluntary; and the products thereof may be quite out of line with any preexistent reality, external sensible or mental-operational: ideas of fantastic voyages and fabulous monsters.[221]

An author's ability to create complex ideas is what makes his claim to a right in his creations stronger. In this way he contributes something beyond what is already known. The mind in this situation transforms a passive capacity into an active power,[222] by making combinations of pre-existing materials: 'for, it being once furnished with simple *Ideas*, it can put them together in several Compositions, and so make variety of complex *Ideas*, without examining whether they exist so together in Nature.'[223] For example, 'complex *Idea* called a tune, which a Musician may have in his mind when he hears or makes no sound at all, by reflecting on the *Ideas* of those Sounds, so put together silently in his own fancy.'[224]

The process of the Lockean version of idea-formation confirms the inherent social constructivist dimension in his epistemology. We see a similar point in Locke's discussion of language, 'the great Instrument and the common Tye of Society.'[225] Furthermore, communication between members of society is vital for

---

which the mind receives 'by reflecting on its own operations within it self' and includes ideas of '*Perception, Thinking, Doubting, Believing, Reasoning, Knowing, Willing…*' E Bk II i 4; and (iii) ideas that are not of sensible qualities or of mental operations such as '*Pleasure*, or *Delight* and its opposite, *Pain,* or *Uneasiness. Power. Existence. Unity.*' E Bk II vii 1.

220 E Bk II i 25.

221 Chappell (n 19 above) 26, 37-38.

222 E Bk II xxiii 7.

223 E Bk II xxii 2.

224 E Bk II xviii 3.

225 E Bk III ii 1.

the success of his theory of ideas as it expands knowledge and allows each of us to experience another's ideas. Thus, Locke opens his note entitled 'Study' with the assertion that '[t]he end of study is knowledge, and the end of knowledge practice or communication.'[226] Similarly, he opens a later essay with the following: 'Reading is for the improvement of the understanding. The improvement of the understanding is for two ends: first, for our own increase of knowledge; secondly, to enable us to *deliver* and make that *knowledge to others*.'[227] This emphasis on communication supports the argument that we all depend on the efforts and labour of others and that copyright works are social entities. Communication necessitates access to external objects, without which the creation of any market of cultural products will not be viable.[228]

In the opening to Book III of the *Essay* Locke asserts that each of us is a 'sociable Creature.'[229] In my discussion of social construction I conclude that as a 'sociable Creature', the author is a social construct. As we see in the *Second Treatise* and the *Essay*, a Lockean author is an evolved being. Authorial and artistic knowledge are not innate, they are socially constructed – creatures of experience and social interaction. As mentioned above, it is arguable that in the *Second Treatise* Locke makes a distinction between 'man' and 'person.' He remarks that 'every Man has a *Property* in his own *Person.* This no Body has any Right to but Himself.'[230] That is, while 'man' is the situation before a person has the benefits of experience, 'person' is a developed entity dependent on and shaped by experience. The appearance of the distinction between a 'man' and a 'person' in his property theory shows that for Locke self-development requires property and, as I already argued, it does not require only tangible assets, but also intellectual properties. Both, tangible and intangible properties improve the conveniences of life.[231] If I am correct in arguing that a copyrighted work is an expressive embodiment of the author's personal identity, labour, ideas, abilities, powers, experiences, and knowledge, then in Lockean terms, an author and his creative expressions are socially constructed and collectively produced entities.

226 J Locke, 'Study' (published 1677) in Goldie (n 21 above) 365, 366.

227 J Locke, 'Some Thoughts Concerning Reading and Study for a Gentleman' (n 216 above) 348, 349.

228 Locke himself is a good example for this. His friendship with Molyneux ended up with the insertion into the second edition of the *Essay* (E II ix 8 145-46) of what has since become known as Molyneux's problem: whether a man born blind and newly restored to sight would be able by sight alone to distinguish between different shapes, such as sphere and a cube. Apart from this, the most notable changes were a whole new chapter 'Of Identity and Diversity' (E Bk II xxvii), and the replacement of the central section of the chapter 'Of Power' (E Bk II xxi) by a largely new and much longer discussion of human volition and freedom. J Milton, 'Locke's Life and Time', in Chappell (n 19 above) 5, 19-20.

229 E Bk III i 1.

230 2nd T: v 27.

231 2nd T: v 44.

Book IV of the *Essay* culminates Locke's attempt to define what is knowledge and describe its origins. Locke tells us that: '*Our Knowledge* therefore is *real*, only so far as there is a conformity between our *Ideas* and the reality of Things.'[232] This reminds us of his insistence that knowledge is never innate, but rather socially constructed – a creature dependent on experience, on exposure and communication. Locke's emphasis on experience and communication demonstrates the role the public plays in the process of idea-formation, knowledge-creation and knowledge-absorption. For example, to know the structure of a triangle is to perceive the *connection* between several *ideas* 'that *the three Angles of a Triangle are equal to two right ones*' and 'that Equality to two right ones, does necessarily agree to, and is inseparable from, the three Angles of a Triangle.'[233] Copyright works are dependent on a similar connection between ideas. They are dependent on the mind's exposure to knowledge. Their essence is based on use of collectively produced and owned simple and complex ideas that once expressed may satisfy the requirements for copyright protection. The notion of the Romantic author would not survive Locke's definition of knowledge and idea-making. What authors, artists and painters know about the world, is what the world cares to tell them. Their works, like Lockean knowledge, are a variation on experience.

If Waldron is correct in claiming that 'Locke and his contemporaries were not much less sophisticated, hermeneutically, than we are',[234] perhaps we can feel confident when we draw analogies between Locke's different writings and reach conclusions that, although not always explicitly stated by Locke, can be found in his philosophy. It would not be too much to say that Locke believed that, in order to preserve our identity as 'sociable creatures', we need to be exposed to as many social events and cultural processes as possible, and to consume collectively produced properties. If this is true, then it also will not be too much to say that Locke was fully aware of the importance of preserving a vibrant public domain to promote the formation of ideas and the evolution of authors. Perhaps that was one of the reasons why we cannot be said to "create" but simply to mix our labour with commonly owned objects. It also might not be too much to argue that Locke saw the limits on authors' rights that he advocated in 'Liberty of the Press' as necessary for the successful creation of complex ideas. In these ways, Locke provides us arguments on which to base re-examination of the justifications and principles we so strongly protect when we discuss copyright.

232 E Bk IV iv 3.
233 E Bk IV i 2.
234 Waldron 2002 (n 19 above) 9.

Chapter 7

Doctrinal Payoffs: The Public as a Joint Author

The Question Posed

An inevitable conclusion from the discussion of the authorial collectivity and the social construction thesis is that collaboration between public and authors is the only way in which copyrighted entities are produced. I referred to intellectual property scholars who embrace this conclusion and see the creative act as a collective enterprise that should be collectively owned. They criticise the propertisation of collectively produced shared symbols and cultural elements and claim that copyrighted entities are collectively produced by both authors and public.[1]

In this chapter I continue my goal to rethink the definition of copyright, with the following question: if authors and their creative expressions are socially constructed, and if copyrighted entities are a collective enterprise between public and authors, to which both contribute, should these entities, when otherwise qualified for copyright protection, be *jointly* owned between public and authors? I examine this question by using existing rules for joint authorship and ask whether the law, as it stands today, guarantees reward to authorial contributions. This chapter then examines whether the law itself can provide the framework on which to base an argument for a public right in copyrighted works, or whether joint authorship is just another principle that shows the weaknesses in our copyright system.[2]

1 See for example, RJ Coombe, 'Objects of Property and Subjects of Politics: Intellectual Property Laws and Democratic Dialogue' (1991) 69 *Texas Law Review* 1853. See above Chapters 1, 4 and 5.

For example, copyright scholars claim that '[t]he production of a "work" that is subject to protection by copyright is an activity undertaken by both author and audience.' M Chon, 'New Wine Bursting From Old Bottles: Collaborative Internet, Art, Joint Works, and Entrepreneurship' (1996) 75 *Oregon Law Review* 257, 264. See also Craig's remark that if '[t]he interdependent nature of human culture means that intellectual works are necessarily the products of collective labour' they 'ought to be owned collectively.' CJ Craig, 'Locke, Labour and Limiting the Author's Right: A Warning Against a Lockean Approach to Copyright Law' 28 *Queens Law Journal* (2002) 1. Scafidi also remarks that as members of a cultural unit we 'already share the same culture and jointly "own" its cultural products.' S Scafidi, 'Intellectual Property and Cultural Products' (2001) 81 *Boston University Law Review* 793, 810.

2 A reader may still have a residual concern and ask whether the public can be a singular author? Although this question will have to remain in need for further research, I was attentive

In order to highlight the difficulties in the reigning definition of joint authorship and its implications for the issue of authorship and the property question in copyright, this chapter takes examples from the US and Canadian copyright experience. Reference to other jurisdictional traditions that hold different attitudes towards joint authorship, to some extent more restrictive that those of English copyright law, will not only show how copyright systems allow denial of authorial contributions, but will reveal the fact that the public's contribution satisfies even the most stringent rules of joint authorship.

Public and Author as Joint Authors

Rules for a Joint Title

Joint ownership of authorial and artistic commodities is a principle which many consider 'fraught with problems.'[3] In particular, the vague formulation of the conditions for joint authorship creates absurd situations in which, although two or more individuals contribute to the creation of a product meriting joint entitlement, copyright 'refuses to acknowledge the existence of 'joint authorship', or does so grudgingly.'[4] The consequences from this practice are manifold and include: denial of 'economic rewards to persons whose creative efforts satisfy the constitutional and statutory concepts of authorship';[5] destabilisation of the economic incentive-based rationale to the ownership of intellectual products; and reinforcement of the concept of the 'lone author' as the sole foundation for copyright ownership.[6] In the public/author paradigm there is no room to question the contribution made by the public, as by their nature, copyrighted commodities are dependent on this contribution.

In the event that two or more individuals jointly own property, the nature of their joint relations and the respective parts to which each is entitled are determined by

---

to it since the beginning of the present study and argued that neither the individual author, nor the public (as a body constituted of individuals), can create alone. In fact, in light of the discussion in previous chapters, this question is almost irrelevant, since the *only* way for a copyrighted entity to form is by way of joint collaboration between public and authors.

3 D Marchese, 'Joint Ownership of Intellectual Property' [1999] *European Intellectual Property Review* 364.

4 P Jaszi, 'On the Author Effect: Contemporary Copyright and Collective Creativity' in M Woodmansee and P Jaszi, *The Construction of Authorship: Textual Appropriation in Law and Literature* (Durham and London: Duke University Press, 1994) 29, 51.

5 M LaFrance, 'Authorship, Dominance, and the Captive Collaborator: Preserving the Rights of Joint Authors' (2001) 50 *Emory Law Journal* 193, 255.

6 Chon also highlights the weaknesses in the current definition of joint authorship as applied to digital works, and remarks that '[t]he bad news about the joint work category is that it seems not to recognise the morphability, flexibility and fluidity of networked digitized works…where multiple authors of a consciously collaborative work exist, we encounter legal interpretations of "joint work" that are influenced by the cult of the romantic author.' Chon (n 1 above) 270.

an agreement between them. The joint relations can take the form of joint tenancy or tenancy in common.[7] Joint tenancy is considered the more perfect form of joint ownership, where the joint owners are treated as one inseparable unit and do not possess individual shares or different parts in the property. They together own the whole item. Despite the presumption in common law that joint tenancy is a more pertinent form of joint ownership, equity will favour the form of tenancy in common, especially in situations of commerce.[8] The form, however, will also be determined by specific words expressed by the parties, showing their intention to own the property in either of the two forms.[9] The law provides clear guidance in the case of patents and copyrights and favours the form of tenancy in common, unless otherwise specified by the parties.[10] As the Court recently held: 'if there are two or more persons who are joint authors they own the copyright in equal shares, but it is suggested that is not an invariable rule because sometimes the authors may be joint tenants rather than tenants in common and in that case until severance there are no shares.'[11] Finally, while tenancies in common and joint tenancies can exist with respect to real and personal property, they do not apply to a chose in action.[12] Intellectual property must be defined as personal property, in order for these forms of joint ownership to apply. The law provides that patents and copyrights are indeed personal properties.[13]

---

7 See M Thompson, *Modern Land Law* (Oxford: Oxford University Press, 2nd ed., 2003) 253-313.

8 The main difference between the two forms is the principle of the 'right of survivorship' (or *jus accrescendi*) according to which, in the event of the death of the joint tenant, the other joint tenant/s obtain the interest. The last survivor will become the sole beneficial owner and will have the right to dispose of the property as he pleases. Because it might be the case that the tenant who had contributed the least might survive the other co-owner/s and thus become the sole beneficiary, equity considers this principle unsuitable in the field of commerce and will determine the right of survivorship according to the share that each of the co-owners has (known as the maxim *jus accrescendi inter mercatores locum non habet*). See for example, *Lake v Gibson* (1729) 1 Eq Rep 290; and in modern law, *Bull v Bull* [1955] 1 QB 234.

9 This is the principle of 'severance' according to which the survival of a joint tenancy will be determined by certain expressions made by the co-owners from which we can learn about their intent not to be regarded as a single owner. For examples, statements such as 'in equal shares' or 'to be divided between' are regarded as preventing the ownership from taking the form of joint tenancy. For a brief account see D Hayton, 'Joint Tenancies – Severance' (1976) 35 *Cambridge Law Journal* 20.

10 See CDPA 1988 s 10(1); PA 1977 s 36(1).

11 *Bamgboye v Reed* [2004] 5 EMLR 61, 74.

12 Choses (or things) are divided into two classes: choses in possession (eg, tangible items capable of being actually possessed and enjoyed, such as a poetry book or a car) and choses in action (eg, a right to recover a debt that can be enforced by legal action). See *Re McKerrell McKerrell v Gowans* [1912] Ch D 648, 650.

13 Under s 90(1) of the CDPA 1988 copyright is transferable as 'personal or moveable property.' Complementing this is s 1(1) which provides that 'Copyright is a property right…';

As with personal property, in copyright the nature of the joint relations and the respective parts to which each is entitled are determined by an agreement between all alleged joint authors, unless the nature of the relationship between the authors involved indicates the method of cooperation.[14] In the case of *Stuart v Barrett*, it was held that in the absence of an agreement between the alleged joint-authors, all share equally as tenants in common, irrespective of their actual contribution in terms of quality, quantity and originality.[15] This rule is of particular importance in the case of public/author joint authorship for two main reasons: an explicit agreement is not a prerequisite, and the difficulty to quantify contribution will not disqualify a contribution for matters of ownership, unless, of course it does not satisfy the requirement of minimum skill and labour and is not original.

Joint authors of a copyrighted works are the initial co-owners of the work. However, co-ownership does not necessarily arise from joint authorship. Co-ownership also applies to situations where, for example, a given interest is transferred or assigned to more than one party or when the work has been produced in the course of employment. Here my main concern is with the way in which joint ownership of copyrighted works comes about when the copyright material is produced by two or more collaborators. The Act specifies that initial ownership of a work is rather straightforward: the first owner of a copyright work is the author of the work.[16] In the case of works of joint authorship, the collaborating two or more authors constitute the 'first owner.' I will deal with initial ownership and will treat the public and authors as constituting the 'first owner' of the work.

---

and s 30(1) of the PA 1977 reads: 'Any patent or application for a patent is personal property (without being a thing in action)...'

Although it is arguable that copyright is a version of chose in action, courts have found that copyright is clearly chose in possession. See for example, *Lauri v Renad* [1892] 3 Ch D 402; *Redwood Music Ltd v B Feldman & Co Ltd* [1979] 1 RPC 1; *Mail Newspapers Plc v Express Newspapers Plc* [1987] FSR 90; and *Bamgboye v Reed* (n 11 above). See generally, S Brodhurst, 'Is Copyright a Chose in Action?' (1895) 11 *Law Quarterly Review* 64; TC Williams, 'Property, Things in Action, and Copyright' (1895) 11 *Law Quarterly Review* 223.

14 *Bamgboye v Reed,* ibid 80.

15 *Stuart v Barrett* [1994] EMLR 448. In *Levy v Rutley*, the earliest recorded case on joint authorship, Byles J found joint authorship to exist although one person had contributed a very small amount of work to the execution. *Levy v Rutley* (1871) LR 6 CP 523, 527-528, 529. See also *Godfrey v Lees* [1995] EMLR 307. For the patent aspect see *Florey and Others' Patent* [1962] RPC 186, 193.

16 CDPA 1988 s 11(1). There is one exception to this rule: in works produced in the course of employment, in the absence of an agreement to the contrary, the first owner is the employer. CDPA 1988 s 11(2). See for example, *Acorn Computers Ltd v MCS Microcomputer Systems Pty Ltd* (1983-85) 4 IPR 214. On this issue see generally, AS Wernick, 'The Work Made for Hire and Joint Work Copyright Doctrines after *CCNV v Reid*: "What! You Mean I don't Own It Even Though I Paid in Full for It?"' (1990) 13 *Hamline Law Review* 287. It should also be noted that under CDPA 1988 s 11(3), 163, and 168, the rule of joint authorship does not apply to Crown or Parliamentary copyright and to copyright of certain international organisations.

Joint authorship does not occur automatically. Copyright law requires authors to satisfy two conditions for there to be a case for joint authorship: collaboration and contribution to produce a copyrightable work of a single kind 'in prosecution of a preconcerted joint design.'[17] The contribution of each of them must not be distinct from that of the other and each must significantly add original creative input to the protectable *expressive* form of the creation.[18] Also, it is somewhat unclear whether English law requires, as do US and Canadian Copyright laws, an intention of the parties to collaborate. Finally, in order to secure the interest of the parties, the law stipulates that no joint author can dispose of the whole or a divisible part of the work without the consent of the other joint authors. I examine each of these elements separately and question whether the collaborative paradigm public/author satisfies them.

Collaboration and Contribution

Under s 10(1) of the CDPA 1988, a claimant to joint authorship must prove that he has contributed to the execution of the copyright work. The contribution should not be separable or distinct from the contribution of any other collaborator and it has to be substantial, but not necessarily equal.[19] That is to say, that the contribution each adds must be significant, inseparable, in pursuant to a common design, and when assembled together, constitutes a unitary copyrightable entity.[20] In the event that the contributions are distinguishable, the work may qualify as a collective work.[21]

---

17 *Levy v Rutley* (n 15 above) 523, 528-529.

18 CDPA s 10(1). Joint authorship will not arise when a work is composed of different parts in which each demands a discrete form of mental activity, for example, an original text and its translation, or the text and soundtrack of a play. CDPA 1988 s 3 and s 10. In such cases there are distinct copyrights. For example, a 'musical work' is defined as 'a work consisting of music, exclusive of any words or actions intended to be sung, spoken or performed with the music.' For example, the lyrics of a song are a separate literary work. CDPA 1988 s 3(1). Also, joint ownership by way of assignment does not arise where different aspects of the copyright (publishing rights, performing rights, etc) are transferred to different people. In this situation each person has copyright over his apportioned subject-matter. CDPA 1988 s 90(2)(a).

19 See *Stuart v Barrett* (n 15 above). Certain copyright works have different criteria for co-authorship (films, CDPA 1988 s 10(1A), and broadcasts CDPA 1988 s 10(2)).

20 The Court in *Stuart v Barrett* mentions these aspects by citing the interlocutory decision in *Najma Heptulla v Orient Longman Ltd (1988)*, [1989] FSR 598 (HC India). *Stuart v Barrett*, ibid 462. *Cf*, *Meltzer v Zoller* 520 F Supp 847 (DNJ 1981).

21 A collective work is a work created by two or more that lacks the coalescence of the requirements for joint authorship. Contributors retain separate copyright. CDPA 1988 s 178 provides that a 'collective work means: (a) a work of joint authorship, or (b) a work in which there are distinct contributions by different authors or in which works or parts of works of different authors are incorporated.' The Act does not specify examples of such works and as such creates unnecessary confusion with what joint authorship consists of, and may also cause abuse of the copyright system by creating artificial rights of non-contributors while diminishing the rights of *de facto* contributors. This matter was considered by the court in

The question of significant original contribution is one of fact and degree,[22] as opposed to whether the parties intended to co-author the work. In the seminal case of *Kenrick v Lawrence* the Court held that sufficient contribution is established only if one contributes to the execution of the idea.[23] The simple reason is that '[t]here is no copyright in ideas. Thus, a person with an original idea is not the author or copyright owner of any work composed by another who makes use of that idea, unless the person with the idea contributes to the *form* in which the copyright exists.'[24] A court will not find joint authorship where it cannot find contribution in the way of *literary labour* to the work.[25] For example, it is not enough that an author thought up a plot of a play or made suggestions for scenic effects, several catchwords, a comic routine to be included, the title, leading characters for the play, or that the author passes on his reminiscences to a ghostwriter.[26] Furthermore, the contribution has to be made during the process leading to the creation of a copyrighted work and not when 'the melody was complete, the chord structure was complete, the rhythm or groove was apparent...and the structure...from start to finish was already laid out.'[27]

The answer to the question of what exactly constitutes sufficient contribution is complex and is fraught with conflicting interpretations. In the case of *Robin Ray v Classic FM*[28] the court was asked to rule on a dispute between a writer and a broadcaster of classical music against the commercial radio station, Classic FM. This dispute concerns the ownership of intellectual property rights in five documents, that contain proposals on how to categorise the tracks of the defendant's music in a catalogue of more than 50,000 items of classical music compiled by the plaintiff over a five-year period, and in a database which includes substantial reproductions of the five documents and of the catalogue. The Court reiterates what exactly are the necessary conditions for joint authorship and emphasises that a joint author

---

Redwood Music v Feldman (n 13 above). *Cf* US 1976 Copyright Act, 17 USC s 101 and s 201(c) and the Canadian Copyright Act RSC 1985, c C-42, s 2. Both Acts provide examples for collective works, such as encyclopaedia, anthology, dictionary or newspaper.

22 See the judgment of Laddie J in *Flyde Microsystems Ltd v Key Radio Systems Ltd* [1998] FSR 449, 456. I further expand on this issue in, L Zemer, 'Contribution and Collaboration in Joint Authorship: Too Many Misconceptions' (2006) 1(4) *Journal of Intellectual Property Law & Practice* 283.

23 *Kenrick & Co v Lawrence & Co* (1890) 25 QBD 99. In contrast, the patent system allows ideas that go to the main principle of the patent to constitute original contribution that would merit joint inventorship. *Smith's Patent* (1905) 22 RPC 57. *Cf, Allen v Rawson* (1845) 1 CB 551, 135 ER 656. See also Marchese (n 3 above) 366.

24 *Stuart v Barrett* (n 15 above) 462.

25 *Ashmore v Douglas-Home* [1987] FSR 553, 563. See also *Tate v Fullbrook* [1908] 1 KB 821; *Tate v Thomas* [1921] 1 Ch 503; *Donoghue v Allied Newspapers Ltd* [1937] 3 All ER 503; and *Wiseman v George Weidenfeld & Nicolson* [1985] FSR 525.

26 *Evans v E Hulton & Co Ltd* [1923-8] Macg Cop Cas 51.

27 *Hadley v Kemp* [1999] EMLR 589, 594.

28 *Robin Ray v Classic FM Plc* [1998] FSR 622.

is required to participate in the writing, and share responsibility for the form of expression in the literary work under dispute. Lightman J held:

> As regards the five documents and the catalogue, there is no doubt that…there were meetings between the plaintiff and representatives of the defendant when discussions took place as to the categories to be adopted and as to the contents of the catalogue, and that the defendant's representatives initiated and developed a number of ideas which the plaintiff incorporated in the five documents and the catalogue. But the plaintiff was solely responsible as author for the writing of the five documents and the catalogue and the way the ideas were expressed in them.[29]

Mere discussions, no matter how valuable they are for the initiation of ideas, cannot serve as the basis for copyright protection unless, in the meetings, work was performed for the tangible fixation of the ideas. The Court was surprised enough with the defendant's argument that an idea or ideas should suffice for contribution, to invite the defendant to kindly 'say no more' and called his argument a 'lapse into heresy.'[30] The Court concludes with the assertion that 'what was required for joint authorship was something akin to penmanship. What was essential was a direct responsibility for what actually appeared on paper.'[31] While the 'sum total' of the defendant's contribution was in the form of ideas, thoughts and material communicated to the plaintiff, the latter was engaged with 'the most important input',[32] namely, tangibly fixing ideas and thoughts.

This strict approach to contribution is distant from an earlier judgment by Laddie J in the case of *Cala Homes v Alfred McAlpine.*[33] Here, dealing with joint authorship of architectural plans, the Court reminds us that skill and labour are core prerequisites for copyright subsistence and states that one's substantial contribution of skill and labour is sufficient for a claim of joint authorship. However, although ideas are insufficient contribution, that does not mean that we should confine our definition of authorship to the person 'who pushed the pen' onto paper. As Laddie J remarks:

> In my view, to have regard merely to who pushed the pen is too narrow a view of authorship. What is protected by copyright in a drawing or a literary work is more than just the skill of making marks on paper or some other medium. It is both the words or lines and the skill and effort involved in creating, selecting or gathering together the detailed concepts, data or emotions which those words or lines have fixed in some tangible form which is protected. It is wrong to think that only the person who carries out the mechanical act of fixation is an author. There may well be skill and expertise in drawing clearly and well but that does not mean that it is only that skill and expertise which is relevant.[34]

---

29 Ibid 637.

30 Ibid 638.

31 Ibid 624, 636. See also *Brighton v Jones* [2004] EMLR 507 (Ch D).

32 *Robin Ray v Classic FM*, ibid.

33 *Cala Homes (South) Ltd v Alfred McAlpine Homes East Ltd* [1995] FSR 818.

34 Ibid 835. *Cf Kenrick v Lawrence* (n 23 above). Here the Court remarked that 'the author must mean a person who has at least some substantial share in putting the touches on

This is a welcome remark by Laddie J which stands in sharp contrast to what Lightman J says about authorship in the *Robin Ray* case while criticising Laddie J's decision.[35] The latter's reference to the important role concepts and emotions play suggests that authorship cannot be reduced to mere physical activity. Although Laddie J's remarks underscore the dependency on contributions from other sources when we create, they invite criticism for running the risk of conveying a definition of authorship, which traditional copyright law does not support. That is, one may argue that sufficient 'skill and expertise' requires something closer to creative input – a higher threshold than 'skill labour and judgement', and as we know, creative input is an alien concept in English copyright jurisprudence.[36]

Laddie J reapplied his reasoning in *Cala Homes* in the later case of *Flyde Microsystems v Key Radio Systems*.[37] This case revolves around the question whether support in testing and debugging software, including consultation on a regular basis in the course of developing software with specific technical functionality, merit joint authorship or an implied licence to use the software. Dismissing the argument for joint authorship, Laddie J clarifies his view on authorship, and remarks that the purpose of CDPA 1988 s 10(1) is not to turn someone who is not an author into an author[38] and the fact that one can learn 'enough about the other's field of expertise to allow them to interchange ideas' does not turn a person into an author of the software even when the 'contributions took a lot of time and were very valuable.'[39] In other words, Laddie J reaches this conclusion through his distinction between authorial skill and labour, and mere skill and labour. While the former may suffice as contribution for joint authorship, the latter, no matter how time-consuming and valuable is, is not enough.[40]

Vaver criticises the restrictive application of the requirement of contribution and remarks that 'what contribution warrants co-authorship may be contentious.'[41] He gives the example 'where A supplies B with all the ideas for the plot of a play and B turns them into a finished work.'[42] Drawing on this example he then explains the flaw inherent in the existing rules of joint authorship:

> This collaboration [between A and B] has sometimes not counted as joint authorship unless A's ideas were independently copyrightable – a result that may promote certainty but that still seems hard. There would have been no play at all without A's input. To elevate

---

to paper.' Ibid 106. See also *Brown v Mcasso Music Production Ltd* [2006] EMLR 3 (Cpwt).

35 *Robin Ray v Classic FM* (n 28 above) 636.

36 See above, Chapter 3.

37 *Flyde Microsystems v Key Radio Systems* (n 22 above) in particular 454-460; For further illustration see *Pierce v Promco SA* [1999] ITCLR 233.

38 *Flyde Microsystems v Key Radio Systems*, ibid 455.

39 Ibid 460.

40 Ibid.

41 D Vaver, *Intellectual Property law: Copyright, Patents, Trade Marks* (Toronto: Irwin Law, 1997) 52-53 (emphasis added).

42 Ibid.

B's contribution and entirely discount A's may discourage some fruitful collaborations. It may also undesirably invite a minute examination and dissection of who said and did what, often long after the event when memory is unreliable. *Any substantial intellectual contribution to a work's composition pursuant to a common design should, in principle, count as co-authorship.*[43]

A line of recent cases restate the rule that contribution must be significant and linked to the expression. These cases show how arbitrary and subjective the assessment of contribution can be. They render legitimate contribution irrelevant. In *Beckingham v Hodgens* the Court of Appeal was asked to rule on the finding of joint authorship of a recording of the Bluebells' song 'Young at Heart' between a professional fiddle player and the leader of the Bluebells.[44] Refusing the appeal, the Court agrees that the parties collaborated in furtherance of a common design but did not satisfy the requirement of inseparable contribution. The court invited musicologists by both parties which confirmed that the violin part in the song – the cause of the claim – is more memorable than any other part of the song. The court upheld the trial judge's decision: 'Having heard the piece played, and reflected on the evidence given, I conclude that the violin part does make a significant and original contribution of the right kind of skill and labour to the Bluebells' version of the song.'[45]

In *Hadley v Kemp* the Court found that nine per cent of the duration of the track was, despite its attractiveness, not enough to qualify the saxophone interlude as significant and original contribution: 'the saxophone solo was only 16 bars in length and occupied under 9 per cent of the duration of the recording. Accordingly the third plaintiff was not a joint author.'[46] In the *Beckingham* case the court did not base its decision on the duration of the violin part, and chose to follow an expert's opinion that the part is merely 'more memorable.' It seems that in *Beckingham* the court applies an objective quality-based test, as opposed to a subjective, rather arbitrary, test in *Hadley v Kemp*. Which test guarantees greater legal certainty?

In *Bamgboye v Reed* the Court reiterates the fact that contribution to musical works is a matter of degree.[47] But similar to Laddie's opinion in *Cala Homes*, the court was looking for something close to '*creative* contribution', and indeed held that Mr Bamgboye makes a significant creative contribution to the musical work.[48] Although it seems the court might have established the beginning of the first English 'creative-step' requirement, something akin to the US decision in *Feist*,[49] this was unnecessary for matters of copyright subsistence. Citing in full the test for joint

43 Ibid (emphasis added).

44 *Beckingham v Hodgens* [2004] 6 ECDR 46 (CA).

45 Ibid 50.

46 *Hadley v Kemp* (n 27 above) 592.

47 *Bamgboye v Reed* (n 11 above).

48 Ibid 62, 78.

49 *Feist Publications Inc v Rural Telephone Service Co* 499 US 340 (1991). See also above, Chapter 3.

authorship as laid down in the *Robin Ray* case the Court again demonstrated how arbitrary the test for contribution is,[50] the Court finds that a contribution of 33 per cent was sufficient creative contribution since it relates to the creation of the musical work and not to the interpretation or performance of the work.[51]

The rules on joint authorship under the CDPA 1988 substantially differ from their US counterpart. This, however, does not mean that the latter works better. As Dreyfuss observes: our policy of joint authorship 'eliminates the possibility that certain contributors…will be protected by the statute.'[52] For example, it is argued that the US Copyright Act of 1976 does injustice in the case of sound recordings and rock music as it does not recognise the complexity of creating a sound recording,[53] or that rock music is a group phenomenon.[54] According to s 101 of the 1976 Act, a joint work is a 'work prepared by two or more authors with the intention that their contribution be merged into inseparable or interdependent unitary whole.' It seems that s 101 mirrors s 10(1) of the CDPA with two main differences: the requirement of intention and the component of interdependency.[55]

50 *Bamgboye v Reed* (n 11 above) 73-74.

51 Ibid 63.

52 R Cooper Dreyfuss, 'Commodifying Collaborative Research' in N Elkin-Koren and NW Netanel (eds.), *The Commodification of Information* (The Hague: Kluwer Law International, 2002) 397, 408.

53 TR Kuda, 'Authorship of Sound Recordings: Why Sound Recordings Should Have Joint Authorship?' (2004) 33 *Southwestern University Law Review* 379, 391-395.

54 GW Hutchinson, Practitioner's Note, 'Can the Federal Courts Save Rock Music?: Why Default Joint Authorship Rule Should be Adopted to Protect Co-Authors under United States Copyright Law' (2003) 5 *Tulane Journal of Technology and Intellectual Property* 77, 79.

55 See P Spyke, 'The Joint Work Dilemma: The Separately Copyrightable Contribution Requirement and Co-ownership Principles' (1993) 40 *Journal of the Copyright Society of the USA*, 463; CS Brophy, 'Joint Authorship under the Copyright Law' (1994) 16 *Hastings Communication and Entertainment Law Journal* 451; and LaFrance (n 5 above) 210-220.

In 1915 Learned Hand J cited *Levy v Rutley* as the authority for his decision in *Maurel v Smith* establishing the test for joint authorship in the United States as composed of the following four elements: intent, contribution, a common design and joint effort. 220 F 195 (USDNY 1915). This should serve as a 'satisfactory analysis' for joint authorship of a copyrighted work, ie, whether 'the extent of the mutual influences between the parts of such a piece' qualifies the work for joint authorship. Ibid 200. For analysis of the case and its influence on the evolution of joint authorship, see E Valachovic, 'The Contribution Requirement to a Joint Work under the Copyright Act' (1992) 12 *Loyola of Los Angeles Entertainment Law Journal* 199, 205-209.

Indeed, until the enactment of the 1976 Act, joint authorship under US copyright law was regulated by common law and looked more similar to the present English model. For example, in *Edward B Marks Music Corp v Jerry Vogel Music Co*, the Court held that for joint authorship to exist 'it makes no difference whether the authors work in concert, or even whether they know each other; it is enough that they mean for their contributions to be complementary in the sense that they are to be embodied in a single work to be performed

In *Thomson v Larson* the Second Circuit rejected a claim of joint authorship, while leaving open the question of whether a contributor of copyrightable material retains an independent interest as the author of his contributions.[56] Although the agreement between Thomson and Larson said nothing about copyright, the collaboration between them brought about a new creation: their joint work resulted in complete rewrite of the *Rent* play script. The question was whether Thomson's and Larson's 'creative contributions rise to the level of joint authorship'?[57] There exist two different approaches to this question. One is that of Nimmer, the other is that of Goldstein. The former argues that each contribution should be 'more than *de minimis*' or that 'more than a word or line…be added.'[58] The latter asserts that each contribution must be independently copyrightable.[59] Although the joint authorship rules under the 1976 Act do not embrace a Goldstein-like condition, common law has created the rule that in order to qualify as a joint author the contribution must be copyrightable. Goldstein's approach attempts, as the Court held in *Childress v Taylor*, to 'carefully draw the bounds of joint authorship so as to protect the legitimate claims of both sole authors and co-authors.'[60]

Can we carefully draw these boundaries by strictly applying rules that ignore contributions made by others? Although under English law the requirement for contribution is closer to Nimmer's *de minimis* approach, both systems require copyrightable contribution and embrace, although on a different scale, Goldstein's approach. This approach seems wrong. First, it discourages authors from creating

---

as such.' 140 F 2d 266 (2d Cir 1944) 267. The principle of joint authorship was also broadly defined in *Shapiro Bernstein & Co v Jerry Vogel Music Co*, in which the Court held that even if an author has no intent to merge a work with another at the time of creation, a joint work will nevertheless be created if that author later shows the necessary intent. 223 F 2d 252 (2d Cir 1955). This was known as the 'Twelfth Street Rag' doctrine (after the name of the song under dispute) but was abolished by the 1976 Act.

56 *Thomson v Larson* 147 F 3d 195 (2d Cir 1998). See Recent Cases, 'Copyright Joint-Authorship: Second Circuit holds that Dramaturge's Contribution to the Musical *Rent* did not Establish Joint-Authorship with Playwright Composer' (1999) *Harvard Law Review* 964; F Buckalew, 'Joint Authorship in the Second Circuit: A Critique of the Law in the Second Circuit Following *Childress v Taylor* and as Exemplified in *Thomson v Larson*' (1998) 64 *Brooklyn Law Review* 549; JD Yarbrough Jr., 'What's Mine Might be Yours: Why We Should Rethink the Default Rule for Copyright Co-Ownership in joint Works' (2001) 76 *Tulane Law Review* 493; and LaFrance, ibid.

57 LaFrance, ibid 193-194.

58 NB Nimmer and D Nimmer, *Nimmer on Copyright* (New York: Matthew Bender & Co, 1998) 6-23.

59 P Goldstein, *Copyright: Principles, Law and Practice* (Boston, Toronto: Little, Brown & Co, 1989) 4.2.1.2. For commentary on the Goldstein and Nimmer approaches, see LaFrance (n 5 above) 196-197, 259-261; and PS Fox, 'Preserving the Collaborative Spirit of American Theatre: The Need for a 'Joint Authorship Default Rule' in Light of the Rent Decision's Unanswered Question', (2001) 19 *Cardozo Arts & Entertainment Law Journal* 497, 507-509.

60 *Childress v Taylor* 945 F 2d 500, 504 (2d Cir 1991).

or providing other creators with valuable ideas, and risks chilling 'the creative process.'[61] As Vaver remarks, it denies contributions without which the work would not at all exist.[62] Second, it strengthens the status of the sole author and further blurs the role of and dependence on the authorial collectivity.

Does the public qualify for the two conditions of collaboration and contribution? I argue the public undoubtedly qualifies for the condition of collaboration. Since no authorial and artistic materials are created *ex nihilo*, every creative author or artist, as a member of the public, is bound to collaborate with it through consumption of cultural and social elements. In a Coombe-like explanation: the creative process is a complex one that requires the availability of publicly accessible symbols.[63] The operation of the copyright creation process is ultimately dependent on the collaboration between public and authors. It is a process that will not exist or yield any results if one of these two collaborators is eliminated from the copyright game.

Given the restrictive interpretation of contribution Courts tend to apply in clear situations of joint input, one may argue that the public does not qualify for the condition of significant contribution and merely adds insignificant raw materials such as ideas and principles. I already showed the difficulties in the idea/expression dichotomy and it seems, following Vaver's view, that these difficulties have a special appeal in the case of joint authorship. Contribution that should merit joint authorship should be distinguished from what is required for sole authorship. When two or more collaborators decide to join efforts in furtherance of a preconcerted joint design, they knowingly participate in a process that would yield results only if their efforts are combined together; the test for significant contribution should be interpreted in light of the shared responsibility collaborators hold for the resulted type of the expression, whether by virtue of pushing the pen onto paper or adding other mental labour in the guise of ideas, concepts and relevant substantial suggestions. If we eliminate invaluable mental contribution, we may end up devising a definition of joint authorship embedded with misconceptions and arbitrary and subjective rules on what amounts to significant contribution, that would not only severely diminish the contribution made by non-joint authors, but also destabilise the incentive system so well ingrained in our vision of copyright. As they stand today, the rules governing joint authorship are just another brick in the wall of our strong and unbalanced conceptions of solitary authorship.

Following the discussion of the authorial collectivity, it is wrong to presume that the public's contribution is insignificant. The social and cultural bond between public and authors dictate that every work requires significant contribution from the public. At the same time, just as there is no 'Romantic sole authorship' there is no 'Romantic public authorship.' Copyright creation is a joint process in which contribution is provided from two sources: public and authors. That is, the public's contribution should amount to authorial contribution for purposes of joint authorship.

61 Fox (n 59 above) 508.
62 Vaver (n 41 above).
63 Coombe (n 1 above).

I find further support to this argument in Laddie J's remarks in *Cala Homes* that '[i]t is wrong to think that only the person who carries out the mechanical act of fixation is an author. There may well be skill and expertise in drawing clearly and well but that does not mean that it is only that skill and expertise which is relevant', and that we should value the contribution coming from 'detailed concepts, data or emotions' and distinct 'expertise.'[64] By analogy, the public contributes invaluable skill and expertise by virtue of maintaining and providing social and cultural properties. The social construction of authors and their creative endeavours emphasise how tangible authorial manifestations are dependent on these properties.

Wilf takes the public in its collective capacity and defends its authorial role in trademarks. A major theme in Wilf's essay 'is the linking together of doctrinal fragments to elaborate the circumstances and implications of the public's role in creating intellectual property.'[65] He defends a public regulatory power in trademarks based on the fact that '[t]rademark doctrine demonstrates a notable reliance upon public perception.'[66] Wilf recognises the dynamics of author-public interaction and concludes that '[a] trademark is not authored by the production/marketing of an object in its package, but by a joint interpretive enterprise between author and public.'[67] This confers on the public property entitlement in trademarks, and 'the public should retain its entitlement.'[68] He defends a joint property title to the public in intellectual creations. By virtue of the fact that every copyrighted entity depends on the authorial collectivity and is a social construct, Wilf's argument neatly applies to copyright.

That is to say, the public's contribution plays a decisive role in the *expression* of any idea. An author cannot be treated as the sole creator or the meaning-maker of a given object and thereby the owner of a copyrighted entity. The contribution the public makes is inseparable from that of the author and amounts exactly to the substantial contribution Courts insist should be found before joint authorship is presumed. Furthermore, following *Levy v Rutley*,[69] both parties, public and authors, benefit from the principle that the quantity of the contribution plays no role.

---

64 *Cala Homes v Alfred McAlpine Homes* (n 33 above) 835.

65 Ibid.

66 S Wilf, 'Who Authors Trademarks?' (1999) 17 *Cardozo Arts & Entertainment Law Journal* 1, 32.

67 Ibid 46-47. Wilf remarks that '[b]y associating a symbol with an object, the public contributes to the authorship of trademarks. This associative power grants a word or icon meaning as the representation of a particular object.' Ibid 1.

68 Ibid 36. Wilf remarks that this joint enterprise between public and authors 'requires a rethinking of the very definition of intellectual property. Intellectual property is different.' Ibid 45-46.

69 *Levy v Rutley* (n 15 above).

Shared Intention

Intent to co-author is what some would call 'the touchstone of joint authorship.'[70] Albeit conflicting views, under English law, as opposed to the US and Canada, intent to co-author, is not a prerequisite for joint authorship. In the recent case of *Beckingham v Hodgens* the court emphasises that the question in joint authorship is one of fact and degree, not of mutual intention, and all that is required to show is collaboration and contribution.[71] Indeed, in the CDPA 1988, intent to co-author as a prerequisite is nowhere to be found. However, it seems, as I shall argue, that intent to co-author has become an implicit requirement.

Intent to co-author as a key condition for joint authorship was examined in the Canadian case of *Darryl Neudorf v Nettwerk Productions.*[72] This case concerns a dispute between a drummer, Darryl Neudorf, and the singer Sarah McLachlan for copyright infringement and a share of the royalties in four musical works. The question was whether Neudorf's contribution was significant according to Canadian copyright law, and whether the parties intended the song to be jointly authored. Cohen J formulated the following three-step test for joint authorship: '(1) Did the plaintiff contribute significant original expression to the songs? If yes, (2) did each of the plaintiff and McLachlan intend that their contributions be merged into a unitary whole? If yes, (3) did each of the plaintiff and McLachlan intend the other to be a joint author of the songs?'[73] With regards the first question, Cohen J held that the contribution to the arrangements of songs is equivocal to the contribution of suggestions and ideas, which is insufficient for claiming joint authorship.[74] Also, contribution of song titles is insubstantial.[75] In other words, Neudorf, as a 'musical arranger', was not successful in using the 'weapons in his armoury' to become co-author of the songs.[76] With regards to the second question, the Court did not find the requisite 'shared intent' between the parties. In reaching this decision, Cohen J was inspired by the English authority of *Levy v Rutley* and concluded that intent to co-author is a requirement when two or more authors collaborate to produce a work of a single kind 'in prosecution of a preconcerted joint design.'[77]

70 Valachovic (n 55 above) 216, 218. For an earlier analysis of the intent to co-author requirement, see TM Brady, Note, 'Manifest Intent and Copyrightability: The Destiny of Joint Authorship' (1989) 17 *Fordham Urban Law Journal* 257.

71 *Beckingham v Hodgens* (n 44 above).

72 *Darryl Neudorf v Nettwerk Productions Ltd & al* [2000] 3 WWR 522.

73 E Simcoe and C Ingram, 'Joint Authorship: A Question of Joint Effort or Intent' (2000) *Copyright World* 18, 19.

74 *Darryl Neudorf v Nettwerk Productions* (n 72 above) 592-599.

75 Ibid 599-600.

76 These were the words articulated by Goff J in the case of *Redwood Music* (n 18 above) cited by J Cohen in *Neudorf* Case, ibid 597-598.

77 Ibid 523, 528-529. Justice Cohen was also motivated by the definition of a joint work under the US Copyright Act of 1976, 17 USC s 101 and s 201(a).

A line of decisions by US Courts has brought many commentators to heavily criticise stringent requirements for joint authorship. The leading authority of *Childress v Taylor* concerns a dispute between actress Clarice Taylor who had an idea for a play and Alice Childress who was hired as playwright.[78] Taylor's contribution was found to consist of ideas, suggestions, frequent discussions and provision of research material, none of which was considered sufficient to qualify her as a joint author of the play. The Court interpreted Goldstein's approach and held that there should be a clear distinction between sole authors and co-authors and found the plaintiff to be a sole author due to lack of contribution on the part of the defendant. In this case the court introduced a two-pronged test requiring that (i) each author's contribution be independently copyrightable; and (ii) each party intentionally regards the other party as a joint author. The second is the more controversial issue. The Court remarks that what distinguishes a given relationship from the 'true joint author relationship is the lack of intent of both participants in the venue to regard themselves as joint authors.'[79] So important is the intent requirement, that the Court asserted that mutual intent requires that each author regard his counterpart as joint author even though he does *not* fully understand the legal consequences of co-authorship relationship at the time of collaboration.[80] As I shall argue, the inherent and unavoidable danger in the intent to co-author condition is denial of authorial contributions.[81]

The far-reaching consequences of the decision in *Childress* were uncovered in *Thomson v Larson*.[82] Although experts considered the collaboration between Thomson and Larson to be the cause for the 'radical transformation of the show'[83] *Rent*, the Court denied the claim for joint authorship on the basis of Larson's lack of intent to co-author. Due to the lack of an agreement between the two, the Court was searching for secondary factors in order to verify whether the two intended to co-author. The Court was looking for a 'window [into] the mind of the party…' and a writer's attribution of the work to himself alone was found persuasive proof that the writer intended the work to represent his authorial contribution alone.[84] The Court then concludes that the way in which Larson 'listed credits on the scripts

78 *Childress v Taylor* (n 60 above).

79 Ibid 507. See also *Respect Inc v Committee on Status of Women*, 815 F Supp 1112 (USND III 1993); *Clogston v American Academy of Orthopaedic Surgeons*, 930 F Supp 1156 (USWD Tex 1996); and *Thomson v Larson* (n 56 above).

80 *Childress v Taylor*, ibid 508. In another case it was held that we should look at the intention of the 'dominant' author, to share authorship. See *Fisher v Klein* 16 USPQ 2d 1795, 1798 (SDNY 1990).

81 Acknowledging this danger, brought Buckalew to ask whether the *Childress* ruling should apply in all situations of collaborative relationship? Buckalew (n 56 above) 580.

82 *Thomson v Larson* (n 56 above).

83 Ibid 198.

84 Ibid 203. The Ninth Circuit adopted this approach and held 'that contribution of independently copyrightable material to a work intended to be an inseparable whole will not suffice to establish authorship of a joint work', and that determinations of co-authorial intent should focus on 'who has decision making authority, how the parties bill themselves, and

strongly supports the view that he regarded himself as the sole author.'[85] It seems that by reaching this decision, the Court itself introduced absurd ways in which authors can rebuff contributors' input even in cases where this input is independently copyrightable.[86] Is not this case a notorious example of a situation where 'a contributor of non-*de minimis* copyrightable material has co-created a joint work within the statutory definition, yet has been denied the rights of joint authorship'?[87] Such decisions render our copyright system 'a system that is ripe for abuse'[88] and shows the fallacies in the way we reward authorial contributions.

A more critical consequence where no protection is secured for nondominant contributors is their inability to protect their moral rights. Honour and dignity, and other personal interests are likely to be affected.[89] The 'Dreyfuss formula' may be found useful to overcome such difficulties:

---

other evidence' of intent to be joint authors. *Aalmuhammed v Lee* 202 F 3d 1227 (9th Cir 2000) 1233-1234.

VerSteeg examines the intent condition in light of copyright and contract theory, and claims that the dominant author's subjective state of mind is not a controlling factor, that one stubborn collaborator cannot be permitted to wrest ownership from nondominant authors, and a person who makes significant contribution should be entitled to restitution, at least in respect of his contribution. R VerSteeg, 'Intent, Originality and Joint Authorship' (2002) 68 *Brooklyn Law Review* 123, 173-176, 177-180.

85 *Thomson v Larson*, ibid 204.

86 In another post-*Childress* case, the Court held that the decision in *Childress* 'may create problems in cases…in which the parties have collaborated in some sense of the term but are at odds as to whether or not there was mutual intent to create a joint work.' *Cabera v Treatro Del Sesenta* 914 F Supp 743 (PR 1995).

The far-reaching implications of the *Childress* decision include consequences on the general definition of copyright. For example, the Ninth Circuit, following the *Childress* test, stressed that originality should be interpreted stringently when the notion of 'independent copyrightable contribution' is at stake, *more than* in situations in which there is a work of individual authorship. *Aalmuhammed v Lee* (n 84 above). See also LaFrance (n 5 above) 246-255.

87 Fox (n 59 above) 515.

88 Hutchinson (n 54 above) 79. A question which the Court left open is whether the contributor whose contribution was denied for purposes of joint authorship retains property rights in his copyrightable input. I am of the view that since the 1976 Act provides that a joint work can be a composition of copyrightable *interdependent* (as opposed to inseparable) parts, the Act itself allows a contributor to retain property in his contribution and the exclusive right to license use of his owned materials. Fox advocates a 'Joint Authorship Default Rule' in such situations. Fox, ibid 525-531.

89 See generally R Rosenthal Kwall, '"Author-Stories": Narrative's Implications for Moral Rights and Copyright's Joint Authorship Doctrine' (2001) 75 *Southern California Law Review* 1. In situations where protection is available, one joint author can waive the moral rights of all other joint authors pursuant to a written agreement. See, Visual Artists Rights Act ("VARA") 17 USC s 106(e)(1) (1990). Such a principle undermined the very idea of a moral right and emphasises the overriding role of economic rights in copyright. See for example, RJ

> What would be better is the codification into intellectual property law a new overarching concept – a principle of proportionality. This principle would acknowledge the special texture of collaborative work products and allocate rights and duties in ways that recognise the distinctive nature of each collaborator's contribution. In copyright, the idea would be to recognise a new category of multiply authored product, the 'collaborative work', which would encompass works that do not qualify as for hire and do not meet the test of joint authorship. The new provision would recognise the authorship status of every participant who has contributed material to such work and give each author pecuniary interests in the work proportional to that party's input.[90]

Despite the centrality of an intention to joint authorship under US and Canadian copyright laws, the Court of Appeal in the *Beckingham* case refers to the requirement of intent as an 'uncertain realm of policy.'[91] The Court held that there is nothing in the wording of the 1988 Act to warrant the imposition of a requirement of intention, and then clarifies why the interpretation of *Levy v Rutley* is mistaken. The latter requires joint labouring in furtherance of a common design '[b]ut the "common design" in that context is not an intention that there should be joint authorship' and what the Court describes in this case 'was the process of jointly creating the work in question: as the judge in the instant case put it…a "common design to produce the work".'[92] Therefore 'there is no basis in the English cases for importing the requirement of an intention as to joint authorship. In Darryl Neudorf, Cohen J followed the United States case of *Childress v Taylor*…In my judgment, the judge in the instant case was clearly right to confine his consideration to the language of s 11(3) and not to look beyond the section into the uncertain realms of policy.'[93]

True, there is no explicit reference in the CDPA 1988 or in English case law that signifies that intent is a requirement for joint authorship. However, the mere fact that contribution must be indistinguishable when infused and directed to a unitary copyrightable whole raises the possibility that intent is presumed. In other words, if a unitary copyrightable work emerges from collaboration between several authors, and if the contribution of each is inseparable, then it is clear that they did not intend their contribution to be alien or distinct from each other's input. If they intended to contribute distinct parts their joint work would not qualify for the requirement of indistinct contribution required under a 10(1) of the CDPA 1988. As Learned Hand J remarks in *Maurel v Smith*, when two or more collaborators '*knowingly* engage in the production of a piece which is to be presented originally as a whole only, they adopt that common design mentioned in *Levy v Rutley*.'[94]

Sherman, 'The Visual Artists Rights Act of 1990: American Artists Burned Again' (1995) 17 *Cardozo Arts & Entertainment Law Review* 373.

90 Dreyfuss (n 52 above) 412.

91 *Beckingham v Hodgens* (n 44 above) 59-60.

92 Ibid.

93 Ibid.

94 *Maurel v Smith* (n 55 above) 199-200 (emphasis added). See also J Cohen in *Neudorf* (n 72 above) 551.

In line with the above, although intention to co-author is not a requirement under English copyright law, Keating J in *Levy v Rutley* writes: 'I fail to discover any evidence that there was any co-operation of the two [authors]...in any improvements either in the plot or the general structure.'[95] Reading this together with the decision of the Court in *Stuart v Barrett*[96] suggests that the intention requirement was created by common law copyright in England. In the latter case, the Court held that the members of the group had composed songs with each of them making contributions, which could not be separated from one another. Composing a joint enterprise then, is, by its very nature, based on some intent on behalf of the parties to collaborate and hence to jointly own the work.

Assuming that intent to co-author is a legitimate criterion for joint authorship,[97] what kind of collaboration will qualify for Justice Cohen's 'shared intent' principle? The requirement for shared intent on the part of both participants sets the threshold for joint authorship 'too high.'[98] In setting the test for intent at this level, the Court, similar to the decision in *Childress v Taylor*, risks denial of copyrightable contributions. Perhaps a better approach would require 'no more than actual co-operation between putative joint authors in the creation of a single work by means of the shared contribution of significant, original expression.'[99] This represents Vaver's approach, and to some extent reflects the implicit requirement of intent to co-author one finds in English case law.

The aim here is to justify joint authorship of copyrighted works between public and authors. How, then, are we to divine whether a creator intended joint authorship with the public? The US Legislative Committee report on the 1976 Copyright Act provides a good sense of conceptual direction. The Committee defines 'intention' in the following way: 'A work is "joint" if the authors collaborated with each other, or if each of the authors prepared his or her contribution with the *knowledge and intention* that it would be merged with the contributions of the other authors as "*inseparable or interdependent part of a unitary whole*." The touchstone here is the intention, *at the time the writing* is done, that the parts be absorbed or combined into an integrated unity...'[100] On the basis of my discussion of authorial collectivity and the public's status as a plural agent capable of intentional states, in the public/

95 *Levy v Rutley* (n 15 above) 529.

96 *Stuart v Barrett* (n 15 above).

97 That intent to co-author is inherent in the very idea of collaborative relationships is also supported by Nimmer's suggestion that 'intent to author' is a missing link in the process of judging copyrightability. D Nimmer, 'Copyright in the Dead Sea Scrolls: Authorship and Originality' (2001) 38 *Houston Law Review* 1, 159. *Cf*, JC Ginsburg, 'The Concept of Authorship in Comparative Copyright Law' (2003) 52 *DePaul Law Review* 1063, 1085-1088. See also, above Chapter 4.

98 Simcoe and Ingram (n 73 above) 20.

99 Ibid.

100 See H R Rep No 1476, 94th Cong, 2d Sess 120 (1976), reprinted in 1976 USCCAN 5659, 5736; S Rep No 473, 94th Cong, 2d Sess 103-104 (1975), cited in LaFrance (n 5 above) 195 (emphasis added).

author collaborative paradigm, both parties are bound to acknowledge that: (i) the authorial contribution each provides is mixed together with the knowledge and an intention to collaborate in the process of making copyrightable inseparable entities. Otherwise there would have been no copyrighted works; and (ii) such knowledge and an intention are present 'at the time the writing is done.'[101] To this I referred in Chapter 5 as 'the copyright moment': the moment in which an authorial or artistic work is born is the moment in which the collaboration between the author and the public yields creative results, i.e., the moment in which collective properties and the author's personal contribution are merged into a unitary whole. At this moment both parties intentionally and knowingly collaborate.

According to the role of the authorial collectivity and the social construction of creative products, the contributions of the public and the authors is inherently inseparable. It is inseparable for the many reasons already outlined and discussed. It is also interdependent because the inner structure of a jointly authored copyrighted work means that inseparability creates dependency between the different components of the work, and without this intra-dependency, the components would not have been able to become unified into one whole, let alone exist at all. Furthermore, where intent to co-author is required, the individual author's intent does not have to be made explicit. By being a member of the public and a consumer of its collectively owned social and cultural properties, the author undertakes a duty to recognise the public's contribution. That is, the requirement of intention to co-author with the public is implicit in the very act of copyright creation. Needless to say, the public, as a plural subject capable of intentional states, satisfies the requirement of intent to co-author by virtue of its responsibility to maintain a stable creative commons, make available cultural and social resources necessary for the copyright creation process, and its inability to guarantee adequate reward commensurate with its contribution.

The Element of Consent

A joint owner of copyright cannot exercise any of the restricted acts in the property (e.g., reproducing the work) without the consent of the other joint owner/s. According to the CDPA 1988 s 173(2), a licensee needs the consent of the other co-owner/s.[102]

101 Ibid.

102 In patents, each co-owner of a patent is permitted under the PA 1977 s 36(2)(a), by himself or his agents and without the consent of others, to do with the co-owned invention any act that otherwise would amount to an infringement act. Pursuant to s 36(3) of the PA 1977, however, consent of the other co-owners is required where a co-owner wishes to grant a licence, assign or mortgage his share in the patent.

As Marchese observes: '…an individual joint owner of copyright is…in a stronger or weaker position than a joint proprietor of a patent, depending on one's point of view – stronger because his agreement is required for any exploitation of the copyright, but weaker in that he cannot himself carry out such exploitation without the co-operation of the others.' Marchese (n 3 above) 367.

In the landmark case of *Cescinsky v George Routledge*,[103] involving an agreement between the parties stipulating that the copyright in several books is vested in both of them equally, the Court held: (i) lending the plaintiff's book to a new writer who intends to publish a book on the same topic is an act that amounts to violation of copyright because it was obvious that such a book will have to rely on the plaintiff's works; and (ii) a reproduction without the consent of all the owners is an infringement of copyright. If the law would waive the requirement of consent, the law would put a co-owner 'at the mercy of his co-owners' 'thus completely ruining the value of the copyright.'[104]

In contrast to the English approach, under US joint authorship rules, irrespective of the amount of their copyrightable contribution, all co-authors own an undivided interest in the co-owned work and each may, without the consent of the other co-author/s exploit the work, or issue non-exclusive licence to third parties.[105] Thus, a composer who is the joint author of a work composed of a sculpture and music can grant a non-exclusive licence for the reproduction of the whole work without the permission of the sculptor. The licensor cannot be sued for infringement by the sculptor because 'you cannot infringe your own copyright.'[106] The co-owner who grants the licence is only required to account to the other co-owner for a rateable share

---

However, courts were willing to accept that one co-owner may sue for infringement without the consent of the other co-owner/s. See for example, *Powell v Head* (1879) 12 Ch D 686. Any damages recoverable are respective of each co-owner's share. In *Prior v Lansdowne Press* J Gowans (citing the authority of *Blackborough v Graves* (1673) 1 Mod Rep 102; 86 ER 765 (one of two tenants in common can recover damages only for a moiety)) remarks that 'on principle, while it is true that an infringement injuring the copyright is an injury done to the copyright as a whole, owned by all the co-owners, one co-owner can only recover compensation in respect of the injury suffered by him, that is, in respect of so much of the copyright as belongs to him.' *Prior v Lansdowne Press Pty Ltd* [1977] RPC 511, 515.

Under PA 1977 s 66(2) a joint owner can bring an action for infringement on his own, but must join in the other co-owners as plaintiffs or, if they refuse to act, as defendants.

103 *Cescinsky v George Routledge* [1916] 2 KB 325.

104 Ibid 330. In *Robin Ray* the Court highlights the fundamentality of consent to the survival of any co-authorship relations and held that absent of consent, a joint owner of a copyright work cannot make copies for the purpose of exploitation of the work abroad. *Robin Ray v Classic FM* (n 28 above) 637; See also *Cala Homes v Alfred McAlpine Homes* (n 33 above) 836.

The requirement of consent is not an invention of modern copyright law. In the early case of *Powell v Head* the Court held that a joint ('part') owner of dramatic copyright cannot license a representation without the consent of the other owners simply because '[i]t is against the very essence of part-ownership or co-ownership that when there is a tenancy in common, one of the two can dispose of the right of the other, there being no partnership or other form of agency.' *Powell v Head* (n 102 above) 690. Therefore, 'where there are two proprietors, the one cannot represent without the consent of the other proprietor.' Ibid.

105 See NF Kugele, 'How Much does it Take?: Copyrightability as a Minimum Standard for Determining Joint Authorship' (1991) *University of Illinois Law Review* 809.

106 Spyke (n 55 above) 470, 483.

of the profits.[107] Waiving the consent requirement, as the Court upheld in *Cescinsky v George Routledge*, would put each co-owner 'at the mercy of his co-owners'[108] and allow imbalance of powers and control. Consent, as one commentator argues, 'reaches a fair balance between recognising artists' desire for control over their own works, and the competing desire to allow the dissemination of creative works.'[109] Moreover, the Court in *Cescinsky v George Routledge* held that since consent is the very essence of joint authorship relations, the common law rule that a joint owner may enjoy the jointly owned property independently in a 'proper manner' (until the property is sold) is inapplicable to copyright.[110]

Joint authors, in other words, are treated as one unit. As Harris observes: 'it is of the essence of joint property that no trespassory rules regarding the asset in question subsist between the joint owners.'[111] There may be no internal trespassory rules between them, as long as their acts are in conformity with the fair dealing doctrine. However, external trespassory rules are imposed on them, which forbid them from performing external acts such as licensing privileges or control-powers to third parties. They can only together issue licences to perform external acts by third parties. The concomitant problem in a joint authorship relations is that the exercise of rights and interests conferred by copyright is indivisible and each co-author can play 'dog in the manger.'

When applied to the public/authors joint authorship paradigm, consent plays an important, but often problematic, role. First, since there is no liberty to reap without sowing, and since copyrighted endeavours are products of the creative collectivity, the two parties that laboured and deserve reaping are public and authors. Any use or disposal of the products of their joint efforts necessitates consent. In the absence of consent the labour of the non-consenting party will not be adequately rewarded and will put this party at the mercy of the other co-owner/s. This generates a difficulty that at first glance may seem insurmountable. If, as collectively produced and owned properties, copyrighted entities require the consent of the public and authors, am I suggesting revival of the famously mocked principle of universal compact prior to appropriation, advocated by Grotius and Pufendorf and strongly rejected by Locke?[112] Should consent then, be eliminated from the public/authors

---

107 See *Childress v Taylor* (n 60 above) 500, 508; and *Community For Creative Non-Violence v Reid* 846 F 2d 1485, 1498 (DC Cir 1988); aff'd, 490 US 730 (1989).

108 *Cescinsky v George Routledge* (n 103 above) 330.

109 Spyke (n 55 above) 491.

110 *Cescinsky v George Routledge* (n 103 above) 330. The Court upheld this rule in *Bull v Bull* (n 8 above) 234, 237. In another case concerning whether a co-owner of business data can prevent the use of the data by another co-owner, the Court held that a co-owner of confidential information should be in no worse position than a co-owner of copyright, that is to say that, he is permitted to use the information only upon receiving the consent of the other co-owners. *Drummond Murray v Yorkshire Fund Managers Ltd* [1998] FSR 372.

111 JW Harris, *Property and Justice* (Oxford: Oxford University Press, 1996) 100.

112 See above, Chapter 6.

joint authorship paradigm?[113] Eliminating the requirement of consent from the public/authors paradigm is like eliminating the public's contribution and merely restating the status quo. This contribution, if it ceases to exist, diminishes the ability of creators to produce and affects the public's ability to renew the stock of cultural and social materials necessary for copyright creation. In the concluding part of this chapter, I will discuss possible doctrinal changes to the present ownership pattern in copyright systems, which attempt to meet this objection and have the inherent value of rewarding the public for its authorial contribution.

Applications

The Method

In this book I claim that every copyrighted work is a joint enterprise between public and authors and that the public satisfies the requirements for joint authorship in *every* incident of copyright. In this part I propose to apply in greater detail the foregoing discussion to the following four cases that shaped the principle of joint authorship: *Godfrey v Lees*,[114] *Darryl Neudorf v Nettwerk Productions*,[115] *Brighton v Jones*[116] and *Thomson v Larson.*[117] It is imperative that I take cases dealing with joint authorship because they emphasise my argument about the public's authorial contribution. These cases illustrate the inherent difficulties in applying joint authorship between collaborators in their individual capacity – difficulties that disappear when it comes to the public/author joint authorship paradigm. They also expose the paradox in placing attention on the author as a sole creator while ignoring authorial input from collaborators in clear cases of joint authorship.

Godfrey v Lees[118]

In this case the Court examines the contribution made to six songs that were allegedly jointly authored and owned. As a tool to assess the level of contribution the Court formulates the 'linking sequence' test, stipulating that the significance of the contribution should be judged in light of the role of a specific and isolated sequence to the whole work.[119] I propose to examine two of the six songs: 'Mocking Bird' and

113 It is indeed possible to argue that the consent requirement is always satisfied because the CDPA 1988 itself represents the general public's consent: it is a piece of legislation adopted in a democratic process, with the participation of the public, and with its conset.

114 *Godfrey v Lees* (n 15 above).

115 *Darryl Neudorf v Nettwerk Productions* (n 72 above).

116 *Brighton v Jones* (n 31 above).

117 *Thomson v Larson* (n 56 above).

118 *Godfrey v Lees* (n 15 above) 328.

119 In other words, the court rephrases the *Robin Ray* test of 'significant creative input' (n 28 above) 636.

'Galadriel.' In the first song, the Court follows the general test for co-authorship in a manner similar to that which led to the decision in *Cala Homes* case.[120]

'Mocking Bird', which the Judge personally finds a 'most attractive work',[121] is composed of three verses, ensuing choruses, and a four bar solo guitar passage which was referred to as 'the sequence.' The Court evaluates 'the sequence' and its inner arrangement and refers to the parties' disagreement regarding authorship of the sequences' most important element – a four note descending harmonic line. In examining this element, the Court refers to the timing of writing the harmonic line, its repetition and originality, and remarks that the sequence, arranged with various orchestral and band overlays, is occasionally repeated throughout the song and 'forms the basis of the climax of the work in bars 57 to 88.'[122] However, since the Court finds that the parties' contribution was merged and is inseparable, it does not base its decision on authorship of the harmonic line and views the song as a unitary whole composed by both parties.

In 'Galadriel' the Court employs the 'linking sequence' test. The song is a 48 bar work and although the main orchestral contribution forms only one eighth of the work's bar-structure[123] it was found to be the cause for the work's great success.[124] In 'Galadriel' Godfrey did not dispute that this song is Lees's masterpiece and that he had no hand in the composition and structure of the song because it was a finished work by the time he was first introduced to it. What Godfrey contributed was the orchestral arrangement of the recorded version. This contribution, it was argued, is the result of the collaboration between Godfrey and Lees. Basing its decision on the six bar sequence, the Court held that contribution should be examined by its intrinsic quality. As the Court remarks:

> The main orchestral contribution to the work is in bars 24 to 29 of this 48 bar work. Those bars form a linking sequence and constitute an integral part of the work. In my view the plaintiff's contribution is sufficient in importance and originality to qualify him as a joint

---

120 *Cala Homes v Alfred McAlpine Homes* (n 33 above).

121 *Godfrey v Lees* (n 15 above) 327.

122 Ibid.

123 Ibid 328. Applying different rules on what amounts to the necessary significant contribution shows the arbitrary nature of the rules on contribution. In *Beckingham v Hodgens* the court called experts to decided on whether the contribution was sufficient (n 44 above); in *Hadley v Kemp* the court found 9 percent not to constitute significant contribution (n 27 above); and in *Bamgboye v Reed,* 33 percent were found sufficient creative contribution (n 11 above).

124 As the court held: 'What the claimant to joint authorship of a work must establish is that he has made a significant and original contribution to the creation of the work .... It is not necessary that his contribution to the work is equal in terms of either quantity, quality or originality to that of his collaborators.' Ibid 325. However, it is not clear from *Hadley v Kemp* whether significant is a quality-based test or quantity-based test: 'It would be surprising if a slight contribution was enough to make a person a joint author and thereby make him an equal owner with another or others who had contributed far more than he had.' *Hadley v Kemp*, ibid 643.

> author of the work. The fact that when composing the six bar orchestral link the plaintiff took the basic melodic and harmonic lines from the song does not deprive the plaintiff share in the authorship of the work in the form in which I heard it. The link passage is, to my ear, an original and cleverly worked adaptation of the song's melodic line.[125]

The requirement of quality, rather than quantity, means that a minimal percentage of bars may be enough to constitute original contribution to the expressive form of a song, and thus, to render it a work of joint authorship. Moreover, the basic ingredient of copyright protection, namely, skill, labour and judgement was found by Blackburne J to be determined not merely by the amount of labour expended on the creation of the whole work, but by the amount of labour and skill expended on the 'linking sequence.'

Setting quality as a condition for joint authorship places the public in an even better position. Even those who deny the public authorial role, would not oppose the argument that the public has at least *some* degree of contribution. Since that degree is to be assessed in qualitative terms it would also be difficult to deny that the dependence on the authorial collectivity always renders the public's contribution substantial. Furthermore, the ubiquitous nature of the public's contribution and the inability to separate it from that of the authors' means that contribution in the public/authors joint authorship paradigm is immeasurable. If one attempts to quantify the contribution the public makes one would find that its quality outweighs that of the individual author.

Neudorf v Nettwerk[126] *and Brighton v Jones*[127]

In the former case the Court dismisses a musician, Neudorf's, claims for joint authorship in four songs attributed to the singer McLachlan who had had a recording contract with the defendant at the relevant time. 'Vox' was one of the songs under dispute and the question was whether the contribution made was significant, although it need not be in equal magnitude. In his testimony, Neudorf argues that he alone contributed the rhythm, the defendant dictated from his parts of the hook melody 'note for note', and that the vocal melody and the chord structure resulted from their collaboration.[128] The defence position was that the hook melody was already present in the guitar chords McLachlan was playing and Neudorf merely replicated the melody using violin sounds.[129] Is a violin version of a guitar style melody, not sufficient to constitute contribution? Cohen J states:

> In my opinion, the plaintiff has failed to establish that he contributed original expression to the hook melody of 'Vox.' The G-C to G-A melody was an expression, but it was not

125 *Godfrey v Lees,* ibid 327.
126 *Neudorf v Nettwerk Productions* (n 72 above).
127 *Brighton v Jones* (n 31 above).
128 *Neudorf v Nettwerk Productions* (n 72 above) 574 (referring to exhibit 19).
129 Ibid 576.

original. The four-chord guitar progression is especially clear in the introduction of the song, and one can easily hear the G-C to G-A melody that is then replicated and used as the violin hook melody in the song. In my view, what the plaintiff did was copy the melody in MaLachlan's chord progression…[130]

The defendant was playing the guitar while Neudorf was in the studio and it seems from the testimony of the parties that both were inspired by the contribution each has made and that this is how the final version of 'Vox' was born. In his testimony regarding the chorus vocal melody, Neudorf remarks that he selected notes for the melody: 'The song 'Vox' originated with both myself and Sarah. She started playing some chords. I selected some notes from what she was playing, provided a rhythm to it that ended up being the riff. From here I came up with the drum bit on the drum machine and Sarah kept playing along, playing along.'[131] He continues and does not deny that it is 'quite feasible to say…that had I not been in the room at the time, Sarah would have continued meandering and continued to meander and perhaps come up with a different chorus' and although it might have been equally powerful as a chorus it would not be the same as with his contribution since, it was his 'selection that changed the direction of the song, and made that into the chorus that it became today.'[132] The Court, however, held that Neudorf's contribution 'falls short of the legal standard for original expression.'[133]

The Court then went to examine the contribution to the verse vocal melody and the chord structure and found the contribution made to both insignificant to merit joint authorship. With respect to the contribution to the verse vocal melody, Neudorf contends that he and the defendant 'were tossing ideas back and forth' and recalled that they were 'collaborating on things.'[134] After all, as Neudorf puts it, '[i]t's very much an interactive process.'[135] True, ideas or suggestions do not amount to significant contribution. However, since it is an 'interactive process', and since both simultaneously agree to join efforts and perform in the studio at the same time, should interaction combined with performance not suffice for contribution?

Neudorf's contribution can be defined using the terms redirection, integration and replication. While redirection and integration mean that one either takes a work of a certain kind in new directions or unites two or more sources that previously are seen as unrelated into a unitary whole, replication is a form of passive contribution in which a certain act leaves the field or the work where it is at present. It seems that Neudorf provides original input which took 'Vox' in new directions and for this reason his contribution is not less than original and significant to the overall musical appearance of 'Vox.' Perhaps the 'linking sequence' test in *Godfrey v Lees*[136]

130 Ibid 577.
131 Ibid 578.
132 Ibid.
133 Ibid 579.
134 Ibid.
135 Ibid.
136 *Godfrey v Lees* (n 15 above).

should be extended to cover situations where unpersuasive contributions should be reviewed in light of their quality and overall impact, which in 'Vox' greatly benefited the end result.

The nature of the collaboration between Neudorf and McLachlan and the unfortunate results from this collaboration are similar to situation between the playwright and the director in the English case of *Brighton v Jones.*[137] The case concerns a dispute between Jones who was commissioned to write the play 'Stones in his Pockets' and Brighton who was the director of the play. The latter's contribution was found insignificant: 'although everyone agrees that changes were made to the script as a result of experience in the rehearsals, no-one can bring to mind at this distance in time (eight years after the event) specific details of any of the changes.'[138] Although the court recognises Brighton's important input into the rehearsals, which came from her strong personality as an experienced theatrical director,[139] it rejects the claim for joint authorship on the basis of insufficient contribution. The Court held that the contribution made was merely in the form of discussions, interpretations and exchange of thoughts, and although 'changes resulted from the experience of the rehearsals and the discussions in the rehearsals',[140] and although Brighton was 'involved in the rehearsals throughout' and 'she probably knew about all the changes before they were made and played', the Court finds that '[i]n terms of the dialogue of the final version of the play…100 per cent of the words spoken (or as near to 100 per cent as makes no difference) were actually composed by Miss Jones.'[141] It is arguable that on the basis of the ruling of Laddie J in *Cala Homes* Brighton's contribution was sufficient to make her a joint author of the work. In that case the Court established that a person might be a joint author, even if he had not himself put the pen to paper and another had effectively written what he had created.[142] In light of this ruling, it was wrong to measure Brighton's contribution on the basis of whether or not she pushed the pen onto paper and for the Court to reach a conclusion that one party can contribute something close to '100 per cent words spoken.'

Vaver warns us to avoid our tendency to leave authorial contributions unrewarded.[143] The *Neudorf* and *Brighton v Jones* cases are notorious examples of situations in which without the contribution of the party who was not recognised as a joint author, the work under dispute would not have come to fruition. This parallels the public/author relations. There is no doubt that the creative act is socially and culturally constructed, there is also no dispute that every author's dependence on and consumption of collectively produced and owned properties is what makes the creative impulse successful. However, copyright law and policy consistently

137 *Brighton v Jones* (n 31 above).

138 Ibid 524.

139 Ibid 526.

140 Ibid 528.

141 Ibid. See in particular, ibid 521-531.

142 *Cala Homes v Alfred McAlpine Homes* (n 33 above).

143 Vaver (n 41 above).

deny this contribution. In fact, the public is not only unrewarded for its contribution, but it seems that – following Courts decisions on joint authorship – the copyright system heads towards an even more stringent conception of sole authorship in which the singular author reigns supreme, and the role of the other joint contributor – the public – is increasingly regarded as non-existent.

Thomson v Larson[144]

In this case the Court was asked to apply the Childress[145] principles to the hit Broadway musical Rent – a modern version of Puccini's classic La Bohême, and to examine whether the relations between a dramaturge's (Thomson) and Rent's creator-composer (Larson) satisfy the requirements for joint authorship.[146] The musical was so successful that it also earned a Pulitzer Prize and a Tony Award. And, the collaboration was so intense that it was recognised as the cause for the 'radical transformation of the show.'[147] Despite the fruitful collaboration between Thomson and Larson that brought about the great success of the show, the identification of Larson as 'sole author' in the agreement (while not mentioning Thomson) was the catalyst that brought the Second Circuit to conclude that Rent did not qualify as a musical work that merits joint authorship.

The process of creating the musical Rent heavily relied on collaboration. In 1989 playwright Aronson teamed up with Larson for the production of the musical which revolves around the lives of New York bohemians. In 1993 Larson signed an agreement with Aronson in which the latter granted the former permission to finish the play without him. In order to complete the play, Thomson was hired as a dramaturge in 1995. Her contract was silent in respect to copyright. Larson and Thomson enjoyed mutual artistic control over the script's direction and made severe modifications to the original draft. Their collaboration was so close that it can be argued that the nature of their relations shifted to that of joint authors.[148] To substantiate this argument: (i) the Thomson-Larson collaboration resulted in rewriting 1,212 of the 2,542 lines of the original script, of which 9 percent were solely contributed by Thomson,[149] and (ii) Larson herself credited Thomson with the responsibility of 'transforming the show.'[150] Due to Larson's unexpected death, negotiations between Thomson and Larson's heirs regarding royalties ensued. The collaboration of Thomson and Larson was judged under the Childress two-stage formula,[151] considering first, that each

144 *Thomson v Larson* (n 56 above).

145 *Childress v Taylor* (n 60 above).

146 This case is one of many post-reactions to the leading authority of *Childress*. See also, *Erickson v Trinity Theatre Inc*, 13 F 3d 1061 (7th Cir 1994); *Cabera v Teatro Del Sensenta* (n 86 above).

147 Recent Cases (n 56 above) 965.

148 Buckalew (n 56 above) 551.

149 Fox (n 59 above) 504 (quoting Brief for Appellant).

150 Ibid.

151 *Childress v Taylor* (n 60 above) 507.

collaborator made an independently copyrightable contribution, and second, that each party intended to treat the other party as a joint author.

The Court denied Thomson's argument for joint authorship on the basis of not satisfying the Childress test. The Court, in other words, held that modifications of nearly half of the lines of the original play including 9 percent exclusive contribution are not sufficient to credit a dramaturge for her contribution. The Court based its decision not on either the quality or quantity of the contribution, but on lack of intent. Treating intent as the core element means that the application of the Childress test denies authors recognition of their contribution, which, in many cases, would include independently copyrightable materials. Also, the fact that intent must be formed 'mutually', makes the test difficult to comply with, since mere words or the manners in which a person listed credits on the scripts are enough to exclude the person from his own contribution.[152] The intrinsic flaws of the Childress case are apparent.

Thomson placed two main issues before the Court: (i) whether she is a joint author with Larson and (ii) whether, in the event of finding against (i), she is entitled to own the copyrightable contributions she made to the play. The Court dealt primarily with the first question. In respect to the second question, the Court tentatively identified the problem but, since Thomson did not raise this matter in the lower Court, the Second Circuit was reluctant to provide a solution. The issue of what happens where two or more collaborators satisfy Goldstein's non-de minimis principle of independently copyrightable contribution but not the requirement of intent, was left open.

As noted above, English law requires that two conditions be satisfied before recognising joint authorship, namely, collaboration and indistinct contribution. Taking the view that Larson and Thomson did extensively collaborate and that each party added contributions to the expression, under the CDPA 1988 Rent would have been declared a work of joint authorship.[153] Following the *Beckingham* case, and in contrast to the *Childress* and Rent decisions, and Cohen J's definition of intent in the *Neudorf* case, intent to co-author plays no role in determining joint authorship under English copyright law, because that would amount to putting Thomson at the mercy of Larson. It is important to emphasise that this argument is premised on the assumption that the Court would find the parts contributed to the play as inseparable and not interdependent since the CDPA does not recognise interdependency as a condition for joint authorship. It is assumed that in the event of interdependently

152 *Thomson v Larson* (n 56 above) 204. The Court also mentions that agreements with outsiders can indicate lack of intention for co-authorship, ibid.

153 Fox, for example, argues that the English test for joint authorship better accommodates the interests of the parties. Fox contends that the English test is clearer than that of the 1976 Copyright Act but could not assist in the *Rent* decision. Fox (n 59 above) 519-522. Spyke argues that US copyright law should be changed in light of its English counterpart, in order to secure appropriate reward for authorial contributions. Spyke (n 55 above) 490.

copyrightable contributions joined together in a unitary whole, the CDPA 1988 might treat the result as a collective work.

Commentators made various suggestions attempting to challenge the Court's reluctance to deal with Thomson's claim to retain exclusive ownership of her copyrightable contribution. For example, a 'Joint Authorship Default Rule' was suggested,[154] as was the application of contract law to theatrical collaboration.[155] However, before the plausibility of these proposals is considered, there are two things to address. First, the 'missing category' effect found in the decisions in *Childress* and *Thomson v Larson* should be considered. The Court seems to have envisioned only two categories of collaborators: (i) joint authors who satisfy all requirements and (ii) non-joint authors with no copyright interests. The latter category includes the 'missing category', those whose contribution reflects Goldstein's approach but do not satisfy the intent condition.

The second point is premised on the first and holds that a reply to Thomson's claim for ownership of her contribution can be found in the Copyright Act itself. Under s 101 of the 1976 Copyright Act a joint work is composed of 'inseparable or interdependent' contributions. Interdependency, as oppose to inseparability, means that a combination of distinct contributions may qualify a work for joint authorship. If the play is composed of interdependent parts – and following Goldstein's approach and the Court's decision that the constituent of contribution has been fulfilled – which are independently copyrightable, then Thomson's claim is a classic copyright claim of an author to have a property right in his copyrightable input. That is to say, that independent copyrighted works exist or that the whole work is a collective work.[156]

A problem may arise in cases in which the parts are inseparable. In that event, I assume that intention would be easier to establish, but if intent is still absent, then, until legislative changes are made, it is recommended that the Courts, in order to account for the 'missing category', apply the rule of independently copyrightable contribution as a threshold in order to guarantee for the non-joint author copyright in his contributions. The Court itself held that a non-author plaintiff might 'have the right to enjoin any use of her contributions in any stage production, book, cast album, or motion picture.'[157] Although the Court did not rule on this point, the problematic result from this argument is that a contributor who did not meet the 'mutual intent'

154 Fox ibid.

155 JC Lee, Comment, 'Upstaging the Playwright: The Joint Authorship Entanglement Between Dramaturge's and Playwrights' (1998) 19 *Loyola of Los Angeles Entertainment Law Journal* 75, 100-105. See also, SE Keller, 'Collaboration in Theatre: Problems and Copyright Solutions' (1986) 33 *UCLA Law Review* 891; D Leichtman, 'Most Unhappy Collaborators: An Argument Against the Recognition of Property Ownership in Stage Directions' (1996) 20 *Columbia-VLA Journal of Law and the Arts* 683; T Yellin, 'New Directions for Copyright: The Property Rights of Stage Directors' (2001) 24 *Columbia-VLA Journal of Law and the Arts* 317.

156 Spyke (n 55 above).

157 *Thomson v Larson* (n 56 above) 206.

condition but satisfies the non-de minimis copyrightable contribution rule 'could hold a collaborative work hostage, or demand its dismemberment.'[158]

Nimmer's more than de-minimis approach constitutes a possible alternative to the approach that considers intent the prime condition for co-authorship.[159] If intent on the part of both contributors exists, why should the Court not set limits to Goldstein's approach and recognise joint authorship?[160] Furthermore, the absurdity in the requirement of intent to co-author is illustrated by the Court in the case of *Childress* where it required the parties to think of the implications of working together, even if they are not familiar with the law. In the words of the Court: the parties should 'entertain in their minds the concept of joint authorship, whether or not they understood precisely the legal consequences of that relationship.'[161]

The 'missing category effect', i.e., the indifference which the Court demonstrated toward contributing non-owners, the requirement of independently copyrightable contribution and the passion infused in the intent condition, all raise the inevitable question: should the public be surprised that its contribution is not recognised? In his examination of the construction of authorship, Jaszi criticises the copyright system for being too individualistic and romantic in respect of the notion of authorship, despite the increasingly 'collective, corporate, and collaborative' nature of writing.[162] Jaszi-like criticism is most suitable for the public/author paradigm. The highly individualistic approach Courts employ creates an obvious paradox: on the one hand the law is keen to protect individual rights at the expense of the public, while on the other hand it seems to exclude those rights where they are fully articulated.

Excluding copyrightable contribution to a work that was not qualified as a work of joint authorship is evidence of the agility with which US Courts: (i) recognise copyrightable contribution; (ii) notoriously insist on mutual intent as the key factor for determination of co-authorship, instead of mutual collaboration and contribution;

158 Recent Cases (n 56 above) 967.

159 It was also argued that Nimmer's approach should be adopted when joint authorship emerges from the relationship between graduate students and a university as it would engender creative activity and afford contributors fair share in the creation. See, SH Patel, 'Graduate Students' Ownership and Attribution Rights in Intellectual Property' (1996) 71 *Indiana Law Journal* 481, 510-512.

160 Valachovic examines Nimmer's approach in greater detail. He takes the example of a celebrity who goes to a ghostwriter in order to write his biography. In the event that no arrangements were made to establish an employment relationship, and the celebrity provided all the material and the writer was assigned the task to structure the material, without the celebrity recording his contribution, under the copyrightability test, the writer was responsible for the execution of the celebrity's ideas and therefore he is the author. Valachovic argues that Nimmer's approach would provide the celebrity the tools to claim joint authorship. He suggests that once intent has been established the rule of more than *de-minimis* should apply. Valachovic (n 55 above) in particular 203-205, 216-218.

161 *Childress v Taylor* (n 60 above) 508 (emphasis added).

162 Jaszi (n 4 above) 38.

(iii) and by doing so, create a system that is uncertain and unfair.[163] These arguments show how Courts disproportionately stretch the edges of authorial individualism, and are not attentive to the non-economic, social and cultural implications of their tendency to deny authorial contributions in clear cases of joint authorship.

In fact, in the *Childress* saga, the Court itself poses the inevitable question: 'If the focus is solely on the objective of copyright law to encourage the production of creative works, it is difficult to see why the contributions of all joint authors need be copyrightable.'[164] The idea that contributions from all joint authors need not be copyrightable strengthens the position of the public when my arguments are confronted by anti-public approaches or opponents of the social construction thesis who embrace an even more stringent conception of the lone author.

This is best illustrated by the examples of theatrical productions which by their nature, following Vickers' critic of Shakespeare's genius, are but a collaborative activity between not only many individuals, but also with the community. Theatrical productions, Vickers asserts, serve as a response to 'outside influences and to social change.'[165] In addition, theatrical productions allow us 'to trace the development of knowledge, as each generation of scholars builds on their predecessors' work, correcting and extending it.'[166] The public role in theatrical creative activities is to nurture and maintain symbols and cultural elements which we collectively share;[167] to guarantee availability of these elements for late-comers and ensure that the creative process does not become stunted.

Finally, although English cases seem to eliminate any allusion to the requirement of intent to co-author, as was emphasised by the Court in *Beckingham v Hodgens*,[168] I argue that, to some extent, they silently embrace it. In the public/author joint authorship paradigm, there is no dispute that intent to co-author exists. The Courts in the *Neudorf* and *Thomson v Larson* cases used the principle of intent to co-author as a weapon against undisputed and decisive contributions in situations of clear joint authorship relationship. As I frequently argue above, the public's status as a plural agent, and the joint responsibility of public and authors to preserve and nurture the storehouse of collective properties we create and own together, makes intent to collaborate implicit, a built-in element, in the very nature of this joint responsibility.

The critique I express highlights the need to re-examine principles dominating our copyright realm, which impose on us many paradoxes and misconceptions of authorship and its limits. It should also urge us to rethink the implications from

163 LaFrance criticises the judicial gloss on the definition of joint works and argues that authorial efforts should be placed as the core feature for establishing whether joint authorship exists. LaFrance (n 5 above).

164 *Childress v Taylor* (n 60 above) 506.

165 B Vickers, *Shakespeare, Co-Author: A Historical Study of Five Collaborative Plays* (Oxford: Oxford University Press, 2002) 119. See also above, Chapter 4.

166 Ibid 147.

167 Coombe (n 1 above).

168 *Beckingham v Hodgens* (n 44 above).

the stringent conditions we set upon authors for joint authorship relations to exist. Perhaps, if our copyright regime was more attentive to contributions coming from sources other than the principal author, the idea behind the public's authorial role would not be a concept alien to contemporary copyright. Whether or not we learn the lessons from our ill-defined principle of joint authorship, the public, as a plural agent capable of intentional states and of making rational choices, and by virtue of its authorial contribution, satisfies even the most stringent of rules copyright laws impose on joint authors.

Alternatives

Restructuring Copyright

There are many ways to restructure our copyright system to accommodate and reward the public's authorial role and recognise its joint title in authorial commodities. The important thing is to increase public access and limit authors' property rights. The alternatives I shall discuss do not provide an exhaustive list, and do not replace the public's joint right in copyrighted entities. They are the immediate consequence of this right.

Several suggestions have been made to replace the present scheme of rights and rewards in copyright with a system of remunerations paid from public funds. Harris examines this option and explains that in such a system there would be no allocation of property right for copyrighted works. The system would recognise that an author should be rewarded for the social wealth he creates by producing creative works. Appropriate schemes of monetary incentives, commensurate with the authors' efforts, and reflective of the potential profit they could have made, will be designed.[169]

Developing this suggestion further, it was suggested that the author could contract with the State to sell his intellectual property right in exchange for adequate reward and compensation (possibly on the basis of sales) to serve as an incentive for future productions.[170] The State would 'use general tax revenue in order to purchase the intangible good for the free use of society as a whole.'[171] The reward could be

---

169 Harris (n 111 above) 298. An earlier attempt from 1960 by the Riksdag, the Swedish Parliament, suggested a bill that proposed to reject the copyright bill and replace it with a grant of 20 million kronors 'for the support and promotion of works of art and literature' to be allocated 'with due consideration towards creative writers and artists having to contend with financial difficulties.' S Ljungman, 'The Function of Copyright in the Present Day Society' (1976) 88 *Revue Internationale du Droit d'Auteur* 51, 55.

170 For further illustration see, RC Guell and M Fischbaum, 'Toward Allocative Efficiency in the Prescription Drug Industry' (1995) *Milbank Quarterly* 525; DG Lichtman, 'Pricing Prozac: Why the Government Should Subsidize the Purchase of Patented Pharmaceuticals' (1997) 11 *Harvard Journal of Law & Technology* 123, 125.

171 BG Damstedt, 'Limiting Locke: A Natural Law Justification for the Fair Use Doctrine' (2003) 112 *Yale Law Journal* 1179, 1213.

determined either *ex ante*, as with the initial proposal, or *ex post* when sufficient information about the worthiness of the intangible has been gathered. Once monetary incentives are allocated, the work is vested in the state which represents the authorial collectivity. It is important to note that this alternative does not mean mere State support to the arts but immediate transference of the property right in the creation to the public domain. In a recent study, Shavell and van Ypersele found that intellectual property rights do not have a special social advantage over reward systems. They favour allowing innovators and authors the choice between the intellectual property right or the reward and advocate separating the monopoly power in the intellectual property right from its viable commercial value.[172] In such a system, eventual public ownership would eliminate the monopolistic distortions intellectual property systems cause. Although an author loses the property right in the work, he still exclusively retains the moral rights in it.

There can be many variations on this proposal. For example, Lessig advocates the option of a public conservancy.[173] This paradigm intends to secure incentives to copyright holders in order to 'build out the creative commons.'[174] In exchange for monetary incentives, rightholders will donate their works, including unfinished works, into a public conservancy that will monitor the dissemination of these holdings to the public. Lessig's formula resembles the public funds alternative, but differs from it as it is based on the will of the individual to cooperate. Its main weakness is that it leaves the choice between preserving the property in the work and donating it in exchange for monetary benefits, too wide.

Another possibility is to adopt a 'rewards for authors' schemes similar to the 'rewards for inventors' schemes which are often used in technology-based organisations.[175] The statutory compensation provisions in the Patent Act recognise the importance of reward for inventions made in the course of employment, and provide that if 'the patent is of outstanding benefit to the employer' then 'the employee should be awarded compensation to be paid by the employer.'[176] The Act is not silent with respect to the fair share of the employee, and provides that the employer is responsible to 'secure the employee a fair share of the benefit which [he] has derived, or may reasonably be expected to derive, from the patent…or from… the property in, or any right in or under, an application for that patent.'[177] Such statutory provisions do not exist for copyright works. Analogously, the author, as an employee, would be rewarded by the state, representing the authorial collectivity, for the works he creates.

---

172 S Shavell and T van Ypersele, 'Rewards Versus Intellectual Property Rights (2001) 22 *Journal of Law and Economics* 525.

173 L Lessig, *The Future of Ideas: The Fate of the Commons in a Connected World* (New York: Vintage Books, 2002) 255.

174 Ibid.

175 PA 1977 s 36.

176 Ibid s 40(1). Sometimes the 'rewards for inventors' schemes operate outside the Act. Ibid s 40(3).

177 Ibid s 41(1).

The public funds, public conservancy and 'rewards for authors' schemes, are proposals that, in other words, advocate separation of the right to the commercial exploitation from the right to property. As Libling once wrote: 'Any expenditure of mental or physical effort, as a result of which there is created an entity, whether tangible or intangible, vests in the person who brought the entity into being, a proprietary right to the commercial exploitation of that entity, which right is separate and independent from the ownership of that entity.'[178] The main drawback of the public fund suggestion and its variants is that it necessitates a difficult reform of the whole copyright system. It is tantamount to abolishing it. At the same time, however, it best explains and illustrates the division of interests in the joint authorship paradigm between public and authors. While the public is concerned with the social value inherent in the copyright work, the author is also interested in fame, reputation and maximising proceeds of the commercial exploitation of the work. This does not mean that the author is not in need of or has less access to the social value of the creation. In fact, if the general public obtains the exclusive right to the social value, then the author enjoys free access to the value by virtue of being a member of the public.

Rethinking Copyright

Authors and the public interest defence An issue that we have to be aware of before we decide on a particular alternative to the present configuration of our copyright system, and its possible success to reach fruition, is that in today's copyright culture, more than ever, legislators are no longer the primary arbiters of public policy. Instead, they are hostages of strong lobby groups whose interests usually prevail over those of the general public. Although they say glibly that they are conferring property rights upon authors as a means of facilitating greater public good, as with traditional property, legislators view copyright from the perspective of the putative owner rather than from the perspective of those whose behaviour he constrains. They are, as Justice Laddie puts it, 'handing out monopolies like confetti while muttering "this won't hurt".'[179]

There are many ways to overcome the present inequity in copyright and the inability of legislators to change our copyright reality. For example, Litman chronicles the many weaknesses of copyright and concludes with the proclamation that '[p]eople don't obey laws that they don't believe in.'[180] Litman believes that civil disobedience with copyright law is justified under certain circumstances and the public rejection of existing copyright policies will eventually persuade legislators to change the law. In addition, recently, she also asserted that in today's copyright

178 DF Libling, 'The Concept of Property: Property in Intangibles' (1978) 94 *Law Quarterly Review* 103, 104.

179 Laddie J, 'Copyright: Over-Strength, Over-Regulated, Over-rated' [1996] 18(5) *European Intellectual Property Review* 253, 260.

180 J Litman, *Digital Copyright* (New York: Prometheus Books, 2001) 195.

reality 'almost all of the copyright rules you hear are made-up rules.'[181] Litman's open cry to disobey copyright rules, while the public is unaware of which rules are real and which are 'made-up' is a possible reaction to the unlimited extension of copyright. However, it is still, worrisome. It may escalate the tensions between the public and authors. Litman's approach may eventually lead to the reappearance of a Lockean state of nature, with all the chaos it entails, in the make-up of contemporary copyright rules.

Alternative and more immediately viable solutions exist that do not require such large changes to the law. For example, if copyright in the UK was more often balanced against certain human rights, in particular, freedom of expression, we might have seen a shift in copyright disputes towards the public interest. Ideally, Drahos writes, 'the human rights community and the intellectual property community should begin a dialogue. The two communities have a great deal to learn from each other. Viewing intellectual property through the eyes of human rights advocates will encourage consideration of the ways in which the property mechanism might be reshaped to include interests and needs that it currently does not.'[182]

Expanding the public interest defence, rendering it in essence an 'escape clause', is another related possibility.[183] Such an 'escape clause' would cover exceptions not found in the 1988 Act, and it would provide courts the means to compensate errors of law incurred in the course of implementing legislation that could not predict, for example, certain technological developments and societal needs. Although this possibility seems as less favourable by courts,[184] in the recent case of *Ashdown v Telegraph Group*[185] the Court of Appeal held that the public interest defence could resolve incompatibilities found between issues of freedom of expression and copyright. In the words of the Court: 'Now that the Human Rights Act is in force, there is the clearest public interest in giving effect to the right of freedom of expression in those rare cases where this right trumps the rights conferred by the Copyright Act. In such circumstances, we consider that section 171(3) of the Act

181 J Litman, 'Ethical Disobedience' (2004) 5 *Ethics and Information Technology* 217, 218.

182 P Drahos, 'Intellectual Property and Human Rights' [1999] 3 *Intellectual Property Quarterly* 349, 370. A dialogue between the human rights community and the intellectual property community was already initiated at the enactment of the Human Rights Act 1998 which, in s 12(4) highlights the fundamentality of freedom of expression. It refers to 'journalistic, literary or artistic material (or to conduct connected to such material)' and to the extent to which this material is 'available to the public' or that it is 'in the public interest for the material to be published.'

183 CDPA 1988 s 171(3).

184 See *Beloff v Pressdram* [1973] RPC 783; *Hyde Park Residence Ltd v Yelland* [2001] Ch 143 (CA); *Ashdown v Telegraph Group Ltd* [2002] Ch 149; *Douglas v Hello! Ltd* [2003] EMLR 31 Ch. See also P Johnson, 'The Public Interest: Is it still a Defence to Copyright Infringement?' (2005) 16(1) *Entertainment Law Review* 1.

185 Ibid.

permits the defence of public interest to be raised.'[186] Limiting the recourse to this option to only 'rare cases', however, deprives it of its potential advantage to properly regulate copyright disputes and defend the public interest.

Definitional changes Definitional changes are also possible. Joint authorship between authors and the public shows that authorship cannot be based on the idea of creations *ex nihilo*; that the social nature of copyrighted entities dictates that authorship is a collaborative activity and that authors can no longer reign supreme. St. Bonaventura, writing in the thirteenth century, identifies four different ways to 'make' a book, none of which corresponds to solitary authorship:

> A man might write the works of others, adding and changing nothing, in which case he is simply called a 'scribe' (*scriptor*). Another writes the works of others with additions which are not his own; and he is called 'compiler' (*compilator*). Another writes both others' work and his own, but with others' work in principal place, adding his own for purposes of explanation; and he is called 'commentator' (*commentator*)...Another writes both his own work and others' for purposes of confirmation; and such a man should be called an 'author' (*auctor*).[187]

Should we substitute the term 'author' with say, 'compilator', 'commentator', 'translator', 'selector', or simply 'penman'? For Litman, the act of authorial creation is more akin to 'translation and recombination.'[188] Likewise, Durham argues that 'authorship is primarily an act of selection from an array of alternatives.'[189] Although definitional changes have the potential to eventually reach legal maturity and find their way into the statute book, like special public funds, they too require substantial modifications to the law and cannot be considered an immediately viable solution.

Trading rights I favour one particular alternative which requires few legal changes, but has the capacity to change the imbalance in copyright and address the concerns I express in this book. It has the inherent value of acknowledging the public authorial role by virtue of ensuring a proper balance between authors' rights and public

---

186 Ibid 170. See generally J Griffiths, 'Copyright Law after *Ashdown* – Time to Deal Fairly with the Public' [2002] 3 *Intellectual Property Quarterly* 240.

187 EL Einstein, *The Printing Press as an Agent of Change: Communications and Cultural Transformations in Early-Modern Europe* (1979) Vol 1, 121-122 cited in M Woodmansee, 'On the Author Effect: Recovering Collectivity' in Woodmansee and Jaszi (n 4 above) 15, 17.

188 J Litman, 'The Public Domain' (1990) 39 *Emory Law Journal* 965, 966.

189 AL Durham, 'Copyright and Information Theory: Toward an Alternative Model of "Authorship"' (2004) *Brigham Young University Law Review* 69, 73. He remarks: 'In important respects, an unromantic, selection-based model of authorship would parallel contemporary literary theory. It would focus attention on the work rather than the author. Originality would be characteristic of the text – or, more precisely, of the text in context of the available alternatives – just as information is a characteristic of a message, not of the message sender.' Ibid 119.

rights. It is a mechanism that develops existing copyright language. I propose an indefinitely renewable copyright term in exchange for an open-ended list of fair dealing exceptions. This formula has two primary advantages, and one weakness. The two advantages are: use of traditional principles, which means re-definition rather than replacement of any of our cherished copyright principles; and a better formula addressing the interests of and rewarding the two extreme in copyright. The weakness concerns reaching a stand-off in the battle between authors and the public. This stalemate, I believe, can be overcome in light of the two advantages. Although it is beyond the scope of the present study to fully explore the practical implications of this formula, it is sympathetic to the interests of both public and authors, and wide enough to call every unforeseeable development into its ambit.[190]

---

190 The CDPA provides a conclusive fair dealing doctrine. CDPA 1988 Chapter III 'Acts Permitted in Relation to Copyright Works.' Chapter III complies with the list of exceptions and limitations provided under Article 5 of Directive 2001/29/EC of the European Parliament and of the Council on the Harmonisation of Certain Aspects of Copyright and Related Rights in the Information Society (22 May 2001). See also above Chapter 3.2(5).

An open-ended list of limitations and exceptions is fundamental for the reasons I mention above. As opposed to the UK and EU approaches, the US fair use doctrine is drafted more generally. The US Copyright Act 1976 states that fair use of a copyrighted work 'for purposes such as criticism, comment, news reporting teaching (including multiple copies for classroom use), scholarship or research' is not an infringement of copyright. This list, as Tushnet explains, 'is not exclusive, and not even inclusive.' R Tushnet, 'Copy this Essay: How Fair Use Doctrine Harms Free Speech and how Copying Serves it' (2004) 114 *Yale Law Journal* 535, 544. In applying fair use exceptions, the Court will have to consider four factors: '(1) the purpose and character of the use, including whether such use is of a commercial nature or is for nonprofit educational purposes; (2) the nature of the copyrighted work; (3) the amount and substantiality of the portion used in relation to the copyrighted work as a whole; and (4) the effect of the use upon the potential market for or value of the copyrighted work.' 17 USC s 107.

According to my proposal there is no need to specify certain educational or other purposes to which the fair use doctrine applies. It would be wrong to freeze the doctrine in the statute, in particular, facing the present rapid technological developments. The UK and EU should adopt a similar approach to that of the US: Courts should be free to adapt the fair use doctrine to particular situations on a case-to-case basis. It is useful to prescribe certain steps to follow in determining the applicability of the doctrine to a give case, but without curtailing the development of the doctrine in the common law tradition. This, however, does not suggest that the US model properly addresses the concerns I express in this study.

For example, Madison criticises the US approach for not sufficiently accommodating certain social and cultural changes and needs. He develops a pattern-oriented approach to fair use and claims, for example, that certain technological advances (eg, file-sharing) are part of some recognised social pattern. MJ Madison, 'A Pattern-Oriented Approach to Fair Use' (2004) 45 *William and Mary Law Review* 1525. I fully agree with Madison's critique of the US fair use model. Its incompatibility with meeting social challenges and cultural needs also emphasises the danger in an ill-defined open-ended fair use doctrine that places the author as its primary object of protection at the expense of recognising the public interest.

How different is this solution from the present state of affairs in copyright? At present, the duration of copyright amounts to a quasi-perpetual right, and in certain situations such as computer technology, it acts as a *de facto* perpetual right since obsolescence precedes expiration of the copyright.[191] But, what about the second part of the formula, i.e., an open-ended fair dealing doctrine?

This paradigm does not create a second-tier copyright protection, something akin to a *sui-generis* right in databases,[192] or a form of protection provided under patent law for new technical advances, known as petty patents or utility models.[193] This formula covers only works that fully meet the conditions for copyright subsistence. According to this proposal, there would be no system of fixed copyright duration. Copyrights will be renewable every five years according to objective parameters, such as creativity and degree of originality over prior art, designed to secure the public interest. Renewal of copyrights and patents was a common practice in eighteenth-century England.[194] In contemporary copyright there is only a fixed term of protection that keeps growing as private property aspirations develop.

Copyright scholars examine the idea of renewal of copyright. Lessig advocates a five-year renewable term. He writes: 'A change in the copyright term would have no effect on the incentives for authors to produce work today. There is no author who decides whether or not to write a book depending upon whether he or his estate will receive money three-quarters of a century from now.'[195] More recently, Landes and Posner advocated an 'indefinitely renewable copyright.'[196] Following empirical analysis, they found that the 'average copyright duration might well be shorter under a system of indefinite renewals than under the current system.'[197] It seems that a renewable copyright term protection would find great support among copyright scholars, especially since studies show it will not destabilise the incentive system in

---

191 An analogy can be drawn from the European Supplementary Protection Certificate for pharmaceuticals which provides for the restoration of the patent term in pharmaceutical (it does not extend the patent per se but grant a *sui generis* supplementary protection certificate which is deemed broadly to have the same effect as a patent). Council Regulation 1768/92 [1992] OJ L/182/1. See G Tritton, *Intellectual Property in Europe* (London: Sweet & Maxwell, 2nd ed., 2002) 177-183.

192 See Directive 96/6/EC of the European Parliament and of the Council of 11 March 1996 on the Legal Protection of Databases, Arts 7-11.

193 See generally, MD Janos, 'Second Tier Patent Protection' (1999) 40 *Harvard International Law Journal* 151.

194 Under the Statute of Anne 1709, new works were protected for an initial term of 14 years, conditional upon registration with the Stationers' Company. The right was renewed for a further term of 14 years provided the author was still living at the expiry of the initial term. Works which were already published were subject to a fixed term protection of 21 years. Ibid s 1, and s 11.

195 Lessig, *The Future of Ideas* (n 173 above) 251-252.

196 WM Landes and RA Posner, 'Indefinitely Renewable Copyright' (2003) 70 *University of Chicago Law Review* 471. See also SL Clemens, 'Copyright in Perpetuity' (2002) 6 *Green Bag* 2d 109.

197 Landes and Posner, ibid 484.

copyright. The danger, however, is that a renewal system alone would perpetuate the imbalance between the public interest and the powers of rightholders who would use their economic strength to revive indefinite copyright via long-term renewals.

A system of renewals, bereft of a strong public dimension, simply recreates the current situation. I argue that in exchange for an indefinite renewable term, an open-ended list of fair dealing exceptions should be introduced. This solution translates the public's powerful joint right into the language of copyright ownership. By accepting the two parts of this formula, we may be able to overcome structural inequity enshrined in copyright law. The denial of the authorial role of the public will gradually end, as this solution would secure rewards for the public equivalent to its right as a joint author of every copyrighted entity. In such a system both public and authors would reign supreme.

Chapter 8

Conclusions: A Blueprint for Just Copyright

Authorship is a joint enterprise between public and authors. This book defends this proposition and introduces a public authorship model. It views the public as a key participant in the creative act of authorship and argues that authorial rights granted to individual creators should be attributed to the public as well. It does not reject the ideal of authorship and values the role of the individual in the process of copyright creation. It does, however, argue against the denial of the public authorial role and arguments viewing the process as a sole territory of the individual. The public authorship model addresses the question of collective social and cultural contribution to authorship. It is the public and authors that participate in the authorship of copyrighted entities and this act of collective labour, I argue, should guarantee the public a stake in copyright works contemporaneous with any private claims. The public authorship model emphasises the sociality of copyright creation and qualifies the public as a joint author of *every* authorial and artistic enterprise.

'Just copyright' is an essentially contested concept. It is a storehouse of many competing conceptions residing under the same legal principle, but pulling towards different poles. This concept has only to allow the conceptions a place where to flourish. It is our task to capture the tension between the various conceptions in a way that best accommodates the interests of members of both poles. This requires us to appropriately structure copyright in a way that balances between private and public interests.

The many different conceptions of 'just copyright' show that the concept satisfies Gallie's formula. These conceptions range from utilitarian, labour-based and personality, to radical social approaches.[1] This study is a variation of the latter. Copyright is a legal and social institution. It confers proprietary entitlement on authors and artists, and correlative duties on the public and consumers. As it stands, however, this structure is not properly defined and balanced.[2] The duties the copyright system imposes on the public are disproportionate. Moreover, these rights erode the social and cultural realities from which copyrighted entities are created, and allow rightholders to disregard the role of the public to the formation of these entities. Every right guarantees authors a private domain. However, in copyright this guarantee also involves violation of collective rights and denial of the legitimate

1 See above, Chapters 1 and 2.

2 See above, Chapter 3.

rights of certain contributors; it also serves 'to deprive us of the optimal cultural conditions for dialogic practice.'[3]

Perhaps a single formula of the right balance in copyright, if at all possible, might be beneficial. However, it is less than desirable. A single, strictly defined, formula would trigger the end of the contested nature of the concept 'just copyright' and the main advantage that it brings to copyright dialogue and to the evolution of copyright policy, namely, the capacity to accommodate unpredictable societal changes and needs. In the current state of affairs in copyright, however, the pendulum is consistently shifting to the author, sanctifying his private realm, and thereby adversely affecting the rights and interests of the public.

Harris rejects any idea of 'full-blooded ownership' in general.[4] I oppose any similar concept in copyright. I base my criticism, *inter alia*, on the fact that copyrighted entities are the defining components of our social and cultural realities, and that the sociality of copyright creation shows that the creation of authorial and artistic properties is quite unlike the vision of Romantic authorship. For reasons similar to Boyle's in rejecting a copyright culture in which '[a]uthors tend to win',[5] I reject the view that the copyright creation is a solitary activity. I do not dismiss the importance of the institution of copyright to cultural stability, and I accept that, to some extent 'authors are the heart of copyright.'[6] I do not announce the 'death of the author' and I support some form of ownership of authorial creations. However, I strongly challenge the status quo and argue that just ownership in a copyright system has to reflect its essentially social nature.

Every copyright work is a creation of the authorial collectivity. Every copyright creation is limited *ab initio* due to its reliance on authorial contributions coming from a source currently unrewarded.[7] This source is the public, or as Wilf puts it, the 'lost public.'[8] There is no author who leaps significantly beyond present knowledge and creates something totally original *ex nihilo*. The originals, as Emerson rightly says, 'are never original.'[9] For originality, as perceived in copyright law to exist, something like innateness would be required. Locke rightly rejected this as a matter of epistemology, and I have found good reasons to follow him as a matter of copyright policy. First, the creative individual is so dependent on the social and

---

3 RJ Coombe, *The Cultural Life of Intellectual Properties: Authorship, Appropriation, and the Law* (Durham and London: Duke University Press, 1998) 69.

4 JW Harris, *Property and Justice* (Oxford: Oxford University Press, 1996) 29-32.

5 J Boyle, *Shamans, Software and Spleens: Law and the Construction of the Information Society* (Cambridge Mass.: Harvard University Press, 1996) 116.

6 JC Ginsburg, 'The Concept of Authorship in Comparative Copyright Law' (2003) 52 *DePaul Law Review* 1063, 1064.

7 See above, Chapter 4.

8 S Wilf, 'Who Authors Trademarks?' (1999) 17 *Cardozo Arts & Entertainment Law Journal* 1, 12-24.

9 RW Emerson, 'Quotations and Originality' in RW Emerson, *Emerson's Complete Works*, Vol 8, *Letters and Social Aims* (London: The Waverley Book Co, Riverside ed., with a note by JE Cabot, 1883) 169, 172.

cultural environment to transform his native inclinations to actual creative abilities, and on already existing works and templates, that the question of innateness is idle. Second, it is the collective that provides, shapes and owns social and cultural processes and collectively produces properties crucial to every individual engaged in creative activity. Authors absorb and translate these properties, and imbue them with unique meaning and subjective interpretation. They also expend physical and mental labour. In this way, a joint enterprise between public and authors is created.

The literature on copyright which advocates its sociality, emphasises the role of social reliance, causality, interaction, and dialogic exchange. It views the audience, the public, as an entity participating in the creation of expressive authorial and artistic properties. Even authorial revision is 'a "collaborative" enterprise involving not only friends and publishers…but the *public* itself…'[10] Only if one places the creative individual in historical and social context, that is, if one attempts to determine what the person knew, how he interpreted that knowledge and how he built new knowledge, is one able to understand the development of even the most radically new works. Through denial of the public authorial role we risk, as Gordon asserts, erosion of 'the creative community's ability to renew itself.'[11] The understanding of how intellectual property is built, the central role of the authorial collectivity, and the status of the public as a plural subject capable of intentional states and of making rational choices, can help design a more appropriate ownership mechanism for copyrighted works.

A natural conclusion from this discussion of authorial collectivity is that authors and copyrighted works are socially constructed and historically contingent. No copyright scholar would reject the general idea behind the statement 'copyright is social', but, I have argued, few realise its full consequences. While apparently accepting the sociality of copyright creation, scholars nonetheless continue to deny the authorial role of the public.[12] This criticism is best reflected by a recent remark by Cornish that many would 'revive the old cry that the creator derives as much, *if not more*, from the culture in which she was born and bred as she gives back in her work, and so deserves no property entitlement. So far, however, these counterclaims appear to have had no more than marginal impact upon the copyright position that has built up over two centuries.'[13]

On the basis of my discussion of the authorial collectivity and the social construction of authors and original works of art and authorship, I conclude that the copyright creation process is a collaborative activity between public and authors. It is an activity that requires the participation of the public in the initiation of the

10 Z Leader, *Revision and Romantic Authorship* (Oxford: Clarendon Press, 1996) 263 (emphasis added).

11 WJ Gordon, 'Authors, Publishers, and Public Goods: Trading Gold for Dross' (2002) 36 *Loyola of Los Angeles Law Review* 159.

12 See above, Chapter 5.

13 W Cornish, *Intellectual Property: Omnipresent, Distracting, Irrelevant?* (Oxford: Oxford University Press, 2004) 50 (emphasis added).

creative impulse and in its subsequent success. That is, the creative act requires that authors and the public collaborate. Collaboration can be viewed in two ways. The first is illustrated by the words of Van Gogh, who, in a letter to Emile Bernard in June 1888, writes:

> Dear Old Bernard,
>
> More and more it seems to me that the pictures which must be made so that painting should be wholly itself, and should raise itself to a height equivalent to the serene summits which the Greek sculptors, the German musicians, the writers of French novels reached, are beyond the power of isolated individual; so they will probably be created by groups of men combining to execute an idea held in common.[14]

Woodmansee and Jaszi, the pioneers who inquired into the construction of authorship in the context of copyright, emphasised collaboration among individuals. The present account proposes a more collective sort of collaboration between public and authors. Adopting a more collective perspective, I devise a proposal for defining the 'copyright moment': a copyrighted entity is born when the contribution of the public and authors is assembled into an inseparable unitary whole.

In support of this view I drew upon Locke's theories of property, copyright and knowledge.[15] But I rejected some common, and influential, misunderstandings of the bearing of Locke's theory on copyright. True, if one confines one's reading of Locke to the property theory in the *Second Treatise*, one may conclude that it praises the individualistic dominion of the labourer. But looking further, there are three ways in which Locke's property theory can be re-imagined.

First, Locke draws a clear distinction between authorial entities and conventional property. In 'Liberty of the Press' and other minor essays, he shows that he is well aware of the social and economic flaws in a system that secures property rights for authors. He defends the rights of both authors and the general public, and challenges the wisdom behind the notion of perpetual copyright and securing a monopoly right vested in a state authority. Second, Locke's theory of property in the *Second Treatise* applies to intellectual property, and therefore limits it in the same ways that conventional property is for Locke limited. Third, I argued that there are social constructionist aspects in Locke's epistemology and philosophy of mind. These not only undermine arguments supporting the Romantic conception of the author, they also highlight the role of the public in authorship.

In my defence of the public authorship model I defend both the author's right to the product of his hands and mind, and the public's right in works of authorship based on the social and cultural contribution it makes to these works. On the basis of our commitment to preserve our cultural reality and the unavoidable dependence between public and authors on each other's authorial input, their joint efforts qualify

14 Cited in J Darracott, *Letters from Artists in the Nineteenth Century* (London: Deirdre McDonald Books, 1997) 37.

15 See above, Chapter 6.

them as joint authors. The author's desire for the commercial exploitation of his labourious creations, and the public's aspirations to retain a right by virtue of its contribution, are at the heart of the collaboration between public and authors. In this regard, I examined whether the collaborative paradigm satisfies the conditions the law imposes on individual collaborators for recognition of joint authorship.[16] Jurisdictions differ in the severity of the conditions they apply but, as I argued, the public/authors collaboration satisfies even the most stringent tests. The joint intentional responsibility to preserve and nurture a stable cultural and social reality and secure our collective identity, creates a special relationship of mutual reliance between public and authors. In this paradigmatic relationship both should acquire a right in the proceeds of their mutual efforts.

The arguments presented in this book attest to the fact that our contemporary concept of copyright incorporates a fantasy. It is a fantasy about authors and their unlimited creative abilities. It is a fantasy that legal systems embrace and cherish. Copyright laws act increasingly as laws of exclusion. They allow certain individuals to possess economic power and knowledge over what are in fact collective products. The public authorship model suggests that, if copyright means anything, it means a principle that defines the mutual commitment authors and the public have undertaken. It is a principle that regulates ownership of cultural and social resources resulting from the collaboration between authors and public in the course of this commitment. Although copyright laws aspire to generate diverse autonomous contributions to our common and cultural discourse, this book exposes the inadequacy in the way copyright laws aim to realise these aspirations.

In the end, I have attempted to open, rather than exhaust, the debate about copyright. Many practical questions are involved in the development of the public authorship model. It may be viewed as a model for a copyright system that declares authorship *without* exclusive ownership. Alternative ways to translate this ideal into workable legislation are manifold. Ensuring a balance between the collaborators in the copyright system is one of my objectives. Grand revolutions that effectively abolish copyright are one strategy for effecting change, but they are difficult to execute, and are unlikely to reach fruition in the present state of affairs in copyright. The solution I advocate consists of trading an indefinitely renewable copyright term in exchange for an open-ended scheme of exceptions and limitations to copyright. This may represent a radical conceptual change, but it does not require substantial legislative reform.

The copyright community is like a tribe, complete with rituals, myths, and stories. It is not a small, close-knit group. It includes each and every one of us. We all contribute to its development. It affects everyone, and its subjects are stamped by virtually everyone's identity. I frequently reiterated in this book, that unlike Locke's land, acorns or apples under the tree, copyright works should never be held hostage to traditional concepts of property. They are by no means sacrosanct. Yet, the copyright community has special affection for the sanctity of property language. It

16 See above, Chapter 7.

celebrates the accumulation and dissemination of knowledge by sanctifying fictitious conceptions of ownership and romantic authorship. The study of "copyright stories" reveals the inadequacy and incompleteness of the romantic view of authorship. I do not exclude the public from this criticism. Copyright is neither the story of the author, nor the story of the public. If we are to use stereotypes of authorship when we talk copyright, we must, by virtue of our collective social and cultural dependence and commitments, invoke these stereotypes with respect to both public and authors.

Bibliography

Aarsleff H, 'Locke's Influence' in V Chappell (ed.), *The Cambridge Companion to Locke* (Cambridge: Cambridge University Press, 1994) 252

Abrams HB, 'The Historic Foundations of American Copyright Law: Exploding the Myth of Common Law Copyright' (1983) *Wayne Law Review* 1119

Adams RM, 'The Locke-Leibniz Debate' in SP Stich (ed.), *Innate Ideas* (Berkeley California: University of California Press, 1975) 37

__ 'Where Do Our Ideas Come From? – Descartes vs. Locke' in SP Stich (ed.), *Innate Ideas* (Berkeley California: University of California Press, 1975) 71

Alchian A and H Damstedt, 'The Property Rights Paradigm' (1973) 33 *Journal of Economic History* 16

Alford F, *The Self in Social Theory: A Psychoanalytic Account of Its Construction in Plato, Hobbes, Locke, Rawls and Rousseau* (New Haven and London: Yale University Press, 1991)

Amabile T, *Creativity in Context* (Boulder: Westview Press, 1996)

Aoki K, 'Authors, Inventors and Trademark Owners: Private Intellectual Property and the Public Domain (Part I)' (1994) 18 *Columbia Journal of Law & Arts* 1

__ '(Intellectual) Property and Sovereignty: Notes Toward a Cultural Geography of Authorship' (1996) 48 *Stanford Law Review* 1293

__ 'Considering Multiple and Overlapping Sovereignties: Liberalism, Libertarianism, National Sovereignty, "Global" Intellectual Property, and the Internet' (1998) 5 *Indiana Journal of Global Legal Studies* 443

Armstrong G, 'From the Fetishism of Commodities to the Regulated Market: The Rise and Decline of Property' (1987) 82 *Northwestern University Law Review* 79

Arthur J, 'Resource Acquisition and Harm' (1987) 17 *Canadian Journal of Philosophy* 337

Astbury R, 'The Renewal of the Licensing Act in 1693 and Its Lapse in 1695' (1978) 33 *The Library* (5th Series) 296

Bagshaw R, 'Legal Proof of Knowledge' in P Mirfield and R Smith (eds.), *Essays for Colin Tapper* (Lexis Nexis: Butterworths, 2003) 73

Baird DG, 'Common Law Intellectual Property and the Legacy of International News Services v Associated Press' (1983) 50 *University of Chicago Law Review* 411

Balkin JM, 'Digital Speech and Democratic Culture: A Theory of Freedom of Expression for the Information Society' (2004) 79 *New York Universtiy Law Review* 1

Bankowski Z and Christodoulidis E, 'The European Union as an Essentially Contested Project', in Z Bankowski and A Scott (eds.), *The European Union and its Order* (London: Blackwell, 2000) 17

Barthes R, 'The Death of the Author', in R Barthes, *Image-Music-Text* in S Heath trans. (ed.), (London: Fontana, 1977) 142

Bartow A, 'Electrifying Copyright Norms and Making Cyberspace More Like a Book' (2003) 48 *Villanova Law Review* 13

Becker LC, 'The Labour Theory of Property Acquisition' (1976) 73 *Journal of Philosophy* 653.

__ *Property Rights: Philosophical Foundations* (Routledge & Kegan Paul, 1977)

__ 'Deserving to Own Intellectual Property' (1992-1993) 68 *Chicago-Kent Law Review* 609

Benkler Y, 'Free as Air to Common Use: First Amendment Constraints on Enclosure of the Public Domain', (1999) 74 *New York University Law Review* 354

__ 'Constitutional Bounds of Database Protection: the Role of Judicial Review in the Creation and Definition of Private Rights in Information' (2000) 15 *Berkeley Technology Law Review* 535

__ 'Siren Songs and Amish Children: Autonomy, Information and Law' (2001) 76 *New York University Law Review* 23

__ 'Through the Looking Glass: Alice and the Constitutional Foundations of the Public Domain' (2003) *Law & Contemporary Problems* 173

Benson P, 'Philosophy of Property Law' in J Coleman and S Shapiro (eds.), *The Oxford Handbook of Jurisprudence and Philosophy of Law* (Oxford: Oxford University Press, 2002) 760

Bentham J, A *Manual of Political Economy* (New York: GP Putnam, 1839)

Bently L, 'Copyright and the Death of the Author in Literature and Law' (1994) 57 *Modern Law Review* 973

Berger P and Luckmann T, *The Social Construction of Reality: A Treatise in the Sociology of Knowledge* (New York: Anchor Books, 1966)

BeView LR, 'Copyright, Trespass, and the First Amendment: An Institutional Perspective' (2004) *Social Philosophy and Policy* 104

Birnhack MD, 'The Idea of Progress in Copyright Law' (2001) 1 *Buffalo Intellectual Property Law Journal* 3

Birrell A, *Seven Essays on the Law and History of Copyright in Books* (London: Cassel and Co, 1899)

Blackstone, Sir William, *Commentaries on the Laws of England* (Butterworth and son, 16th ed. 1825)

Boden M, *The Creative Mind: Myths and Mechanisms* (New York: Basic Books, 1992)

__ *Dimensions of Creativity* (Boston: MIT Press, 1994)

Bogart JH, 'Lockean Provisos and the State of Nature' (1984-1985) 95 *Ethics* 828

Boxer S, 'Artists Duelling, Curators Dealing: A Show is Born' *The New York Times*, 'Arts & Leisure', Sunday, February 9, 2003, Section 2, 1

Boyle J, 'A Theory of Law and Information: Copyrights, Spleens, Blackmail, and Insider Trading' (1992) 80 *California Law Review* 1415

__ *Shamans, Software and Spleens: Law and the Construction of the Information Society* (Cambridge Mass.: Harvard University Press, 1996)

__ 'A Politics of Intellectual Property: Environmentalism for the Net' (1997) 47 *Duke Law Journal* 87

Brady TM, Note, 'Manifest Intent and Copyrightability: The Destiny of Joint Authorship' (1989) 17 *Fordham Urban Law Journal* 257

Bratman ME, 'Shared Intention' (1993) 104(1) *Ethics* 97

Brennan TJ, 'Copyright, Property and the Right to Deny' (1992-1993) 68 *Chicago-Kent Law Review* 675

Breyer SG, 'The Uneasy Case for Copyright' (1970) 87 *Harvard Law Review* 28

__ 'Copyright: A Rejoinder' (1972) 20 *UCLA Law Review* 75

Bridy A, 'Sheep in Goat's Clothing: Satire and Fair Use After Campbell v Acuff-Rose Music Inc.' (2004) 51 *Journal of the Copyright Society of the USA* 257

Briggs J, 'The Genius Mind' (1984) 92 *Science Digest* 74

Brodhurst D, 'Is Copyright a Chose in Action?' (1895) 11 *Law Quarterly Review* 64

Brophy CS, 'Joint Authorship under the Copyright Law' (1994) 16 *Hastings Communication and Entertainment Law Journal* 451

Brown RS, 'Eligibility for Copyright Protection: A Search for Principled Standards' (1985) 70 *Minnesota Law Rev* 579

Buckalew F, 'Joint Authorship in the Second Circuit: A Critique of the Law in the Second Circuit Following *Childress v Taylor* and as Exemplified in *Thomson v Larson*' (1998) 64 *Brooklyn Law Review* 549

Buckle S, *Natural Law and the Theory of Property: Grotius to Hume* (Oxford: Clarendon Press, 1999)

Burke S, *The Death and Return of the Author: Criticism and Subjectivity in Bathes, Foucault and Derrida* (Edinburgh: Edinburgh University Press, 2nd enlarged ed., 1998)

Burkitt D, 'Copyrighting Culture – The History and Cultural Specificity of the Western Model of Copyright' [2001] 2 *Intellectual Property Quarterly* 146

Buss TV and Mansfield RS, *The Psychology of Creativity and Discovery* (Chicago: Nelson Hall, 1981)

__ 'The Blooming of Creative Scientists: Early, Late and Otherwise' (1981) *Gifted Child Quarterly* 63

Byrne C, MacDonald R and Carlton L, 'Assessing Creativity in Musical Compositions: Flow as an Assessment Tool' (2003) 20(3) *British Journal of Music Education* 277

Caenegen van, W, 'The Public Domain: Scientia Nullius?' [2002] 6 *European Intellectual Property Review* 324

Callies DL and Breemer JD, 'The Right to Exclude Others from Private Property: A Fundamental Constitutional Right' (2000) 3 *Washington University Journal of Law and Policy* 39

Canaday J, *What is Art? An Introduction to Painting, Sculpture and Architecture* (London: Hutchinson, 1980)

Carr EH, *What is History?* (New York: Vintage Books 1961)

Carrell N, *Bach the Borrower* (London: George Allen & Unwin, 1967)

Carroll N, *Philosophy of Art: A Contemporary Introduction* (London & New York: Routledge, 1999)

Carter A, *The Philosophical Foundations of Property Rights* (New York and London: Harvester Wheatsheaf, 1989)

Carter SL, 'Does it Matter Whether Intellectual Property Is Property?' (1993) 68(2) *Chicago-Kent Law Review* 715

Carter WB, 'The Classification of Ideas in Locke's Essay' (1963-1964) 2 *Dialogue* 25

Carty H, 'Advertising, Publicity Rights and English Law' [2004] 3 *Intellectual Property Quarterly* 209

Chafee Z Jr., 'Reflections on the Law of Copyright: I' (1945) 45 *Columbia Law Review* 503

__ 'Reflections on the Law of Copyright: II' (1945) 45 *Columbia Law Review* 719

Chappell V, (ed.), *The Cambridge Companion to Locke* (Cambridge: Cambridge University Press, 1994)

__ 'Locke's Theory of Ideas' in V Chappell (ed.), *The Cambridge Companion to Locke* (Cambridge: Cambridge University Press, 1994) 26

Cherensky S, 'A Penny for Their Thoughts: Employee-Inventors, Preinvention Assignment Agreement, Property and Personhood' (1993) 81 *California Law Review* 597

Cherno M, 'Locke on Property: A Reappraisal' (1957) 68 *Ethics* 51

Child JW, 'The Moral Foundation of Intangible Property' (1990) 73(4) *The Monist* 578

Chon M, 'New Wine Bursting From Old Bottles: Collaborative Internet, Art, Joint Works, and Entrepreneurship' (1996) 75 *Oregon Law Review* 257

Christman J, *The Myth of Property* (Oxford University Press, 1994)

Ciolino DS, 'Why Copyrights are not Community Property' (1999) *Louisiana Law Review* 127

Clemens SL, 'Copyright in Perpetuity' (2002) 6 *Green Bag* 2d 109

Cohen AB, 'Copyright Law and the Myth of Objectivity: The Idea-Expression Dichotomy and the Inevitability of Artistic Value Judgements' (1990) 66 *Indiana Law Journal* 175

Cohen FS, 'Dialogue on Private Property' (1954) 9 *Rutgers Law Review* 357

Cohen GA, *'Marx and Locke on Land and Labour'* (London, 1985)

Cohen M, 'Property and Sovereignty' (1928) 13 *Cornell Law Quarterly* 8

Cohen P, Morgan J and Pollack ME (eds.), *Intentions in Communication* (Cambridge MA.: MIT Press, 1990)

Colendich KM, 'Who Owns "The Law"? The Effect on Copyrights when Privately-Authored Works are Adopted or Enacted by Reference into Law' (2003) 78 *Washington Law Review* 589

Colman J, *John Locke's Moral Philosophy* (Edinburgh: Edinburgh University Press, 1983)

Cook-Gumperz J (ed.), *The Social Construction of Literacy* (Cambridge University Press, 1986)

Coombe RJ, 'Objects of Property and Subjects of Politics: Intellectual Property Laws and Democratic Dialogue' (1991) 69 *Texas Law Review* 1853

__ 'Author/izing the Celebrity: Publicity Rights, Postmodern Politics, and Unauthorized Genders' (1992) 10 *Cardozo Arts & Entertainment Law Journal* 365

__ 'Challenging Paternity: Histories of Copyright' (1994) 6 *Yale Journal of Law and the Humanities* 397

__ 'Critical Cultural Legal Studies' (1998) *Yale Journal of Law and the Humanities* 463

__ *The Cultural Life of Intellectual Properties: Authorship, Appropriation and the Law* (Durham and London: Duke University Press, 1998)

__ 'The Recognition of Indigenous Peoples' and Community Traditional Knowledge in International Law' (2001) 14 *St. Thomas Law Review* 275

Coombe RJ and Cohen J, 'The Law and Late Modern Culture: Reflections on Between Facts and Norms from the Perspective of Critical Cultural Legal Studies' (1999) 76 *Denver University Law Review* 1029

Cooper Dreyfuss R, 'Collaborative Research: Conflicts on Authorship, Ownership, and Accountability' (2000) 53 *Vanderbilt Law Review* 1161

__ 'Commodifying Collaborative Research' in N Elkin-Koren and NW Netanel (eds.), *The Commodification of Information* (The Hague: Kluwer Law International, 2002) 397

Copyright and Design Law: Report of the Committee to Consider the Law on Copyright and Designs (Cmnd 7632) (HMSO 1977)

Cornish W and Llewelyn D, *Intellectual Property* (London: Sweet and Maxwell, 5th ed., 2003)

Cornish W, 'Moral Rights Under the 1988 Act' (1989) *European Intellectual Property Review* 449

__ *Intellectual Property: Omnipresent, Distracting, Irrelevant?* (Oxford: Oxford University Press, 2004)

Cotter TF, 'Pragmatism, Economics, and the Droit Moral' (1997) 76 *North Carolina Law Review* 8

Coulter J, *The Social Construction of Mind* (London and Basingstoke: Macmillan, 1979)

Craig CJ, 'Locke, Labour and Limiting the Author's Right: A Warning Against a Lockean Approach to Copyright Law' (2002) 28 *Queens Law Journal* 1.

Crew KD, 'Copyright Duration and the Progressive Degeneration of a Constitutional Guarantee' (2005) 55 *Syracuse Law Review* 189

Csikszentmihalyi M, *Creativity: Flow and the Psychology of Discovery and Invention* (New York: HarperPerennial, 1996)

Dagan H, 'The Distributive Foundation of Corrective Justice' (1999) 98 *Michigan Law Review* 138

Dallon CW, 'Original Intent and the Copyright Clause: Eldred v Ashcroft Gets it Right' (2006) 50 *Saint Louise University Law Journal* 307

Daix P, *Picasso: The Cubist Years 1907-1916* (London: Thames and Hudson, 1979)

Damstedt BG, 'Limiting Locke: A Natural Law Justification for the Fair Use Doctrine' (2003) 112 *Yale Law Journal* 1179

Darracott J, *Letters from Artists in the Nineteenth Century* (London: Deirdre McDonald Books, 1997)

Davies G, *Copyright and the Public Interest* (London: Thomson, Sweet & Maxwell, 2nd ed., 2002).

Davison MJ and Hugenholtz PB, 'Football Fixtures, Horseraces and Spin Offs: The ECJ Domesticates the Database Right' (2005) 27(3) *European Intellectual Property Review* 113

Day JP, 'Locke on Property' (1966) 16 *Philosophical Quarterly* 207

De Beer ES (ed.), *The Correspondence of John Locke* (Oxford: Clarendon Press 1979)

Deazley R, *On the Origin of the Right to Copy: Charting the Movement of Copyright in Eighteenth Century Britain* (Oxford: Hart Publishing, 2004).

Denicola R, 'Copyright in Collections of Facts: A Theory for the Protection of Nonfiction Literary Works' (1981) 81 *Columbia Law Review* 516

__ 'Freedom to Copy' (1999) 108 *Yale Law Review* 1661

Dietz A, 'The Artist's Right of Integrity Under Copyright Law – A Comparative Approach' (1994) 25 *International Review of Industrial Property and Copyright Law* 177

Dinwoodie GB, Hennessey WO and Perlmutter S, *International Intellectual Property Law and Policy* (New York: M Bender, 2001)

Doherty M and Griffiths I, 'The Harmonisation of European Union Copyright Law for the Digital Age' [2000] European Intellectual Property Review 17

Dommering E and Hugenholtz P (eds.), *Protecting Works of Fact: Copyright, Freedom of Expression and Information Law* (Deventer: Kluwer, 1991)

Drahos P, *A Philosophy of Intellectual Property* (Dartmouth: Ashgate 1996)

__ 'Intellectual Property and Human Rights' [1999] 3 *Intellectual Property Quarterly* 349

Drassinower A, 'A Right-Based View of the Idea/Expression Dichotomy in Copyright Law' (2003) 16 *Canadian Journal of Law and Jurisprudence* 3

Dreier T, 'Balancing Proprietary and Public Domain Interests: Inside or Outside of Proprietary Rights?', in R Dreyfuss, LD Zimmerman and H First (eds.), *Expanding the Boundaries of Intellectual Property: Innovation Policy for the Knowledge Society* (Oxford: Oxford University Press, 2001) 295

Dreyfuss R, Zimmerman LD and First H (eds.), *Expanding the Boundaries of Intellectual Property: Innovation Policy for the Knowledge Society* (Oxford: Oxford University Press, 2001)

Drury SB, 'Locke and Nozick on Property', (1982) 30 *Political Studies* 28-41.

Dunn J, *The Political Thought of John Locke* (Cambridge: Cambridge University Press, 1969).

Durham AL, '"Useful Arts" in the Information Age' (1999) *Brigham Young University Law Review* 1419

__ 'The Random Muse: Authorship and Indeterminacy' (2002) 44 *William and Mary Law Review* 569

__ 'Copyright and Information Theory: Toward an Alternative Model of "Authorship"' (2004) *Brigham Young University Law Review* 69

Durkheim E, *Sociology and Philosophy* (Glencoe, Illinois: The Free Press, trans. DF Pocock, 1953)

Dworkin G, 'Moral rights in English Law – The Shape of Things to Come' (1986) *European Intellectual Property Review* 144

Dworkin R, *Taking Rights Seriously* (London: Duckworth, 1977).

Eindhoven JE and Vinacke WE, 'Creative Processes in Painting' (1952) 47 *The Journal of General Psychology* 139

Einstein EL, *The Printing Press as an Agent of Change: Communications and Cultural Transformations in Early-Modern Europe* (1979) Vol 1

Elkin-Koren N, 'Copyright Law and Social Dialogue on the Information Superhighways: The Case Against Copyright Liability of Bulletin Board Operators' (1995) 13 *Cardozo Arts & Entertainment Law Journal* 345

__ 'Cyberlaw and Social Change: A Democratic Approach to Copyright Law in Cyberspace' (1996) 14 *Cardozo Arts & Entertainment Law Journal* 215

__ 'A Public-Regarding Approach to Contracting Over Copyrights', in R Dreyfuss, LD Zimmerman and H First (eds.), *Expanding the Boundaries of Intellectual Property: Innovation Policy for the Knowledge Society* (Oxford: Oxford University Press, 2001) 191

__ 'Of Scientific Claims and Proprietary Rights: Lessons from the Dead Sea Scrolls Case' (2001) 38 *Houston Law Review* 445

Elkin-Koren N and Netanel NW (eds.), *The Commodification of Information* (The Hague: Kluwer Law International, 2002)

Elster J, *Explaining Technical Change* (Cambridge: Cambridge University Press, 1983)

Emerson RW, 'Quotations and Originality' in RW Emerson, *Emerson's Complete Works*, Vol 8, *Letters and Social Aims* (London: The Waverley Book Co, Riverside ed., with a note by JE Cabot, 1883) 169

Epstein R, 'Possession as the Root of Title' (1979) 13 *Georgia Law Review* 1221

__ 'On the Optimal Mix of Private and Common Property' (1994) 11 *Social Philosophy and Policy* 117

__ 'Liberty versus Property? Cracks in the Foundations of Copyright Law', Chicago John M Olin Law & Economics Working Paper No 204 (2d Series) (April 2004) 28

Eysenck HJ, 'Creativity and Personality: Suggestions for a Theory' (1993) 4 *Psychological Inquiry* 147

Fallon RH, "'The Rule of Law' as a Concept in Constitutional Discourse' (1997) 97 *Columbia Law Review* 1.

Feist GJ, 'A Meta-Analysis of Personality in Scientific and Artistic Creativity' (1998) 2 *Personality and Social Psychology Review* 290

Ferguson S, 'What Makes Locke's Simple Ideas Adequate? A Response to Bemúdez' (1996) 27 *The Locke Newsletter* 31.

Ferrante-Wallace J and Brown P, *The Social Construction of Race and Ethnicity in the United States* (New York: Longman, 1998)

Fisch E, *Guernica by Picasso* (London and Toronto: Associated University Press, 1988)

Fisher W, 'Property and Contract on the Internet' (1998) 73 *Chicago-Kent Law Review* 1203

__ 'Theories of Intellectual Property', S Munzer (ed.), *New Essays in the Legal and Political Theory of Property* (Cambridge: Cambridge University Press, 2001) 168

Fitzpatrick D, 'Searle and Collective Intentionality: The Self-Defeating Nature of Intentionalism with Respect to Social Facts' (2003) 62(1) *American Journal of Economics and Sociology* 45

Foucault M, 'What is an Author?' in P Rainbow (ed.), *The Foucault Reader* (New York: Pantheon Books, 1984)

Fox Bourne HR, *The Life of John Locke* (London: Henry S King, 1876) Vol 2

Fox PS, 'Preserving the Collaborative Spirit of American Theatre: The Need for a "Joint Authorship Default Rule" in Light of the Rent Decision's Unanswered Question', (2001) 19 *Cardozo Arts & Entertainment Law Journal* 497

Frefogle ET, 'The Construction of Ownership' (1996) *University of Illinois Law Review* 173

Frey BS, 'State Support and Creativity in the Arts: Some New Considerations' (1999) 23 *Journal of Cultural Economics* 71

__ 'Creativity, Government and the Arts' (2002) 150(4) *De Economist* 363

Friedman B, Note, 'From Deontology to Dialogue: The Cultural Consequences of Copyright' (1994) 13 *Cardozo Arts & Entertainment Law Journal* 157

Gallie WB, 'Essentially Contested Concepts' (1955-1956) 56 *Proceedings of the Aristotelian Society* 167

Garnett K, JR James and G Davies, *Copinger and Skone James on Copyright* (London: Sweet & Maxwell 14th ed., 1999)

Garon JM, 'Normative Copyright: A Conceptual Framework for Copyright Philosophy and Ethics' (2003) 88 *Cornell Law Review* 1278

Garver E, 'Essentially Contested Concepts: the Ethics and Tactics of Argument' (1990) 23 *Philosophy & Rhetoric* 251

Gaus GF and Lomasky LE, 'Are Property Rights Problematic?' (1990) 73(4) *The Monist* 483

__ 'Property, Rights and Freedom' (1994) 11 *Social Philosophy and Politics* 209

Geist M, The Ninth Annual Honorable Helen Wilson Nies Memorial Lecture in Intellectual Property, 'All Rights Reserved? Cultural Monopoly and the Troubles with Copyright' (2006) 10 *Marquette Intellectual Property Law Review* 411

Gergen KJ, 'The Social Constructionist Movement in Modern Psychology' (1985) 40 *American Psychologist* 266

__ 'Meaning in Relationship' in M Gergen and KJ Gergen (eds.), *Social Construction: A Reader* (London: Sage Publications, 2003) 148

Gergen M and Gergen KJ (eds.), *Social Construction: A Reader* (London: Sage Publications, 2003)

Gervais DJ, 'Feist Goes Global: A Comparative Analysis of the Notion of Originality in Copyright Law' (2002) 49 *Journal of the Copyright Society of the USA* 949

__ 'Canadian Copyright Law Post-CCH' (2004) 18 *Intellectual Property Journal* 131

Ghiselin B (ed.), *The Creative Process: Reflections on Invention in the Arts and Sciences* (Berkeley: University of California Press, 1952)

Ghosh S, 'Copyright as Privatization: The Case of Model Codes' (2004) 78 *Tulane Law Review* 653

Gibbard A, 'Natural Property Rights' in RM Stewart (ed.), *Readings in Social and Political Philosophy* (New York: Oxford University Press, 1986) 237

Gifford DJ, 'Innovation and Creativity in the Fine Arts: The Relevance and Irrelevance of Copyright' (2000) 18 *Cardozo Arts & Entertainment Law Journal* 569

Gilbert M, 'Modelling Collective Belief' (1987) 73 *Synthese* 186

__ *On Social Facts* (Princeton: Princeton University Press, 1989)

__ 'Walking Together: A Paradigmatic Social Phenomenon' (1990) 15 *Midwest Studies in Philosophy* (1990) 1

__ *Living Together, Rationality, Sociality, and Obligation* (New York: Rowman & Littlefield, 1996)

__ 'The Structure of the Social Atom: Joint Commitment as the Foundation of Human Social Behavior' in FF Schmitt (ed.), *Socializing Metaphysics: The Nature of Social Reality* (Lanham, MD: Rowman and Littlefield, 2003) 39

Ginsburg J, 'Creation and Commercial Value: Copyright Protection for Works of Information' (1990) 90 *Columbia Law Review* 1865

__ 'A Tale of Two Copyrights: Literary Property in Revolutionary France and America' in B Sherman and A Strowel (eds.), *Of Authors and Origins: Essays on Copyright Law* (Oxford: Clarendon Press, 1994) 131.

__ 'The Concept of Authorship in Comparative Copyright Law' (2003) 52 *DePaul Law Review* 1063

__ 'The Right to Claim Authorship in US Copyright and Trademarks Law' (2004) 41 *Houston Law Review* 263

Gleicher J, 'The Bard at the Bar: Some Citations of Shakespeare by the United States Supreme Court' (2001) 26 *Oklahoma City University Law Review* 327

Gobetti D, *Private and Public: Individuals, Households, and Body Politic in Locke and Hutcheson* (London and New York: Routledge, 1992)

Golan D, *Inventing Shaka: Using History in the Construction of Zulu Nationalism* (Boulder: L Rienner 1994)

Goldie M (ed.), *John Locke: Political Essays* (Cambridge: Cambridge University Press, 1997)

Goldstein P, *Copyright: Principles, Law and Practice* (Boston, Toronto: Little, Brown & Co, 1989)

__ *International Copyright: Principles, Law, and Practice* (Oxford: Oxford University Press 2001)

Gordon RW, 'Paradoxical Property', in J Brewer and S Staves (eds.), *Early Modern Conceptions of Property* (London: Routledge, 1996) 95

Gordon WJ, 'An Inquiry into the Merits of Copyright: The Challenges of Consistency, Consent, and Encouragement Theory' (1989) 41 *Stanford Law Review* 1343

__ 'The Norms of Copyright and the Problem of Private Censorship' (1990) 57 *The University of Chicago Law Review* 1009

__ 'On Owning Information: Intellectual Property and the Restitutionary Impulse' (1992) 78 *Virginia Law Review* 149

__ 'Reality as Artifact: From Feist to Fair use' (1992) 55 *Law & Contemporary Problems* 93

__ 'A Property Right in Self-Expression: Equality and Individualism in the Natural Law of Intellectual Property' (1993) 12 *Yale Law Journal* 1533

__ 'Authors, Publishers, and Public Goods: Trading Gold for Dross' (2002) 36 *Loyola of Los Angeles Law Review* 159

__ 'Intellectual Property Law' in P Crane and M Tushnet (eds.), *Oxford Handbook of Legal Studies* (Oxford: Oxford University Press, 2003) 167

__ 'Render Copyright unto Caesar: On Taking Incentives Seriously' (2004) 71(1) *The University of Chicago Law Review* 75

Gordon WJ and Bone RG, 'Copyright' in B Bouckaert and G de Geest (eds.), *Encyclopaedia of Law & Economics: Volume II* (Edward Elgar: Cheltenham, UK, 2000) 189

Gordon WJ and Watt R (eds.), *The Economics of Copyright: Developments in Research and Analysis* (Cheltenham: Edward Elgar, 2003)

Gorman RA and Ginsburg JC, *Copyright: Cases and Materials* (New York: Foundation Press, 6th ed., 2002)

Gray J, 'On the Essential Contestability of Some Social and Political Concepts' (1977) 5 *Political Theory* 331

__ 'On Liberty, Liberalism and Essential Contestability' (1978) 8 *British Journal of Political Science* 385

__ 'Political Power, Social Theory, and Essential Contestability' in D Miller and L Siedentop (eds.), *The Nature of Political Theory* (Oxford: Clarendon Press, 1983) 75

Gray K, 'Property in Thin Air' (1991) 50 *Cambridge Law Journal* 252

__ 'Equitable Property' (1994) 47(2) *Current Legal Problems* 157

Gredley M, 'Parody: A Fatal Attraction?' (1997) *European Intellectual Property Review* 339

Green L, *The Authority of the State* (Oxford: Clarendon Press, 1990)

Greenlee D, 'Locke and the Controversy Over Innate Ideas' (1972) 33(2) *Journal of the History of Ideas* 251

Grey TC, 'The Disintegration of Property' in JR Pennock and JW Chapman (ed.), *Property*, Nomos, XXII (New York: New York University Press, 1980) 85

Griffiths J, 'Copyright in English Literature: Denying the Public Domain' [2000] *European Intellectual Property Review* 150

__ 'Copyright Law after *Ashdown* – Time to Deal Fairly with the Public' [2002] 3 *Intellectual Property Quarterly* 240

Grunebaum J, *Private Ownership* (London: Routledge & Kegan Paul, 1987)

__ 'Ownership as Theft' (1990) 73(4) *Monist* 544

Guell RC and Fischbaum M, 'Toward Allocative Efficiency in the Prescription Drug Industry' (1995) *Milbank Quarterly* 525

Hacking I, *Rewriting the Soul: Multiple Personality and the Sciences of Memory* (Princeton: Princeton University Press, 1995) 21

__ *The Social Construction of What?* (Cambridge Mass.: Harvard University Press, 1999)

__ 'The Looping Effects of Human Kinds' in D Sperber (ed.), *Causal Cognition* (New York: Clarendon Press, 1995)

Haddad BM, 'Property Rights, Ecosystem Management, and John Locke's Labour Theory of Ownership' (2003) 46 *Ecological Economics* 19

Hadfield GK, 'The Economics of Copyright: An Historical Perspective' (1992) 38 *Copyright Law Symposium* (ASCAP) 1

Hamilton MA, 'The Distant Drumbeat: Why the Law Still Matters in the Information Era' (2002) 20 *Cardozo Arts & Entertainment Law Journal* 259

Hamilton WH, 'Property – According to Locke' (1932) 41 *Yale Law Journal* 864

Hampshire S, *Thought and Action* (New York: Viking Press, 1959)

Harris J, 'Leibniz and Locke on Innate Ideas' (1974) 16 *Ratio* 226.

Harris JW, *Property and Justice* (Oxford: Oxford University Press, 1996)

Hart HLA, *The Concept of Law* (Oxford: Oxford University Press, 2nd ed. 1994)

Haslanger S, 'Ontology and Social Construction' (1995) 23 *Philosophical Topics* 127

__ 'Social Construction: The "Debunking" Project', in FF Schmitt (ed.), *Socializing Metaphysics: The Nature of Social Reality* (Lanham, MD: Rowman and Littlefield, 2003) 301

Hatch OG, 'Toward a Principled Approach to Copyright Legislation at the Turn of the Millennium' (1998) 59 *University of Pittsburgh Law Review* 719

Häyrinen-Alestalo M, 'Is Knowledge-Based Society a Relevant Strategy for Civil Society?' (2001) 49(4) *Current Sociology* 203

Hayton D, 'Joint Tenancies – Severance' (1976) 35 *Cambridge Law Journal* 20

Hegel GWF, *Philosophy of Right* (1821) (Oxford: Oxford University Press, TM Knox trans., 1967)

Held V, 'John Locke on Robert Nozick' (1976) 43 *Social Research* 16-95

Heller M, 'The Tragedy of the Anticommons: Property in the Transition from Marx to Markets' (1998) 111 *Harvard Law Review* 621

__ 'The Boundaries of Private Property' (1999) 108 *Yale Law Journal* 1166

__ 'Symposium: Critical Approaches to Property Institutions: Three Faces of Private Property' (2000) 79 *Oregon Law Review* 417

Hertzman E, 'Mozart's Creative Process', in PH Lang (ed.), *The Creative World of Mozart* (New York: Norton, 1991) 17

Hetcher S, 'Changing the Social Meaning of Privacy in Cyberspace' (2001) 15 *Harvard Journal of Law & Technology* 149

Hettinger EC, 'Justifying Intellectual Property' (1989) 18 *Philosophy & Public Affairs* 31

Hilton T, *Picasso* (London: Thames and Hudson, 1975)

Hindriks F, 'Social Groups, Collective Intentionality and Anti-Hegelian Skepticism' in M Sintonen, P Ylikoski, and K Miller (eds.), *Realism in Action: Essays in Philosophy of the Social Sciences* (Dordrecht: Kluwer, 2003) 213

Hofkosh S, *Sexual Politics and the Romantic Author* (Cambridge: Cambridge University Press, 1998)

Hohfeld WN, 'Fundamental Legal Conceptions as Applied in Judicial Reasoning' (1913) 23 *Yale Law Journal* 16

__ *Fundamental Legal Conceptions* (Yale University Press: 1919)

Honderich T (ed.), *The Oxford Companion to Philosophy* (Oxford: Oxford University Press, 1995)

Honoré AM, 'Ownership', in *Making the Law Bind* (Oxford: Clarendon Press, 1987) 166-179

Hornsby J, 'Collectives and Intentionality' (1997) 57(2) *Philosophy and Phenomenological Research* 429

Hudson L, 'The Question of Creativity' in PE Vernon (ed.), *Creativity* (Penguin Books, 1970) 217

Hugenholtz PB, 'Copyright and Freedom of Expression in Europe' in R Dreyfuss, LD Zimmerman and H First (eds.), *Expanding the Boundaries of Intellectual Property: Innovation Policy for the Knowledge Society* (Oxford: Oxford University Press, 2001) 343

Hughes J, 'The Philosophy of Intellectual Property' (1988) 77 *Georgetown Law Journal* 287

Hundret EJ, 'Market, Society and Meaning in Locke's Political Philosophy' (1977) 15 *Journal of the History of Ideas* 15

Hurt RM and Schuchman N, 'The Economic Rationale of Copyright' (1966) 56 *American Economic Review* 421

Hutchinson GW, Practitioner's Note, 'Can the Federal Courts Save Rock Music?: Why Default Joint Authorship Rule Should be Adopted to Protect Co-Authors under United States Copyright Law' (2003) 5 *Tulane Journal of Technology and Intellectual Property* 77

Innocent R, 'Copyright Problems as Experienced by Visual Artists' (1988) 10(7) *European Intellectual Property Review* 203

Janos MD, 'Second Tier Patent Protection' (1999) 40 *Harvard International Law Journal* 151

Jaszi P, 'Towards a Theory of Copyright: The Metamorphoses of "Authorship"' (1991) *Duke Law Journal* 455

__ 'On the Author Effect: Contemporary Copyright and Collective Creativity' in M Woodmansee and P Jaszi (eds.), *The Construction of Authorship* (Durham and London: Duke University Press, 1994) 29

__ 'Goodbye to All That – A Reluctant (and Perhaps Premature) Adieu to a Constitutionally-Grounded Discourse of Public Interest in Copyright Law' (1996) 25 *Vanderbilt Journal of Transnational Law* 595

__ 'Caught in the Net of Copyright' (1996) 75 *Oregon Law Review* 299

Jaszi P and Woodmansee M, 'The Ethical Reaches of Authorship' (1996) 95 *South Atlantic Quarterly* 947.

Johnson P, 'The Public Interest: Is it still a Defence to Copyright Infringement?' (2005) 16(1) *Entertainment Law Review* 1

Johnson ST, Note, 'Internet Domain Name and Trademark Disputes: Shifting Paradigms in Intellectual Property' (2001) 43 *Arizona Law Review* 465

Jones M, 'Eldred v Ashcroft: The Constitutionality of the Copyright Term Extension Act' (2004) 19 *Berkeley Technology and Law Journal* 85

Jones R, 'The Myth of the Idea/Expression Dichotomy in Copyright Law' (1990) *Pace Law Review* 551

Joyner JK, 'Future Technology Clauses: Would Their Lack of Compensation Have Discouraged Shakespeare's Creativity and Denied Society's Access to His Works in New Media?' (2002) 31 *Southwestern University Law Review* 575

Kaplan B, *An Unhurried View of Copyright* (New York: Columbia University Press, 1967)

Kearns P, *The Legal Concept of Art* (Oxford: Hart Publishing, 1998)

Keller SE, 'Collaboration in Theatre: Problems and Copyright Solutions' (1986) 33 *UCLA Law Review* 891

Kewes P, *Authorship and Appropriation: Writing for the Stage in England, 1660-1710* (Oxford: Clarendon Press, 1998)

__ '"A Play, Winch I Presume to Call Original": Appropriation, Creative Genius, and Eighteenth-Century Playwriting' (2001) 34(1) *Studies in the Literary Imagination* 17

Kim H, 'Locke on Innatism' (2003) 3 *Locke Studies* 15

Knowles D, *Political Philosophy* (London: Routledge, 2001)

Koestler A, *'The Act of Creation'* (New York: Lineright, 1964).

Koleman KJ, 'Copyright Law and Economics in the EU Copyright Directive: Is the Droit d'Auteur Passé?' (2004) 35(6) *International Review of Intellectual Property and Competition Law* 603

Kramer MH, *John Locke and the Origin of Private Property: Philosophical Explorations of Individualism, Community, and Equality* (Cambridge: Cambridge University Press 1997)

Kuda TD, 'Authorship of Sound Recordings: Why Sound Recordings Should Have Joint Authorship?' (2004) 33 *Southwestern University Law Review* 379

Kugele NF, 'How Much does it Take?: Copyrightability as a Minimum Standard for Determining Joint Authorship' (1991) *University of Illinois Law Review* 809

Lacey LJ, 'Of Bread and Roses and Copyrights' (1989) *Duke Law Journal* 1532

Laddie H, 'Copyright: Over-Strength, Over-Regulated, Over-rated' [1996] 18(5) *European Intellectual Property Review* 253

Laddie H et al, *The Modern Law of Copyright and Designs* (London: Butterworths, 3rd ed. 2000)

LaFrance M, 'Authorship, Dominance, and the Captive Collaborator: Preserving the Rights of Joint Authors' (2001) 50 *Emory Law Journal* 193

Landes WM and Posner RA, 'Trademark Law: An Economic Perspective' (1987) 30 *Journal of Law & Economics* 265

__ 'An Economic Analysis of Copyright Law' (1989) 18 *Journal Of Legal Studies* 325

__ 'Indefinitely Renewable Copyright' (2003) 70 *University of Chicago Law Review* 471

Lange D, 'Recognizing the Public Domain' (1981) 44 *Law & Contemporary Problems* 147

Larschan B and Brennan BC, 'The Common Heritage of Mankind Principle in International Law' (1983) 21 *Columbia Journal of International Law* 305.

Laslett P, 'Introduction', in Locke J, *Two Treatises of Government*, P Laslett ed., (Cambridge: Cambridge University Press, 2nd ed., 1988) 3

Latour B and Woolgar S, *Laboratory Life: The Construction of Scientific Facts* (Princeton: Princeton University Press, 1986)

__ *Laboratory Life: The Social Construction of Scientific Facts* (Beverly Hills: Sage, 1979)

Leader Z, *Revision and Romantic Authorship* (Oxford: Clarendon Press, 1996)

Lee JC, Comment, 'Upstaging the Playwright: The Joint Authorship Entanglement Between Dramaturge's and Playwrights' (1998) 19 *Loyola of Los Angeles Entertainment Law Journal* 75

Leenheer Zimmerman D, 'Authorship Without Ownership: Recognizing Incentives in a Digital Age' (2003) 52 *DePaul Law Review* 1121

Leichtman D, 'Most Unhappy Collaborators: An Argument Against the Recognition of Property Ownership in Stage Directions' (1996) 20 *Columbia-VLA Journal of Law and the Arts* 683

Lemley MA, 'Romantic Authorship and the Rhetoric of Property' (1997) 75 *Texas Law Review* 873

__ 'The Economics of Improvement in Intellectual Property Law' (1997) 75 *Texas Law Review* 989

__ 'Beyond Preemption: The Law and Policy of Intellectual Property Licensing' (1999) 97 *California Law Review* 111

__ 'Property, Intellectual Property, and Free Riding' (2005) 83 *Texas Law Review* 1031

Lessig L, *Code and Other Laws of Cyberspace* (New York: Basic Books, 2000)
__ *The Future of Ideas: The Fate of the Commons in a Connected World* (New York: Vintage Books, 2002)
__ 'Copyright's First Amendment' (2001) 48 *UCLA Law Review* 1057, 1068
__ *Free Culture: How Big Media Uses Technology and the Law to Lock Down Culture and Control Creativity* (New Your: The Penguin Press, 2004)
Leval PN, 'Fair Use or Foul? The Nineteenth Donald C Brace Memorial Lecture' (1989) 36 *Journal of the Copyright Society of the USA* 167
Leyden W, 'John Locke and Natural Law' (1956) 31 *Philosophy* 23-35
Libling DF, 'The Concept of Property: Property in Intangibles' (1978) 94 *Law Quarterly Review* 103
Lichtman DG, 'Pricing Prozac: Why the Government Should Subsidize the Purchase of Patented Pharmaceuticals' (1997) 11 *Harvard Journal of Law & Technology* 123
Lim TH, MacQueen HL and Carmichael CM (eds.), *On Scrolls, Artefacts and Intellectual Property* (Sheffield: Sheffield Academic Press, 2001)
Lipton J, 'Information Property: Rights and Responsibilities' (2004) 56 *Florida Law Review* 135, 177-181
Litman J, 'Copyright, Compromise, and Legislative History' (1987) 72 *Cornell Law Review* 857
__ 'The Public Domain' (1990) 39 *Emory Law Journal* 965
__ 'Copyright as Myth' (1991) 53 *University of Pittsburgh Law Review* 235
__ *Digital Copyright* (New York: Prometheus Books, 2001)
__ 'Ethical Disobedience' (2004) 5 *Ethics and Information Technology* 217
Littrell R, Note, 'Towards a Stricter Originality Standard for Copyright' (2001) 43 *Boston College Law Review* 193
Ljungman S, 'The Function of Copyright in the Present Day Society' (1976) 88 *Revue Internationale du Droit d'Auteur* 51
Locke J, *An Essay Concerning Human Understanding* (first published 1690) edited with an Introduction by PH Nidditch (Oxford: Clarendon Press, 1971)
__ 'Labour' (published 1693), M Goldie (ed.), *John Locke: Political Essays* (Cambridge: Cambridge University Press, 1997) 326
__ 'Law', in M Goldie (ed.), *John Locke: Political Essays* (Cambridge: Cambridge University Press, 1997) 328
__ 'Liberty of the Press' (published 1694-1695) in M Goldie (ed.), *John Locke: Political Essays* (Cambridge: Cambridge University Press, 1997) 329
__ *Essays on the Law of Nature* in M Goldie (ed.), *John Locke: Political Essays* (Cambridge: Cambridge University Press, 1997) 79
__ *Some Thoughts Concerning Reading and Study for a Gentleman* (published 1703) in M Goldie (ed.), *John Locke: Political Essays* (Cambridge: Cambridge University Press, 1997) 348
__ *Two Treatises of Government*, P Laslett (ed.) (Cambridge: Cambridge University Press, 2nd ed., 1988) 265

Loewenstein J, *The Author's Due: Printing and the Prehistory of Copyright* (Chicago: Chicago University Press, 2002)

__ *Ben Jonson and Possessive Authorship* (Cambridge: Cambridge University Press, 2002)

Longino H, *The Fate of Knowledge* (Princeton and Oxford: Princeton University Press, 2002)

Lord King, *The Life and Letters of John Locke* [1884] (New York: Burt Franklin repr. 1972)

Lubens R, 'Survey of Developments in European Database Protection' (2003) 18 *Berkeley Technology Law Journal* 447

Lunney GS Jr., 'Reexamining Copyright's Incentives-Access Paradigm' (1996) 49 *Vanderbilt Law Review* 483

__ 'The Death of Copyright: Digital Technology, Private Copying, and the Digital Millennium Copyright Act' (2001) 87 *Virginia Law Review* 813

Lutz KB, 'Patents and Science: A Clarification of the Patent Clause of the U.S. Constitution' (1949) 18 *George Washington Law Review* 50

Lynch M and Woolgar S (eds.), *Representation in Scientific Practice* (London: MIT Press, 1990)

Macaulay TB, *History of England from the Accession of James II*, in CH Firth (ed.), (London: Macmillan, 1913) Vol V

__ A Speech Delivered in the House of Commons on 5th February 1841 in Lady Trevelyan (ed.), *The Works of Lord Macaulay* (London: Longmans, Green and Co, 1866) 195

Macherey P, *A Theory of Literary Production* (London: Routledge and Kegan Paul, Geoffrey Wall trans., 1978)

Machlup F and Penrose E, 'The Patent Controversy in the Nineteenth Century' (1950) 10 *Journal of Economic History* 1

MacIntyre A, 'The Essential Contestability of Some Social Concepts' (1973) 84 *Ethics* 1

MacKinnon DW, 'IPAR's Contribution to the Conceptualization and Study of Creativity' in IA Taylor and JW Getzels (eds.), *Perspectives in Creativity* (Aldine: Chicago IL, 1975) 60

Macpherson CB, *The Political Theory of Possessive Individualism: Hobbes to Locke* (Oxford: Oxford University Press 1972)

__ *Property: Mainstream and Critical Positions* (Oxford: Basil Blackwell Publishing, 1978)

Madison MJ, 'Complexity and Copyright in Contradiction' (2000) 18 *Cardozo Arts & Entertainment Law Journal* 125

__ 'Comment: Where Does Creativity Come From? And Other Stories of Copyright' (2003) 53 *Case Western Reserve Law Review* 747

__ 'A Pattern-Oriented Approach to Fair Use' (2004) 45 *William and Mary Law Review* 1525

Madow M, 'Private Ownership of Public Image: Popular Culture and Publicity Rights' (1993) 81 *California Law Review* 127

Maniatis SM, 'Trade Mark Rights – A Justification Based on Property' [2002] 2 *Intellectual Property Quarterly* 123

Marchese D, 'Joint Ownership of Intellectual Property' [1999] *European Intellectual Property Review* 364

Marcuse H, *Technology, War and Fascism* (London: Routledge, D Kellner (ed.), 1998)

Martindale C and Dailey A, 'Creativity, Primary Process Cognition and Personality' (1996) 20(4) *Personality and Individual Differences* 409

Masten J, *Textual Intercourse: Collaboration, Authorship, and Sexualities in Renaissance Drama* (Cambridge: Cambridge University Press, 1997)

Mautner T, 'Locke on Original Appropriation' (1982) 19 *American Philosophical Quarterly* 259

McCrae RR, 'Creativity, Divergent Thinking, and Openness to Experience' (1987) 52 *Journal of Personality and Social Psychology* 1258

__ 'Openness to Experience as a Basic Dimension of Personality' (1993) 13 *Imagination, Cognition and Personality* 39

Meijers A, 'Can Collective Intentionality be Individualized' (2003) 62(1) *American Journal of Economics and Sociology* 167

Menell PG, 'Intellectual Property: General Theories' in B Bouckaert and G de Geest (eds.), *Encyclopedia of Law & Economics: Volume II* (Edward Elgar: Cheltenham, UK, 2000) 129

Merges RP and Glenn HR, 'The Proper Scope of the Patent and Copyright Power' (2000) 37 *Harvard Journal on Legislation* 45.

__ 'A New Dynamism in the Public Domain' (2004) 71(1) *University of Chicago Law Review* 185

Merrill TW and Smith HE, 'The Property/Contract Interface' (2001) 101 *Columbia Law Review* 773

Merrill TW, 'Property and the Right to Exclude' (1998) 77 *Nebraska Law Review* 730

Miller K, 'Commitments' in M Sintonen, P Ylikoski, and K Miller (eds.), *Realism in Action: Essays in Philosophy of the Social Sciences* 169

Milton J, 'Locke's Life and Time', in V Chappell (ed.), *The Cambridge Companion to Locke* (Cambridge: Cambridge University Press, 1994) 5

Moore AD, 'A Lockean Theory of Intellectual Property' (1997) 21 *Hamline Law Review* 65

__ 'Intangible Property: Privacy, Power, and Information Control' (1998) 35 *American Philosophical Quarterly* 365

__ 'Towards a Lockean Theory of Intellectual Property' in AD Moore (ed.), *Intellectual Property: Moral, Legal and International Dimensions* (New York and Oxford: Rowman & Littlefield, 2001) 81

Mossoff A, 'What is Property: Putting the Pieces Back Together' (2003) 45 *Arizona Law Review* 371

Munzer S, *A Theory of Property* (Cambridge: Cambridge University Press, 1990)

__*New Essays in the Legal and Political Theory of Property* (Cambridge: Cambridge University Press, 2001)

Nance DA, 'Owning Ideas' (1990) 113 *Harvard Journal of Law and Public Policy* 757

Naumann FM, *Making Mischief: Dada Invades New York* (Whitney Museum of Art: Harry N Abrams, 1996)

Netanel NW, 'Copyright Alienability Restrictions and the Enhancement of Author Autonomy: A Normative Evaluation' (1993) 24 *Rutgers Law Journal* 347

__ 'Copyright and a Democratic Civil Society' (1996) 106 *Yale Law Journal* 283

__ 'Assessing Copyright's Democratic Principles in the Global Arena' (1998) 51 *Vanderbilt Law Review* 217

__ 'Locating Copyright Within the First Amendment Skein' (2001) 54 *Stanford Law Review* 1

Nimmer D, 'The End of Copyright' (1995) 48 *Vanderbilt Law Review* 1385

__ 'Copyright in the Dead Sea Scrolls: Authorship and Originality' (2001) 38 *Houston Law Review* 1

Nimmer NB and Nimmer D, *Nimmer on Copyright* (New York: Matthew Bender & Co, 1998)

Norwich JJ, *Shakespeare's Kings: The Great Plays and the History of England in the Middle Ages: 1337-1485* (London: Scribner, 1999)

Notkiewicz M, 'Samuel Pufendorf: Obligation as the Basis of the State' (1983) 21 *Journal of the History of Philosophy* 15

Nozick R, *Anarchy, State and Utopia* (Oxford: Basic Books, 1974)

O'Neill S, 'Flow Theory and the Development of Musical Performance Skills' (1999) 141 *Bulletin of the Council for Research in Music Education* 129

O'Rourke MA, 'Beyond Microsoft: Antitrust, Technology, and Intellectual Property' (2001) 16 *Berkeley Technology Law Journal* 561

Oddi AS, 'The Tragicomedy of the Public Domain in Intellectual Property Law' (2002) 25 *Hastings Communications & Entertainment Law Journal* 1

Olivecona K, *'Law as Fact'* (1971)

__ 'Appropriation in the State of Nature: Locke on the Origin of Property' (1974) 35 *Journal of the History of Ideas* 221

__ 'Locke's Theory of Appropriation' (1974) 24 Philosophical Quarterly 220

Osborne T, 'Against 'Creativity': A Philistine Rant' (2003) 32(4) *Economy and Society* 507

Palmer TG, 'Are Patents and Copyrights Morally Justified? The Philosophy of Property Rights and Ideal Objects' (1990) 13 *Harvard Journal of Law & Public Policy* 817

Patel SH, 'Graduate Students' Ownership and Attribution Rights in Intellectual Property' (1996) 71 *Indiana Law Journal* 481

Patterson LR, 'Nimmer's Copyright in the Dead Sea Scrolls: A Comment' (2001) 38 *Houston Law Review* 431

Peeler CD, 'From the Providence of Kings to Copyrighted Things (and French Moral Rights)' (1999) 9 *Indiana International and Comparative Law Review* 423

Pegrum MA, *Challenging Modernity: Dada Between Modern and Postmodern* (New York and Oxford: Berghahn Books, 2000)
Penner J, *The Idea of Property in Law* (Oxford: Clarendon Press, 1997)
__ 'The Bundle of Rights Picture of Property' (1996) 43 *UCLA Law Review* 711
Perkins DN, *The Mind's Best Work* (Cambridge Mass.: Harvard University Press, 1981)
Perron Tollefsen D, 'Collective Intentionality and the Social Sciences' (2002) 32(1) *Philosophy of the Social Sciences* 25
Pessach G, 'A Theoretical Basis for Copyright' (2001) 31(2) *Mishpatim* 359 (in Hebrew)
__ 'The Legacy of *Feist* Revisited: A Critical Analysis of the Creativity Requirement' 36 (2002) *Israel Law Review* 19
Pigou AC, *The Economics of Welfare* (London: Macmillan, 1921)
Pinker S, *The Blank Slate: The Modern Denial of Human Nature* (New York: Penguin Books, 2003)
Plant A, 'The Economic Aspects of Copyright in Books' (1934) 1 *Economica* 167
Policastro E, 'Creative Intuition: An Integrated Review' (1995) 8 *Creativity Research Journal* 99
Poquette BR, 'Information Wants to be Free' (2000) 22 *Hamline Journal of Public Law and Policy* 175
Port K, 'The Unnatural' Expansion of Trademark Rights: Is a Federal Dilution Statute Necessary?' (1994) 18 *Seton Hall Legislative Journal* 433
Powell M, 'The European Union's Database Directive: An International Antidote to the Side Effects of Feist?' (1997) 20 *Fordham International Law Journal* 1215
__ 'Networks of Learning in Biotechnology: Opportunities and Constraints Associated with Relational Contracting in a Knowledge-Intensive Field' in R Dreyfuss, LD Zimmerman and H First (eds.), *Expanding the Boundaries of Intellectual Property: Innovation Policy for the Knowledge Society* (Oxford: Oxford University Press, 2001) 252
Quinton A, 'Social Objects' (1975) 76 *Proceedings of the Aristotelian Society* 1
Radin MJ, 'Property and Personhood' (1982) 34 *Stanford Law Review* 957
__ 'Market Inalienability' (1987) 100 *Harvard Law Review* 1849
__ 'The Liberal Conception of Property: Cross Currents in the Jurisprudence of Takings' (1988) 88 *Columbia Law Review* 1667
__ *Reinterpreting Property* (Chicago: Chicago University Press, 1993)
Rand B (ed.), *The Correspondence of John Locke and Edward Clarke* (Cambridge Mass.: Harvard University Press 1927)
Ransom H, *The First Copyright Statute: An Essay on the Act for the Encouragement of Learning, 1709* (Austin: University of Texas Press, 1956)
Rawls J, *A Theory of Justice* (Oxford: Oxford University Press, 1971 (ed 1999))
Recent Cases, 'Copyright Joint-Authorship: Second Circuit holds that Dramaturge's Contribution to the Musical *Rent* did not Establish Joint-Authorship with Playwright Composer' (1999) *Harvard Law Review* 964

Reed C and Angel J (ed.), *Computer Law* (Oxford: Oxford University Press 5th ed., 2003)

Reese RA, Note, 'Reflections on the Intellectual Commons: Two Perspectives on Copyright Duration and Reversion' (1995) 47 *Stanford Law Review* 707

Reeve A, *Property* (London: Macmillan, 1986)

Regnier T, 'Could Shakespeare Think Like a Lawyer? How Inheritance Law Issues in Hamlet May Shed Light on the Authorship Question' (2003) 57 *University of Miami Law Review* 377

Reich C, 'The New Property' (1964) 73 *Yale Law Journal* 733

Reichman JH and Samuelson P, 'Intellectual Property Rights or Data?' (1997) 50 *Vaderbilt Law Review* 51

Reitan E. 'Rape as an Essentially Contested Concept' (2001) 16(2) *Hypatia* 43

Resnik DB, 'A Pluralistic Account of Intellectual Property' (2003) 46 *Journal of Business Ethics* 319

Reytblat J, 'Is Originality in Copyright Law a "Question of Law" or a "Question of Fact?": The Fact Solution' (1999) 18 *Cardozo Arts & Entertainment Law Journal* 181

Ricketson S, 'People or Machines? The Berne Convention and the Changing Concept of Authorship' (1991) *Columbia Journal of Law & the Arts* 16

Ricketson S and Ginsburg JC, *International Copyright and Neighbouring Rights*, Vol I-II (Oxford: Oxford University Press, 2nd ed., 2006).

Rogers GAL (ed.), *Locke's Philosophy: Content and Context* (Oxford: Clarendon Press, 1994)

__ 'Innate Ideas and the Infinite: The Case of Locke and Descartes' (1995) 26 *The Locke Newsletter* 49

Rolt R and Allen J, *The Steam Engine of Thomas Newcomen* (New York: Science History Publications, 1977)

Romer PM, 'Endogenous Technological Change' (1990) 98(5) *Journal of Political Economy*, S71, S73-S74.

Rose CM, '"Enough and as Good" of What?' (1987) 81 *Northwestern University Law Review* 429

__ 'Property as the Keystone Right?' (1999) 71 *Notre Dame Law Review* 329

Rose M, *Authors and Owners: the Invention of Copyright* (Cambridge Mass.: Harvard University Press, 1993)

__ 'Copyright and Its Metaphors' (2002) 50 *UCLA Law Review* 1

Rosen A, 'Reconsidering the Idea/Expression Dichotomy' (1992) 26(2) *University of British Columbia Law Review* 263

Rosenthal Kwall R, '"Author-Stories": Narrative's Implications for Moral Rights and Copyright's Joint Authorship Doctrine' (2001) 75 *Southern California Law Review* 1

Roslansky JD (ed.), *Creativity* (Amsterdam and London: North-Holland Publishing Co., 1970)

Ross T, 'Copyright and the Invention of Tradition' (1992) 26(1) *Eighteenth Century Studies* 1

Rubenfeld J, 'The Freedom of Imagination: Copyright's Constitutionality' (2002)112 *Yale Law Journal* 1
Rubin EL, 'Due Process and the Administrative State' (1984) 72 *California Law Review* 1044
Rushton M, 'An Economic Approach to Copyright in Works of Artistic Craftsmanship' (2001) 3 *Intellectual Property Quarterly* 255
Ryan A, *Property and Political Theory* (Oxford: Blackwell, 1984)
Samuelson P, 'The Quest for Enabling Metaphors for Law and Lawyering in the Information Age' (1996) 94 *Michigan Law Review* 2029
__ 'Should Economics Play a Role in Copyright Law and Policy' (2003-2004) 1 *University of Ottawa Law & Technology Journal* 1
Sandel MJ, *Liberalism and the Limits of Justice* (Cambridge: Cambridge University Press 2ed., 1998) 62
Sanders JT, 'Justice and the Initial Acquisition of Private Property' (1987) 10 *Harvard Journal of Law and Public Policy* 367
__ 'Projects and Property' in D Schmidtz (ed.), *Robert Nozick* (Cambridge: Cambridge University Press, 2002) 34
Sartorious R, 'Persons and Property' in RG Frey (ed.), *Utility and Rights* (Minneapolis, MN: University of Minnesota Press, 1984) 196
Saunders D, *Authorship and Copyright* (London: Routledge, 1992)
Scafidi S, 'Intellectual Property and Cultural Products' (2001) 81 *Boston University Law Review* 793
Schaffner JE, 'Patent Preemption Unlocked' (1995) *Wisconsin Law Review* 1081
Schiffman LH, *Reclaiming the Dead Sea Scrolls* (Philadelphia: Jewish Publication Society, 1994)
Schlatter R, *Private Property: The History of an Idea* (George Allen & Unwin, 1951)
Schmidtz D, 'When is Original Appropriation Required?' (1990) 73(4) *The Monist* 504
__ (ed.), *Robert Nozick* (Cambridge: Cambridge University Press, 2002)
Schneider M, 'The European Union Database Directive' (1998) *Berkeley Technology Law Journal* 551
Schocet G, '"Guards and Fences": Property and Obligation in Locke's Political Thought' (2000) 21(3) *History of Political Thought* 365
Schwartz MP and Treanor WM, 'Eldred and Lochner: Copyright Term Extension and Intellectual Property as Constitutional Property' (2003) 112 *Yale Law Journal* 2331
Searle JR, *Intentionality* (Cambridge: Cambridge University Press, 1983)
__ 'Collective Intentions and Actions', in P Cohen, J Morgan and ME Pollack (eds.), *Intentions in Communication* (Cambridge MA.: MIT Press, 1990)
__ *The Construction of Social Reality* (New York: The Free Press, 1995)
__ 'Précise of *The Construction of Social Reality*' (1997) 57(2) *Philosophy and Phenomenological Research* 427

Seville C, 'Copyright's Bargain – Defining Our Terms' [2003] 3 *Intellectual Property Quarterly* 312

__ 'Peter Pan's Rights: "To Die Will Be an Awfully Big Adventure"' (2003) 51(1) *Journal of the Copyright Society of the USA* 1, 7

Shapin S, *The Scientific Revolution* (Chicago: Chicago University Press, 1996)

Shapiro I, *The Evolution of Rights in Liberal Theory* (Cambridge: Cambridge University Press, 1986)

__ 'Resources, Capacities, and Ownership: The Workmanship Ideal and Distributive Justice' (1991) 19 (1) *Political Theory* 47

__ (ed.), J Locke, *Two Treatises of Government and A Letter Concerning Tolerance* (New Haven: Yale University Press, 2003)

Shavell S and van Ypersele T, 'Rewards Versus Intellectual Property Rights' (2001) 22 *Journal of Law and Economics* 525

Sherman B and Bently L, *The Making of Modern Intellectual Property* (Cambridge: Cambridge University Press, 1999)

__ *Intellectual Property Law* (Oxford: Oxford University Press, 2001)

Sherman B and Strowel A (eds.), *Of Authors and Origins: Essays on Copyright Law* (Oxford: Clarendon Press, 1994)

Sherman RJ, 'The Visual Artists Rights Act of 1990: American Artists Burned Again' (1995) 17 *Cardozo Arts & Entertainment Law Review* 373

Shiffrin SV, 'Lockean Arguments for Private Intellectual Property' in S Munzer (ed.), *New Essays in the Legal and Political Theory of Property* (Cambridge: Cambridge University Press, 2001) 138

Shouksmith G, *Intelligence, Creativity and Cognitive Style* (London: Batsford, 1970)

Siebert FS, *Freedom of the Press in England 1476-1776: the Rise and Decline of Government Control* (Urbana: University of Illinois Press, 1952)

Simcoe E and Ingram C, 'Joint Authorship: A Question of Joint Effort or Intent' (2000) *Copyright World* 18

Simmons AJ, *The Lockean Theory of Rights* (Princeton, Oxford: Princeton University Press, 1992)

__ 'Original Acquisition Justifications of Private Property' (1994) 11(2) *Social Philosophy and Policy* 63

__ 'Makers' Rights' (1998) 2 *The Journal of Ethics* 197

Singer J, 'The Legal Right Debate in Analytical Jurisprudence from Bentham to Hohfeld' (1982) *Wisconsin Law Review* 975

Singh R, 'John Locke and the Theory of Natural Law' (1961) 9 *Political Studies* 105

Sintonen M, Ylikoski P, and Miller K (eds.), *Realism in Action: Essays in Philosophy of the Social Sciences* (Dordrecht: Kluwer, 2003)

Smith SM, Ward TB and Finke RA (eds.), *The Creative Cognitive Approach* (Cambridge Mass.: MIT Press, 1995)

Sofer A, 'Joint Authorship: An Uncomfortable Fit with Tenancy in Common' (1998) 19 *Loyola of Los Angeles Entertainment Law Journal* 1

Spector HM, 'An Outline of a Theory Justifying Intellectual Property Rights' [1989] 8 *European Intellectual Property Review* 270

Spence M, 'Intellectual Property and the Problem of Parody' [1998] 114 *Law Quarterly Review* 594.

Sperber D (ed.), *Causal Cognition* (New York: Clarendon Press, 1995)

Spinello RA, 'The Future of Intellectual Property' (2003) 5 *Ethics and Information Technology* 1

Spyke P, 'The Joint Work Dilemma: The Separately Copyrightable Contribution Requirement and Co-ownership Principles' (1993) 40 *Journal of the Copyright Society of the USA*, 463

Sreenivasan G, *The Limits of Lockean Rights in Property* (New York: Oxford University Press, 1995)

Stallman R, 'Re-evaluating Copyright: The Public Must Prevail' (1996) 75 *Oregon Law Review* 291

Stanley SL, 'A Dangerous Step Toward the Over Protection of Intellectual Property: Rethinking Eldred v. Ashcroft' (2003) 26 *Hamline Law Review* 679

Stehr N, 'The Social and Political Control of Knowledge in Modern Societies' (2003) 55(4) *International Social Science Journal* 643

Steiner H, 'The Natural Right to the Means of Production' (1977) 77 *Philosophical Quarterly* 41-49

Sterk SE, 'Rhetoric and Reality in Copyright Law' (1996) 94 *Michigan Law Review* 1197

Sterling JAL, *World Copyright Law* (London: Sweet and Maxwell, 1998)

__ 'International Codification of Copyright Law: Possibilities and Imperatives' (2000) 33 *International Review of Industrial Property and Copyright Law* (IIC) 270

Sternberg R (ed.), *The Nature of Creativity: Contemporary Psychological Perspectives* (Cambridge: Cambridge University Press, 1987)

Stevens JP, 'The Shakespeare Canon of Statutory Construction' (1992) 140 *University of Pennsylvania Law Review* 1373

Stich SP (ed.), *Innate Ideas* (Berkeley California: University of California Press, 1975)

Stillinger J, *Multiple Authorship and the Myth of Solitary Genius* (New York: Oxford University Press, 1991)

Stillman PG, 'Property, Freedom, and Individuality in Hegel's and Marx's Political Thoughts' in JR Pennock and JW Chapman (ed.), *Property*, Nomos, XXII (New York: New York University Press, 1980) 130

Stokes S, *Art & Copyright* (Oxford: Hart Publishing 2003)

Suler JR, 'Primary Process Thinking and Creativity' (1988) 88 *Psychological Bulletin* 144

Tawney RH, 'Property and Creative Work', in CB Macpherson, *Property: Mainstream and Critical Positions* (Oxford: Basil Blackwell, 1978) 133

Tedrowe CC, 'Conceptual Severance and Takings in the Federal Circuit' (2000) 85 *Cornell Law Review* 586

Tehranian J, 'ET TU, Fair Use? The Triumph of Natural-Law Copyright (2005) 38 *U C Davis Law Review* 465

Thakur N, 'Database Protection in the European Union and the United States: The European Database Directive as an Optimum Global Model' (2001) 1 *Intellectual Property Quarterly* 100

Thomas K, 'Beyond the Privacy Principle' (1992) 92 *Columbia Law Review* 1431

Thompson M, *Modern Land Law* (Oxford: Oxford University Press, 2nd ed., 2003)

Thomson J, *The Realm of Rights* (Cambridge, Harvard University Press, 1992)

Torremans P, *Holyoak and Torremans Intellectual Property Law* (Oxford: Oxford University Press, 4th ed., 2005)

Tritton G, *Intellectual Property in Europe* (London: Sweet & Maxwell, 2nd ed., 2002)

Tuomela R, 'We Will Do It: An Analysis of Group-Intentions' (1991) 51(2) *Philosophy and Phenomenological Research* 249

__ *The Importance of Us: A Philosophical Study of Basic Social Notions* (Stanford: Stanford University Press, 1995)

__ 'Collective Acceptance, Social Institutions, and Social Reality' (2003) 62(1) *American Journal of Economics and Sociology* 123

Tully J, *A Discourse on Property: John Locke and His Adversaries* (Cambridge: Cambridge University Press, 1980)

__ *An Approach to Political Philosophy: Locke in Contexts* (Cambridge: Cambridge University Press, 1993)

Tushnet R, 'Copy this Essay: How Fair Use Doctrine Harms Free Speech and how Copying Serves it' (2004) 114 *Yale Law Journal* 535

Tyerman BW, 'The Economic Rationale for Copyright Protection for Published Books: A Reply to Professor Breyer' (1971) 18 *UCLA Law Review* 1100

Underkuffler LS, 'On Property: An Essay' (1990) 100 *Yale Law Journal* 127

Underkuffler LS, *The Idea of Property: Its Making and Power* (Oxford: Oxford University Press, 2003)

Vaidhyanathan S, *Copyrights and Copywrongs: The Rise of Intellectual Property and How it Threatens Creativity* (New York and London: New York University Press, 2001

Valachovic E, 'The Contribution Requirement to a Joint Work under the Copyright Act' (1992) 12 *Loyola of Los Angeles Entertainment Law Journal* 199

Van den Bergh R, 'The Role and Social Justification of Copyright: A 'Law and Economics' Approach' (1998) *Intellectual Property Quarterly* 17

Vandervelde K, 'The New Property of the Nineteenth Century: The Development of the Modern Concept of Property' (1980) 29 *Buffalo Law Review* 325

Vaver D, 'Intellectual Property Today: Of Myths and Paradoxes' (1990) 69 *Canadian Bar Review* 98

__ 'Translation and Copyright: A Canadian Focus' (1994) 16(4) *European Intellectual Property Review* 159

__ 'Abridgements and Abstracts: Copyright Implications' (1995) 17(5) *European Intellectual Property Review* 225

__ *Intellectual Property Law: Copyright, Patents, Trade Marks* (Toronto: Irwin Law, 1997)

__ 'Moral Rights Yesterday, Today and Tomorrow' (1999) 7(3) *International Journal of Law and Information Technology* 270

__ 'Patently Absurd' [2000] *Oxford Today* 21-22. Inaugural Lecture, University of Oxford

__ 'Intellectual Property: The State of the Art' (2000) 116 *Law Quarterly Review* 621

Velleman JD, 'How to Share an Intention' (1997) 57(1) *Philosophy and Phenomenological Research* 29

Vernon PE (ed.), *Creativity* (Penguin Books, 1970)

VerSteeg R, 'Rethinking Originality' (1993) 34 *William & Mary Law Review* 801

VerSteeg R, 'Sparks in the Tinderbox: Feist, "Creativity", and The Legislative History of the 1976 Copyright Act' (1995) 56 *University of Pittsburgh Law Review* 549

__ 'Intent, Originality and Joint Authorship' (2002) 68 *Brooklyn Law Review* 123

Vickers B, *Shakespeare, Co-Author: A Historical Study of Five Collaborative Plays* (Oxford: Oxford University Press, 2002)

Wald J, 'Legislating the Golden Rule: Achieving Comparable Protection Under the European Union Database Directive' (2002) 25 *Fordham International Law Journal* 987

Waldron J, 'Enough and as Good Left for Others' (1979) 29 *Philosophical Quarterly* 319

__ (ed.), *Theories of Rights* (Oxford: Oxford University Press, 1984) 1

__ *The Right to Private Property* (Oxford: Oxford University Press, 1988)

__ 'From Authors to Copiers: Individual Rights and Social Values in Intellectual Property' (1992-1993) 68 *Chicago-Kent Law Review* 841

__ 'Vagueness in Law and Language: Some Philosophical Issues' (1994) 82(3) *California Law Review* 509

__ 'Is the Rule of Law an Essentially Contested Concept (in Florida)?' (2002) 21 *Law and Philosophy* 137

__ *God, Locke, and Equality: Christian Foundations in Locke's Political Thought* (Cambridge: Cambridge University Press, 2002)

Wall G, 'Locke's Attack on Innate Knowledge' (1974) 49 *Philosophy* 414

Wallas G, *The Art of Thought* (New York: Harcourt Brace, 1926)

Walterscheid EC, 'To Promote the Progress of Science and Useful Arts: The Background and Origin of the Intellectual Property Clause of the United States Constitution' (1994) 2 *Journal of Intellectual Property* 1

Warren S and Brandeis L, 'Privacy – The Right To' (1890) 4 *Harvard Law Review* 193

Watson J, *The Double Helix* (New York: Signet, 1968)

Weinreb L, 'Copyright for Functional Expression' (1998) 111 *Harvard Law Review* 1149

Weisberg R, *Creativity: Beyond the Myth of Genius* (New York: WH Freeman, 1993)

Welsh GS, 'Creativity and Intelligence: A Personality Approach' (2nd ed, 1977).

Wernick AS, 'The Work Made for Hire and Joint Work Copyright Doctrines after *CCNV v Reid*: "What! You Mean I don't Own It Even Though I Paid in Full for It?"' (1990) 13 *Hamline Law Review* 287

Wicklund RA, 'The Appropriation of Ideas' in PB Paulus (ed.), *Psychology of Group Influence* (New Jersey and London: Lawrence Erlbaum Associates Publishers 2ed, 1989) 393

Wilf S, 'Who Authors Trademarks?' (1999) 17 *Cardozo Arts & Entertainment Law Journal* 1

Wilkinson M, 'Constituting Europe: Flexibility or Finalité' (2002) 22 *Oxford Journal of Legal Studies* 177

Williams TC, 'Property, Things in Action, and Copyright' (1895) 11 *Law Quarterly Review* 223

Wilmer F, *Social Construction of Man, the State and War* (Taylor & Francis Books Ltd Routledge, 2002)

Winchester SJ, 'Locke and the Innatists' (1985) 2 *History of Philosophy Quarterly* 411

Winfrey JC, 'Charity Versus Justice in Locke's Theory of Property' (1981) 42(3) *Journal of the History of Ideas* 436

Wolcher LE, 'The End of Technology: A Polemic' (2004) 79 *Washington Law Review* 331

Wolf C, 'Contemporary Property Rights: Lockean Provisos and the Interests of Future Generations' (1995) 105 *Ethics* 791

Wolfradt U and Pretz JE, 'Individual Differences in Creativity: Personality, Story Writing, and Hobbies' (2001) 15 *European Journal of Personality* 297

Wood P, *Diversity: The Invention of a Concept* (San Francisco: Encounter Books, 2003)

Woodmansee M, 'The Genius and the Copyright: Economic and Legal Conditions of the Emergence of the "Author"', (1984) 17 *Eighteenth-Century Studies* 425

__ *The Author, Art, and the Market: Rereading the History of Aesthetics* (New York: Columbia University Press 1994)

__ 'On the Author Effect: Recovering Collectivity' in M Woodmansee and P Jaszi (eds.), *The Construction of Authorship* (Durham and London: Duke University Press, 1994) 15

Woodmansee M and Jaszi P (eds.), *The Construction of Authorship* (Durham and London: Duke University Press, 1994)

__ 'Introduction' in M Woodmansee and P Jaszi (eds.), *The Construction of Authorship* (Durham and London: Duke University Press, 1994) 1

Woolhouse R, 'Locke's Theory of Knowledge' in V Chappell (ed.), *The Cambridge Companion to Locke* (Cambridge: Cambridge University Press, 1994) 146

Wright RG, 'Is Natural Law Theory of Any Use in Constitutional Interpretation?' (1995) 4 *Southern California Interdisciplinary Law Journal* 463

Yarbrough JD Jr., 'What's Mine Might be Yours: Why We Should Rethink the Default Rule for Copyright Co-Ownership in Joint Works' (2001) 76 *Tulane Law Review* 493

Yellin T, 'New Directions for Copyright: The Property Rights of Stage Directors' (2001) 24 *Columbia-VLA Journal of Law and the Arts* 317

Yen AC, 'A First Amendment Perspective on the Idea/Expression Dichotomy and Copyright in a Work's "Total Concept and Feel"' (1989) 38 *Emory Law Journal* 393

__ 'Restoring the Natural Law: Copyright as Labour and Possessions' (1990) 51 *Ohio State Law Journal* 517

__ 'The Interdisciplinary Future of Copyright Theory' in M Woodmansee and P Jaszi (eds.), *The Construction of Authorship* (Durham and London: Duke University Press, 1994) 159

Yolton JW, 'The Concept of Experience in Locke and Hume' (1963) 1 *Journal of the History of Philosophy* 53.

__ 'Ideas and Knowledge in Seventeenth-Century Philosophy' (1975) 13 *Journal of the History of Philosophy* 145

Yu PK, 'The Escalating Copyright Wars' (2004) 32 *Hofstra Law Review* 907.

Zaibert LA, 'Collective Intentions and Collective Intentionality' (2003) 62(1) *American Journal of Economics and Sociology* 210

Zemer L, 'The Making of a New Copyright Lockean' (2006) 29(3) *Harvard Journal of Law & Public Policy* 871

__ 'On the Value of Copyright Theory' (2006) 1 *Intellectual Property Quarterly* 55

__ 'The Conceptual Game in Copyright' (2006) 28(3) *Hastings Communications and Entertainment Law Journal* 409

__ 'Contribution and Collaboration in Joint Authorship: Too Many Misconceptions' (2006) 1(4) *Journal of Intellectual Property Law & Practice* 283

Zimmerman DL, 'Is There a Right to have Something to Say? One View of the Public Domain' (2004) 73 *Fordham Law Review* 297

Zionkowski L, 'Aesthetics, Copyright and the Goods of the Mind' (1992) 15 *British Journal for Eighteenth Century Studies* 167

Zuckert P, 'Do Natural Rights Derive from Natural Law?' (1997) 3 *Harvard Journal of Law & Public Policy* 695

Index